During the period between his conversion in A.D. 386 and his ordination to the priesthood in 391, Augustine developed a theory of man and a perception of Christianity that influenced all his early works. Intending from the first to refine his understanding of the Christian faith, Augustine also meant to do justice to what he deemed valid in the other schools of thought of his time, including Stoicism, the philosophy of Cicero, and even Manichaeism. The theory that he developed centered on the notion that man is a "fallen soul" who turned away from the Divine Beauty and plunged from a state of contemplative bliss into the world of body, time, and action. In Plotinus' *Enneads* Augustine discovered the most comprehensive framework for such a concept.

Father O'Connell approaches Augustine through Plotinus in order to demonstrate that the Plotinian frame furnishes the matrix for the elements of Christianity which the young Augustine was attempting to understand. He presents convincing evidence to show that Augustine's tendency to undervalue such human concerns as sex and love, culture, art, and scientific research arises not directly from the Christian message but from that message as passed through a Plotinian filter.

In his Introduction, the author establishes the legitimacy of his use of a number of Plotinus' *Enneads* as keys to Augustine's early thought. The body of his study is divided into three parts, "Divine Soul," "Fallen Soul," and "Christian Soul." In each part he begins by comparing Plotinus' Greek text with Augustine's Latin, noting the various links of language, idea, and image between them. He then focuses on Augustine's own initial questions and suppositions, tracing his intellectual development through his early works to the point where he thought he had found provisionally satisfactory answers to his initial problems. In this way Father O'Connell argues that Plotinian Neo-Platonism, far from making fragmentary contribution to Augustine's speculations, provided him with a theory of man that helps clarify Augustine's fascination with omnipresence, his attacks on the "idolatry" of the soul's pretensions at divinity, the puzzling treatise *On the Immortality of the Soul,* and finally the relation of faith to understanding and of both to Christ's function in promoting the soul's eventual return to the vision it once enjoyed in the heavenly Jerusalem.

Robert J. O'Connell, S. J., is Associate Professor of Philosophy at Fordham University.

ST. AUGUSTINE'S EARLY THEORY OF MAN

ST. AUGUSTINE'S EARLY THEORY OF MAN, A.D. 386-391

ROBERT J. O'CONNELL

THE BELKNAP PRESS
OF
HARVARD UNIVERSITY PRESS
CAMBRIDGE, MASSACHUSETTS, 1968

Distributed in Great Britain by Oxford University Press, London
Library of Congress Catalog Card Number 68-21981
Printed in the United States of America

MATRI
primo
caeterisque
MAGISTRIS
pie dicatum

PREFACE

It is always hazardous to guess what future ages will think of the period through which one is living. Their perspective may flatten out the promontories that seem to us so formidable. Yet it is difficult to imagine that they will remain unmoved by the ferment we find so striking in Christianity today. The ecumenical consciousness that has become nearly a fever since the Second Vatican Council is only one of its most dramatic manifestations.

Yet more than one observer has remarked that Vatican II was long in coming and slowly prepared, more slowly and in greater depth than the uninformed would suspect. It climaxed, in fact, a painstaking and laborious effort of decades during which Christian thinkers of all denominations were grappling with the deeper common problem of striving afresh to measure the chasm that seemed to separate Church and World, the religious and what has come to be called the "secular." What stance must the Christian adopt before, and in, the "world"? How does his Christian vision relate to the human values, the ends of human life toward which—rightly or wrongly—unbelievers so widely felt the Church was indifferent, if not hostile? Human love and friendship, scientific research and art, social justice and the human concern for building the earth: how do such contemporary "absolutes" fit in with the Christian vision?

It would be tiresome here to cite the litany of thinkers, both Christian and non-Christian, who have struggled with various facets of this problem. Suffice it to say that two conclusions at least seem gradually to have emerged from the discussion of these past decades. First, it became progressively clear that a central, if not the central, issue was the vision of man. Second, a dawning awareness that dated philosophic frameworks had possibly pulled the Christian vision out of shape crystallized into a call for "return to the sources": the assumption was that a renewed contact with Scripture and with the great minds of the early Church would aid us today in finding fresh starting points for this perennial dialogue between Church and World.

Among those great minds Augustine's place is secure, if not impregnable. But his crucial importance for our ecumenical century is even more impressive. How often has it been said and written that Protestant Christianity remains Augustinian over against a Roman Catholicism become Thomist? One need not entirely agree with such vast categorizations to recognize the foundation of truth on which they rest.

Is it possible, then, that recapturing the Augustinian vision of man will help us, not only to establish some greater measure of ecumenical understanding, but also to reply to the questions of modern man with a message warmer, more human than the one which Christians now are everywhere renewing?

A vast question, that. For, to stay with only part of it for the moment, what is Augustine's vision of man?

It once seemed to me that the substance of that vision could be explicated without venturing out on the shifting terrain of *Quellenforschung*. And yet, as time went on, a number of obscurities in Augustine's works forced this task upon me. It may appear strange to read that after centuries of commentary and generations of interpreters, certain passages of the Saint's writings never received adequate explanation. What is more clear, for instance, than the "common-proper" distinction so crucial in Augustine's later works? However, the first massive introduction of that distinction seemed to me far from explicable. It prompted exploration of possibilities others had suggested, and led to findings that caused me to suspect that similar research on other apparent anomalies might result in comparable illumination.

The difficulties were presented by Augustine's own text. In almost every case, it was Plotinus who helped most in clarifying what Augustine said, and what he meant by what he said. As a result, I have been led to underline Plotinus' influence on

Augustine to an extent unknown since Bouillet, Grandgeorge, Alfaric, and Nörregaard were apparently discountenanced by the work of later scholars—Theiler, Henry, and O'Meara among them.

Much of what is presented here in support of my view has already appeared in article form.[1] There, however, it was necessary to take another approach than the one taken in these pages. The main burden of proof centered on establishing the plausibility, at least, that Augustine had read, meditated, and assimilated into his synthesis much more of Plotinus' philosophy than had recently been admitted as demonstrable. The orientation, style, and order of these articles was dictated by this burden of proof. It meant that one Plotinian treatise after another had to be added to the list; that the method of proving such dependence had to become the focus of explicit examination; that comparisons between Plotinus and Augustine be carried out in painfully technical fashion, Latin being set against Greek; that subsequent articles should build upon the evidence which had preceded and earlier articles not presuppose the evidence which was to appear later. The result was largely an approach to Augustine through Plotinus, one in which successive treatises of the former were focused on partial areas of Augustine's work, before any fuller orchestration of the Saint's own writings could come into play. The increased scope of Plotinus' influence had to be proved in terms of its power to illumine key themes in Augustine's work. But the Plotinian influence tended to occupy center-stage, and the Augustinian themes themselves in their own meaning, interrelation and development became secondary.

What these articles may be thought to have accomplished, however, is at least to have established the plausibility of adducing an added number of precisely identifiable Plotinian treatises as part of Augustine's intellectual armory. A number of scholars working in this area have been good enough to communicate both their (sometimes qualified) assent to this proposition, and in

[1] In their order of conception: "*Ennead* VI, 4–5 in the Works of St. Augustine," *Revue des Études Augustiniennes* (hereafter cited as *REA*) 9: 1–39 (1963); "The Plotinian Fall of the Soul in St. Augustine," *Traditio*, 19: 1–35 (1963); "The *Enneads* and St. Augustine's Image of Happiness," *Vigiliae Christianae*, 17: 129–164 (1963); "The Riddle of Augustine's *Confessions:* A Plotinian Key, "*International Philosophical Quarterly*, 4: 327–372 (1964). A critical review of these articles, by Goulven Madec, may be found in *REA* 11: 372–375 (1965). Olivier Du Roy, in his *L'Intelligence de la Foi en la Trinité selon Saint Augustin* (Paris, 1966) also makes occasional critical comments on them; I regret his work reached me too late for me to accord it the careful consideration it deserves.

more than one case their reservations on the implications that seemed to be drawn from it. But if the proposition may be considered as at least plausible, another approach to the problem may help to clarify its implications and eliminate misunderstandings on the corollaries some seemed to detect were being drawn about Augustine's synthesis. One challenge several of these scholars raised may be mentioned here, for it has often been raised—and too often justly—against such efforts of *Quellenforschung*. Does it manage to smother and destroy, or, on the contrary, bring the individuality of the "dependent" author into higher relief? Does "my" Augustine remain Augustine?

I intend, therefore, to take, in the main, a new approach to the materials already presented in the articles mentioned. One result of this approach is that it permits a much less technical handling of those materials. Instead of comparing Plotinus' Greek with Augustine's Latin, the parallels will be handled for the most part in English, the key Latin and Greek expressions appearing in parentheses.

A second feature of the approach taken here is that the materials have been rearranged, reoriented, and considerably expanded in order to provide far fuller exposition of Augustine's own development. Each of the book's main Parts begins with a comparison with Plotinus; but then, the examination focuses on the contours of Augustine's intellectual landscape, attempts to isolate his set of initial questions and suppositions, explores the linkage whereby one work follows from another, and traces the development of his thought up to the point where he is provisionally persuaded that he has come to satisfactory articulation of a view that answers to his initial problems. These Augustinian explorations, then, attempt to counter the objection that Plotinian illumination tends more to deform than clarify the Saint's own personal thought.

Hence the build of the work: the Introduction means to establish the legitimacy of using a considerable number of *Enneads* as keys for unlocking the inner recesses of Augustine's early thought-world. Then, in the opening chapter of each Part, this claim of legitimacy is buttressed by comparison between Augustine's text and certain treatises of Plotinus. It is then confirmed by showing its explanatory value through a careful study of Augustine's own writings, a study which, at every step of the way, claims to let Augustine remain Augustine. That explanatory value implies that Plotinian Neo-Platonism contributed not merely one or another piece to the Augustinian mosaic, but, more important than that, that its dominating influence illumines the entire sequence of Augustine's early works, a sequence that then becomes manifestly the unified product of a developing intellectual quest.

Some may prefer to consider the unity of Augustine's early writings a subsidiary hypothesis. There are still many who contend that he was a far more occasional and far less organized writer than such a contention would imply. For those who view him that way, therefore, this book will appear as the simultaneous attempt to confirm two distinct, interweaving hypotheses. In that case, confirmation of them both must be allowed gradually to emerge as the explanation of Augustine's intellectual task proceeds. Only when the entire picture has been traced can valid judgment on its accuracy be leveled. But in the course of drawing that picture, the reader must permit me sometimes to interpret certain themes, as they are announced in an earlier work, in the light of their clearer and fuller development in later writings. For there are times when only later, fuller statement allows us to see what was implied, or explicitly but only elliptically stated, in earlier expressions. Only one who has seen the oak can know what the acorn was in the first place—not, assuredly, an oak full-grown, but an oak in embryonic form.

The claim of this work is, therefore, that looking at Augustine through Plotinus does not necessarily deform the portrait of Augustine: quite the contrary. It must be admitted, though, that the inverse accusation may be leveled with far more justice. The understanding of Plotinianism may well have been "Augustinized" throughout these pages. Students of that great, subtle, but difficult thinker will have a generous list of indictments in this regard. They may find his mythological language taken with a seriousness so literal as to seem at times naïve: the "two worlds" represented more imaginatively than intelligibly, the soul's "fall and return" consequently shorn of some of its most sophisticated nuances, the oppositions between action and contemplation, between omnipresence and emanation thinking, stressed almost to the point of caricature.

To all such accusations the only possible plea is guilty, but with extenuating circumstances. Not that the presentation of Plotinus' thought here is entirely indefensible: where an Emile Bréhier, for example, finds an "undeniable contradiction" and a Jean Trouillard labors with patient finesse to eliminate or attenuate it, there is still reason to suspect the contradiction may have been there in the first place. The point is, though, that a perfectly adequate and sophisticated idea of Plotinus' philosophy of man would be not only unnecessary but at times confusing and inappropriate for the task of illumining Augustine's adaptation of that philosophy: he was simply incapable of understanding Plotinus all that well. Even when directly exposing Plotinus' thought, accordingly, I take the liberty of presenting the idea of him that Augustine's limited philosophic background would, and (as his writings show) did, allow him to form.

It would be much fairer to say, therefore, that I have come at Plotinus through Augustine, rather than the reverse. But if Augustinians insist I have Plotinized their Saint, and Plotinians object with equal vehemence that I have Augustinized their philosopher, the central affirmation of this work may only stand the firmer for it: the resemblance between the two thinkers seemed so compelling that either sin (or an amalgam of both) may be forgiven.

Fordham University
December 1967

R. J. O'C.

ACKNOWLEDGMENTS

My thanks must go in the first place to Professor Henri-Irénée Marrou, under whose sunny guidance the core of this work first appeared as a thesis for the Sorbonne. I hope that his help and advice received at that time still shows through this finished product. Help came from so many others, though, that the list would lengthen indefinitely. But nothing would excuse my omitting such names as: Frs. Régis Bernard, Francis O'Connor, Joseph Moingt, and Paul Henry, who distinguished themselves as true "brothers in Christ" in a variety of ways, both then and since; Professors Jean Guitton and Pierre Courcelle, whose criticisms and suggestions at the thesis defense have since proved valuable; Professors A. H. Armstrong, J. J. O'Meara, A. Solignac, John F. Callahan, and G. Madec, who have been both kind and candid in giving me their views on the portions of this work which have appeared in article form; Fr. William Grimaldi, of Fordham, whose Greek learning has illumined a number of Plotinus' nettling passages for me.

I must thank, as well, the students both graduate and undergraduate who have aided me in sharpening many of the views conveyed here; Fr. James M. Somerville, Chairman, and other members of the Fordham Philosophy Department, particularly

Fr. W. Norris Clarke, with whom discussion of these ideas has always been as lively as it was invaluable; and the authorities of Fordham University who kindly accorded me a Faculty Fellowship year to put this work into final form.

I am grateful, also, to the following publishers for their permission to quote extensively from translations of Scriptures, Augustine, and Plotinus (I append fuller publication data below): to the University of Chicago Press, who permitted my use of *The Bible, An American Translation*; to Doubleday and Company, New York, who allowed me to use John K. Ryan's translation of the *Confessions*; to Faber and Faber, London, and to Pantheon Books, a division of Random House, Inc., New York, who allowed use of the MacKenna-Page version of the *Enneads*; to the Newman Press, Westminster, Md., and to Longmans, Green and Company, Ltd., London, who permitted me to use the translations of the *Contra Academicos*, *De Quantitate Animae*, and *De Libero Arbitrio* which have appeared in their *Ancient Christian Writers* series; and to the Catholic University Press, who have allowed me to quote from the following volumes of the *Fathers of the Church* series: from Volume 5 (*De Beata Vita*, *De Ordine*, *Soliloquia*); from Volume 4 (*De Immortalitate Animae*, *De Musica*, and *De Utilitate Credendi*); and from Volume 38, an extended portion of *Sermon* 197.

Finally, I must thank the editors of the *Revue des Études Augustiniennes*, *Vigiliae Christianae*, *International Philosophical Quarterly*, and of *Traditio* (published by Fordham University Press) who have kindly permitted me to use substantial portions of articles (fully cited below) originally published in their respective journals.

FORMS OF CITATION

For simplicity of reference, the following forms of citation have been used throughout:

(*a*) Research instruments

Augustinus Magister, Acts of the Augustinian Congress, 3 vols. (Paris, 1954) = *AM*, I, II, III depending on the volume.

Real-Encyklopaedie der Klassischen Altertumswissenschaft, Pauly-Wissowa-Kroll-Witter (Stuttgart, 1894ff) = *RE*.

(*b*) Texts and translations used

Bibliothèque Augustinienne series of *Oeuvres de Saint-Augustin* (Paris, 1933ff) = *BA* plus the volume number (e.g., *BA* 6).

Ancient Christian Writers series (Westminster, Md., 1946ff) = *ACW* plus the volume number (e.g., *ACW* 22).

Fathers of the Church series (New York [later, Washington, D.C.], 1948ff) = *FC* plus the volume number (e.g., *FC* 1).

When referring to critical editions and translations of the works of Augustine and Plotinus, I designate them simply by the editor's or translator's name.

The English translation of Augustine's *Confessions* regularly quoted is that of John K. Ryan in the *Image Books* series (New

York: Doubleday, 1960). I have consulted other versions also, principal among them those of Vernon J. Bourke, published as *FC* 21 (New York, 1953), Frank J. Sheed (New York: Sheed and Ward, 1954), E. B. Pusey (reprinted in *Everyman's Library*, London, 1953), William Watts (originally issued in 1631, revised by W. H. D. Rouse for the Loeb Classical Library, Cambridge, Mass., 1912). The French versions by Pierre de Labriolle (Paris, Guillaume Budé Collection, "Les Belles Lettres," 1925) and by Eugène Tréhorel and Guilhem Bouissou in volumes 13 and 14 of the *BA* series (Paris, 1962) have also proved valuable.

The *ACW* series has been used for translations of the *Contra Academicos* (by John J. O'Meara, 1950), the *De Quantitate Animae* (by Joseph M. Colleran, 1950), and the *De Libero Arbitrio* (by Dom Mark Pontifex, 1955). I have drawn on the *FC* series for translations of: the *De Beata Vita* (by Ludwig Schopp), the *De Ordine* (by Robert P. Russell), the *Soliloquia* (by Thomas F. Gilligan; all the foregoing from volume 5, 1948); and for translations of the *De Immortalitate Animae* (by Ludwig Schopp), the *De Musica* (by R. C. Taliaferro) and the *De Utilitate Credendi* (by Sr. Luanne Meagher, O.S.B.; these three works contained in volume 4, 1947). The translation of *Sermon* 197 is that of Sr. Mary Muldowney, R.S.M., from *FC* 38, 1959. For the *De Vera Religione*, John H. S. Burleigh's translation has been used (in The Library of Christian Classics, volume VI, *Augustine*: *Earlier Writings*, London: *SCM* Press, 1963).

I have occasionally altered the translations referred to above, in each case parenthesizing the corresponding Latinism to justify my rendition. For the *De Genesi contra Manichaeos* and the *De Moribus Ecclesiae et Manichaeorum*, I have made my own translations. Throughout, I have regularly worked from the Latin text of Augustine's works recommended by the editors of the *Clavis Patrum Latinorum*, 2d ed. (= *Sacris Erudiri*, III), Steenbrugge: Eligius Dekkers and Aemilius Gaar, 1961.

Translations from Plotinus' *Enneads* are taken, unless otherwise indicated, from the version of Stephen MacKenna, 3d ed. revised by B. S. Page (London: Faber and Faber; New York: Pantheon Books, a division of Random House, Inc., 1962). Reference is made in standard form, *Enn* VI, 4, 7, 21–23, for example, indicating a quotation drawn from lines 21 to 23 of the seventh chapter of the fourth treatise of the Sixth *Ennead*. I have also profited from the translations contained in Emile Bréhier's edition; in Richard Harder's *Plotins Schriften* as reworked by Rudolf Beutler and Willy Theiler (Hamburg, 1956ff), in A. H. Armstrong's *Plotinus* (New

York, 1964). Changes in MacKenna's translation are accompanied by the corresponding Greek phrase in parentheses, and occasionally by reference to one or other of the above translators.

The text of the first five *Enneads* is that of the critical edition being done by Fr. Paul Henry and Hans-Rudolf Schwyzer (Museum Lessianum, Series Philosophica, volumes 33 and 34, Paris: Desclée De Brouwer, 1951 and 1959 respectively). For *Ennead* VI, Émile Bréhier's text was used (from the 2d ed. of *Les Ennéades*, vol. VI, parts I and II [referred to as *Ennéades* VI^1 and VI^2 respectively], Paris: Guillaume Budé Collection, "Les Belles Lettres," 1954). The only exceptions are those sections quoted at length from *Ennead* VI, 4 and *Ennead* VI, 5, for which Fr. Henry was gracious enough to furnish the readings he and Schwyzer had provisionally settled upon for their edition. For that kindness, my sincere thanks go to both these eminent and indefatigable scholars.

For extended quotation, I have used *The Bible, An American Translation*, translated and edited by J. M. P. Smith and E. J. Goodspeed, Copyright 1935 by the University of Chicago Press. In cases where it seemed advisable to remain more literally faithful to the Latin Version that Augustine cites, the translations are my own.

(*c*) Works of St. Augustine

Those frequently cited are referred to in title abbreviations taken (in slightly adapted form) from those suggested by the editors of *Folia*, Supplement II, Worcester, Mass., November 1954. The issue receives its title from its principal contribution, by Herbert Hohensee, "The Augustinian Concept of Authority." Latin titles (in chronological order), English translations, and corresponding abbreviations as used throughout the book are as follows:

Contra Academicos	Against the Academics	*Acad*
De Beata Vita	On the Happy Life	*Vita*
De Ordine	On order	*Ord*
Soliloquia	Soliloquies	*Sol*
De Immortalitate Animae	On the Immortality of the Soul	*Immort*
De Quantitate Animae	On the Greatness of the Soul	*Quant*
De Moribus Ecclesiae et Manichaeorum	On the Morals of the Church and of the Manichees	*Mor*

De Genesi contra Manichaeos	On Genesis, against the Manichees	*Gen Man*
De Libero Arbitrio	On Freedom of Choice (or: of the Will)	*Lib*
De Magistro	On the Teacher	*Mag*
De Vera Religione	On True Religion	*Ver*
De Utilitate Credendi	On the Usefulness of Believing	*Util*
De Musica	On Music	*Mus*
Confessiones	Confessions	*Conf*
De Trinitate	On the Trinity	*Trin*
De Civitate Dei	The City of God	*Civ*
Retractationes	Retractations	*Retr*
Epistolae	Letters	*Ep* (+number, e.g. *Ep* 7).

In citing from Augustine's works, the chapter numbers are regularly omitted except for those works where they are indispensable (for example, *Civ, Retr*); only the book and section is given. Thus, for example, *Conf* V, x, 19 is shortened to *Conf* V, 19.

The pronouns He and You, when referring to God or Christ, are capitalized throughout. This typographical device has been settled on to avoid confusion in the reader's mind, especially when quoting from Augustine's frequent dialogues with the Divinity. It might otherwise be difficult to tell when the "he" refers to Augustine himself.

CONTENTS

ST. AUGUSTINE'S EARLY THEORY OF MAN

The Fatherland is There whence we have come
and There is the Father.
What then is our course, what the manner of
our flight? This is not a journey for feet . . .
you must close the eyes and call instead upon
another vision which is to be waked within you.

Plotinus, *Ennead* I, 6, 8.

Not on foot, and not by distance of place
do we depart from You or return to You.
That younger son of Yours did not . . . make
a journey on foot.

Confessions I, 28.

You closed my eyes . . .
and I awoke in You and I saw . . .
and this vision was not derived from the flesh.

Confessions VII, 20.

INTRODUCTION

AUGUSTINE'S EARLY PLOTINIANISM

The properly skeptical reader, especially if he is abreast of the scholarly controversies that have surrounded the issue of Augustine's Neo-Platonism, will find his critical sense awakened by the use I make of Plotinus' *Enneads* in the following study. Two questions particularly will occur to him: What warrant do I have for using the number of treatises I use? How legitimate is my manner of using them?

One not so well acquainted with the history of the question may be inclined to place the objection further back: What warrant is there for even supposing that Plotinus exercised any influence, to say nothing of the powerful influence on Augustine's early thinking that I suppose in the pages that follow? Ill-equipped though he appears to have been for reading Greek philosophical writings in the original,[1] there was, after all, a considerable amount of

[1] The classic work on Augustine's education and on the extent of his "culture" is Henri Irénée Marrou, *Augustin et la Fin de la Culture Antique* (Paris: Boccard, 1938); hereafter cited as *Culture Antique*. The second volume, entitled *Retractatio*, appeared in 1949. It is not my view that Augustine was able, especially in this early period, to read Plotinus' difficult Greek in the original—nor, indeed, that he was ever able to do so. For the fairest summary and safest verdict I know on this controverted issue, see Marrou's *Retractatio*, pp. 631–637. Wherever in this work I refer to Augustine as "reading the *Enneads*," consulting or echoing Plotinus' "text," I hope the reader will understand these elliptical expressions as referring to the Latin translation of Marius Victorinus

diffuse Platonism circulating throughout the ancient Latin-speaking world. Augustine could have drawn many of his Platonic ideas from translations of Plato's *Phaedo* and *Timaeus* which were extant and accessible or from Platonic strains which show up in the philosophic writings of Cicero, in the *florilegia* and in the doxographies which made cultivated reading for the *rhetor* of his time. What need is there to suppose that in addition to all these, he must have read Plotinus?

Before directly confronting that final question, let me plainly admit that I recognize in the preceding paragraph a warning, and a challenge I do not mean to evade. A Plotinian interpretation of Augustine of the sort proposed here must, if it is to commend itself as sound, coherently relate his Plotinianism to the intellectual strata left by the preceding stages of Augustine's intellectual development.[2] To isolate what each of these stages left as its contribution to his final view, account must be taken of each of them in turn. Augustine was not only a Bishop and Father of the Church, he became that by passing through a provisional set of identities, each one of which shaped his final being.

(on which subject, see below). That translation has been lost to us, so the best indication we have of what it contained is obviously the Greek of the *Enneads* themselves: hence the device used here of comparing with the original text. If, upon occasion, I compare what I consider to be Plotinian "echoes" in Augustine with the Latin counterparts employed by Marcilius Ficinus in his Renaissance translation of the *Enneads*, my meaning is not (obviously) that Augustine read Ficinus' translation, as one critic thought was being implied. My point in these instances is to confirm my findings. When the resources of the Latin language are exploited by two different authors to render Plotinus' sometimes special phraseology, the likelihood is that the Latin renderings will be similar. I call attention to such verbal similarities as occur between Augustine and Ficinus for the value they have in pointing to the Plotinian "source" common to both.

[2] Aimé Solignac presents an excellent summary along with some new materials on this question of Augustine's intellectual development, in his valuable Introduction to *Les Confessions*, vol. 13 of the *BA* series of Augustine's works; see especially pp. 85–112. Also, by the same author, "Doxographies et manuels dans la formation philosophique de saint Augustin," in *Recherches Augustiniennes*, I (Paris, 1958), pp. 113–148.

In his study of Augustine's early theory of man, *Das Sein und der Mensch: Die Existenzielle Seinsentdeckung des Jungen Augustin* (Freiburg: Alber, 1959), Franz Körner quite rightly argues (pp. 27–40, esp. p. 33) that the interpreter must reach the point where he leaves off exploring the thought-world that influenced Augustine, in order to do justice to the originality he brought to creatively reshaping its lines of influence. The question is, however, when is that point reached? My conviction is that Körner took this "leap" after inadequate investigation of Plotinian influences and consequently failed to notice that the "principle of interiority" so pivotal in his view (see pp. 58ff; cf. pp. 80ff) represents far more Augustine's Neo-Platonic *interpretation* of his experience; hence the interpretation, different from mine, which Körner presents of "pride" in its connection with "outer" realities (pp. 36ff), of the soul's (not, as Körner repeatedly puts it, "man's") existential situation (pp. 46–47 and 59), and of Augustine's attitude toward pantheism (p. 193).

He began as a North African, educated, H. I. Marrou has shown, as a *rhetor* in the Roman tradition. This experience exposed him to the culture and literature that formed the mind and sensibility of his epoch: Vergil and Terence are not only names he often mentions; they formed his imagination to a great extent. On the philosophic side, reliable studies in recent years have underlined the influence of Varro's encyclopedic learning, of Seneca and Apuleius, of the doxographies which flooded the ancient world with thumbnail sketches of the welter of philosophic positions that competed for the mind's allegiance.

But in all this early period of training, Cicero[3] holds a unique position as not only the model of the ancient *rhetor*, but also the urbane Academician who had set himself the ambitious task of transposing the thought of the Greeks into the Roman tongue. His *Hortensius* fired Augustine's "first conversion" at the age of nineteen.

That conversion was, however, not to one or other philosophic point of view. It made Augustine a lover of wisdom, inserting into a heart aflame with worldly ambition and seduced by the bright promise of his own great talents an ideal to rival that of the *rhetor:* the dream of the "philosophic" way of life. To abandon the life of the law courts and the public forum, and devote oneself unreservedly to the pursuit of truth and wisdom was the invitation which, centuries before, Aristotle's *Protreptikos* had held out to his contemporaries. Cicero had recaptured a similar invitation in his own work, modeled as it was on Aristotle's. It takes Augustine years to come to terms with that invitation, eventually to acquiesce in it; but it furnishes a golden thread which runs throughout his conversion story.

Cicero's offer was, however, never made more concrete than that. His dialogues show Stoic and Epicurean each presenting their rival views on life's key questions—the nature of the Gods, the ends of human life—only to be answered at the end in the Academic's cultivated but skeptical tones. Cicero not only does not know the answer to such questions, he wonders whether man can ever know them. Wisdom for man consists in questing for the truth, resigned to the likelihood it can never be found.

Augustine tells us it was the absence of Christ's name in Cicero that prompted him to turn to the Scriptures. The lowliness of their style repelled him: his youthful pride left him easy prey to the traps of the Manichees. Part of the reason was that the

[3] See Maurice Testard, *Saint-Augustin et Cicéron*, 2 vols. (Paris, 1958).

name of Jesus was always on their tongue. The indications are, however, that their promise that "truth" could be found was also of key importance in his conversion. To confirm this impression one need only reflect that when finally he is brought to doubt this new-found faith, the yawning chasm of skepticism opens to tempt him seriously as it seems never before to have done.

The next decisive influence on Augustine's mind comes through the preaching of Ambrose and his reading of the "Platonic books." The very conjunction Augustine thought he saw in Ambrose's interpretation of the Bible and Plotinus' philosophic interpretation of human life may justify the fact that this study concentrates on Plotinus' influence with only passing reference to Ambrose. This is not the place to detail the reasons why the latter's preaching (and later, writing) seems mainly to have created in Augustine's mind an attitude receptive to a Neo-Platonized version of Christianity. Others, Fr. Charles Boyer and Pierre Courcelle chief among them, have done that work already, and it is my conviction that a careful study of the *Confessions* corroborates this aspect of their views. Aside, however, from creating this favorable "climate of understanding," a study of Ambrose's works will show, I think, that he contributed far less crucially than Plotinus did to the eventual *structure* of Augustine's Christianity. Wherever a piece of the Ambrosian mosaic corresponds to a matching piece in Augustine's, study of the design into which the piece fits will show Plotinus' synthetic spirit at work. Ambrose was, admittedly, capable of preaching sermons that pirate, at times parrot, the thoughts of Philo, Origen, and Plotinus himself. But that is, after all, a modest achievement at best and far from adequate ground for calling him a "philosopher" in any genuine sense of that term.

My exact contention here is that the *Enneads* provided the early Augustine with a comprehensive philosophic matrix, an intellectual frame. So promising did Plotinianism appear to him that it inspired a "confidence" that all he deemed valid in the other influences shaping his mind could find a natural place within that matrix. Occasionally, they might have to be reinterpreted to fit the matrix. Occasionally, too, he is clearly conscious that the opposite might be true: the contours of Plotinianism might require adjustment in order to accommodate some insight coming from another source. As time goes on and his development proceeds, the matrix itself is more severely tested. At points, it breaks under the strain, though Augustine is not always conscious of the break. But even through the *Confessions*, *De Trinitate*, and as late as the *De*

Civitate, the "Platonists" claim a special place in Augustine's esteem: they, of all philosophers, came closest to the Christian truth. Even when he has abandoned large sections of the Plotinian synthesis, his positions can best be understood by relating them to the initial synthesis he has seen the need of reforming.

That contention goes far to explain the method followed throughout this study. Its validity depends on the supposition that when attempting to disengage the structure of Augustine's developing Christianity, his language must be regarded as embodying a thought-world that receives particularly illuminating interpretation when it is compared with that (for want of a better term) central "source," Plotinus' *Enneads*. Once he encountered them, the *Enneads* not only brought together what earlier philosophical and religious influences had bequeathed to his thinking, they also continued to nourish and predominantly form his subsequent intellectual development. Although I consider that proposition valid over a much greater span, I make it here only of the early period (A.D. 386 to 391, from his conversion until his ordination to the priesthood) during which the recent convert was engaged in an effort to work out his first synthesis. Where later works, such as the *Confessions*, are used in evidence, their function is always to illumine the works of this period.[4]

So much, therefore, for the relationship supposed here between his Plotinianism and the other currents running in Augustine's thought-world. It is time now to confront the question raised by my equating *platonici* with Plotinus. All that I have said above about the influences playing on Augustine's intellectual development is put quite clearly in the first six books of the *Confessions*. But when in the Seventh Book he describes how his thought-world finally came together, the catalytic readings are anonymously designated as "Platonic books," nothing more. Who might these *platonici* be?

First of all, they are obviously not the authors of whatever Platonic writings he might have read before this time. The intellectual revolution recounted in the Seventh Book of the *Confessions* is plainly not to be attributed to such strains of "diffuse Platonism" as had already entered Augustine's intellectual bloodstream during the course of his studies and later activity as a *rhetor*. Whatever

[4] Erich Dinkler's *Die Anthropologie Augustins* (Stuttgart, 1934) eschews careful study of this early period, preferring to expose the more settled anthropological views which Dinkler (pp. 4–5) assumes Augustine incorporated in the works of his maturity, from the *Confessions* onward. How well the works of maturity can be understood apart from the development that gave them birth is a large question.

effect such readings may have had on his mind, it must be distinguished from the "incredible conflagration" (*Acad* II, 5) sparked in his thirty-second year by contact with what he describes as Latin translations of certain "books of the platonists": *libri platonicorum* (*Conf* VII, 13). There was something about these books which was new to him; new, and so powerful, that they took whatever random chords of Platonism Augustine had encountered before and succeeded in bringing them into harmony. His disorganized intellectual world, he suddenly felt, had fallen into place.

Up until 1888, when Adolph von Harnack wrote his celebrated study on "*Die Höhepunkte in Augustins Konfessionen*,"[5] scholars could still interpret the intellectual revolution Augustine relates in Book VII of the *Confessions* as though it had been ignited by the works of Plato. After all, doesn't Augustine, in a parallel description in *De Beata Vita* 4, specify that these works—*lectis autem Platonis paucissimis libris*—were Plato's own?

Later scholarship has thrown that reading into serious doubt. The manuscript tradition presents strong arguments for a copyist's error at this point; it seems so probable that the original reading was *Plotini* that one may safely take it as practically certain.[6] There are, as well, crucial mentions of Plotinus in comparable contexts throughout Augustine's early works. However, some legitimate doubt may remain. Attribution in the ancient world was hardly the careful thing we have made it today. There are precedents indicating the *possibility* that when Augustine wrote "Plotinus" he *could* have meant Plotinus' leading disciple, the editor of his *Enneads* and the best known, most widely read popularizer of the master's thought, Porphyry. Time and subsequent scholarship have accordingly shifted the ground on which Harnack once so confidently walked. No major scholar today would hold that *Confessions* VII, 13–23 refers to readings in Plato. The alternatives have become either Plotinus, or Porphyry, or both. But how did these two come into the picture?

THE CASE FOR PLOTINUS

An important chapter in this story was written in the mid-nineteenth century when Bouillet began translating Plotinus'

[5] Harnack's classic essay is reprinted in *Reden und Aufästze*, I (Giessen, 1904), pp. 51–79.

[6] See Paul Henry, *Plotin et l'Occident* (Louvain, 1934), pp. 82ff.

Enneads.[7] His far-ranging erudition and more particularly his close familiarity with Augustine's writings prompted him to suggest a considerable series of loci where he seemed to be borrowing now from Plotinus, now from Porphyry. These parallels were, it must be admitted, largely of a doctrinal nature. Bouillet seldom pushed the question into close examination of linguistic resemblances.

But they were striking enough to encourage Grandgeorge, toward the end of the century, to make a somewhat more scientific study of them.[8] His conclusion was that Augustine's doctrine was at many points substantially the same as that found in Plotinus. Subsequent students of Augustine's intellectual development, Alfaric, Boyer, and Nörregaard most prominent among them,[9] carried on the effort to uncover what writings might have been influential in Augustine's conversion in A.D. 386. Both Alfaric and Nörregaard felt confident enough to draw up generous lists of such treatises, drawn primarily from Plotinus' *Enneads*. This nascent consensus held firm throughout the 1920's. It was momentarily shaken by Willy Theiler's contention, in 1933, that Augustine read no Plotinus whatever, but only exposés of the master's thought coming from the pen of his disciple-editor, Porphyry.[10] That radical position was challenged a year afterward by Fr. Paul Henry, whose epoch-making *Plotin et l'Occident* proved, to the satisfaction of most co-workers in the field, that despite his weakness in Greek, Augustine could have read Plotinus in a translation by Marius Victorinus Afer, and that he did, in fact, undergo the detectable influence of *Ennead* I, 6, and probably of *Enneads* V, 1, III, 2, and IV, 3 around the time of his Milanese conversion. Turning the tables on his adversary, Henry then attempted to show that the Neo-Platonic strains in Augustine's thought that Theiler had attributed to Porphyrian writings could better be explained as deriving from Plotinus' *Enneads* as both Augustine's and Porphyry's common "source." Henry buttressed his argument by referring to the fact that Augustine informs the addressees of his first two works that "very few" of these books had been responsible for the intellectual (and, to some extent, spiritual) conversion he had recently undergone. The fewness of these

[7] M. N. Bouillet, *Les Ennéades de Plotin*, 3 vols. (Paris, 1857–1861).

[8] L. Grandgeorge, *Saint Augustin et le Néo-Platonisme* (Paris, 1896).

[9] See Prosper Alfaric, *L'Evolution Intellectuelle de saint Augustin* (Paris, 1918); Charles Boyer, *Christianisme et néo-platonisme dans la formation de saint Augustin* (Paris, 1920; reissued with minor changes, Rome, 1953); and Jens Nörregaard, *Augustins Bekehrung*, German translation from the Danish original (Tübingen, 1923).

[10] Willy Theiler, *Porphyrios und Augustin* (Halle, 1933).

writings, then, made it all the more imperative that proof for Porphyrian readings be rigorously established and by comparison of textual, not merely doctrinal, parallels. In other words, by the same type of evidence as had underpinned Henry's own case for Augustine's dependence on Plotinus. For the same reasons, Henry took earlier scholars like Alfaric and Nörregaard to task for claiming so large a number of Plotinus' writings as influential in Augustine's conversion.

Subsequent scholars have in the main heeded Henry's warning that proving Augustine's dependence on one or other precise treatise, whether of Plotinus or Porphyry, must be a more exacting business than pre-Theiler studies sometimes made it out to be; but his insistence that the proof invariably be based on "textual" rather than "merely doctrinal" parallels, as though there were no middle ground between those two, has since been seriously eroded. His confidence that Augustine read "very few" books of Plotinus has suffered a similar fate. Nörregaard, for example, was clearly aware that Augustine's first contact with these *libri platonicorum* was contact with very few books. Indeed, the situation could hardly have been otherwise. What Nörregaard had legitimately assumed is that Augustine's expressions about "very few books" refer exactly to that first, soul-stirring contact; the recent convert is describing the effect which even those few treatises has on him. "Very few drops" (*guttas paucissimas*) were required to enkindle the "incredible conflagration" that enveloped him (*Acad* II, 5). Writing to his friend Mallius Theodorus (*Vita* 4) his point is the same as in the parallel remark to Romanianus cited above. He means to emphasize the "burning" impression these books made upon him, the power that could be packed into "very few" of them, hence only accessorily the fewness of the books in question. Considering this stress, not only does it seem likely he would continue with these readings, but given Augustine's insatiable intellectual appetite at this time, the opposite appears psychologically inconceivable.

Now even between this first contact and the composition of the Dialogues of Cassiciacum, there is a time-gap considerable enough (June to November, 386, according to Fr. Aimé Solignac's dating of these events[11]) to give free play to that intellectual appetite. Even for the earliest of Augustine's extant writings, therefore, Nörregaard's presumption is valid: one might fully expect to find traces of more than "very few books." The only way to check on

[11] *Les Confessions*, *BA* 13, pp. 205–206.

such a presumption is to look, and this, though his method might perhaps have been tighter, Nörregaard did, finding an affirmative answer.

Not surprisingly, then, and despite the limitations imposed by more rigorous method, scholars since Henry have been steadily working toward what amounts to reinstatement of the "long lists" he had found so disturbing in Alfaric and Nörregaard. Courcelle, O'Meara, Solignac, Armstrong, and Verbeke (limiting the enumeration to recognized leaders in the field) have all contributed to this growing consensus.[12] As a result, writing in 1962,[13] Solignac felt entitled to say that Augustine "surely" read *Enneads* I, 6 "On Beauty," I, 8 on "The Nature and Source of Evil," V, 1 on "The Three Initial Hypostases," V, 2 on "The Origin and Order of the Beings Following on the First," III, 2–3 the treatise (which Porphyry arbitrarily divided into two) "On Providence." He adds that Augustine "very probably" read *Enneads* V, 3 on "The Knowing Hypostases and the Transcendent," VI, 6 "On Numbers," and VI, 9 "On the Good, or the One," as well as several treatises from the fourth *Ennead*, notably *Ennead* IV, 7 on "The Immortality of the Soul." My own researches have led me to agree substantially with Solignac's judgment, and further to conclude (with the obviously modest type of certitude one can come to in such matters) that Augustine "surely" read *Ennead* III, 7 on "Eternity and Time," IV, 3–5, the triple-treatise on "Problems concerning the Soul," IV, 8 on "The Soul's Descent into Body," V, 8 "On the Intellectual Beauty," and VI, 4–5, the

[12] See Pierre Courcelle, *Recherches sur les Confessions* (Paris, 1950), esp. pp. 157–167. In his earlier *Les Lettres Grecques en Occident* (Paris, 1943) Courcelle had criticized Theiler's exclusivism (159–161), expressed agreement with Henry (161–163), then qualified both statements by presenting (164–182) a learned personal case for a wider array of Neo-Platonic influences, including both Porphyry and Plotinus. See J. J. O'Meara's Introduction and notes to his translation *Against the Academics*, *ACW* 12 (Westminster, Md., 1950), esp. pp. 160ff; *The Young Augustine* (London, 1954), pp. 131–155; "Augustine and Neoplatonism," *Recherches Augustiniennes*, 1: 91–111 (1958); and *Porphyry's Philosophy from Oracles in Augustine* (Paris, 1959). In *The Charter of Christendom* (New York, 1961), O'Meara applies the same thinking to the interpretation of *The City of God*. In contrast to O'Meara, Heinrich Dörrie, "Porphyrios als Mittler zwischen Plotin und Augustin," in *Antike im Mittelalter*, 1: 26–47 (Berlin, 1962) adds little if anything to the Theiler–Courcelle case for Porphyry (see esp. pp. 39–41). Solignac's contributions include "Réminiscences plotiniennes et porphyriennes dans le début du *De Ordine* de saint Augustin," *Archives de Philosophie*, 20: 446–465 (1957), hereafter cited as "Reminiscences," and the extended Note in *Les Confessions*, *BA* 13, pp. 682–689. For A. H. Armstrong's suggestions, see "Spiritual or Intelligible Matter in Plotinus and St. Augustine," *AM* I, 277–283, and for Gérard Verbeke's suggestions, "Spiritualité et immortalité de l'âme chez saint Augustin," *AM* I, 329–334, hereafter cited as "Spiritualité."

[13] In his Introduction to *Les Confessions*, *BA* 13, p. 110.

double treatise "On the Integral Omnipresence of the Authentic Existent."

THE USE OF PLOTINUS

But it must be obvious that the manner of proving the influence of one or other *Ennead* on Augustine supposes an idea of how such influences betray themselves. This, in turn, supposes an idea of how Augustine himself "used" the *Enneads*, how he underwent their influence, mastering and to greater or lesser extent transforming the expressions and ideas he took from them.

If, for example, one imagines Augustine must have read Plotinus' writings, and virtually copied them word for word, then proving his dependence on any fragment of the *Enneads* implies one can produce so close a linguistic correspondence between fragments of their writings that (allowing for the differing resources of the Greek and Latin languages) the mind comparing both fragments is compelled to judge that Augustine's very expression derives from Plotinus'. On the other hand, if one allows for the case where Augustine may have read a treatise, pondered it, personally assimilated it to the point of making it his own, and then reproduced, not a servile copy of his expression, but an original reformulation of Plotinus' insight, then the task of proving Augustine's dependence on the original Plotinian model becomes considerably more complex and delicate. It is not too unfair to say that the method of textual parallels advanced by Henry, and employed with sometimes astonishing fruitfulness by Courcelle, Jean Pépin, and Solignac, *ideally* supposes the first, more servile type of dependence. The ambiguous term "source" then comes to mean something reasonably precise: the linguistic model from which another linguistic fragment is derived without the intervention of any significant creative transformation on the part of the "influenced" author. The method of "merely doctrinal" parallels, on the other hand, would claim the virtue of allowing for the influenced author's having brought a certain originality to the way he exploited the writings that inspired him. It requires that we look in the influenced author, not for the duplication of his master's expression, but for the creative reproduction of his insight. Here, then, the term "source" assumes a slacker sense: it designates the original utterance that inspired the insight eventually formulated by the influenced author, but formulated in a way that, linguistically, may be quite original.

Clearly, though, there will be cases of this second type of "source" which later exploration can never confidently discover. The more the influenced author brings his creative originality into play, the more he elaborates original and personal expression of a borrowed insight, so much the more does he make it difficult for subsequent students of his writings to trace back a given fragment of his work to the font of its inspiration. The difficulty is only enhanced when inspiration from one "source" has combined and been transfused with inspiration drawn from another, or from several other, sources. The original will inevitably be so masked in this process of personal re-creation that it may become impossible confidently to trace the resulting formulation back to any one of its several "sources."

In the light of such possible difficulties, stubborn reliance on close linguistic correspondences, insistence on "textual" combined with suspicion of "merely doctrinal" parallels, seems to commend itself as sage counsel. The tenants of this method would accordingly be interpreted as advising that, instead of launching out into guesswork, we modestly, prudently limit our efforts to what can really be "proved." Not every source can reliably be demonstrated as having functioned as a source; but then, man cannot hope, especially in historical matters, to know all he would like to know, and that is the end of that. We must settle for the limitations imposed by sound method and the canons of evidence it entails.

It is understandable, then, why proponents of this method have tended to look down on merely "doctrinal" parallels. They have preferred to argue from the "harder" type of evidence, where an Augustinian expression reproduces so closely an expression in Plotinus that even the most biased mind would be forced to capitulate before the need to explain the correspondence as pointing to literary dependence.

But this advance in method came with inbuilt temptations; they eventually became clear in time. André Mandouze, in his witty (and faintly malicious) contribution to the Augustinian Congress of 1954[14] examined a test case which, while in some respects extreme, was nonetheless symptomatic. He showed how three authors, treating Augustine's vision at Ostia (*Conf* IX, 23–25) by dealing in minute fragments of text, came to quite precise but discordant conclusions on the "sources" active in Augustine's account. Even in the modest task for which it was designed, the method of "textual parallels" had broken down: Why? One

[14] André Mandouze, "L'extase d'Ostie," in *AM* I, 83ff.

reason was that the very nature of the method persuaded its adherents to focus more or less statically on words and phrases, to isolate fragments of text and thereby (too often) lose sight of the sense, context, movement, and unity of thought embodied in the documents being compared. It is, for instance, seldom if ever possible to track down a single source for any relatively common phrase,[15] one which Augustine could have drawn from Plotinus, Porphyry, Cicero, the *florilegia* or doxographical literature, even from the relatively cultivated conversation of the epoch. But even patently philosophical phraseology of a more technical cast presents at times surprising difficulties. Assume what would appear to be the easiest case of all, where extrinsic evidence grounds the confidence that some precise phrase of Augustine is, *de facto*, modeled on some corresponding phrase in Plotinus' *Enneads*. The difficulty is that certain phrases occur almost identically in several Plotinian treatises.[16] When (allowing for the transposition of Greek into Latin) closely resemblant phraseology is found in Augustine, how can it confidently be attributed to this, rather than another, competing treatise? It is possible, obviously, only by taking the wider context into consideration. Thus, at this point, the air-tight distinction between "textual" and "doctrinal" parallels has sprung something of a leak. Or, to be more just, it becomes plain that the argument from textual parallels develops persuasive power only when it takes into account both fragments' organic connection with the entire movement of thought and image embodied in the two documents in question. It is mythical to claim one is inspecting purely linguistic correspondences in abstraction from "doctrinal" content. In that case it would no longer be language one is inspecting, only words. But a perfectly antiseptic abstraction from surrounding context and doctrinal content is equally impossible. However camouflaged, the consideration of context and content must creep back in. And only when the scholar is fully aware that both these elements have crept

[15] See the observations of Christine Mohrmann, *AM* III, 34–38, and the subsequent discussion, *ibid.*, pp. 41–48. Du Roy's notion of rigor in tracing sources remains expressly modeled on Fr. Henry's (*L'Intelligence de la Foi*, p. 69, n. 5). It is not surprising that he should find the method outlined above lacking in that kind of "rigor," p. 73, n. 5, p. 189, n. 5, p. 252, n. 4.

[16] It might be objected at this point that each Plotinian fragment is, to some extent, individualized by being embedded in the context of a treatise which is characterized by a special preoccupation, hence an individual "point" which gives it a direction and "thrust" not shared by any other single treatise (else why should Plotinus have felt the need to write *this* treatise at all?) Considered in context, therefore, it is true to say that no fragment recurs quite *identically* in Plotinus; they are always *analogues*. But this consideration of context is precisely what I am arguing for.

back in, and takes their re-entry into lucid account, does his argument carry conviction.

Much of my own reflection on this problem of tracing the "sources" of Augustine's thought was stimulated by the discussion sparked by Mandouze's paper. But it may have been a benign providence that inspired A. H. Armstrong to submit to that same Congress a valuable little essay[17] contending that Augustine's exegesis of the "Heaven of Heaven" in the Twelfth Book of the *Confessions* reflected the doctrinal pattern of *Ennead* II, 4 on "The Two Kinds of Matter," but vested in the language of several other treatises, notable among them *Enneads* V, 8 "On the Intelligible Beauty," III, 7 "On Eternity and Time," and IV, 8 "On the Descent of the Soul," plus *Enneads* V, 3 on "The Knowing Hypostases and the Transcendent" and VI, 7 "How the Multitude of Ideas Came Into Being, and on the Good." In the light of Mandouze's paper, one feature of Armstrong's contribution seemed to me then particularly remarkable: his insouciance respecting "accepted" philological exigencies in executing textual comparison. His proof for *Ennead* II, 4 is conducted on a frankly philosophic level. He argues from a striking parallel of "idea-patterns" (the expression is my own) in both authors; the linkage of ideas in Plotinus on the one hand, and Augustine on the other, shows to Armstrong's satisfaction that Augustine's doctrine faithfully reflects Plotinus', once allowance is made for the adaptations required by Christianity. Only at the end of his essay does Armstrong raise the question of linguistic correspondences, and then, he sends us off to scrutinize quite different treatises from the one that centrally concerned him!

At first the thought occurred that Armstrong had simply gone back to the old method of merely "doctrinal" parallels, but closer examination led me to suspect that the methodological implicits of his study were considerably more sophisticated than that. For one thing, his demonstration of Plotinian influence, brief and dense though it was, was for me convincing in a way that neither doctrinal nor textual comparisons had ever seemed to be. On further scrutiny, that power to convince seemed more and more clearly to stem from his application of the insight that language must be related to thought, thought kept inseparable from image, and the whole "pattern" of language-thought-and-image considered precisely as a "pattern" which boasts not only shape but movement also.

[17] See n. 12, above.

It appeared, from his essay, that Armstrong had studied the compound of thought and image expressed (indeed, embodied) in the language of Augustine and Plotinus. But he had examined that compound, not as though it could exist entirely apart from, independent of, its linguistic embodiment, but nonetheless with keen awareness that various linguistic patterns can express and embody what remains "essentially" the same pattern of thought and image. For each content-pattern, of course, there exists in any language only a limited variety of linguistic patterns to embody it. Men thinking alike will tend to talk alike; a man adopting another's way of thinking and imagining will tend to fall into analogous, if not identical, ways of expressing his thought and imaginings. Hence linguistic correspondences normally point to corresponding contents. But thought and image can still correspond, can still be "borrowed" by one author from another, and that correspondence be more or less effectively disguised by shifts in language. A bungling plagiarist reproduces another's expressions; a talented one steals another's content and, within the limits set by the language he is working in, makes the expression of it his own.

This flexible relation between dynamic thought-and-image patterns and their variable linguistic embodiments not only seemed psychologically realistic; it reflected what would frequently happen to a Plotinian insight once it passed through the mind of an Augustine. Hence it offered a clue as to how one might, at least in certain instances, persuasively argue back from the eventual Augustinian product to the original Plotinian "source." But the term "source" now came to designate something defined by the method itself: the original dynamic pattern of thought, image, and language, which inspired another mind to create a thought-image-language pattern analogous to it. Analogous—that is, manifesting the differences that result from the "influenced" author's having brought his personal creativity to bear, and yet still betraying enough of the contour and dynamism found in the "source" that it was possible still to trace its process of formation back to that source.

Depth of Assimilation

Just such a supple notion of "source" and "influence" seemed required for handling the problem of gauging Augustine's dependence on Plotinus. Traces of that dependence might be expected to show up in various ways, according to the depth at which the Saint assimilated a given feature of Plotinus' thought.

At first, while the thought is relatively unassimilated, he might find himself so dependent on the text of a given treatise that whole gobs of its expression find their way into his writings. Here textual comparisons win their brightest triumphs. As time goes on, however, Augustine may, like any dependent author, personalize his grasp of the content and individualize his mastery of the underlying images, and the expression will consequently become more and more his own. Even then, however, reconsulting one or other treatise of the Neo-Platonist may refresh and tighten, not only the Saint's grasp of the content, but the linkage of both with a style of linguistic expression, thus making linguistic correspondence more detectable. But in general it may be said that the more thoroughly a "source" is assimilated, the more profound and enduring its effective influence is, the more freely the influenced author will be able to manipulate, recombine, and re-express materials that eventually he makes so much his own that he may even come to forget that once, long ago, he found them in another's work, approved them, and then proceeded to appropriate them.

Talent and Task of the Borrower

This transmutation of thought once borrowed from another will obviously vary with the power, originality, and richness of the mind at work; but it depends as well on the complexity of the intellectual project he has set himself. Now Augustine sets himself as complex and ambitious an intellectual task as could be conceived. He brings to it, moreover, a richly furnished and rarely gifted mind.

His continued study of Plotinus went hand in hand with meditation on the Bible and the effort to construct an "understanding of the Faith" in which the two would blend as validly as possible. From the *Contra Academicos* forward this intention is plain. After a personal history of philosophy in which Plato's "purest and most clear" doctrine is said to have "shone forth especially in Plotinus" (that "Plato came to life again": *Acad* III, 41), he announces his own resolve "in nothing whatever to depart from the authority of Christ." But at the same time, "as to that which is sought out by subtle reasoning," he is confident "at the moment that I shall find it with the Platonists, nor will it be at variance with our sacred mysteries" (*Acad* III, 43).

But the *Contra Academicos* calls to mind another complicating factor in Augustine's intellectual task: his determination to show that what was valid in other philosophical traditions in the ancient world was not negated, but assumed into and fulfilled in Plotinianism. His treatment of the Academics is designed to show that they were not merely skeptics, but that their skepticism was a tactic they resorted to in defense of their secret positive teaching: the same Platonism which shone forth anew in Plotinus' writings. The *De Beata Vita*, we shall have occasion to see, strives to establish a similar concordism between the Stoic and Plotinian ideals of happiness. Augustine's task in this regard had perhaps been facilitated to the extent that the frequently eclectic tendencies of the ancient philosophic world had already succeeded in "Platonizing" these rival systems of thought. In any event, he does not feel he is forcing them out of shape when he accepts a number of elements from Roman philosophers such as Cicero, Varro, and Seneca, and then proceeds to subordinate them to, inform them by, what he accepts from Plotinus. He was convinced not only that Aristotle and Plato had shared profound agreement (*Acad* III, 42), but that other apparently rival systems also really became themselves and said with limpid clarity what they had been obscurely stammering when given utterance by that *os Platonis*, the author of the *Enneads* (*Acad* III, 41).

But there is a third feature of Augustine's intellectual endeavor disclosed as early as the *Contra Academicos* and running through all the writings of the period we are about to study: his polemic preoccupation with Manichaeism. The work is dedicated to Romanianus, his former patron, in whose conversion to Manichaeism Augustine played an important role. He feels obliged to undo that work now, not only in Romanianus' interest, but on behalf of others he had proselytized as well. His *intellectus fidei* is constantly beamed in this direction: to show that the Manichees' central claim, to have solved the problem of evil by their dualistic conception, was unfounded. His own synthesis of Plotinus and the Bible could, he felt, provide more satisfying answers to their problem than they had. His thought is sharpened, polarized by this polemic focus. His expression, too, is often keyed to taking over their language and imagery, transposing and transforming it when that was needed to purify it of its errors and inadequacies. This preoccupation with a certain audience, therefore, introduces a further twist into Augustine's assimilation of Plotinus, an additional factor of "disguise."

Parallel "Patterns"

In the final state of such a complex assimilation, philological comparison, professing to remain antiseptically on the level of language, is often incapable of uncovering a "source" that may still be exercising an influence all the more decisive for its being subterranean. And yet, it may still be permissible to look "below" (so to speak) the surface layer of expression, and possible to find not merely fragmentary doctrinal parallels, but what I have termed "parallel patterns" of thought and image. These will consist not merely in concepts and images taken atomically one by one, but in complex constellations of them, arranged in patterns both formal and dynamic. Given the intention, thrust, and movement of any individual Plotinian treatise, certain ideas will call for their natural successors, certain images for their natural partners. My contention is that, in certain instances at least, the reappearance of such a distinctive cluster in Augustine's work may be established just as "objectively" as any linguistic cluster. For thought and image have contours as firm, and represent a type of evidence as "hard," as the black and white of words on paper. And, though their contours may shift somewhat in the process of intellectual assimilation and development, it may still be possible to identify varied stages of their genesis with considerable confidence.

The process I have outlined for ferreting out Plotinian patterns in Augustine's thought also defines the "use" I make of Plotinus' writings for illumination of Augustine's text. The latter is simply an attempt to reconstruct the same process but considered as running in the opposite direction. I have, in short, tried to discern and respect the manner in which Augustine "used" Plotinus—taking into account the complexity of the intellectual task he set himself, the concordist assumptions that presided over his effort, and the varying injection of creative originality he brought to its execution—and thereby giving an account of the problems a modern would have with the results of his synthetic activity.

Such problems moderns have had, and continue to have. Unable to share Augustine's assumption of basic concord between rival schools and Plotinianism, more than one scholar has felt forced to opt between *either* a Plotinian *or*, say, a Stoic or Ciceronian "source" for, and interpretation of, certain Augustinian propositions. Reluctant to countenance—or even to acknowledge—his optimistic view of the kinship shared by Plotinianism and Christianity, a whole array of literature has felt obliged to inquire whether Augustine's Milanese conversion in A.D. 386 was to Christianity *or* to Neo-Platonism, as though, at that point in his career, these would have appeared mutually exclusive entities.[18]

[18] A good presentation of this controversy can be found in the Introduction to M. P. Garvey, *Saint Augustine, Christian or Neoplatonist?* (Milwaukee, 1939). Sister Garvey's way of answering that question merits a more reserved judgment.

A special problem arising from Augustine's concordist views touches his use of the Bible. And here I mean the Bible as Augustine found it interpreted by authorized spokesmen for the *Catholica*, notably by Ambrose of Milan. Its pages, often enough, warrant Augustine's rejection of some tenet of Plotinianism—Trinitarian subordinationism, for example. But he is not always free from the temptation to interpret what the *Catholica* teaches in terms of what Plotinian philosophy will permit it to say. The result, in one of Solignac's happy coinages, is an occasional "hybrid formation" where Augustine has reached some uneasy compromise between Christianity and Plotinianism.

This tendency of Augustine's to "inform" all other sources with a selective Plotinianism should warn the reader of an attitude it would be illegitimate to bring to the evaluation of what follows: an "either-or" mentality, which demands that this or that feature of Augustine's thought be accounted for *either* by a Plotinian, *or* by a Biblical, or by some other *single* source.

To concentrate on the Bible for a moment: in the Seventh Book of the *Confessions*, Augustine introduces his account of his Platonic readings with an *apologia* (VII, 13–15) designed to show that he is clearly aware both of the agreement and occasional disagreement —*ibi legi, . . . ibi non legi*—between the *platonici* and the Bible. This illustrates the method whereby he read both Plotinus and Scripture, from his earliest works up to and including the *Confessions*. What strikes him is the series of coincidences between the two. Of these coincidences, many are purely verbal to our modern understanding, but they meant a great deal more to a *rhetor* educated, as Augustine was, in a predominantly literary culture. When he discovers the same term or image in both Plotinus and the Bible, he is often rather too easily convinced that Plotinus' expression is saying much the same thing as a "spiritual exegesis" of Scripture will yield. To ask whether he drew a term or image from the Bible, rather than from Plotinus, is to bring an either-or question to an intellectual development running on a different track entirely. Augustine's is far more a "both-and" mind; what interests him is what he finds both in philosophy and in Scripture. What is important is the fresh creation that emerges once he has gone to work on such correspondences.

By the very nature of the case, though, some of those creations are calculated to unsettle Biblical scholars. But their discomfort will often afflict Plotinian scholars, too. We have already seen the problem involved in finding Plotinian fragments in Augustine's work and tracing them back to one or other of the *Enneads*. Such fragments can occur twice or even more frequently in various loci. Oftentimes, though, the meaning of two such fragments is subtly different owing to the context, movement of thought, and the contribution Plotinus intends each to make toward the individualized "point" of the treatise in question. Multiple occurrences of this sort help to account for the many cases of "interference" in Augustine's mind between one Plotinian treatise and another. The Saint is seldom if ever merely repeating the master's words, regurgitating undigested chunks of Plotinianism shorn of all contextual relation. Nor is he in the habit of referring mentally to one treatise hermetically sealed off from the total context—as he understands it—of Plotinus' work. He has seen various themes recur and over time has developed his power of thinking out themes of one treatise in relation to the same or analogous themes as Plotinus exposes them elsewhere. The result is that in any given section of Augustine's writings one or other Plotinian treatise may dominate, but seldom, if ever, to the hermetic exclusion of others.

This is particularly true when a thematic relation between several treatises is close enough to make it normal and natural that a certain mutual interference be expected. It would be strange, for instance, if (granted that he read them both) Augustine developed his thought on beauty by unique reference to *Ennead* I, 6 "On Beauty," without his understanding of that treatise resonating with what Plotinus says in his much later *Ennead* V, 8 "On the Intelligible Beauty." There is, therefore, a certain unity and cohesion to Plotinus' thought-world, and Augustine was intelligent enough to grasp it to a great extent and put that grasp to work.

But there are also strains and inconsistencies in Plotinus. Certain problems internal to his thought lead him to a perceptible "shift of accent" as the years advance. By the time he addresses himself to "The Intelligible Beauty," for instance, the violent anti-Stoic animus of the early treatise "On Beauty" has largely evaporated. We cannot expect Augustine always to have recognized the initial strains and the consequent development they brought about; his frequent practice of combining the contextual thrusts of treatises that date from different periods of Plotinus' life will, accordingly, sometimes lead him to deform the problematic line of both the treatises in question. The result, more often than not, is a bastardized Plotinianism which modern scholars would refuse to honor with the master's name.

We cannot, therefore, expect Augustine always to have understood Plotinus in the way contemporary scholars claim he must be understood. Nor, in consequence, may we require that he use the master's thought only in ways that modern scholarship would deem legitimate.

THE POSSIBLE INFLUENCE OF PORPHYRY

But what right does one have to interpret Augustine's early thought without taking into account the influence of Plotinus' editor and disciple, Porphyry? My fundamental reason for doing so is that since Theiler, no proponent of Porphyrian influence on Augustine is inclined to deny he was also strongly influenced by Plotinus.[19] Once this Plotinian influence is granted, however, I have found no scholar who could offer convincing proof that, before the composition of the *De Consensu Evangelistarum* around the year A.D. 400, Augustine read any Porphyry whatever. For every case that initially seemed to point to Porphyrian *as distinct from* Plotinian influence turns out, on closer scrutiny, to be *better* explained by tracing the Augustinian element in question back to the *Enneads*.

It is central to this question to notice that the case for Porphyry has always, and indeed must, suppose that the Porphyrian form of Neo-Platonism had some philosophic accent clearly distinguishable from the Plotinian. Theiler rested his case on alleged thematic differences; O'Meara, more recently, has done the same, stressing not Theiler's, but a different set of themes.[20] Even though often arguing from a more fragmentary kind of evidence, Courcelle and Solignac have worked from the same principle: the expressions or doctrinal accent represented by those fragments must, they submit, be accounted for by works of Porphyry as distinguished from the *Enneads* which both of them, along with O'Meara, admit Augustine read. Such contentions, we shall see when we come to a study of the themes in question, invariably rest on indirect evidence. More than that, as I shall have occasion to argue, the reasoning invoked often supposes a "Porphyrian" interpretation of Augustine which is sometimes a distortion, almost always at least questionable.

The claimant for Porphyrian influence on Augustine must, in addition, cope with a problem that Solignac candidly admits makes his contentions "difficult to verify."[21] Almost none of Porphyry's writings have come down to us. The significant

[19] See the references to Theiler, Courcelle, O'Meara and Solignac given above, nn. 10 and 12.

[20] For more on these alleged thematic differences, see below, pp. 21ff.

[21] Introduction to *Les Confessions*, *BA* 13, pp. 111–112.

exception is the *Aphormai*, or in their Latin title, *Sententiae ad Intelligibilia Ducentes*, which the evidence suggests Porphyry wrote as a kind of résumé-introduction to the *Enneads*. It may well be that they were wholly or partially translated by Marius Victorinus and prefaced the translation of Plotinus from which Augustine drew his inspiration. It is clear from this work, however, that its effect would hardly be to acquaint Augustine with a Porphyrian brand of Neo-Platonism distinct from his master's. Quite the contrary is true. Porphyry is precisely introducing the reader to the *Enneads*, something which requires that his résumé be faithful to Plotinus' thought. It is symptomatic that in at least one instance where he claims to find echoes of the *Sententiae* in Augustine's *De Ordine*,[22] Solignac is subsequently led to admit that the Porphyrian influence very probably worked "inside"—somewhat like a minor eddy in the larger current of—the Plotinian influence borne by the particular treatise of the *Enneads* Porphyry was summarizing. That treatise, Solignac goes on to assert, Augustine very likely read. The implicit admission is, therefore, that in this instance Porphyry's influence merely sharpened and underlined one aspect of Plotinus'—something one would fully expect from the very nature of the *Sententiae*. The case supposes more of an identity than a distinction between Plotinian and Porphyrian Neo-Platonism. For the purposes of the interpretation presented in these pages, therefore, the *Enneads* could safely be taken as embodying the single philosophic accent both master and disciple can be considered to have shared.

But did the Porphyry of those writings that have not survived to us, or survived only in fragments, citations, and allusions embedded in the writings of other authors (including Augustine), did *that* Porphyry exhibit any peculiar philosophic accent whose traces can be uncovered alongside, and distinguishable from, traces of Plotinian influence? If, so, it would obviously make a difference in the interpretation of Augustine which of these two language-and-thought-worlds one supposed an Augustinian proposition as emerging from, and still, to some extent at least, embodying.

So, for example, Theiler contended that the Augustine of the early synthesis incorporated in the *De Vera Religione* (A.D. 391) differed from Plotinus in emphasizing the ethical, subjective side of the individual soul's fall toward nonbeing from its "Mid-being" position (*μέση οὐσία*) in the order (*τάξις*) of reality. That emphasis, he contended, coupled with one on the soul's salvific return to

[22] Solignac, "Reminiscences," pp. 461–462.

the realm of being. It led, in turn, to his stressing the triadic fault of pride, curiosity, and concupiscence as rooting that fall, and to the connection between "curiosity" and the need for battling against "fantasy" and its images.[23] Since (Theiler claims) none of these themes is to be found in exactly the same connections or emphasized with equal intensity by Plotinus, Augustine must have found them, neatly packaged for him it would appear, in the writings of Porphyry. Augustine is given little if any credit for creative originality; his intellectual project is viewed as transmitting faithfully the riches of Porphyrian philosophy. It never seriously enters Theiler's mind that he might have found elements of such a synthesis as *membra disjecta* in Plotinus and subtly transposed them in forging his personal synthesis. There is little if any allowance made for the possibility that Augustine was a powerfully original thinker, an authentically Christian thinker, engaged in the complicated task of elaborating an "understanding of the faith," and that in doing so his thought (and use of Neo-Platonic materials) might have undergone a five-year development which reached its first culmination in, but hardly started from, the *De Vera Religione*.

Plainly, then, opting for Porphyry as a dominant influence on Augustine's thought can make, and has made, a difference in the eventual view of Augustine's intellectual development. The same must be said of O'Meara's markedly different case for Porphyrian, but in addition to Plotinian, influence.

No summary of O'Meara's rich and highly sophisticated presentation of what he takes to be Porphyrian themes in Augustine can hope to avoid injustice. One can only attempt to outline the main lines of his case without deforming them too greatly.[24] Having admitted that Augustine read Plotinus—he even goes to the trouble of pointing to where four of the treatises Henry had proposed have left discernible traces in the earliest Dialogues of Cassiciacum—O'Meara makes a clear distinction between Augustine before and after the *De Consensu Evangelistarum*: he has, by this time, evidently read Porphyry's attack *Against the Christians*. The question that concerns us here is whether he had read him at the time of his conversion in A.D. 386, and whether the writings of 386–391 must be interpreted accordingly. O'Meara thinks they

[23] Theiler and, following him, Rudolf Beutler (in his article "Porphyrios," *RE* XXII, 1, cols. 275–313, esp. 301–312) lists other features he considers distinctive of Porphyry vis-à-vis Plotinus, but I limit this enumeration to those that directly affect the allegation of detectable Porphyrian influence on Augustine's early theory of man.

[24] See the reference to O'Meara's contributions in n. 12, above.

must, and he classifies as Porphyrian two types of theme. In both cases O'Meara's argument is parallel: he fixes on those themes that Augustine himself identifies as Porphyrian—in the *De Civitate Dei* and in the *Retractations*—and attributes those same themes to Porphyrian influence where they show up in Augustine's early works.

The first class of themes the older Augustine mentions with the intention of rejecting them. Thus, for example, the aging Bishop censures a series of expressions in his early works, warning the reader that they ought not be interpreted as implying the Porphyrian contempt of sense-knowledge or the Porphyrian doctrine of "flight from the body." The argument may at first seem paradoxical, even subject to retort. Augustine, one is tempted to say, is warning the reader against the false impression that these phrases indicate the very Porphyrian influence for which O'Meara is arguing. But there is something unreal about that retort: it seems at least natural to surmise that Augustine is trying to correct some early missteps as gracefully as possible, and as a Bishop having attained the prominence he had, one can understand why. For it is not always easy to find another meaning for these censured expressions besides the one Porphyry would have intended by them also. There is every likelihood that they bore the same sense for Augustine when he wrote them; hence they *might* be importations from Porphyry. But there is a stronger and more real objection to O'Meara's argument: numerous loci in the very Plotinian treatises O'Meara has admitted that Augustine read contain analogues of these offensive phrases and a doctrine very like the one he attributes to Porphyry. If, furthermore, those "Porphyrian" expressions in the early works are put to careful scrutiny, their cast and context frequently argue more convincingly for Plotinian than for Porphyrian origin. The fact that Augustine, once he has rejected the doctrinal implications of those expressions, prefers to lay them at the disciple's rather than at his master's door could easily be understood in the light of the anti-Porphyrian polemic so prominent in the *De Civitate Dei*. He wishes to preserve Plotinus as free of taint as he can for those instances where he can use the master for refuting the disciple. But—and this is where the impact on interpreting Augustine comes into play—even were one to insist on identifying such themes as having in fact been drawn from Porphyry, one must at the same time admit that precisely inasmuch as Augustine could have found exhortations to turn away from sense and flee the body in the *Enneads*, they do not represent a Porphyrian emphasis *distinct from* his master's. To that extent then, using the *Enneads* to illumine the import of such themes where they occur in Augustine, and omitting all reference to Porphyry, would not result in any notable deformation of Augustine's thought. It still stands as a legitimate procedure for interpreting Augustine.

This is not quite so true for the second class of themes O'Meara holds to be Porphyrian: the class the older Augustine still approves and assumes into his synthesis.

The Saint interprets Porphyry as having sought a "universal way"—*via universalis*—whereby not only the favored few, but the unlettered many, could attain to the beatifying possession of Truth. For this he receives nothing but praise. Augustine tries to show that this *via universalis* is Christ himself incarnate, both Truth and Way to Truth, indeed, Truth become Way. This theme, too, O'Meara finds already forming in the young Augustine. The entire relation of faith and reason as Augustine conceives of it derives, O'Meara thinks, from this Porphyrian conception of the *via universalis*, adapted at need for the Christian context.

To this point the main objections are two. First of all, the passage (*Civ* X, xxxii) that Augustine produces from Porphyry to indicate that he was seeking this *via universalis* is a very shaky one. The theme is far from evidently there and might just as conceivably have been read into Porphyry by an Augustine whose polemic point is uppermost in his mind. The *via universalis* theme is unquestionably Augustinian; it may well be Neo-Platonic to the extent that Augustine, anxious to secure a hearing from the Neo-Platonists, exerts his wits to foist it upon them.

The second objection is more relevant to this study because it directly affects the interpretation of Augustine. O'Meara's insistence on handling this theme as peculiarly "Porphyrian" (as distinct from Plotinian) has led him, I suggest, to misinterpret the faith-reason dialectic in Augustine's early works. The danger is one that dogs all efforts of *Quellenforschung*—that of reading the allegedly "influenced" author's work through the lens of the "source" that is held to have influenced him. Looking for "Porphyrianisms" or "Plotinianisms" in Augustine can lead one to find them, and in the finding, to miss the real Augustine. To be specific, O'Meara proposes that Augustine found in Porphyry a theory of philosophic reason as the "way of the few," whereas oracles, and theurgy more generally, would constitute a "universal way" for the "many," unsuited as they are to the philosophic mode of ascent. Transforming this theory of the two ways to fit the Christian context, Augustine then proposes (O'Meara reasons) both faith in Christ and philosophic reason as *coordinate* ways, on equal footing, for the arrival at truth. My suggestion is (and the proof for this contention will have to wait the proper point for its development) that the early Augustine does indeed speak of two ways, the way of reason and the way of authority. Christ functions in both ways, but in a peculiar manner in the way of authority. Finally, this way of authority is for the many. At this point, however, I must part from O'Meara's understanding of the matter. The way of authority, far from being coordinate, is definitely subordinated to the way of reason, and a Neo-Platonic source—along with others—is active in persuading Augustine of this subordination. But the Saint's slow elaboration of his theory of the "Ways," and of their relation to each other, can be understood better, and without distortion, by appealing to Plotinus as the Neo-Platonist in question, rather than to Porphyry.

More precisely, Plotinus rather than a Porphyry whose influence on Augustine's early anthropology is conceived of as distinguishable from, and to that extent running counter to, Plotinus' influence. I do not mean to outlaw the possibility that Augustine read *any* Porphyry during these years; nor do I claim that such readings could not have had and did not have *any* discernible influence alongside and distinguishable from Plotinus' influence. My claim is both more modest and more precise: when it comes to understanding those aspects of Augustine's developing theory of man that are handled in this book and during the period that it covers (A.D. 386–391), the most rewarding procedure is that of considering the *Enneads* as the dominant Neo-Platonic influence on his thinking, so dominant that any *competing* influence from Porphyry can safely be ignored. Hence, a Porphyrian can quite well accept the interpretation I give of Augustine, to the extent that he admits that Plotinus represents the Neo-Platonism to which Porphyry gave substantial allegiance.[25] The same would be true for one who held that some of Augustine's Neo-Platonism could have come to him from other quarters. In either of these cases, the *Enneads* are a defensible key to Augustinian exegesis, so

[25] The same could be said of many cases where a scholar like Du Roy, for example, interprets one or another passage of Augustine by a different Plotinian fragment than I have adduced as its "source" (see *L'Intelligence de la Foi*, p. 73, n. 5, p. 189, n. 5, p. 252, n. 4). The fragment he chooses leads him into the whole Plotinian world-view it reflects in little, so that his resulting interpretation of Augustine shares wide areas of agreement with the one I have presented. See especially, in this connection, his explanation of authority and its relation to reason, pp. 109–148, of beatitude, pp. 149–161, and of "Admonition," pp. 161–165.

long as the interpretation does not do violence to Augustine's own text as it stands, but illuminates its meaning in a manner consistent with his use of the same expressions in others of his early works.

The test of any such angle of vision as I have adopted in this study is its capacity to give account of Augustine's rich complexity without distortion or impoverishment. My claim is that Plotinus' influence was both rich and complex enough to evoke the Augustine we know and recognize. It must, accordingly, be asked whether the interpretative use that is here made of Plotinus' doctrine is rich and complex enough to let Augustine remain Augustine and to illumine what he said and what he meant by what he said, with due regard for the succeeding stages of his intellectual development.

THE OBJECT: UNDERSTANDING AUGUSTINE

This concern is the real business of source-research as it is employed in these pages. Its purpose is not to smother, but to uncover and place the individuality of the influenced author in the sharpest possible focus; not to show that Augustine is saying what Plotinus said, as though he were saying it without addition, subtraction, or remainder, but to measure accurately what Augustine himself says and what he means by what he says.

To apply this for a moment to a problem alluded to earlier, and subsequently left in the shadows: isn't there every reason to think that a renewed and broadened emphasis on Augustine's Plotinianism will only bring to life the dormant question of his "conversion"? Doesn't it suggest, again, that Augustine was converted at Milan far more to Neo-Platonism than to Christianity?

Confronted by this issue, I have not felt entitled to take cover behind Courcelle's thesis that Augustine's acquaintance with Plotinianism was mediated by St. Ambrose. There is still too much of the problematical in that position. But the central contribution of Courcelle's *Recherches sur les Confessions* appears to be, first, his proof that Ambrose—whose dependence on Origen, Philo, and the Cappadocians is a matter of record—at one point in his career even preached Christianity decked out in Plotinian language—consequently his warning, issued in terms even more telling than Boyer's before him, against the anachronism of stressing an opposition between Christianity and Neo-Platonism conceived in terms quite foreign to Augustine's own time.[26] The question of

[26] The references throughout this work are limited for the most part to relatively recent studies which have taken the optic represented by those referred to above: that

Augustine's sincerity as a Christian, then, seems more than ever a false problem, one that serves only to mask the real question at issue: how adequate, objectively, was the Neo-Platonic *intellectus* which Augustine—sincerely, though perhaps at points mistakenly—believed to correspond to the content of the *fides catholica*?

But, it might be objected, that way of reframing the question really rests on another grand assumption: can one be confident that from Cassiciacum onwards Augustine was embarked on this conscious quest for an *intellectus fidei*? Can this be proved from a study of what he has written?

The contention here is that it can be proved—once the study of his writings produces the fruit of understanding what he is driving at. And for that understanding, it is indispensable to know exactly how, and how much, Plotinus functions in his thinking.

To resume the main contention of this work again, therefore: Augustine conceives of Plotinus as an invaluable ally in his task of developing an "understanding of the faith," an *intellectus fidei* wherein both terms must be accorded equal importance. Principally against the Manichees[27]—they are never far from his attention—he insists upon "faith," and the faith of the *Catholica*. But against those within the *Catholica* who would rest on a purely undigested, unreflected "simple faith," he is more and more openly warning of the need to rise to "understanding," a spiritual understanding somewhat analogous to Clement's Christian *Gnosis*. To use the terms Jean Guitton proposes,[28] his *esprit*, and therefore his subjective sincerity, are never in doubt; but in this delicate task the *mentalité* and language of an age constantly bring him close to betrayal of that "spirit." But once we know how, and how much, Plotinianism is at work in Augustine's intellectual development, a paradoxical result occurs. We are enabled to see how Augustine's progressively firmer grasp of Christianity advances *pari-passu* with a

---

Augustine's thought can best be illumined by carefully setting it against the intellectual background of his time, with special attention to Neo-Platonism. The specialized character of that optic may excuse my passing over in silence some studies which, though recent, have chosen to ignore, or (to my way of thinking) underestimate the importance of approaching Augustine's thought from that angle.

[27] François Chatillon, "En attendant le retour de Mani," *Revue du Moyen Age Latin*, 10: 185–190 (1954) points to the importance of Manichaeism for an understanding of Augustine's thought; I could not agree more. For what remains the most reliable work on this sect as Augustine knew it, see H. C. Puech, *Le Manichéisme, son fondateur, sa doctrine* (Paris, 1949). Alfaric, *L'Evolution* also presents a mine of information on Augustine's views of his former heresy.

[28] In *Le Temps et l'Eternité chez Plotin et Saint Augustin* (Paris, 1933), pp. xi and following.

surer understanding of Plotinus' teaching; we come to see that certain conflicts are inevitable; and we are in a position to measure accurately how Augustine reacts to those conflicts. Each time that conflict becomes clear *to him*, Augustine's reaction is resoundingly Christian, as we shall have several occasions to demonstrate. Accordingly, the further he advances the more he shifts his emphasis to those points of the Plotinian synthesis that are more easily Christianizable and begins to sense at the same time the limitations of Plotinus in this regard. The picture that emerges is one of an initial commitment to Christianity which slowly unfolds, an "intellectual evolution," if you will, become gradually more conscious of the corollaries—and internal strains—contained in its premises from the very start.

ONE: THE DIVINE SOUL

1 GOD AND THE SOUL

It may seem strange, particularly in our epoch, to open an inquiry into a thinker's theory of man by plunging right off into his thinking about God. If strange it be, then Augustine was a strange man: but that, at all events, is the kind of man he was. God-haunted, he would have found it passing strange that we might think his tack even faintly out of style. The talk among Christians of a God who is "dead" would have puzzled one for whom, in Harnack's ringing phrase, the living God was always his highest good, the very "life" of his soul.

But this preoccupation with God was not exclusively affective, not merely an affair of sentiment or aspiration. Intellectually, Augustine was convinced, one of man's most decisive exigencies, if he was to arrive at any just idea of himself, of his situation, and of his destiny, was to think rightly about God. Again and again he diagnoses his former religious failings as having stemmed, on the intellectual level, from his inability to form an adequate notion of God.

But, disconcerting for a modern though it be, one of the first things the recent convert had to get clear was a reasoned conviction of the soul's *distinction* from God. For the Manichees had claimed the soul was "by nature" one with God, a fragment of the luminous deity. Even after his disappointment with Faustus' attempt to solve his difficulties against Manichee doctrine, it took Augustine a considerable while to shuck off all remnants of that central tenet. The very philosophers, whose teachings on the physical world had brought him to see the weaknesses of Manichee cosmology, came round to assuring him in other terms of the soul's "divinity." That teaching, we shall see, is what the more mature Augustine refers to when he uses the term "idolatry."

Even after the encounter with the "books of the Platonists" at Milan, this issue was not firmly settled in his mind. The reason was that alongside all the correctives those writings brought to his former thought-ways, they still contained occasional phrases redolent of the error that had so long been his—phrases that insinuated that the soul was still "divine," in some sense "one" with God. To follow the turnings of Augustine's development on the soul's distinction from God, to understand the view of the soul he later rejects when he accuses the "Platonists" of "idolatry," but at the same time to measure the tensions that earlier brought him to toy with the notion of the soul's "divinity," it is important and illuminating to appreciate from the outset how, and how deeply, he underwent the influence of Plotinus' twin-treatise on Omnipresence, *Ennead* VI, 4–5. For from this treatise Augustine drew not only the underlying principles whereby he relates the "other" world to "this," but also a series of powerful images he employs to represent God's omnipresent "care" for fallen souls at each step of their journey through human life. To understand what the Augustine of this early period thought of "man," one must probe deeply into what he meant by that "journey."

Importance of the Omnipresence Theme for Augustine

For Augustine, from beginning to end, the opening question of philosophy was always: what is man's highest good, the good whose attainment will make him happy? Similarly, the primary fact of human consciousness for Augustine was man's ineradicable desire for happiness.

Often, however, and especially so in his earlier works, Augustine's awareness of man's desire for happiness is coupled with an equally acute awareness of the misery of human life as we experience it. The Manichees had made capital of this dark side of the human condition. The soul's experience of evil was the starting point for their proof that it must be native to another world, a fragment of the Divine Light, in fact alienated from its primordial bliss by some original catastrophe and taken prisoner in the darkness of this material realm.

Little wonder, then, that the earliest work he completed after his conversion was the Dialogue "On the Happy Life," *De Beata Vita*. It represents an interlude between the first and second books of the *Contra Academicos*, a work in which he is bent on showing that man is not condemned only to "seek" the truth, as the Academics thought; he may legitimately aspire, in the Gospel's phrase, to "find" it as well. The existential bearing of that question is brought out, not only in the third book of the *Contra Academicos*, but in the *De Beata Vita* as well. The agreement with the *Confessions* is striking, for Augustine from the very beginning places happiness in the "finding" and "possession" of the Truth; this is the "food" for which the soul hungers. But Truth's true name is God.

Moreover, Augustine already sees that his problem has an ontological dimension: how can the soul's alienation from God be reconciled with God's unfailing presence to all his creatures, including the soul? The difficulty is that to "seek" God implies that the seeker does not yet "possess" Him. Yet God is present to all His creatures so that they do, after all, "possess Him." The dialogue puts the solution to the difficulty in a paradox that comes from the lips of Monica: "I believe that everyone possesses God, but, if one lives righteously, he has God favorable to him, and if wrongly, hostile" (*Vita* 19).

Deum habere propitium, *Deum habere infestum*. Across the years that same paradox echoes in Augustine's query to God in the *Confessions*: whither does the wicked man go, "or where does he flee, except from you well-pleased (*placido*) to you all wrathful (*iratum*)"? (IV, 14). The supposition in both cases is the same. Everyone "possesses" God, that is, participates in His Being in order to exist at all; hence God is present to all creatures—even to those who choose "absence" from him through sin. Flee though man may, God remains ineradicably present, with an angry presence now, but present: for the heart of all participation, its deepest core, is omnipresence.

So it is that from Cassiciacum onwards Augustine is struck by those paradoxes of omnipresence. But his fascination with the theme is never more evident than in the *Confessions*. The very opening paragraphs find him already launched on a series of queries on God's presence to man, even to the man who would be absent from Him. Cayré and, more recently, Grabowski have both devoted studies to this theme's centrality for understanding Augustine and his *Confessions*.[1] In variants and harmonics the same

[1] Fulbert Cayré, *Dieu présent dans la vie de l'esprit* (Paris, 1951); Stanislaus J. Grabowski, "St. Augustine and the Presence of God," *Theological Studies*, 13: 336–358 (1952); *The All-Present God* (St. Louis, 1954).

leitmotiv spans the work from beginning to end, its recurrence relieved of monotony only by the Saint's masterful handling of a set of mighty images which portray Augustine seeking God "outside" him, when He is all the while "within," and yet, not only within, but "behind," "before," "above"—at times, in some bewildering way, all of these at once.

But the obverse of that leitmotiv is equally important. Augustine spares no pains to remind us throughout the first seven books of the *Confessions* that the key to his error was precisely his incapacity to conceive of God in spiritual terms. He did not know how to think of God "except as a corporeal mass, for I thought that anything not a body was nothing whatsoever. This was the greatest and almost the sole cause of my inevitable error"—*maxima et prope sola causa . . . inevitabilis erroris meae* (V, 19).

The intellectual side of his conversion will, accordingly, involve a breakthrough to the "spiritual." One can, therefore, understand why Henry could feel so confident that *Enneads* I, 6 and V, 1 provided adequate "illustration" for that conversion process.[2] For both insist on leaving sense behind, turning away from the inferior world of bodies, and emerging into the higher, intellectual world. Seen through the lens of these two treatises, therefore, the *Confessions* seem indeed to conduct Augustine to that Neo-Platonic illumination of Book Seven, under the guise of a quasi-ecstatic "ascent to the spiritual." This, in essence, is the interpretation put upon those crucial paragraphs by Pierre Courcelle in his *Recherches sur les Confessions*,[3] and there is much truth in it.

But not the whole truth. For closer inspection of the loci where Augustine exposes this nagging intellectual difficulty finds a deeper common trait. If we compare Augustine's work with these two treatises, as Mandouze has observed, it is impossible not to be struck by "a radical difference of tonality"; it is "God's perpetual presence in the *Confessions* which changes everything."[4] This is the

[2] *Plotin*, p. 128.

[3] *Recherches*, pp. 157–167.

[4] Mandouze, "L'extase d'Ostie," in *AM* I, 83ff. G. Madec complains (in *REA* 11: 373 [1965]) that I have misused this observation. Mandouze "was certainly not thinking of the Plotinian theme of omnipresence" but rather of the "difference of tonality" introduced by the fact that Augustine is writing "before God's gaze" and constantly addressing his God. Granted the second (Christian) element, was its precise flavor not made possible by the transformation of the religious imagination operated by the first (Plotinian) element? The second is quite conceivable without the first. Compare, for instance, the prayer of the *Soliloquies*: Augustine is certainly addressing his God, writing before his "gaze"; but one senses far more God's "distance" than the *Confessions*' atmosphere saturated with His Presence. The reason, I suggest, is that the effect of such treatises as I, 6 and V, 1 has meantime been brought within the orbit of the Omnipresence treatise.

deeper common trait pervading all Augustine's descriptions of his difficulty. The text just cited, for example, is bracketed by the realization that this difficulty prevents him from realizing that God is present everywhere (V, 16) and everywhere present "entire" (VI, 4). The same is true for virtually every locus where the *Confessions* deal with this issue. A spiritual conception of God is essential, but because only such a conception can do justice to His omnipresent relation to creatures. And neither of the treatises that Henry and Courcelle have put to work can account for the sophisticated complexities of Augustine's manner of thinking out God's omnipresence.

Importance of the Omnipresence Theme for the Neo-Platonist

Looming large in Theiler's case for Porphyry were text upon text concerning omnipresence. For want of extant texts, Theiler makes appeal to Porphyry's *Sententiae*—that work in which the disciple is providing an introduction to his master's thought. He cites *Sententia* 40 (as Solignac does also for the *De Ordine*) and analyzes it at length to show how Augustine faithfully reflects its doctrine and corollaries.

But in the *Sententiae*, as we have noted, Porphyry's fidelity to his master makes it difficult at times to distinguish him from Plotinus. What Theiler's evidence points to is the crucial importance the notion of omnipresence had assumed for Plotinus and his school.

Ennead VI, 4–5

Theiler's evidence points to something even more precise: the importance of Plotinus' classic twin-treatise on Omnipresence, *Ennead* VI, 4–5. Here we have another instance of a single treatise dismembered by Porphyry's editing. Its title claims that "Being is integrally everywhere, one and the same." It takes its start from Plato's *Parmenides*, in which the young Socrates is pictured as being forced by the Eleatic Stranger to probe some of the central difficulties in participation theory. This was the work largely responsible for impressing the Neo-Platonists with the importance of omnipresence as the condition that permitted the world of experience to participate in the perfection of the Ideal World.

More than one modern commentator has paid homage to this treatise' brilliance and singular importance for a grasp of Plotinus' most mature thought.[5] One may wonder, therefore whether *Ennead* VI, 4–5 made a comparable impression on Plotinus'

[5] Emile Bréhier, "Images plotiniennes, images bergsoniennes," in *Etudes de Philosophie Antique* (Paris, 1955), pp. 292–307, hereafter cited as "Images"; A. H. Armstrong, "Emanation in Plotinus," *Mind*, 46: 61–66 (1937), hereafter cited as "Emanation."

disciples. Once the question is asked, it suddenly dawns that not only *Sententia* 40, on which Theiler placed such stress, but the entire series of *Sententiae* from the thirty-third to the forty-fourth (over a third of Mommert's text in the Teubner edition) may legitimately be regarded as little more than an extended paraphrase of this twin-treatise.

Porphyry's *Life* of his master informs us that it ushered in the writings of Plotinus' "mid-period" which "display the utmost reach of his powers" and generally "attain the highest perfection." We are encouraged to bear in mind that this period coincided with Porphyry's own "association" with his master and that the editor-disciple was present at, and presumably contributed to, "the Conferences" at which these questions were "threshed out." Indeed, Porphyry specifically adds that Plotinus composed the very twin-treatise in question "under persuasion from Amelius and myself" (*Life of Plotinus*, 5–6). Not only, then, did Porphyry consider the treatise peculiarly important, it is also likely that he strongly agreed with its tenor.

Would it therefore have been likely that Marius Victorinus excluded it from his translation? On the contrary, it would have impressed him as a "must," if his intention was, as we may surmise, to make Plotinus' thought accessible to the Latin world. The presumption is, therefore, that this treatise was available in Latin translation and came into Augustine's hands.

A QUESTION OF DEPENDENCE

State of the Question

Perhaps the move to *Ennead* VI, 4–5 is premature. Solignac, for example, regards *Sententia* 40 as a comment upon *Ennead* VI, 9 instead, and in justice it must be said that no early Plotinian treatise is more remarkable than this for kinship to the one we are now considering. But holding final solution to that question in abeyance, it should be noted that other scholars are of another mind. From the earlier consensus only Grandgeorge seems to have singled out *Ennead* VI, 4–5 as influential in Augustine's thinking, but Theiler, in an effort to show that certain elements of Augustine's omnipresence doctrine were incorporated in the lost works of Porphyry, found himself obliged to appeal to this very Plotinian treatise as evidence for that contention: if the master said it, the disciple *must* have.[6] It is one of the ironies of Henry's work that he, too, pointed momentarily to the same possibility. Confronted

[6] *Porphyrios*, pp. 28, 43ff.

with Theiler's suggestion of Augustinian dependence on *Sententia* 40, Henry's rejoinder is that the Augustinian and Porphyrian texts could both more easily be explained as reflecting a common source, the second part of Plotinus' treatise on Omnipresence.[7] That, however, is where Henry stops short. He never pursues the question further.

There the matter rested until Richard Harder, famous as a student and translator of Plotinus, brought it to the fore again in a final contribution just before his death. He delivered the *Vortrag* in question to an imposing group of Plotinian scholars brought together by the Hardt Foundation for discussion of the "Sources of Plotinus' Thought." Its published version is reconstructed from notes by the participants and leaves many questions hazy.[8] It is not clear whether he was arguing for Augustine's general dependence on the Plotinian doctrine of omnipresence—something which could be satisfied by appeal to Porphyry—or for direct dependence on this precise treatise. At one point he speaks suggestively of "exact citation" of *Ennead* VI, 4–5. He points to several of Augustine's descriptions of God's presence—*tota simul* among them—and connects them with Plotinian descriptions occurring in this same treatise. Henry, also a participant, notes only that he had years before connected one fragmentary parallel, which Harder had drawn from Augustine's *De Immortalitate Animae*, with *Ennead* IV, 2 rather than with VI, 4–5. Plotinus points out in *Ennead* IV, 2 that the soul's presence to the body is not to be compared to the presence of the color white to the various bodily parts it affects. The soul, he goes on to observe cannot "take distance from itself." The same remarks occur in Augustine; *ergo*, the saint read *Ennead* IV, 2 and *not* VI, 4–5. But not surprisingly, remarks of this sort, as closely parallel to Augustine's, occur in other *loci* of Plotinus' works, and notably in *Ennead* VI, 4–5. If the situation be conceived of in either–or terms, therefore, then surely the context-connections on both sides must be examined.

But need we conceive this as an either–or situation? Perhaps so, if one holds that Augustine read "very few books" of Plotinus. But we have already seen the weaknesses in that presumption. Why could Augustine not have read both treatises in question? Given the present movement of scholarly consensus toward widening the circle of Augustine's readings in the *Enneads*, it is more probable

[7] *Plotin*, pp. 71ff.

[8] *Entretiens sur l'Antiquité Classique*, Hardt Foundation, 5, "Les Sources de Plotin" (Vandoeuvres-Geneva, 1960), pp. 325–332; hereafter cited as *Sources de Plotin*.

that he read both than that he read only one. And had he read both, he would have found that *Ennead* VI, 4–5, a longer, more mature, immensely richer work than *Ennead* IV, 2, contains every insight of the latter with such superabundance as to make him almost forget it in favor of *Ennead* VI, 4–5. But what *Ennead* IV, 2 lacks and *Ennead* VI, 4–5 contains argues for his having almost certainly read the latter.

The same solution may be found to hold in respect to *Ennead* VI, 9. Many of the omnipresence elements contained in that treatise reoccur in *Ennead* VI, 4–5; but again, there are no grounds for making these two mutually exclusive alternatives. It is a priori likelier than not that Augustine read both. But even in the event one were to insist on making it an either–or question, it might well turn out on examination that *Ennead* VI, 4–5 contains a certain "surplus" not to be accounted for by *Ennead* VI, 9. It may be, too, that the elements found in both of them are individualized by the intention, thrust, and movement of the treatise on Omnipresence. The contention in these pages is that *Ennead* VI, 4–5 has, in fact, a different "point" than Plotinus' earlier treatise "On the One, or the Good" (VI, 9), and that its point is exactly the one required to account for the function that many elements, common to both treatises, serve in the *Confessions*.

The Problem of Method

But, before any persuasive evidence can be presented that Augustine did read *Ennead* VI, 4–5 and undergo its profound influence, both a broadening of perspective and a modification of method are indispensable.

A broadening of perspective is necessary because if we consent to limit the debate to a fragment from the *De Immortalitate Animae*, as Henry and Theiler seemed inclined to do, it seems impossible to decide whether Augustine read *Ennead* IV, 2, *Ennead* VI, 4–5, or both—or, for that matter, neither. The area of search must be expanded; once it includes the *Soliloquies*, the work *On Freedom of Choice*, and the *Confessions*, it will become plainer that we are dealing with three distinct stages in Augustine's meditation and profound assimilation at least of *Ennead* VI, 4–5.

But this, in turn, imposes a modification of method: specifically, it requires us to compare, not merely "doctrinal," nor merely "linguistic" parallels, but parallel "patterns" of thought, image, and expression, examined as organically interlocking units and resituated with respect to the over-all thrust, the individual "point" of Plotinus' Omnipresence treatise.

CHARACTER OF *ENNEAD* VI, 4–5

Participation and Omnipresence

Plotinus is attempting to show how the relation between the "two worlds" or Neo-Platonism is to be thought. The inferior world must be conceived as participating in the superior, of course—but what he now insists upon is that for a right understanding of participation theory, one must see that at the heart of it and grounding its very possibility is the omnipresence of the higher world to the lower. The twin-treatise in question is, significantly, 22–23 in the chronological sequence of his writings, much later than *Enneads* I, 6 and V, 1 and (to adapt Mandouze's phrase to another context) "radically different in tonality." For what is tested is the relative "separateness" of the two worlds which pervades these earlier treatises. Even the classic "emanation" image will undergo profound recasting in the process.

Difficulties, and a Method for Handling Them

But it would scarcely be enough to connect the *Confessions* and *Ennead* VI, 4–5 merely because they both focus on the issue of God's omnipresence. Here, it is important to note that throughout the first seven books of his work, Augustine is describing the difficulties he had in conceiving of that omnipresence. This is the first specific similarity between the two works under consideration: Plotinus is focusing on the difficulties to be overcome before the omnipresence notion can properly be grasped. Bréhier's *Notice* characterizes the distinctive trait of this twin-treatise as presenting, not a marshaled set of arguments, a series of proofs all in form. Rather, Plotinus tries to jog the mind into an ever deeper, ever sharper insight into the thesis he is exposing. Instead of demonstrations in the strict sense, he

> makes use of images, persuasive analogies which he then corrects in order to afford his reader a just view of the matter. He appeals to common sense, . . . to common religious belief. But above all (and he comes back to this frequently) he shows that if the thesis of being's omnipresence is found difficult to admit, the fundamental reason for that difficulty lies in the peculiar trait of the human imagination which makes us consider omnipresence incompatible with the real, because we invincibly imagine the real as an extended body subject to division.[9]

"He comes back to this frequently": indeed, Plotinus repeats, insists, and never tires of repeating those methodological pointers.

[9] *Les Ennéades de Plotin*, text and translation (Paris: Collection Guillaume Budé, 1924–1938), VI[1], 162; hereafter cited as Bréhier, *Ennéades*.

If one were to search for the treatise of all his works which describes, diagnoses, and answers to the difficulty that Augustine just as tirelessly describes as his own, a better would never come to hand. The reader will have noted also the paradox of method to which Bréhier alludes here: the use of the imagination to purify the imagination, of image to dispel imagery. The bearing of that paradox on our question will become manifest shortly.

The Individuality of This Treatise

It is exactly this emphasis on methodology, this painful diagnosis of the difficulties involved in forming a correct conception of omnipresence, describing its nature, root, and consequences in minute detail, then applying the corrective, illustrating again and again the *manner* of thinking that must be applied, in short, this extended effort of philosophical *manuductio*, which is characteristic of this treatise as of no other that Plotinus ever wrote. Others —*Ennead* VI, 9 among them—present this or that element of the finished doctrine, or suppose it in passing; none of them presents its mode of genesis. And once we examine the treatise from this, its proper point of view, we are struck by how regularly Augustine's own descriptions of his difficulty, its root and nature and consequences, the terms, images, and linkage of ideas, the diagnosis applied, and the expression of the final insight with all its paradoxes, all read like faithful echoes of Plotinus' twin-treatise.

PLOTINUS AND AUGUSTINE: A PARALLEL PATTERN OF DOCTRINE

The Difficulty, Root and Branch

The root of the difficulty can be variously expressed, but in both authors, as Bréhier notes of Plotinus, it comes down invariably to the same thing: we conceive of the relation of the superior world (which includes the soul, the Ideas, and God) to the inferior world in terms drawn from sense, in terms appropriate to concrete sensible reality and to the working of our imagination, rather than to intelligence in its genuine operation. Put another way, we do not draw our principles from the appropriate intelligible realm, but from the inferior, corporeal realm.

What, then, is the result? Note that for Plotinus the problem is entirely analogous whether stated of the soul, the Ideas, or of God, so we may express it for brevity in terms of Augustine's dominating interest, God. For both authors, the result is that, having imagined God after the fashion of an extended body, we automatically consider Him as spatial, hence as distributed part-for-part over a vast area, hence received part-for-part (as a property or form) by corporeal beings. We use such images as these: God is "poured out" into the containers of inferior reality, or "diffused" throughout and "filling," "penetrating" them. He is described as "more" in a large body than in a small, or (in an effort to correct such images) we place God "above" corporeal beings in such a way that He would be more distant from some than from others, or, worse yet, supported by them. We are tempted to imagine Him as a kind of power, a light, say, streaming down on material things in such a way as eventually to dwindle off into darkness where His light would "fail."

What, then, is the correct vision? Again, the accord is flawless. It involves the realization that there are two distinct orders of reality, radically different one from the other; that the higher realm is nonbodily, nonspatial, utterly partless, hence, if present at all, then present *entire*, integrally, to each unity of the inferior world—and hence, common to them all, and the property of none. God is not in the realm of flux and thus not in any sense "poured out"; He is not contained "in" inferior realities, but rather, He contains them. Nor is He more "here" than "there," more in this being than in that in any sense where distance, space, or quantity would have any role to play. Their possession of Him is measured by their capacity, competence, rank. He is "above" the inferiors, not as a material light is above the things it lights up, but with a distanceless superiority which is that of producer to produced; He does not rest on them, they rest in Him and from Him receive all their stability. But they are in Him, not as in a place or in an envelope, not as in some space formerly part of the Void, for this would only be a more subtle way of putting God Himself in place. He is, on the contrary, utterly placeless, and this placelessness is the very condition for His being integrally present to things in place.

Paradox? Then here is another. Or, rather, the same paradox in its most acute formulation. In order to be really "common" to all, hence integrally present to each, God must become the property of none, must remain self-infolded, in Himself, and not go forth from Himself. To be present, He must remain forever "apart," with a distanceless distance, at once self-enclosed and not so. Only by remaining fast in Himself will He truly be the "unfailing," will there be no place or being in the inferior world to which His power (identical with His Presence) fails to reach. Even this ultimate refinement, this final paradox, Augustine has firmly grasped and put to work.[10]

The Question of Source: a Question of Formal Structure

If considered only from the viewpoint of their number, this correspondence of elements is almost bewildering. It stamps Augustine's doctrine of omnipresence as in any case distinctively related to the one held and taught by Plotinus, whatever be his direct source for that doctrine. We shall shortly see that his account of the *libri platonicorum* and his presentation of the metaphysic he found there puts that relation to Neo-Platonism beyond all question.

But again, is it possible that Augustine gleaned this variety of elements from hither and yon in any number of Neo-Platonic writings? Not impossible, perhaps, but the rule of choosing the simplest of available hypotheses counsels that we settle on one treatise that best accounts for all the elements concerned, rather than burrow into a number of others that will do the job much less well.

The appeal to a number of other treatises, furthermore, would utterly fail to explain the formal aspect of the correspondence, the tight unity of conception that links this number of elements into a *pattern* which is parallel to that found in *Ennead* VI, 4–5. One is reminded of the hypothesis that envisaged one monkey, one typewriter, reams of paper, and an indefinite lapse of time, all as adding up to the complete works of Shakespeare. All the elements are there; the only thing lacking is "soul," and precisely the soul of Shakespeare, to bring them together and transform them with a new meaning. And the omnipresence doctrine, in Mandouze's phrase, is not just one element alongside of a number of others in the *Confessions*, it is precisely *ce qui change tout*, what en-souls them all, transforms them and puts them into an entirely new register. And this it does precisely by virtue of its own internal laws, its own formal structure and dynamic, a structure and dynamic which suggest that Augustine must have found them in a source where the same presiding conception was already powerfully at work.

Plotinus, Porphyry, or Both?

Now among the Neo-Platonists, our only realistic choice lies between Plotinus and Porphyry. Theiler, for one, would have us choose Porphyry to the exclusion of Plotinus, but the grounds for

[10] In nn. 32 to 36 to my article on this subject (*REA* 9: 8–11 [1963]) the reader will find this concatenation of doctrinal parallels more fully catalogued, with reference to both works in question.

making this an either-or matter have gradually been eroded by subsequent scholars. Other tenants of the Porphyrian hypothesis—O'Meara, Courcelle, and Solignac, most notably—would now freely admit that Augustine did, after all, read Plotinus, and in more generous doses than Henry had previously imagined. Finally, Theiler's most striking piece of evidence for the Porphyrian derivation of Augustine's thinking on omnipresence is *Sententia* 40. A paraphrase of Plotinus more faithful than that contained in *Sententiae* 33–44, however, would be difficult to imagine. If, therefore, we are entitled to consider the *Sententiae* as representative of Porphyry's thinking when dealing with this precise question—everything points to this being likely, and Theiler's own practice shows we have no other recourse—there is no serious warrant for attributing to Porphyry's omnipresence doctrine a philosophic accent clearly distinguishable from his master's. And only such a clear distinction would justify choosing Porphyry *to the exclusion* of Plotinus. His "association" with Plotinus during this period, his outspoken admiration for the quality of its production, his participation in the "Conferences" that preceded the composition of the very twin-treatise he claims to have urged Plotinus to write on the matter, all argue for the opposite: that his own thought on this crucial and important issue, at least while writing the *Sententiae*, would be faithfully Plotinian. The most cursory examination of *Sententia* 40 confirms that presumption. For the moment, therefore, we may take Theiler's appeal to that text as not excluding, but actually inviting closer examination of what may have been the common font of Porphyry's and Augustine's teaching on omnipresence: *Ennead* VI, 4–5.

That it functioned as their common source will shortly be made clear by a careful analysis of the *Confessions*' account of Augustine's "platonic" readings at Milan. But that analysis requires in its turn that we situate those readings in terms of the problematic that Augustine has gone to some lengths to evoke.

ILLUMINATION AT MILAN

The "Difficulty" of Omnipresence, the "Problem" of Evil

"Difficulty" and "problem" are not quite the same thing. A difficulty, as we use the term here, must be surmounted before the problem can be resolved. And the main problem of the *Confessions* is still, at bottom, the Manichaean problem: whence comes evil? That problem Augustine presents at length in Manichaean terms in the account he gives, in Book III (10–18) of his conversion to that sect. The order of presentation there dovetails closely with the solution he claims to have found in Neo-Platonism. What put the problem beyond solution, he assures us (*Conf* III, 12) was the difficulty he experienced in transcending corporeal imagery and forming a spiritual conception of God, a conception that would permit him to understand that the Divine Presence is *tota ubique*, omnipresence. Hence his only resort was to conceive both of God and of Evil as material substances, mutually exclusive one of the other. In Book VII, accordingly, we must not be surprised to hear his claim that, having arrived at that conception of omnipresence, he found that he could readjust his vision of the world's relation to God, and thus resolve the problem of evil in non-dualistic terms.

Resolve it, that is, in its intellectual dimension. Meanwhile, however, he has repeatedly pointed out (III, 12; V, 20; VII, 4–7) that the question of *whence* Evil comes cannot be answered until one sees clearly on the prior question, *what* evil is. This solution, in turn, becomes accessible only when the "darkened heart," the *acies mentis obscurata*, has been cleansed and enlightened. For this very "darkening" with its resulting incapacity to break through the veil of corporeal imagery, is a "sickness," an *insania*, a punishment for a primal "iniquity" whose root-identity is pride, *superbia* (VII, 11). In Augustine's mind, then, there is an organic connection between the *iniquitas* of man and his incapacity to rise to a proper conception of God's omnipresence. The difficulty that makes his problem intellectually irresoluble is itself an outgrowth of that problem in its existential and religious dimension.

Only when God has succeeded in bringing low his proud head has the "opportune time" come (cf. VI, 17 and 24) for Augustine to attain to a spiritual conception of Him and His relation to creatures. How had this been achieved? Augustine sees two means, exactly those which the Manichees rejected: the humble submission of faith (VI, 6; VII, 7) and the purifying "heat" of sufferings (V, 14; VII, 12) which God's omnipresent Providence applies to cauterize the wound of the heart, bathe the film on his inner eye, reduce the swelling whereby his *inflata facies* prevents him from seeing. In another image, Augustine is turned outwards, *foras* (and downwards) to the "lowest things," to "vanity" rather than "Truth," away from the *Summa* which is God dwelling forever "within," "in the heart." The cure that opens his inner, spiritual eye, will also "turn" his gaze from outer to inner, from lower to higher. Not before giving us a final summary of this entire complex of conversion-imagery, one which makes clear the relation between evil and the incapacity to conceive of omnipresence, and at the same time suggests that he is at last ready to accept the "admonition" which he is about to receive, does Augustine open his account of his Neo-Platonic readings (VII, 12–13).

This effort to "situate" the paragraphs recounting those readings in a context that Augustine has prepared with consummate care will help us avoid seeking a message there that corresponds much more to our own preoccupations than to his. For Augustine's description here is a tight unity, and bound in unity to the rest of the *Confessions*. The danger in lifting these paragraphs out of that context, or of dismembering their unity, is the one which presides at all major surgery: that the patient after the operation may not be quite the same organism as was wheeled into the amphitheater. And a little scrutiny reveals that Augustine's account in *Confessions* VII, 13–26, is quite literally organic. The sutures that bind it together are living tissue; no one member can be understood except in functional relation to the others and to the whole.

An Organic and Logical Account

Having begun (VII, 13–15) with what Fr. Henry has aptly called a "spiritual apology" to justify his enthusiastic allegiance to Neo-Platonism, Augustine presents us with the fruit of those readings (VII, 16–23). A reflection on the Incarnation (VII, 24–25) leads into a final summary of the entire experience (VII, 26). Against all reductions that would see in the central section (VII, 16–23) a movement that is unilaterally "ecstatic," it must be remarked that Augustine's concern is not only with the lies that the Manichees—for he has them plainly in mind—had spread about God, but also with those they uttered respecting His *opera*, His creatures (cf. III, 10). The movement of the entire account, accordingly, is not so much "upward" as "oscillating"—from God to creatures and back again. To stay with purely formal indices for the moment, Augustine's vision of God's true nature—*vidi te*—issues in every case into a corrected vision of creatures in their true relation to God: "I beheld other things below you," he says (VII, 17), "I looked back over other things, and saw" (VII, 21), and, finally, he passes upward "gradually from bodies" to a glimpse of "what is" (VII, 23) and summarizes the entire experience without failing to mention his certainty "that all other things are from you" (VII, 26). Even on the basis of purely philological considerations, nothing could be plainer: both God and creatures are involved throughout, and the account oscillates from one to the other just as it does throughout the *Confessions*, with an oscillation commanded by the relational character of the participation, and hence the omnipresence, notion.

Another evidence for the organic unity of the account is the progress of the philosophical *Weltanschauung* it transmits. We shall later show some interesting relationships between the order of this account and the progression of content and problematic in Augustine's early works. But we shall stay for the moment with the archiclassic movement which presents us first with a vision of God as "Being," the "other things" (to use the classic terms) as "beings by participation" (VII, 16–17); God as "Supreme Good," creatures as "good by participation" (VII, 18–19); God as Eternal Truth, inferior realities as "temporally true," their "temporal order" (VII, 20–22) complementing the "order of place" referred to earlier (VII, 18–19). At this point, the vision of "iniquity" represents the denouement permitting Augustine to perform the only true "ascent" (VII, 23) of the entire account, one which starts from corporeal beauty and arises to the Divine Beauty which ultimately grounds their power of attraction. Being, Good, Truth, Beauty—nothing could be more classical. The progress of the account, therefore, is not only organic, but logical as well. There is no indication whatever of a series of discrete "events," only a continuously developed view of reality under the sign of participation theory.

The Problem of Evil Solved

It may seem disconcerting to claim that the "high point" of this entire section lies, not in this or that vision of God, but in the insight into "iniquity." And yet, nothing else is more coherent with the close connection that Augustine has set up between his omnipresence difficulty and the problem of evil. This explains why the transcendent "food of grown men" which Augustine is too "infirm" to eat (VII, 16) is counterpointed later by the "food mingled with flesh" of the Incarnate Word (VII, 24–25). The insights prompted by his readings issue in certainties—"I saw . . . was certain . . . it was made manifest to me"—but just as important, in a sense of his own infirmity. This infirmity, against the Manichaean denial of our responsibility for our fall, Augustine must trace ultimately to his own "iniquity." Thus, his inability to form a correct conception of God and creatures, a conception in which God's omnipresence plays the crucial role, is due to his own "perversity," his own lack of order. Only when his *insania* has abated can he enjoy the insight that is the hinge of the entire account, namely, that the question "whence evil comes" is answered with the single term, *iniquitas*. The ascent of VII, 23 is made possible only when his former Manichaean "presumption" has been turned (inchoatively at least) into "confession," when his own perversity is recognized and implicitly avowed for what it is.

The Difficulty of Omnipresence Banished

The main contribution of the readings, then, was to cut through Augustine's difficulty, and thereby solve his problem, precisely by conducting him to a right notion of God's *nature and relation to the world*, a notion commanded by the Plotinian doctrine of participation and hence of omnipresence. The oscillation already noted suggests this strongly; the concern is with God and "other things," the *cetera*, the *alia*. But closer examination will put that interpretation beyond doubt.

For this account fairly bristles with omnipresence elements. I will explain shortly my reasons for thinking that the vision of "unchangeable light" (VII, 16) supposes *Ennead* VI, 4–5. Suffice it to call attention for the moment to the phrase "Truth . . . diffused neither through finite nor through infinite space." When taken in connection with its analogies throughout the *Confessions*, and with the difficulty that has haunted him till now, this correction manifestly refers not only to God's spirituality, but ultimately to His omnipresence.

"I beheld other things below you" (VII, 17)—this brings us to note of God that "he abides in Himself, and renews all things"—a Biblicism which shows that Augustine found in the Wisdom books the same paradoxical doctrine (to be present, God must remain "in Himself") as he had discovered in Plotinus. This is perhaps why he had already evoked it earlier (VII, 14), when showing the basic agreement between the *platonici* and Scripture.

The little treatise "on evil" of paragraphs VII, 18–19 betrays the same orientation. The declaration that there is nothing "outside" (*extra*) the created universe which could "break in and corrupt" its order invincibly recalls the terms in which, just before these readings, the problems of evil and omnipresence are posed: "where then is evil, whence and by what means has it crept in here?" (VII, 7). And there, the "spatial" image of God was the root of his misconception.

In paragraph VII, 20, Augustine is getting to the core of the problem that has been central to all his difficulties. He alerts us to that fact by interrupting the positive side of his development. One final time, he resumes his former Manichaean views. He adds a sketch of his post-Manichaean Stoicism; the terms in both instances perfectly parallel former statements (in III, 10ff; VII, 1–3, 7) where the omnipresence preoccupation is unquestionable. That same context is echoed faithfully here by the imagined "god that filled all the places in infinite space," a misconception that is then corrected as he looks "back over other things"—for the relation is suddenly inverted and Augustine sees that "all things are *in You* . . . (though) not as in a place"—God is not "contained," He is, rather (as Plotinus had insisted) "container"—provided always that we understand that term correctly, for He is indeed "infinite, though in a different way."

One need only compare the description of the *Verbum* in VII, 24 with that in VII, 14 and 17 to find its "supereminent" station implying He is "above all times" so that He "abides in Himself"—all notions crucial to Plotinus' doctrine of omnipresence.

The final summary in VII, 26 only adds to the presumption already formed. Augustine advises us that he was "certain . . . that you are infinite, though not diffused through space . . . and that all other things are from you." The relation of God and creature is uppermost in his mind. The key to that relation is participation, and the heart of participation is omnipresence.

Iniquitas: and the Neo-Platonic *Aversio*

Augustine is, therefore, presenting us with an organic and progressive vision which may best be described as a Christian-Platonist religious philosophy. Turning back now to the heart of the account, we find the vital problem, the *unde malum* of the Manichees, resolved in the final phrase of paragraph VII, 22.

And I asked, "What is iniquity (*iniquitas*)?" and I found that it is not a substance. It is perversity of will, twisted away from the Supreme Substance, Yourself, O God, and towards lower things, and gushing forth its insides, and swelling outwards: *detortae in infima voluntatis perversitatem proicientis intima sua et tumescentis foras.*

Here we are confronted with a variation on the classic Neo-Platonic couple of "turning away—turning back" which Theiler has attributed to the influence of Porphyry, partially on the strength of comparison with *Sententia* 40. Henry, we observed, points out in this same connection that dependence on the finale of Plotinus' twin-treatise on Omnipresence is at least equally probable. We shall try to pare that finale to what is directly relevant.

It opens on a note that is absent from Porphyry: a lapidary question-answer that may well have provided the seed of Augustine's celebrated name for God, the "life of souls, the life of lives, living yourself, O life of my Soul" (III, 10). The changes I make in Mackenna's translation are in the interests of a more literal fidelity to the new text of Henry-Schwyzer. "To return," Plotinus asks, "how is that Power present to the universe?" And he answers:

> As a One Life: Ὡς Ζωὴ μία.
>
> Consider life in any living thing: it . . . is omnipresent; . . . in it there is no Matter to make it grow less and less according to the measured mass.
>
> Conceive it as a power of an ever-fresh infinity, brimming over with its own vitality. If you look to some definite spot and seek to fasten on some definite thing, you will not find it. The contrary is your only way; you cannot pass on to where it is not; you will never halt at a dwindling point where it fails at last and can no longer give; you will always be able to move with it—better, to be in its entirety (ἐν τῷ παντὶ) and so seek no further; denying it, you have strayed to something of another order and you fall; looking elsewhere, you do not see what stands there before you: παρὸν οὐκ ἰδῶν τῷ εἰς ἄλλον βλέπειν.
>
> But supposing that you do thus "seek no further," how do you experience it?
>
> In that you have entered into the All (πᾶς) and have not remained in some part of it (ἐν μέρει αὐτοῦ). You do not say: "so much is me" (τοσοῦτός εἰμι) but laying aside that "so much" you become the All (τὸ πᾶν). No doubt you were the All from the first, but something other than the All has been added to you, and that addition diminished you; for the addition was not from the All (οὐ γὰρ ἐκ τοῦ παντός)—you can add nothing to the All—but from what is not the All (τοῦ μὴ παντός). It is on account of this non-being that you are become some-one (τις), and you are not the All except by putting that non-being away. You increase, then, by letting go of the "alien" (τὰ ἄλλα); cast aside the alien and there is the All, present . . .
>
> No need for it to come to you in order to be present; when it is not present it is rather you who have departed; to depart does not mean to put distance between you and the All, for it is still present; but (more exactly) you did not depart: still near to it, you turned about to the contraries: ἀλλὰ παρὼν ἐπὶ τὰ ἐναντία ἐστράφης.

It is rare that one can enjoy even the illusion of agreeing with everybody, yet here is a text which encourages that utopian dream. It needs only to be compared with Porphyry's interminable paraphrase (he is convinced his reader is not very bright) for it to become clear that all the elements of Plotinus' masterful text are at least represented. And yet, it must be admitted that a reasonably intelligent reader (and Augustine could lay modest claim to that) might have spelled out those virtualities for himself, particularly with the aid of other Plotinian treatises. To this extent, then, we find ourselves in agreement with Henry against Theiler.

And yet it must be acknowledged that the latter has amassed an impressive series of texts which show Augustine playing variations on a number of the themes we have just seen, among them the "turning away" to non-being, a diminishing addition which makes the soul "less" in its very being, reducing it to a "plenteous poverty" because it has lost the "whole" in pursuit of the "part."[11]

But a number of other instances could be added to these: some of them are presented in Theiler's Porphyrian commentary on the *Confessions*.[12] Augustine never tires of that final paradox of God remaining present even to the man who has "departed," remaining with us even when we are not with Him, because He does not desert us, it is we who did the deserting. Here, too, is a quite probable source—along with *Ennead* VI, 9—for the Augustinian image of God as "center," with the other things as "opposites," on an outer periphery.[13] Sinners, in a phrase of Jeremias to delight a Plotinian's heart, "turn their backs on you, not their face to you" (II, 6); hence Augustine can say of himself, "I had my back to the light and my face turned towards the things upon which the light fell" (IV, 30).

These are only some of the reasons which suggest that Theiler's instinct was correct; the doctrine he underlines as Augustine's in a number of instances manifestly reflects the omnipresence doctrine of the Plotinian school, whether drawn from *Ennead* VI, 4–5, or Porphyry's *Sententiae*, or conceivably even both.

Plotinus or Porphyry: a Parallel Pattern of Imagery

But the text just cited also hints at the means of showing that in excluding *Ennead* VI, 4–5 Theiler's instinct betrayed him after all: for *Ennead* VI, 4–5 presents us with an *image*—a metaphysical image, if you prefer, one that Plotinus offers to purify our habitual images—but the image of the center is there, nonetheless. And at this point the paradox pointed to in Bréhier's *Notice* to this treatise promises to hold a precious clue. For few works more teem with

[11] See Theiler, *Porphyrios*, pp. 25–28 and 46ff for a series of these parallels, with references to *Ennead* VI, 4–5 as well. Note the correlation whereby Plotinus connects "part" and (our) *prop*-erty; our part-icularity, for instance, is what makes us some one "apart" from the All.

[12] *Porphyrios*, pp. 60–69.

[13] This is quite likely a variant of the *omphalos* image common to primitive religions, as Huguette Fugier has claimed, "L'Image de Dieu-Centre dans les *Confessions* de saint Augustin," *REA* 1: 379–395 (1955). But closer identification and specification of the source than Miss Fugier was inclined to attempt, can clarify the meaning and the psychological value of the image as Augustine uses it.

imagery than the *Confessions*; and the same must be said for Plotinus' treatise on Omnipresence. Comparing the imagery both works employ to convey that notion of omnipresence will facilitate our task of establishing at least Plotinian (with or without resonance from Porphyrian) dependence. It will also pave the way for a sharper understanding of the import those images have for Augustine.

IMAGES OF OMNIPRESENCE

The Absence of Image in Porphyry

Why are the images we are about to study entirely absent from the *Sententiae*? If one wished to be unkind, one could press on Theiler that their omission was systematic; that Porphyry, great enemy of the imagination that Theiler has made him out to be, would have dropped them intentionally.

But aside from Porphyry's right to violate his preaching in practice—as Plotinus does—the irony of the situation is that Porphyry's rejection of the imagination is at least partially a construct of Theiler's, starting from the condemnation of imagery he finds in Augustine's *De Vera Religione*. "Give me a man who can see without being influenced by imaginations," says Augustine at one point, and from such utterances Theiler has spelled out an entire Porphyrian polemic against the *phantasia*.[14] Despite that theoretical rejection of the imagination, however, Augustine too remains a literary artist of the first order, an "image-maker" of undeniable brilliance, and a powerful image evokes in him a response that proves he is one of us after all, a man to whom image remained forever consubstantial to his thinking.

That irony is perhaps only more intense when we consider Plotinus' intention in this treatise on Omnipresence. Despite all his warnings against imaged thinking (and we shall see how closely they elbow some of his most stunning efforts of metaphysical imagination) this twin-treatise alone would certify him as one of the most potent wielders of image who ever wrote philosophy. So struck has Bréhier been by the method of "dynamic image" we are about to see in action, he has devoted a special study to the process. Armstrong, too, has been led to make a comparable study.[15] And both of them have had to deal with images taken precisely from this treatise.

[14] *Porphyrios*, pp. 36ff, 57.
[15] See n. 5, above.

There are four important images in *Ennead* VI, 4–5 which, for our purposes, we may reduce to three distinct types. First, and most characteristic of Plotinus' method, are the two dynamic images of the Light and of the Hand. The second type is represented by the image of the Head, and here the strictly dynamic character is gone and something more akin to paradox has taken its place. The third type is represented by the image of "Eros waiting at the door." Its influence on Augustine is more unmistakably traceable than that of the others; for the purposes of the argument, accordingly, I may be excused for examining it first. Neither dynamic nor paradoxical, it occurs in *Ennead* VI, 5, 10. But, to begin with, a word of explanation on its function in the argument.

"Eros Waiting at the Door"

The relation that Plotinus means to exclude is one whereby the superior reality—ὄντως ὄν, what "truly exists"—will compose with the beings of the inferior world, becoming a "form" ap-*prop*-riated by one being to the exclusion of others. Such a relation would prevent its remaining integrally present to each and *common* to all of them.[16]

The difficulty in conceiving this relation is the same as always. We insist on imagining it in terms of sensible reality, in terms of beings whose mass makes them subject to mutual exclusion in place, so that part of them must be possessed by this, another part possessed by another being. Plotinus offers his reader several examples (*Enn* VI, 4, 12) to illustrate the relation he wishes him to grasp: diverse subjects can see the *whole* of the same object, hear the same sound *in its entirety*. The resulting knowledge from our study, he will repeat in the text we are about to cite, and wisdom itself, are both *common* to all of us, without being parceled out part for me and part for you.

Having seized on this relation of appropriation of the part against community in the whole, Augustine presents a long *manuductio* in the second book of the *De Libero Arbitrio* (15–33). He systematizes Plotinus' different suggestions into an ascending consideration which shows that the lower senses (taste, smell) necessarily possess only this or that part of the shared object—Augustine and Evodius cannot eat the same piece of honey in its entirety—since the operation of these senses involves an appropriation of the object, a transformation whereby it becomes part of the individual nature of the sentient. The higher senses (hearing and

[16] Plotinus' clearest statement of this principle occurs in *Ennead* VI, 4, 3, 11ff.

sight), on the contrary, furnish a more adequate analogy of spiritual community in the possession (of Beauty, Truth, or Wisdom); for in both the object is left entire and unchanged, still common to both subjects of knowledge. This *manuductio*, some twenty paragraphs of the text, has been treated by commentators either as an anomaly to be ignored or as a mere digression. Yet the importance of the *commune-proprium* distinction in Augustine's subsequent writings, and the fact that he puts it to work in the culminating definition of sin here,[17] show that it had a functional import to him. That import, we suggest, involves a profound and decisive adaptation of the source from which he drew these diverse elements. From paragraph 20 to paragraph 38 of the second book of the *De Libero Arbitrio*, the Saint has strewn generous traces of the Eros image from *Ennead* VI, 5 which clearly betray that source. We assemble them here, underlining on either side the corresponding elements which, despite the transformation which Augustine has worked, still (beneath surface dissimilarities) answer one to another.

Ennead VI, 5

10, 1–50: It remains, then, poised in wisdom within itself (*Μένει οὖν ἐν ἑαυτῷ*); it could not enter any other (*οὐκ ἐν ἄλλῳ γένοιτο*); those others look to it and in their longing find it where it is. This is that "Love waiting at the door" (*ὁ θυραυλῶν Ἔρως*), ever coming up from without, striving towards the beautiful, happy when to the utmost of its power it attains (*ἐφιέμενος τοῦ καλοῦ καὶ ἀγαπῶν ἀεὶ οὕτως ὡς δύναιτο μετασχεῖν*). Even here the lover does not so much possess himself of the beauty he has loved as wait before it (*οὐ δεχόμενος τό κάλλος, ἀλλὰ παρακείμενος οὕτως ἔχει*). That Beauty is abidingly self-enfolded (*ἐφ' ἑαυτοῦ μένει*) but

De Libero Arbitrio II

34: . . . That truth, however, abiding in itself (*in se manens*), gains nothing . . . and loses nothing (*nec proficiat . . . nec deficiat*) . . . but whole and incorrupt, gladdens with its light those who are turned towards it (*integra et incorrupta . . . conversos laetificet lumine*) . . .

35: Behold Truth Itself (*ipsa veritas*). Embrace (*amplectere*) it if you can, and enjoy it (*fruere ea*) . . .

33: You could not call this yours or mine or any man's, but it is present and offers itself in common to all (*omnibus . . . [cernentibus] praesto esse ac se praebere communiter*) . . . No one could say that anything which is present and com-

[17] *De Libero Arbitrio* II, 53. Once one admits that the second book stands as a kind of *retractatio* of the first, where the unique object of their research was the definition of sin (I, 34), then this definition of sin assumes particular importance, becoming, in fact, the "point" of the second book. See P. Séjourné, "Les conversions de saint Augustin d'après le *De Libero Arbitrio* I," in *Revue des Sciences Religieuses*, 89–90: 359, n. 2 and 360 (1951). He likens the second book to an "édition revue et corrigée" of the first.

its lovers, the Many, loving it as an entire, possess it as an entire when they attain, for it was an entire that they loved (*οἱ ἑνὸς ἐρασταὶ πολλοὶ ὅλου ἐρῶντες ὅλου ἔχουσιν οὕτως, ὅταν ἔχωσιν· τὸ γὰρ ὅλον ἦν τὸ ἐρώμενον . . .*).

Similarly wisdom (*τὸ φρονεῖν*) is entire to all (*πᾶσιν ὅλον*), and thus (in the well-known saying) "common to all" (*ξυνὸν τὸ φρονεῖν*);[18] it is not distributed parcelwise (*οὐ τὸ μὲν ὧδε, τὸ δὲ ὡδὶ ὄν*); it cannot without absurdity be fixed in place (*τόπου δεόμενον*) . . . in any true participation in wisdom it must itself be one, a whole in union with itself (*εἴπερ ὄντως μετέχομεν τοῦ φρονεῖν, ἓν δεῖ εἶναι τὸ αὐτὸ πᾶν ἑαυτῷ συνόν*).[19]

So must it be in our participation in the Supreme; we shall not take our several portions of it,

mon to all who have reason (*quod communiter omnibus ratiocinantibus . . . praesto est*) belongs exclusively to the nature of one individual (*ad ullius eorum proprie naturam pertinere*).

25: What should we think of Wisdom Itself (*ipsa sapientia*)? Do you suppose that each individual has his own individual Wisdom, or that one Wisdom is present to all in common, so that each man is wiser the more fully he shares in it (*An vero unam praesto esse communiter omnibus, cuius quanto magis quisque fit particeps, tanto est sapientior*)?

37: But no one can be separated from [Truth and Wisdom] by spatial distance (*Nemo locis separari ab ea . . . potest*) . . . We have, therefore, in Truth, a possession which we can enjoy equally and in common (*aequaliter atque communiter*). There is nothing straitened or defective in it (*nullae . . . angustiae, nullus . . . defectus*). It receives all its lovers (*omnes amatores*) without stirring their envy; it is common to all (*omnibus communis*) and is chaste with each (*singulis casta*). One does not say to another: go back and let me approach; take away your hands and let me embrace it too (*ut etiam ego amplectar*). All cling to it, all touch the self-same reality (*omnes inhaerent, id ipsum omnes tangunt*)

[18] I adjust MacKenna's "shared by all" in the light of Harder's "*Daher das Wort: 'Gemeinsam das Denken.'*" Plotinus is referring to the saying of Heraclitus: *ξυνόν ἐστι πᾶσι τὸ φρονέειν*, and the lexical force of *ξυνόν*, "common to all," allows that meaning to show through Plotinus' ellipsis. Cf. Frg. 113 in Hermann Diels' *Fragmente der Vorsokratiker*, I (Berlin, 1912), p. 99.

[19] Again an adjustment of MacKenna. Cf. Harder's more faithful *eines und dasselbe sein muss . . . ganz bei sich selber*.

[20] Harder's *erfassen* reproduces more graphically the image of "laying hold" (as with the hands) which the immediate context shows Plotinus has in mind. MacKenna translates more neutrally, "possess."

nor you some separate entire and I another (οὐ μοίρας αὐτοῦ λαβόντες, οὐδὲ ὅλον ἐγώ, ὅλον δὲ καὶ σύ, ἀποσπασθὲν ἑκάτερον ἑκατέρου . . .).

Or take our souls in the way they lay hold of the good (ὡς ἐφαπτόμεθα τοῦ ἀγαθοῦ);[20] it is not one good that I, and another that you lay hold of; it is the same for both (Οὐ γὰρ ἄλλου μὲν ἐγώ, ἄλλου δε καὶ σὺ ἐφάπτῃ, ἀλλὰ τοῦ αὐτοῦ) . . . giver is in contact with taker and gives not as to a recipient outside but as to one in intimate contact . . . It is therefore by identification that we see the good and lay hold of it (ὁρῶμεν τἀγαθὸν καὶ ἐφαπτόμεθα αὐτοῦ), brought to it by becoming identical with what is of the Intellectual in ourselves . . .

And what is there to hinder this unification (τί δὲ καὶ ἐμπόδιον τοῦ εἰς ἕν)? There is no question of one member pushing another out as occupying too much space (Οὐ γὰρ δὴ τὸ ἕτερον ἀπωθεῖ θάτερον τόπον οὐ παρέχον), any more than happens in our own minds where we take in the entire fruit of our study and observation, all uncrowded (ὥσπερ οὐχ ὁρῶντες πᾶν μάθημα, καὶ θεώρημα καὶ ὅλως ἐπιστήμας πάσας ἐπὶ ψυχῆς οὐ στενοχωρουμένας).

. . . It is a food which is divided in no part (*nulla ex parte discerpitur*); you drink nothing from it which I cannot drink . . . what you take from it still remains whole for me too (*et mihi integrum manet*) . . . No one ever takes anything of it exclusively as his own, but it is wholly common to all at the same time (*Non . . . fit cuiusquam unius proprium, sed simul omnibus tota est communis*).

36: Since the supreme good (*summum bonum*) is known and grasped in the Truth (*cognoscitur et tenetur*) and since that Truth is Wisdom, let us see in Wisdom the Supreme Good, grasp and enjoy it (*cernamus in ea teneamusque summum bonum*).

38: Even if the music of a singer could last forever, his admirers (*studiosi*) would struggle and vie with each other to hear him (*certatim . . . venirent*); they would crowd each other . . . fight for places (*coarctarent sese atque pugnarent de locis*) each one anxious to get near the singer . . . But no thronging crowd of hearers keeps others from approaching the beauty of Truth and Wisdom. . . it does not move from place to place (*At illa veritatis et sapientiae pulchritudo . . . nec multitudine audientium constipata secludit venientes . . . nec migrat locis . . .*). It is close (*proxima*) to all its lovers (*qui diligunt eam*) throughout the world [if they] turn towards it (*ad se conversis*) . . . It is in no place, yet nowhere absent (*nullo loco est nusquam deest*) and . . . itself is never changed for the worse (*a nullo in deterius commutatur*).

20: The law and truth of numbers (*ratio et veritas numeri*) is present to all who reason (*omnibus ratiocinantibus praesto est*) . . . Their truth presents itself equally to all who can grasp it (*aequaliter omnibus se praebeat valentibus eam capere*) . . . It is not changed and turned into a kind of food of the perceiver (*perceptoris quasi alimentum*) but itself remains whole and true (*vera et integra permanente*) . . .

Along with both authors' presiding intention of contrasting "common" possession with individual "appropriation" of any desired good, the first thing that strikes one on examination of this parallel is the initial identity of basic image: it is a question in both cases of Beauty—in characteristic feminine form—being sought by her many lovers. But although Plotinus soon drops this image, Augustine continues with it, and simply assumes Plotinus' other illustrations under it, fusing them with it. Here, as throughout the *manuductio* which has led to it, he combines Plotinus' other examples of *μάθημα*, *θεώρημα*, and the objects of *ἐπιστήμη* more generally, with the notion of *φρονεῖν*; the resulting whole becomes that hypostatized "Beauty of Truth and Wisdom," *veritatis et sapientiae pulchritudo* which, from the context, is paradoxically identical with the Eternal Christ (cf. *Lib* II, 37–38). Both authors take care to eliminate all limitations of place, hence to avoid all species of "crowding" proper to the sensible sphere, so that despite their multitude, the lovers need not elbow each other out of possession. Augustine's *singulis casta* shows Plotinus' *οὐ δεχόμενος* in moralistic dress. Yet despite the "distanceless distance" implied in both expressions, all the lovers possess the beloved by intimate contact, that contact, moreover, going out to the same "whole" and not to different wholes or one or other partial fragment. The fundamental reason for this is the same for both authors: Wisdom "remains in itself" and does not go forth to become the "property" of this or that participant, remaining, on the contrary, "common" to all her lovers. The possession of the good Plotinus presents as an additional example, and it is interesting to find the Saint so faithfully reproducing the allusions to both sight and touch (*ὁρῶμεν τἀγαθὸν καὶ ἐφαπτόμεθα*; *cognoscitur et tenetur*; *cernamus . . . teneamusque*; cf. II, 26–27 where this combination occurs four times). But this, too, Augustine (with Trinitarian intentions, doubtless) has assumed into the basic image with which Plotinus had begun, reminding his reader that *in* that Truth (Christ) we hold and behold the highest good, that is, the Father. Despite all this fusion of elements, despite the occasional vivacity that Augustine brings to their development, the identity of fundamental image and of the metaphysical insight it transmits is manifest.

But this parallel is remarkable in another way. Not only are the doctrinal patterns of thought and image in close correspondence, but it is also striking how many particular expressions seem borrowed (through Marius Victorinus' translation) straight from Plotinus. The likelihood is that Augustine either had the *Enneads* to hand when writing the *De Libero Arbitrio*, or, at very least, had its turns of phrase quite fresh in memory.

Compare, in this connection, the form another reminiscence of this image takes in the *Soliloquies*. It is quite possible that Augustine did not have a copy of the *Enneads* with him at Cassiciacum. This would explain the fact that the reminiscence takes a less exuberant form as to detail. And yet, the structure and implications of the basic image he could have firmly grasped at Milan, with the result that certain parallels in expression follow naturally. Italics indicate expressions that recur later in the *De Libero Arbitrio*.

> [Reason]: Now, we are trying to discover what kind of a *lover of wisdom* (*amator sapientiae*) you are: that wisdom which you *desire to behold and possess with purest gaze and embrace* (*castissimo conspectu atque amplexu . . . videre ac tenere desideras*), with no veil between and, as it were, naked: such as wisdom allows to very few and these the most chosen of *its lovers* (*amatoribus suis*). If you were inflamed with love of some beautiful woman, would she not rightly refuse to give herself to you if she discovered that you loved anything but herself? And will the *purest beauty of wisdom* (*sapientiae . . . castissima pulchritudo*) reveal itself to you unless you burn for it alone?
>
> [Augustine, after protesting the singleness of his love]: What limit can there be to my *love of that Beauty* (*illius pulchritudinis amor*) in which I not only do not *begrudge it to others* (*non invideo caeteris*), but even look for *many* (*plurimos*) who will *long for* it with me (*mecum appetant*), *sigh for* it with me (*inhiant*), *possess it* with me (*teneant*), *enjoy it* with me (*perfruantur*); they will be all the dearer to me the more we share that *beloved in common* (*quanto erit nobis amata cummunior*) (*Sol* I, 22).

The passage of years will transform this image. So powerfully does it polarize the convert's subconscious that it cannot be expected to crop up in the *Confessions* without drawing with it the accretions resulting from that intervening work of time. Its transformation works in a twofold direction: as certain accidentals of Plotinus' presentation are absorbed by forgetfulness, other features are marshaled to replace them. From the storehouse of Augustine's memory they come, Plotinian, Biblical, literary, and experiential images. They cluster about the basic frame that was there at the start, to form a single constellation resonating with poetic ambivalences. So powerful is the resulting product that in the end it gathers to itself all the implicits of his slow conversion process, all the multiple facets of God's work in his behalf, and charges a single word with power to express them all. But, to trace more clearly the genesis of Augustine's central expression of "conversion," other elements of the final image must first pass in review.

Light: a Dynamic Image and a Metaphysical Correction

The second image to consider is the dynamic Light-image which Plotinus presents in *Ennead* VI, 4, 7. To bring out the steps in the correction process, we divide it into three paragraphs:

> Or imagine a small luminous mass serving as centre to a transparent sphere, so that the light from within shows upon the entire outer surface, otherwise unlit: we surely agree that the inner core of Light, intact and immobile, reaches over the entire outer extension; the single light of that small centre illuminates the whole field.
>
> The diffused light is *not due to any bodily magnitude* of that central point, which illuminates not as body but as body lit, that is, *by another kind of power than corporeal quality*.
>
> Let us then abstract the corporeal mass, retaining the light as power: we can no longer speak of the light in any particular spot; it is equally diffused throughout the entire sphere. We can no longer even name the spot it occupied . . . we can but seek and wonder as the search shows us the light simultaneously present at each and every point in the sphere.

The movement of thought, therefore, involves three steps: first, the presentation of an initial image of the corporeal order, the luminous core. Then comes a correction, consisting in the reminder (the underlining is meant to bring it out) that light, in Plotinus' view,[21] is an incorporeal phenomenon. In the third and radical step, Plotinus asks us to "abstract the corporeal mass," and the initial image is shattered and at the same time lifted out of the corporeal, into the intelligible realm. It is in this moment of "shatter" that Plotinus expects insight to occur.

But what was Augustine to do with this dynamic correction if he did not hold Plotinus' somewhat specialized theory on the

[21] See Bréhier, *Ennéades* VI[1], 186, n. 1; also Armstrong, "*Emanation*," pp. 64ff.

incorporeality of light? Paradoxically enough, Plotinus himself offered a way out, and in this very treatise. Later on, he is compelled to return to his favorite image of "emanation" and submit it to a profound correction. It is a compliment to Augustine's alertness that he seems to have grasped the relation of that correction with the one we have just seen. The changes I make in MacKenna's translation here are in the interests of a more literal fidelity to the text.

It is not reasonable, it is even impossible in our opinion, to conceive of the Ideas and Matter as lying apart (*χωρὶς*) with Matter illumined from them as from somewhere above (*πόρρωθεν ἄνωθέν ποθεν*), a meaningless conception, for what could the words "far" and "separate" mean here (*τί γὰρ ἂν εἴη τὸ «πόρρω» . . . καὶ τὸ «χωρίς»*)? The theory of participation would not be the most obscure and difficult of all if it could be made understandable through such images (*παραδείγμασιν*).
When we ourselves speak of illumination, it is not to suggest the mode in which sensible light pours down on sensible objects (*ὡς ἐπὶ τῶν αἰσθητῶν . . . εἰς αἰσθητὸν*); but since, on the one hand, the Ideas hold the rank (*τάξιν*) of Archetypes with respect to material things, their images (*εἴδωλα*), and since, on the other hand, there is an analogous "apartness" (*τοιοῦτον οἷον χωρὶς*) between illumination (*sic*: *τῆς ἐλλάμψεως*) and illuminated, this is why we talk as we do.[22]
But now we must speak more precisely. We do not mean that the Idea is locally separate from Matter (*ὡς χωρὶς ὄντος τόπῳ*) showing itself in Matter like a reflection in water; Matter is at all points in contact (*ἐφαπτομένην*) with the Idea.
It is because the Idea, say, of Fire, is not *in* the Matter (*ἐν τῇ ὕλῃ*) that the Fire itself, not having become the form of Matter (*οὐκ ἐγγενόμενον αὐτὸ τῇ ὕλῃ μορφὴν*) can produce (*παρέξεται*) the form of Fire in the entire enfired mass; . . . that single Fire . . . produces an image (*εἰκόνα*) of itself . . . yet it is not spatially separate (*τόπῳ χωρὶς ὂν οὐ παρέξει*).

Now it would seem that what Augustine has done, with benefit, as we shall have occasion to see, of other Plotinian reminiscences, is this: he has combined both treatments of the light-image to the point where they coalesce. The incorporeality of light becomes an unnecessary postulate, and yet the dynamic movement of correction is retained to a remarkable degree. In the first paragraph of his reflections on the *libri platonicorum* he states:

Admonished thence (*scil*: by those books) to return to myself, under your leadership I entered into my inmost being: *intravi in intima mea.*

[22] For a treatment of some technical difficulties involved in this passage, the reader may consult nn. 87 and 88 to my article in *REA* 9: 26 (1963).

This I could do, for you became my helper. I entered there, and by some sort of eye-of-my-soul I saw, above that eye-of-my-soul, above my mind, an unchangeable light. It was not this common light, plain to all flesh, nor bigger (*grandior*), as it were, but of the same kind (*ex eodem genere*), as though that light were to shine many times more bright and with its greatness (*magnitudine*) fill the universe (*totumque occuparet*). Not such was that light, but other, entirely other from all such lights: *aliud, aliud valde ab istis omnibus*. Nor was it above my mind as oil is above water or sky above earth: above my mind it was, because it made me, and I beneath it because made by it: *superior quia ipsa fecit me, et ego inferior, quia factus ab ea* (*Conf* VII, 16).

If we compare them to similar expressions in connection with the omnipresence difficulty in the *Confessions*, the terms "inmost being" and "eye-of-my-soul" are Augustine's way of reminding us that his insight on this occasion was at last a truly intelligible one. The "unchangeable light" could, at first glance, be attached to any number of Plotinian light-images; again, it is more than probable that other reminiscences are at work here. But Augustine's warnings that he is not speaking of "common" light, sensible light ("plain to all flesh"), ring a special note. It is a light, he continues, of a different order entirely (*non ex eodem genere*)—the distinction, as Plotinus had insisted, is one of *τάξις*. "Above" it is, and Augustine repeats the term several times, but not "above" as one sensible object is "higher" than another, not "above . . . as oil is above water, or sky above earth." This would imply the spatial relation Plotinus insists must be eliminated, bring in images of "far and separate" which have nothing to do with the case, suppose that corporeal realities of the same order were in question. But this light is "other"—*aliud, aliud valde*—its superiority is exactly as Plotinus had described it, one of true being to its image, of producer to produced, *superior quia ipsa fecit me, et ego inferior quia factus ab ea.*

So much for the second of Plotinus' corrections: Augustine has encased the first, dynamic correction inside the process we have just examined. And he has done it, we would suggest, not through some slavish comparison of one text with the other, nor through mere verbal memory, but precisely because he has so firmly grasped the movement of the thought and the dynamism of the image-correction involved. Note for a moment the almost feverish pace of that movement: *supra . . . supra . . . non . . . nec . . . tamquam si*! The phrase hurtles forward with the same dynamism sensed in Plotinus' correction. A light, assuredly: but "unchangeable," "above my mind," not this "common light"—and at this point

Augustine sketches his own dynamic correction in three bold strokes. Imagine, he seems to be saying, imagine this light as quantitatively "bigger" (*grandior*). Then imagine this bigness coupled with a qualitative intensification of its brightness: *multo multoque clarius claresceret*. And now, imagine it expanding, beaming outward to embrace the "all" (*totum*). Then, after this penultimate correction, let your mind leap: this light was "other, entirely other." A light, but not alone a bigger light, nor only so much bigger *and* brighter that (like that in Plotinus' earlier illustration) it virtually ceases to be a localizable source, but spreads outward and ends by "occupying the entire mass of the sphere." The difference is one of "order," hence the image must be shattered. Augustine attempts to shatter it by bringing Plotinus' later correction into play.

Brief, pointed, metaphysically condensed to a degree that demonstrates a philosophical talent of a high order, Augustine's text leads the mind straight to the *Veritas* which alone "truly exists," though not "diffused through finite nor through infinite space": the familiar terms of the omnipresence problem are with us once again.

The Hand—from Dynamic Image to Paradox

The extremely sophisticated process of "dynamic correction" we have just examined was developed by one of human history's greatest thinkers, on the basis of an immense philosophic culture and after years of teaching activity. It shows Plotinus, beyond any doubt, a true "professional." What is astonishing is that Augustine, much less seasoned, far less learned, immensely talented, doubtless, but with the brilliance that from time to time betrays the amateur, Augustine seems nonetheless to have grasped the secret of a process which may well have eluded the faithful Porphyry.

But Augustine is not giving lessons in philosophic method; nor is his native gift the dynamic image. It is in handling paradox that he is a master of another sort. The very opening paragraphs of the *Confessions*, to cite but that instance, show an intensity of treatment—image paired off against counter-image, terms colliding with their contraries, the stab of paradox everywhere—which provides an admirable lens for metaphysical vision. This remark on the style of Augustine's imagination may help us to understand the transformation he has worked on the second of Plotinus' dynamic images, that of the Hand. It occurs in the same paragraph of Plotinus' treatise as the dynamic light-image, and is absent, just as its partner was, from the *Sententiae*. Its purpose is to show that a being can control another with its energy without splitting up into parts corresponding to the parts of the extended being controlled.

> A hand may very well hold[23] an entire mass, a long plank, or anything of the sort; its power is distributed throughout and yet, it is not distributed unit for unit over the objects being held: the power is felt to reach over the whole area, though the hand is only a hand-long, not taking on the extension of the mass it holds.
>
> Lengthen the object, and provided the total is within its strength, the power extends to this new body-mass without the need of being divided into as many parts as the new mass possesses.
>
> Now let us eliminate the corporeal mass of the hand, retaining the power it exerted: is not that power, the indivisible, present throughout that assemblage of bodies, and present in the same way to each part?

The Head—and a Tug at the Hair

Again, the three-stage process is evident: an initial image, an intermediate correction, then a correction so radical that the image shatters. Before passing on to see what happens to it in the *Confessions*, we present the last image that concerns us: that of the Head. It, too, is absent from Porphyry.

First, a remark on the doctrine which it is meant to illustrate. As in the finale of *Ennead* VI, 5, quoted above, Plotinus is here insisting that we are all one being, identical with the universal being, the All. The thesis in question is what Armstrong speaks of—precisely in reference to these same two texts—as "outspoken pantheism."[24] The consequences of that will come to light shortly; the relevant text concerns us now.

> We reduce to Real Being, all that we have and are; to that we return, as from that we came. We have knowledge (*νοοῦμεν*) of what is there, not images (*εἴδωλα*) or even impressions (*τύπους*) and to know without images is to be those things (*Εἰ δὲ μὴ τοῦτο, ὄντες ἐκεῖνα*) . . . We are

[23] Plotinus uses the term *κρατοῦν*. Exactly translated, this becomes MacKenna's "control"; but Ficinus uses *tenere*, Bréhier, "tenir levé," and I have taken the liberty of inserting this more obvious term here. One may suppose that such a neutral term (*tenere*) was probably present in the translation Augustine used: see the *omnitenens manu veritate*, *Conf* VII, 22. Courcelle kindly offers the information that the *omnitenens* with respect to God is repeated in *Conf* XI, 15—and, we would add, in explicit connection with repeated evocations of the "hand" image (XI, 13–15), and in the same time-eternity connection as here, *Conf* VII, 21. Courcelle observes also that in *Tractatus In Joannem* CVI, 5, Augustine assures his hearers of the equivalence between the Latin *omnitenens* and the Greek *παντόκρατωρ*, thus returning to Plotinus' term, *κρατοῦν*. This, however, may well be no more than a curious coincidence.

[24] Armstrong, "Emanation," p. 62. It should be clear that neither Armstrong nor I intend to characterize Plotinus' *over-all system* as "pantheistic." The thrust of this problematic has brought him in these two instances to go much farther in this direction than he usually does, or would.

(true beings) while we are also one with all: therefore we and all things are one (*Πάντα ἄρα ἐσμὲν ἕν*).

When we look outside of that on which we depend, we are not conscious of that unity; *we are like a single head with many visages*, the many *visages turned outwards*, but *on the inner side, all one head*: *Ἔξω μὲν οὖν ὁρῶντες ἢ ὅθεν ἐξήμμεθα ἀγνοοῦμεν ἓν ὄντες, οἷον πρόσωπα πολλὰ εἰς τὸ ἔξω πολλά, κορυφὴν ἔχοντα εἰς τὸ εἴσω μίαν.*

If a man could but be turned about (*ἐπιστραφῆναι*)—by his own motion or by a lucky pull of Athena—he would see at once God, and himself, and the All: *θεόν τε καὶ αὑτὸν καὶ τὸ πᾶν ὄψεται* (*Enn* VI, 5, 7, 1–14).

There is no effort of dynamic correction, here: the image is pure paradox. Considering Augustine's penchant in that direction, we must not be surprised if it enjoys a certain future in his works. Like the finale of VI, 5, it supposes the whole-part couple with frankly pantheistic implications; it presents us with an *εἴσω-ἔξω* that strongly recalls Augustine's "within-without"—*intus-foras*. It features a conversion-image as well, one that uses the same term as before, *ἐπιστραφῆναι*, but here the context, and especially the *ἕλξις* of Athena, which Bréhier translates as a "tug at the hair," gives this image of turning-about a violence that is not present in the former text. Bréhier remarks in another place on the difference in quality between the more usual Plotinian image of conversion and Bergson's "torsion,"[25] a difference in quality that should be evident. But could it be that Bergson's image is Plotinian after all? Granted one would never be tempted to translate the conversion image of *Ennead* VI, 5, 12 (or of *Sententia* 40) by the term *torquere*; but for the image we have just seen, that translation would hardly be out of place.

Central Image of Conversion

All three of these images—Eros, the Hand, the Head turned about—can be detected at the heart of Augustine's account of his Neo-Platonic illumination, or, to use the more usual but misleading designation, of his "intellectual conversion." Rather than remaining three distinct images, however, they fuse into one—and, paradoxically, they are held in fusion by a single term, the Latin verb *fovere*.

But proving that involves, among other things, tracing Augustine's progressive exploitation of that term and his orchestration of its attendant images. This brings us to a second major phase in verifying the hypothesis that *Ennead* VI, 4–5 exercised a profound

[25] Bréhier, "Images," p. 298.

and lasting influence on his thinking. This phase consists in showing the explanatory value of the hypothesis: its power to lay bare the often subtle, sometimes almost hidden resonances of meaning locked in the Saint's writings. But the meaning, in every case, must be the meaning of the text—in the text and not merely read into it. The test of our hypothesis is this: does it permit Augustine to remain Augustine? And the text itself, though it may have to be read sometimes with painful care, must always decide that question. *Caveat lector* . . .

2 FOVISTI CAPUT NESCIENTIS

DISSECTING AN IMAGE

Prelude to Insight

Augustine's first step in recounting the fruit of his Neo-Platonic readings is to present his vision of the transcendent Light, and then turn back to a new vision of the *cetera*, the "other things" below God. He then goes on to glimpse God as Good, and all temporal realities as good in their own order. This brings him to a solution of the question "what evil is," and lays the groundwork for coming to his central problem, resolution of the question "whence evil comes."

In a book as carefully composed as the *Confessions*, it is significant that Augustine here abruptly stops the forward progress of his account. He wishes to warn us of the crucial importance of what he is about to tell us. He moves backward in time and takes the trouble of resuming once again two stages of the difficulty that has been his throughout the *Confessions*: the difficulty of conceiving God's relation to the world in terms that will permit solution of the question, "whence is evil?"

The first stage is familiar. As a Manichee he thought it impiety to ascribe to God's doing whatever he looked upon as "evil" in the universe. Unable, at the same time, to conceive of God and universe except in corporeal and imaginative terms, he was driven into the dualistic theory of "two substances," one Good, one Evil—one Divine, one anti-god.

The second stage of his difficulty results from the view he gradually adopted after leaving Manichaeism (*inde rediens*). Then God was imagined as infinite, rather than (as the Manichees had taught) infinite on all sides save the one bounded by the "hordes of darkness." But He is still envisaged as diffused through space (*per infinita spatia locorum omnium*). Now, in terms which will come up for more careful scrutiny later, Augustine rejects that view as well. Having resumed his difficulty in these two stages, then, he gets to the heart of the matter: to the vision in which he saw God and creatures in their proper relation at last.

The Central Image

Ryan translates this crucial passage as follows:

> But afterwards, you soothed my head, unknown to me (*fovisti caput nescientis*) and closed my eyes, lest they see vanity (*vanitatem*); I turned a little from myself, and my madness was lulled to sleep (*consopita est insania mea*). I awoke in you (*evigilavi in te*) and saw that you are infinite, although in a different way (*aliter*), and this vision was not derived from the flesh (*a carne*).
>
> I looked back over other things (*respexi alia*) and I saw that they owe their being to you, and that all finite things are in you (*in te*). They are there, not as though in a place, but in a different fashion (*aliter, non quasi in loco*), because you contain all things in your hand by your truth: *quia tu es omnitenens manu veritate* (*Conf* VII, 20–21).

Fovisti caput. Omnitenens manu veritate. Augustine's head, the Divine Hand, and, linking the two, that apparently innocent term *fovisti.* Here we have the Saint's incredibly condensed expression of conversion, the very heart of the *Confessions.*

The Hand: a Biblical Image "Plotinized"

The function of the image of the Hand here is to express that space-defying relationship of all creation to an omnipresent God Who upholds them (*omnitenens*) in a hand that is neither place nor in place. As such, the image is assuredly charged with a host of Biblical connotations. Psalm 139 immediately comes to mind, that hymn to the Divine Omnipresence and Omniscience which unquestionably threads its way in and out of Augustine's conversion story. There the Psalmist praises the God Who

. . . dost enfold me behind and before
And dost put thy hand upon me . . .
If I take up the wings of the dawn
And dwell at the back of the sea
Even there thy hand will guide me
And thy right hand will hold me (Ps. 139: 5, 9–10).

But here, as generally in Scripture, the "hand of God" does not formally and properly symbolize God's integral omnipresence in the precise way Augustine's *omnitenens manus* does. In the Bible, God's "arm" is imaged as "long," the "hand" of His power "reaches out" to the ends of the earth. But Augustine has too carefully set up the omnipresence problem, too explicitly evoked it here, to be content with such "uncorrected" imagery. Not only would it solve nothing in the context, it would merely tumble us back into the most primitive formulation of the question. What he has done is typical of his entire intellectual endeavor: he has taken a Biblical image and (as Ambrose had shown was both necessary and legitimate) "spiritually interpreted" it according to the logic of Plotinus' dynamic correction. In so doing, he has impregnated it with this new meaning, the only one directly relevant and required by the context. Again, it is not a question of "either-or"; both the Bible and Plotinus are at work here, the latter providing the "understanding" of the former's imagery.

The other elements in the presentation only reinforce this view: to bring such relatively disparate Plotinian images into collision at the heart of his account Augustine's powerful imagination had to go to considerable lengths. But collide they do.

To glimpse the Truth, which is his lapidary expression for Plotinus' "true being" (ὄντως ὄν), Augustine must allow his querulous "madness" to be "lulled to sleep," must let God close his eyes to "vanity." But "vanity" is invariably his term in the *Confessions* (IV, 26; V, 17 and 20; VII, 1; cf. III, 10–12) for those empty fantasies the "vain" soul fabricates in her efforts to imagine God, and spiritual realities more generally, on the pattern of bodies seen through the "outer" eye of the "flesh" (*a carne*).[1] Hence a presumption is already forming: the vision of truth will be attained only after Augustine is enabled to see with the "inner" eye, not of the body, but of the mind, to pierce the veil of

[1] Louis Chevalier and Henri Rondet, in "L'Idée de vanité dans l'oeuvre de saint Augustin," *REA* 3: 221–234 (1957) suppose (p. 234) that man was truly incarnate in paradise. Release this supposition, take account of the development required to shape the concordism between the Biblical notion and the Plotinian counterpart, and the texts they adduce from the *Confessions* can, I submit, be interpreted uniformly in the sense I have proposed.

"phantasms" (cf. VII, 11–12) and catch sight of reality's intelligible shape. And so he does. Having gained an intellectual insight, he sees that God is not properly *in* things, but as Plotinus had insisted, the very reverse is closer to the truth: *in te cuncta finita, sed aliter.* All finite realities are in Him, but in another fashion: not as in place—and at this point the grammatical anomaly which has driven translators to every variety of desperate solution, is fully intended. God up-holds all things, not *manu veritatis*, "in the hand of truth," as one might expect. He up-holds them, rather, *manu veritate*, in His "truth-hand": sheer juxtaposition of two ablatives, one correcting the other almost to the point of cancellation, almost to the strain and rupture Plotinus produces when he calmly suggests we "now eliminate the corporeal mass of the hand"—and thereby shatters his image before our gaze.

The Head—and the *Parvulus Conversus*

But *fovisti caput nescientis*: what warrant is there for saying this is the head of Plotinus' image? On the face of it, there seems not the remotest possibility that *fovere* could ever mean "tug" or "twist about," as the Plotinian image surely requires.

Yet the term is pregnant with ambiguities. Its most general dictionary meaning is to "warm," as a mother-bird might do by folding her wings about her young. It can also mean to "bathe" or "foment" a wound in some (presumably warm) solution designed to "heal." The passage to transferred senses then becomes self-explanatory: *fovere* comes to mean such things as "foster," "support or favor," "cherish" or "caress"—as a mother might do with a child on her lap or bosom.

Ryan's translation, "soothe," follows Pusey's in choosing a compromise between the "bathing" and "caressing" images. Just previous to this account of the Platonic readings, Augustine has pictured God as a physician who with "secret hand" makes his "swelling wound" subside and thereby brings his "mind's afflicted and darkened eyes" back to health; he has, moreover, repeatedly evoked the notion of "sickness" throughout his account. Hence the common practice of translating *fovere* in the largely medical sense, a practice surely authorized by the context.

But here again, we may not have an either-or situation: translation may force us to choose between alternatives which the original language organically combines. Pierre de Labriolle's translation may, at first, appear arbitrary: *Vouz avez attiré ma tête contre vous*, "you drew my head against you." Yet the appearance of arbitrariness vanishes once we note how artfully Augustine has evoked another of the term's familiar images: *sinu*, or *gremio fovere*, the tender action of a mother or nurse, drawing a fretful child upon her breast to comfort him. Here the term *fovere* would acquire a definite imaginative suggestion of "turning about."

No sooner is this possibility entertained than a number of corroborative indices in the text cluster immediately about it. Augustine has regularly associated the vital step of passing from looking on "vanity" to "seeing Truth" with a "turn inward" from looking "outward." The verse of Psalm 118, which he is partially citing here, embodies that same image. Originally, it read *Averte oculos meos ne videant vanitatem*, "*turn my eyes away* lest they look on vanity." Augustine has inserted the term for head, and qualified it with an "unknowing" (*nescientis*) that strongly recalls Plotinus' ἀγνοοῦμεν ("we do not know") from the context of the head-image in *Ennead* VI, 5, 7. He has further polarized the ambivalence of the term *fovere*, accordingly, by making it replace an *averte* with which his readers were familiar and which they would dimly, half-consciously, supply. He has intensified that polarization by setting the phrase in the unbroken movement of this entire subsection (VII, 20–21) toward the vision that climaxes it—the vision of that "iniquity" which is the primordial counterpart of "conversion": the "per-versity" of a will that is "twisted away" (*detortae*) from God the Supreme and spews forth its "insides," swelling outward, *foras*.

And for a moment we are faced with a difficulty. Even in the bizarre logic of imagery—and most of the linkages here were forged in the depths of Augustine's poetic unconscious—the violence of that primal "dis-tortion" seems to call for an equally violent "re-torsion" or "twisting back." But that violent movement Augustine has saved for the Eighth Book account of what is often (accurately?) termed his "moral" conversion. Few readers of the *Confessions* will have forgotten the dramatic moment when

> Ponticianus told us this story, and as he spoke, you O Lord *turned me back* (*retorquebas*: kept turning me back?) *upon myself*. You took me from *behind my own back* (*a dorso*) where I had placed myself because I did not wish to look upon myself. You *stood me face to face with myself* so that I might see how foul I was, how dis-torted (*distortus*) and defiled, how covered with stains and sores. I looked, and I was filled with horror, but there was no place for me to flee to away from myself. If I tried to *turn my gaze from myself* (*a me avertere aspectum*), he still went on with the story he was telling, and once again you *placed me in front of myself*, and *thrust me before my own eyes*, so that I might find out my iniquity and hate it: *me rursus opponebas mihi et inpingebas me in oculos meos* (VIII, 16).

The italics added serve to bring out the variants on the basic image of "re-torsion": it is at work throughout the account, linked with the primal "de-tortion" that constitutes "iniquity." *Opponebas, inpingebas, retorquebas*: God's action is obviously patterned here on the insistent, almost heartless, gesture of a master engaged in housebreaking a young puppy. Conversion is, therefore, in the logic of Augustine's imaged thought, quite literally a "turning back" of what once was "turned away"—another index, albeit indirect, that the term *fovere*, central to his so-called "intellectual" conversion, also has something of this imaginative connotation.

But the movement *fovere* implies is gentler, distinctly maternal: it has nothing of the violence of the image in this second form. Why then did Augustine split Plotinus' image in two? To answer that question, one must first uncover the imaginative implicits at work on either side, to find out, to begin with, how the term *fovere* ever acquired the "turning" connotation in the first place. This analysis will lead back to the image of Eros-waiting-at-the-door, and then compel us to trace out the successive stages of its bewildering metamorphosis over the years, until it becomes the dominant in Augustine's image of conversion.

But first, a curious paradox: one which confirms, as though confirmation might be needed, the opinion that holds the *Confessions* are an astonishing work of art. The term *fovere* occurs only one other time in the *Confessions*, in Book XIII, where it appears in a reference to St. Paul's first letter to the Thessalonians. And yet, no word occurs more frequently in the early works, and almost invariably in a "conversion" context. But even when the term itself is absent, its various senses and attendant images are active, and in a way foreshadowing the central image of the *Confessions*.

FOVERE IMAGES AT CASSICIACUM

Philosophy and Her Lovers

Among the first words we have from Augustine's pen after his conversion at Milan are those in which he dedicates the *Contra Academicos* to Romanianus. There he speaks of "true philosophy" who "promises to make clear to her true devotees" (*veris amatoribus suis*) that what men call "fortune" is really Divine Providence (I, 1).

Awakening the slumbering soul

The reverses Romanianus attributes to fortune are, therefore, "the secret work of a providence [which] has decided to rouse [his] divine element . . . lulled to sleep (*sopitum*) somehow by the lethargy of this life" (I, 3). *Evigila, evigila*: "Awake, awake I beg you" Augustine urges; he himself was in the same state of somnolence until an illness forced him to abandon his *rhetor's* position and retire to Cassiciacum.

A mother's lap and breasts

That retirement has made it possible for him to "take refuge in the lap of philosophy": in *philosophiae gremium*. "She now nourishes and cherishes me": *nutrit et fovet* (I, 3)—that same "philosophy from whose breasts (*ubera*) no age can complain that it is excluded. And so that I may incite you all the more eagerly to cling to her and drink of her (*avidius retinendam et hauriendam*) . . . I send you a foretaste" (I, 4).

Strength for a fledgling

The opening paragraphs of Book II resume the dedication. "Come with me then to philosophy," Augustine urges his former patron; he would repay past kindnesses to a Romanianus "who had expended care upon the cradle and, as it were, nest of my studies (*cunabula et quasi nidum . . . foveras*) and [later] supported me in my first efforts when I ventured to fly alone" (II, 3).

The fires of love

Indeed, Romanianus exercised a providential function in preparing Augustine for the new "flight" he is presently embarked upon, the philosophic life he has resolved to lead. For Augustine and his companions had "never ceased to yearn after philosophy." But since as yet they were "untouched by that great fire which was to consume us, we thought that the slow fire with which we burned was the greatest." And here the Saint describes the "incredible conflagration" caused by the Platonic readings. Now, none of his former desires hold any more charm for him.

Return to self: a tug, and the voyager looks backward

"Swiftly did I begin to return entirely to myself (*totus in me . . . redibam*). Actually, all that I did—let me admit it—was to look backward from a journey, as it were (*respexi . . . quasi de itinere*) to that religion which, implanted in us in our childhood days, is bound up in the marrow of our bones. But she indeed was drawing me, unknowing, to herself": *ipsa ad se nescientem rapiebat* (II, 5).

Again, Philosophy's beauty

Augustine then recounts his comparison of these readings with those of St. Paul, whose writings he read through "entirely, with the greatest attention and care" (II, 5). The result is once again expressed in terms of the Eros-image: "And then, indeed, whatever had been the little radiance that had surrounded the face of philosophy before that moment, she now appeared so great that if I could show it . . . even to [Romanianus' enemy] . . . he would fly, an impassioned and holy lover, amazed and glowing with excitement, to this beauty of philosophy": *ad huius pulchritudinem blandus amator et sanctus, mirans, anhelans, aestuans advolaret* (II, 6).

The soul's upward flight

For even his *Philocalia*, his "love of beauty," is sister to the "love of wisdom," *Philosophia*, being like a bird "dragged down from her heavenly abode by the birdlime of wantonness, and locked up in an ordinary cage." Her sister, meanwhile, who alone knows of *Philocalia's* heavenly origin, "winging her way unrestrained, frequently takes notice of her in her wingless squalor and poverty, but rarely sets her free" (II, 6).

Healing and opening the inner eye

But if Romanianus' adversary "who so loves the false, could with healed and open eyes look upon the true beauty even for a moment, with what delight would he take refuge in the lap of philosophy": *quanta voluptate philosophiae gremio se involveret* (II, 7).

Summary: "Philosophy" and her features

There is a close correspondence between these variants of the Eros-image and Augustine's central image of conversion in the *Confessions*. *Philosophia* is obviously a personification. Her relationship to other personifications, like Truth and Wisdom, must await further clarification; but she has breasts, bosom, and lap; she is beautiful once her glory has been glimpsed; her "true lovers" are invariably "inflamed" and drawn to her, leaving all other charms behind.

But being drawn to her implies a "conversion." As in the *Confessions*, there is question of returning to the self, falling asleep to the outside world and waking to a splendid vision. This sleeping and waking is associated with Philosophy's turning one's head, redirecting the mind's eye till it is looking back toward the starting point of the "journey" the soul is pursuing. Here, too, the soul is said to be "unknowing."

At first, therefore, "Philosophy's" bridal character predominates: Augustine has yearned and burned to plunge himself into her lap, cast himself upon her bosom, catch sight of her naked splendor—the erotic overtones to his image of the "happy life" it would be idle to deny. Her countenance is beautiful with the true beauty his *Philocalia* sought in false beauties "outside." Happiness, he notes in the *De Beata Vita*, is found in a "temperance" which—like the "lady Continence" of the Eighth Book of the *Confessions*—is a kind of "bride" of the soul; her ardent lovers will abandon all else to win her favors, glimpse, hold fast, cling to her.

But then, almost imperceptibly, *Philosophia's* function becomes a maternal one as well. Conversion to Philosophy, Augustine notes, was one, for him, with conversion to (or "by") the "religion" of infancy, drunk in with his mother's milk; but now at Philosophy's "breasts" he drinks as well, rejoicing that no age-group is forbidden to do so. She fondles, caresses him—*fovet*—but (to recall that key term's other senses) her action is a favoring, fostering, and strengthening one: *nutrit et fovet*. Romanianus' action, expressed by the same verb, was like that of a parent-bird strengthening its chick for mature flight on its own; but such, too, is *Philosophia's* care, lavished on Augustine now. Wingless like *Philocalia*, he hopes *Philosophia* will help him grow wings again, wings for flying back to happiness.

He hopes, as well, that her action will effect the "healing and strengthening" of his inner eye, so he can gaze unflinching at the splendid sun of Truth, and so be bathed in unabating bliss: a final sense of the term *fovere*, but once again, like all the others here, a sense active in the *Confessions* as well.

The Wanderer Come Home

Already interweaving with the Eros-image, however, is another image of "conversion," basically different in structure and implications, yet ready to be drawn into the orbit of the first. This phenomenon of image-fusion is common in Augustine. But it might have surprised him to realize that it was a word—*fovere*—that operated as the catalytic agent.

The Odysseus image

For happiness is spoken of not only as vision, possession, embrace, and union. It is also imaged as "arrival," after stormy voyaging, the entry into port, into the calm of safe harbor. Here O'Meara seems on sure ground: the Odyssey-image of the ancient world, and notably of *Ennead* I, 6, is obviously at work. For Odysseus was the figure of the unhappy, wandering soul, far from his "homeland," tossed and crossed by wind and wave, yearning to have the buffeting behind him and "return" home at last.

Biblical resonances

But the image is not uniquely secular. Augustine's fond familiarity with the Psalms, his practice of interpreting the history of Israel as symbol of the Christian's life, certainly led him to the identical image in Psalm 107.

> Those who go down to the sea in ships,
> And do business in the great waters,
> They saw the works of the Lord,
> And his wonders in the deep,
> For he spoke and raised up the storm-wind,
> Which lifted up its billows on high.
> They mounted to the heavens, they descended to the depths.
> They were dissolved in their distress.
> They reeled and staggered like a drunken man,
> And were at their wits' end.
> When they cried to the Lord in their trouble,
> He delivered them from their distress.
> He stilled the storm to a whisper,
> And the waves were hushed.
> Then they rejoiced because they were quiet,
> And he brought them to their desired haven (Ps. 107: 23–30).

Connection with the soul's "flight"

But the image of "arrival" takes another form in Augustine's earliest works: a variant on the figure—already seen in connection with *Philosophia*—of the winged soul, classic in Neo-Platonic tradition. The flight of the soul is also, like Odysseus' journey, a "return"—*reditus*. Here, in the *Contra Academicos* (III, 3), the legend of Daedalus intervenes, and Augustine speaks of the "flight" as winging across the seas.

The Prodigal: a journey overland

Finally, there looms up to join both Daedalus and Ulysses the figure of the Prodigal (*Sol* I, 5). Restless in his Father's house, he left his home to fall eventually into misery and want. His suffering brings him "to himself," however; it reminds him of the Father's house on which he turned his back and inspires him to return. Significantly, the journey here is overland: like the trek to Larissa of which Socrates speaks in the *Meno*, or the journey Augustine mentions in the *Contra Academicos* to Alexandria, or a trip to any nameless city one desires to go to (I, 11–12; III, 34). Here the Exodus history of wandering in the desert comes into its own as image of the pilgrim soul. Illustrative again is Psalm 107.

They wandered in the wilderness, in the waste,
They found no way to an inhabited town.
They were hungry and thirsty,
Their courage collapsed within them,
When they cried to the Lord in their trouble,
He delivered them from their distress,
And guided them in a straight way,
So that they came to an inhabited town . . .
For he satisfied the thirsty spirit,
And the hungry heart he filled with good (Ps. 107: 4–9).

In quest of a city

Was Augustine familiar with Psalm 107 at the time of his conversion at Milan? Very probably. It is certain, however, that his first move after reading Plotinus was to take up St. Paul's Epistles and read them *attentissime*, with the express purpose of finding whether they agreed with the Neo-Platonist. Now the Epistle to the Hebrews Augustine certainly deemed Paulinian; the figure of the journey to a city must have struck him when he came to its commendation of Abraham, the pilgrim called to be a "stranger in the land he had been promised ... For he was looking forward to that city with the sure foundations, designed and built by God" (Heb. 11: 9–10). All the Old Testament saints recognized, in fact, that "they themselves were only strangers (*peregrini*) and foreigners here on earth . . . in search of a country of their own . . . a better, a heavenly country . . . for [God] has prepared a city to receive them" (Heb. 11: 13–16). That city later gets a name: "Mount Zion, . . . the city of the living God, the heavenly Jerusalem" (12: 22), in comparison with which "we have no permanent city here on earth, but are in search of a city that is to come" (13: 14).

The wanderer's hunger and thirst

It is hardly surprising that Augustine associates his pre-conversion wandering with the hunger and thirst that afflicted the Prodigal and the Israelites. Arrival is accordingly associated with assuagement, refreshment—and the journey-image begins to slip into the orbit of the maternal image.

The soul's food

But this was merely one more point where Plotinus and the Bible agreed. The *De Beata Vita* means to prove that the hungering soul's true food is Truth, the subsistent and beatifying Truth Whose true name is God. Plotinus had assured him of nothing different, in his glowing portrait of the Intelligible Heaven, when he spoke of Truth as "mother, nurse, existence and sustenance" to them there. This, however, is the "food of grown men," as the *Confessions* puts it (VII, 16–17). The soul will feed on it at journey's end. But how are we to "grow" in order to arrive at it?

STRENGTH FOR THE JOURNEY

How Lies the Way?

The question Plotinus had asked was a telling one: how does one make the journey? In terms of the foregoing images: sea voyages require ships and gear; a bird must grow sturdy wings before it can fly; even when journeying on land, a man must inquire about the road and gather strength to travel it. Three images: but all posing an identical question, and one which will bring them all under the sway of a fourth, the Eros-image.

Fortune and Providence

Right from the first, Augustine is keenly aware that he had needed help and had received it. Was it supplied by chance fortune, or is "fortune" another name for God's secret, universal Providence? We know the answer he insinuates to Romanianus: his help, too, extended to Augustine when preparing for his flight into the *rhetor's* profession, was providential: *foveras*. The mistress-mother of his soul, *Philosophia*, is strengthening him now for a new flight: *nutrit et fovet*. The breasts of mother and nurse had done the same to turn his infancy into eventual manhood: *foverunt*.

This is precisely the point at which Augustine's imagination works a paradoxical fusion between the maternal Eros-image and the images of "voyage," "journey," and "flight." The *Contra Academicos* allows us to surprise that process of fusion just as it gets underway: Augustine is arguing with Alypius that though the accomplished sage may dispense with, in fact, ought to "despise" them, "fortune" and its gifts may nonetheless be needed for the novice on the "way" to *becoming* "wise." In the course of the argument, his mind flits swiftly over three analogies that illustrate his point: when we were infants we had "need of woman's breasts" to nourish us to the point where we were then able to "live and grow strong without them"; similarly, the ship one uses to cross the Aegean, the wings Daedalus used for his flight, are discarded and even "contemned" on arrival at the "port of wisdom, and, as it were, the steadfast and pleasant country" (*Acad* III, 3). From that point forward, these three images, along with the image of a "journey" overland (*Acad* I, 11–12; III, 33), will invariably evoke one another, interweave in a kind of fugue, but then regularly resolve as both "voyage" "flight" and "journey" melt into the first, so that "return" becomes return to the maternal care of that "Beauty, ever ancient, ever new."

"*Fove Precantes, Trinitas*"

As the *De Beata Vita* means to prove, his present flight to "happiness" leads straight to the very bosom of the Godhead. How is the strength for that journey to be won? The answer comes in Monica's exclamatory prayer toward the end of that Dialogue: *Fove precantes, Trinitas* (35). The line is taken from the final strophe of Ambrose's *Deus creator omnium*, a hymn that made a strong impression on Augustine. The *Confessions* (X, 50) later recounts how deeply the recent convert was affected by the hymnody in Milan's basilica. This very hymn, in fact, comes to his mind as consolation after Monica's death (*Conf* IX, 32), and as example for metrical analysis in both *De Musica* VI and the Eleventh Book of the *Confessions* (XI, 35). It had been sung in the weary night vigils, and (suggestively) Monica is described as uttering it here *evigilans in fide*: "awakening in faith," bringing forcibly to mind Augustine's own response to God's *fovere*-action in the Confessions: *evigilavi in te.*

Fove precantes, Trinitas, then: but how is God's care mediated to men in need of it? Augustine's view is already firm: Plotinus' teaching on the universality of Providence (cf. *Ennead* III, 2–3) makes not only men like Romanianus "ministers" of God's activity, it arranges all things in concert for bringing the soul back home.

Paul and His Care for the "Little Ones"

Typically, comparison with St. Paul showed Christianity in striking agreement, agreement expressed in the same basic imagery. The text Augustine quotes in the Thirteenth Book of the *Confessions* reads: "And we became little ones (*parvuli*) in your midst, as if a nurse (*nutrix*) were to care for (*foveat*) her children" (I Thess. 2: 7; cf. *Conf* XIII, 32). But the association Augustine has by that time developed is plain from the way he introduces this theme: Paul, he informs us, was encouraging his readers to " 'be reformed in the newness of [their] mind' lest he always keep them as babes (*parvulos*) whom he would have to nourish with milk and care for (*foveret*) as a nurse." No longer, then, in Augustine's imagination, is Paul himself the "little one" in question; the faithful are that. Paul is depicted as a "nurse," regretting that he must treat them as he treated the Corinthians, not "as spiritual persons [but] as babies (*parvulis*) in Christ. I fed you with milk, not solid food, for you were not ready for it" (I Cor. 3: 1–2). The same theme Augustine must in this same period have found orchestrated in the Letter to the Hebrews: its addressees are told they cannot understand the *grandis sermo*; they have "come to need milk instead of solid food (*solido cibo*). For anyone who is limited to milk . . . is only an infant (*parvulus*). But full-grown men have a right to solid food: *perfectorum autem est solidus cibus* (Heb. 5: 11–14).

Catholica, Mother and Nurse

Already at Cassiciacum, then, the answer to Augustine's question is taking form. To awaken us to our misery, to nourish, foster, strengthen us for the journey homeward, for the voyage to our native land, to fledge us for the flight that will allow us to feed on the *cibus grandium* (*Conf* VII, 16), there must be a nurse, a mother who feeds us temporarily on "milk" till we are "grown." "And so," in the words of a text slightly more mature,

> those whom the Catholic Church holds up as sucklings at her breast (*vagientes . . . ubera sustentat*) . . . are nourished, each according to his capacity and strength. In one or other manner they are all conducted, first to this stage of "perfect manhood," then to the ripeness and white hairs of wisdom; each is permitted, as they will it, both to live and to live happily (*Mor* I, 17).

The Church and Christ

The instrument of Omnipresent Providence and God's "maternal" care is the *Catholica*, accordingly. She is mother and nurse of little ones humble enough to believe and accept her fostering care for them. But her work is continuation of the work of Christ, Who "mingled that food [the *cibus grandium*] which I was unable to receive, with our flesh, for 'the Word was made flesh' so that your Wisdom . . . might provide milk for our infant condition . . . He heals their swellings and nourishes their love . . . so that in their weariness they may cast themselves upon the [humbled Godhead], while it arises and lifts them up" (*Conf* VII, 24). The *De Libero Arbitrio* had identified the Eternal Christ with the "Beauty of Wisdom" for whose caresses the soul yearns; now He has become vested with all the images responding to the term *fovere*. He is healer, nurse, mother, upholder, this Christ who, like a mother-bird, proclaimed his desire to take us all, like "chicks," beneath fond protecting wings.

So close is the relation of Church and Christ that Augustine never tires of quoting to the Manichees that Pauline text which says "No man ever hates his own flesh; rather, he nourishes and fosters it (*nutrit et fovet*) as Christ does the Church" (Eph. 5: 29). Providential instrument and bride, the very "flesh" of Christ, the Church (in the light of omnipresence teaching) "upholds" her infants with God's own Truth-Hand, gives them, as Augustine's childhood nurses did, milk which comes immediately from God's own breasts.

For all of this, if Providential, is God's own work; and if God be Omnipresence, then His Truth-Hand is the one that fondled and supported the infant Augustine, and now has twisted his head about to let him glimpse the homeland he left behind him on his wanderings, glimpse the Truth which "truly exists."

HUMAN SUFFERING AND DIVINE CARE

If left as it stands, however, Augustine's portrait of the tender care He images in the figure of maternal omnipresence would have been fatally defective in the eyes of the readers for whom it was primarily drawn—his former co-religionists, the Manichees. He has, it is true, justified the *Catholica's* appeal for simple faith in those of her children who are still "little ones": they must mature before the food of grown men can be set before them. But stark against Augustine's confession of the Biblical God's love for men the Manichees set the patent fact of evil, the searing reality of human suffering.

Here again, Augustine is convinced, the Bible's answer came in one word: "care." Evils themselves could embody God's providential care for us; our sufferings could be medicinal. The author of the Letter to the Hebrews, to stay within the circle of Augustine's readings at this time, compares God to the father in Proverbs 3: 11–12. Speaking of the sufferings they are undergoing, he counsels them:

> My son, do not think lightly of the Lord's discipline,
> Or give up when he corrects you.
> For it is those whom the Lord loves that he disciplines,
> And he chastises every son that he acknowledges.
> You must submit to it as discipline. God is dealing
> with you as his sons. For is there a son whom his
> father does not discipline? (Heb. 12: 5–8).

Plotinus' double-treatise "On Providence," *Ennead* III, 2–3, probably directed against a gnosticism akin to Manichaeism, made much the same point: rather than let them persuade us Providence was not universal, we must learn to ferret out the providential value of what evils befall us, what sufferings we are called upon to endure. This, too, is the point of Augustine's imagery. If life held no tempests for us, we might never pursue the voyage to the safety of home; were desert travel pleasant, we might settle there and never dream of the delights awaiting us once the desert is crossed; had the Prodigal not experienced the pangs of hunger, he might never have returned to himself, and to his father's house; if here we enjoyed a lasting city, we would never be aroused by longing for the heavenly Jerusalem. Augustine's recent sickness was a providential thing: it occasioned his retirement to the philosophic calm of Cassiciacum. So, indeed, were all the sufferings he had endured. They served to awaken him, sever his soul from the attractions of earth, set his heart on that other world to which all earthly life is a journey. Indeed, he wonders, could the soul be awakened any other way than by such providential tempests? (*Vita*, 1.) Would that Romanianus, too, might find his present difficulties signs of God's omnipresent providential care for him; let them awaken him, return him to his true self, bring him to the haven of "philosophy." The doctor must hurt in order to heal; the sun that warms us (*fovet*) sometimes burns as well. That burning, though, can be a medicinal thing, melting the ice of our sinfulness, cauterizing the wound that festers. And Christ the Healer is also the warming, burning, strengthening Sun, "from whose heat no man can hide" (*Conf* V, 1; IX, 8; cf. Ps. 18: 7).

ONLY AN IMAGE, ONLY A WORD . . .

There are several ironies in the contention put forth in the preceding pages. For if there is one claim Augustine seems to deem important for his message, it is that, unlike the Manichees, he had at last been taught by Plotinus how to think without his thought being dominated by images; "phantasm" is, for him, a nasty word. More than one literary critic of recent times has demonstrated, though, that a man's use of imagery reveals far more transparently his deeper life of thought and affectivity than all the abstract generalities he may enunciate. What does "conversion" mean for Augustine? The answer lies at least as much in appreciating the implicits of this single powerful image, as in all the disquisitions on his theory of grace, providence and predestination. His theories on these matters, although they admittedly developed *pari passu* with the slow genesis of this central image of "care," are far more commanded by it than Augustine, surely, would ever have thought they were.

But that the whole process should have been catalyzed by a single word and encountered in various sources at a particularly critical point in the life of his imagination Augustine would have found close to scandalous. No one is more repeatedly insistent on the importance of distinguishing, and even opposing, realities and their verbal expression: *res*, he tirelessly reminds us, *non verba*. There are, as we shall see, deep anthropological implicits in this insistence. Yet nothing tests Augustine's anthropology more severely than his *rhetor's* sensitivity to words, than the power they wield over his poetic imagination. Nothing is more revealing on the working of his mind and sensibility than his use of language.

But again, no crucial item in his language can be studied merely as a blob of black and white upon a page. It functions as a kind of magnet, drawing to itself a world of thought-and-image, and must be understood in organic linkage with that world. This is what we have tried to do with the term *fovere*. There are few terms in Augustine's writings that more luminously reveal the organic relationship between the Biblical faith he heard "spiritually interpreted" by Ambrose and the Plotinian understanding which, from then up to the time of the *Confessions*, he considered in substantial accord with that faith.

Plotinian Christianity in Genesis

One may quarrel with one or other suggestion we have made in trying to conjecture when and where Augustine hit upon the various materials he finally fuses into this single decisive image: *fovisti caput nescientis*. But quarrels on detail should not call into question the substance of the explanation—or its implications. One of those implications deserves mention in passing. On the level of image (and images of this sort do not "lie") there is a profound consonance between Augustine's descriptions of his conversion in the *Confessions* and in his earliest works. But another of those implications is this: at no moment can Augustine's development of an *intellectus fidei* be conceived of as exclusively, or even unilaterally, Plotinian. Whether or not we agree with his understanding and use of them, it is far from negligible that the images Augustine gleans from progressively familiar contact with the Bible constantly enrich, and encourage, the process of developing a Plotinian expression of Christianity.

In addition to the Biblical materials we have already seen,

Isaias, for example, pictures God as shepherding his people, nursing, carrying, comforting his lambs—as mother, feeding them from the breasts of His great consolation. The Psalmist continually begs to be sheltered in the shadow of His pinions, and in the Gospels Christ Himself is depicted as mother-hen taking her chicks under her wings, as doctor healing and opening blind eyes. The Israelite journey through the desert will become, for Augustine, the figure of the Christian's "journey" through this temporal life, with God forever fostering, protecting, chastening, and feeding him with "bread from heaven." As his effort to think out the "faith" advances, Augustine finds his imagination saturated with an increasing number of Biblical images; but at the same time he finds each one of these images drawn into the field of force of, electrified by, the corollaries of Plotinus' doctrines of Providence and Omnipresence.

By the time of the *Confessions*, therefore, it is hardly an exaggeration to claim that, to Augustine's teeming imagination, one word —*fovet*—says everything that need be said on God's unceasing, omnipresent activity toward man.

Flowering of an Image: The *Confessions*

His opening meditation on infancy (in Book One) is peopled with images of mother, nurse, and generous breasts whose milk is really God's nourishing care for him. The infant, he advises us, is symbol of the "little one" who must believe what mother and nurse tell him, accept their treatment of him—including punishment—as for his good; he must put his trust in, cast his cares entirely upon them (I, 30). Augustine takes St. Matthew's verse on the "little one" quite literally, but in the terms above suggested: "for of such is the Kingdom"—they are the model of the faithful Christian, and conversion consists in "becoming a child" again.

The Second Book continues the process, picturing God's omnipresent wrath raised above an Augustine who "knew it not" (2), His omnipotence "not far" even from one "far" and wandering farther from Him (3). God's "gentle hand" is portrayed as powerful to "stretch forth . . . and soften the thorns" (3), at a time when there was no other "hand to root out" the "briars of unclean desires spread thick over [Augustine's] head" (6). Had he remained chaste, he "would have looked with greater joy to [God's] embraces" (3). "Exiled" then "from the joys of [God's] house," he now sees God was "always present to aid . . . merciful in [His] anger," careful to salt his pleasures with bitterness and disgust so that he might eventually find pleasure without disgust in God. "For you fashion sorrow into a lesson for us. You smite so that you may heal" (4).

And still his "perverse will, tending down towards lower things," propels him along those "crooked ways on which walk those who turn their back on [God] and not their face to [Him]" (6). Monica "admonishes" him with an admonition he now realizes was God's, but then, he "knew it not" (7). Now, as a "sick man who has been healed" by the divine "physician," he confesses the past sins God has "dissolved . . . as if they were ice" (15) and proclaims his "desire" for the "beautiful and comely" God from whom he once "fell away" and "went astray," thereby becoming a "land of want" (18), tormented with hunger for that "inner food" which is God Himself (III, 1).

But from Book IV, 1 to Book V, 2 he rings all the changes on his hidden key term in a fugue which features all the key images of *Ennead* VI, 4–5 resonating fully with their Biblical counterparts.

He begins by describing himself as a "little one" (*parvulus*) on God's own breast, "sucking Your milk" (*sugens lac tuum*) (IV, 1). He continues his meditation with the reminder that the "hand" of the proconsul—one "skilled in the art of medicine"—was placed on his "head," but not to cure him. Only the divine physician could have cured his illness (IV, 4–5). He reminds his reader of the omnipresence atmosphere: he was, he says, looking for beauties "outside" (*foras*) when God was all that time "not far," ever present, in fact, could he only have turned about to look within his own heart (IV, 25ff). He returns to another image commanded by his key term by evoking the "nest of faith" where "food" is none other than the Pauline "milk" spoken of at the beginning of the book, where the wings that protect are none other than God's (IV, 31). God's is the "physician's hand" (*manus medicinalis*) forever and everywhere at work to heal Augustine's swollen head (V, 1), and from that therapeutic "heat" no man can hide (V, 1).

But His is also the maternal hand that carries us (IV, 31): *tu portabis*, "You will carry us"—but whither? As if to answer, Augustine rings the changes on the terms *vertere* and *torquere* once again (IV, 31), reminding us that the terminus of that divine action is always a "re-turn" which makes man once again an infant "mouth turned back to You" (*os conversum ad te*), a suckling child quite literally come back to the breast of a "maternal" omnipresence. In the climax to this fugue he weaves these images together with amazing power; the atmosphere is charged with omnipresence, but the basic image is obviously that of a child returning to its mother. He prays

that our soul may arouse itself to You out of its weariness . . . passing on to You . . . for with You is refreshment and true strength: *refectio et vera fortitudo*.

Whither do [the wicked: *iniqui*] flee, when they flee from Your face? . . . They fled away . . . that being blinded (*excaecati*) they might stumble upon You (*in te offenderent*)—Who forsake nothing that You have made—that they, the unjust, might stumble upon You . . . withdrawing themselves from Your gentleness, stumbling against Your righteousness, and falling upon Your severity: *offendentes in rectitudinem tuam et cadentes in asperitatem tuam*. In truth, they do not know (*nesciunt*) that You are everywhere (*ubique sis*), for no place can enclose You, and You alone are present even to those who have set themselves far from You (*praesens etiam his qui longe fiunt a te*). Let them be converted (*convertantur*) and seek You . . . let them be converted, and behold, You are there within their hearts, within the hearts of those who confess to You, and cast themselves upon you, and weep upon Your breast after all their rugged ways: *in corde confitentium tibi et proicientium se in te et plorantium in sinu tuo*. When You gently wipe away their tears, . . . You, Lord, who made them, can remake [or feed?] them, and give them consolation: *reficis et consolaris eos* (V, 1–2).

Here, then, we have the full orchestration of the *fovere* theme as Augustine's imagination produced it. To assure us there is no mistake, he repeats the performance again in Book IX. All the themes and paradoxes of omnipresence are there, the contrast of inner and outer, vanity and truth, the coupling of blindness and *nescientia*; and blending with them is God's omnipresent action, warming, burning, and healing—nourishing, shadowing with his wings, and caressing as a mother does to draw her infant to her in the turning movement of conversion.

Here, then, we also have Augustine's own implicit exegesis of the central image of Book VII—*fovisti caput nescientis*—where like a child, tired after the long day's play at games that only leave him fretful and unfulfilled, he climbs back up at last onto his mother's lap, still wailing his childish complaints against the hard world. Gently the maternal hand wipes the scalding, blinding tears from his eyes, strokes his feverish head, closes his eyes, turns his head against her breast. And like an infant he is soothed, casts his cares upon this mothering God, *cessavi de me paululum*. He stops his fretting and drowses off—*consopita est insania mea*—and awakens to the realization that the "righteousness" he hurtled against that day, the "roughness" on which he fell, was this same "gentle" God's, though he knew it not: *nesciunt, quod ubique sis*. And the hand that healed, carried, soothed, and comforted, this too was God's, *omnitenens*, the only truly existent, omnipresent Truth.

Fove precantes, Trinitas: in the long vigils at Milan, Monica, that faithful mother, prayed.

Fovisti caput nescientis: years afterward, her son can find no better word to express the maternal tenderness of God's answer to that prayer.

Image and Import

There is obviously a theory of human life implied in Augustine's use of these *fovere*-images—a theory in which man, or perhaps more exactly "soul" (though this must await closer study) is viewed as having "departed" on a "journey" away from God, is "cared" for in multiple ways, until the results of that care show forth in "conversion" and "return" to God. In another variant of the basic image, the departure was a "fall," and return is an upward "flight" of the soul to the longed-for homeland. We know what was meant by the Plotinian counterparts of this constellation of images. Plotinus saw the soul as fallen from a premundane state of contemplative bliss into the temporal world of body and action; its principal concern was therefore to "awaken" to its misery, find and take the upward way, return to the bliss from which it had fallen. Return, he warns, is "not a journey for feet"; the soul must "close the eyes and call . . . upon another vision which is to be waked" within it (*Enn* I, 6, 8). "Not on foot," Augustine echoes him, "do we depart from You or return to You" (*Conf* I, 28), then, after God had "closed [his] eyes" for him and he "awoke," he saw—with another vision—one "not derived from the flesh" (*Conf* VII, 20). A striking correspondence of language and imagery: but does Augustine mean to imply by using it the same theory of soul, fallen and bent upon return, as Plotinus intended?

It would be premature to answer that question now; too many elements are still missing from the picture. Moreover, Augustine's adaptation of Plotinian materials to the task of elaborating an "understanding" of the Biblical faith should warn us to allow for creative transpositions on his part. The resemblances between his view of man and Plotinus' may turn out to be more superficial than the differences he may have been led to introduce.

One of those differences, and a radical one, underlies a textual anomaly noted in the course of this chapter; slight at first viewing, it may turn out to be deceptively slight. We noted that the maternal mildness of Augustine's *fovere*-image is already an adaptation of the brusquer Plotinian "twist" of the head. Is it enough to say that Augustine had worked the change to remind us of God's tireless goodness? It would not appear so: for in that case, why reintroduce the almost cruel twisting motif at the moment of the so-called "moral" conversion in Book Eight? What prompted him to split this image into two, present it in these distinct stages in the *Confessions*, when those stages seem to telescope throughout the earlier works? Does he mean to convey something by this split? And if so, what?

The answer to that question will lead to a more balanced view of Augustine's attitude toward Plotinus. Up to this point he has found him in remarkable agreement with the Bible as Ambrose had presented it to him at Milan. But there are points where that agreement falters and breaks down. The splitting of the head image means to underline one of those points, for it signifies Augustine's frank rejection of what he thought was a momentary Plotinian lapse into what he means by "idolatry."

3 IDOLATRY

Augustine has gone to great lengths to prepare the ground for his central moment of insight in the *Confessions*. Stopping the forward progress of his account, as we have seen, he explains how he had refused to believe that anything evil could come from God. "And from there, [my soul] turned to the theory of the two substances, but found no rest in it, and prattled nonsense: *aliena loquebatur* (VII, 20).

God and corporeal creation are here envisaged as two opposing, antithetic substances. But in that manner of envisaging them there was, as Plotinus later brings him to see, a basic flaw of method. Grasping the contours of the participation insight requires that the central relation of Archetype to the participant ectypes be kept intact: that relation is omnipresence. But this in turn requires that one really *think*. The radical defect in Manichaean method was that their image of God was exactly that, an image; they imagined everything in "phantasmal," hence corporeal, terms. The Divine, in their way of viewing it, was like a great sea of light, infinite on all sides except the one where the "hordes of darkness" lay over against it like a quarter-slice of cosmic pie.

Having recalled this image briefly, Augustine passes on immediately to a later stage in his unrelenting effort to form a conception of God. Having left Manichaeism—*inde rediens*—"my soul fashioned for itself (*fecerat sibi*) a god that filled all places in infinite space." The correction to Manichaeism is evident: God is now infinite in all directions, though still imaginatively envisaged. But there is yet a radical defect.

It thought that this god was You, and set it up in its heart: *collocaverat in corde suo*. Thus it again became the temple of its own idol, a thing abominable before You: *et facta erat rursus templum idoli sui abominandum tibi* (VII, 20).

Fecerat sibi, collocaverat—even without the explicit occurrence of the later *templum idoli*, it would be clear that Augustine is describing his efforts to conceive of God in terms suggesting an artificer's operations in fashioning and setting up an idol. But there are two puzzling features about this: first, that the *soul itself* is made the temple of the idol, the "god" being set up in its "heart"—*in corde suo*. And second, that troubling *rursus*: Augustine is plainly indicating that whatever "idolatry" was applicable in the second instance was equally applicable in the first. Now this seems immediately to exclude the possibility that "idolatry" is being used in its ordinary meaning, for in that sense, how can Manichaeism justly be considered "idolatry"? More to the point, perhaps, could Augustine himself, at any stage of his development, be properly spoken of as an "idolater" in the ordinary understanding of the term? If not, then what does he mean by the term as used of himself, the Manichees, and whatever thinkers suggested the spatial-infinite image of God he is referring to here?

Again, the problem is one of Augustinian language; solution of it requires that we re-examine closely what he has previously said of these two stages in his theological views. Even if all is not equally clear and certain once that examination is finished, it may sharpen our understanding of what he means by certain of these same phrases when applied to the *libri platonicorum* and round out the picture of his attitude towards Neo-Platonism. Finally, the seemingly innocent fact that the Augustine of the *Confessions* chose to split the Plotinian head-image into two will disclose its real implications: he has broken cleanly with the Plotinian conception of the soul's "divinity."

THE IDOLATRY OF MANICHAEISM

Man, a Part of "Creation"

Magnus es, Domine: "Great art Thou, Lord." Thus does Augustine open his *Confessions*, with an exclamation of praise. Indeed, one of the Biblical senses of the term "confess" implied exactly that: praise. "And man," he then goes on to say, "who is part of Your creation, wishes to praise You, man who bears about his mortality, bears about testimony to his sin and testimony that You resist the proud. Yet man, this part of Your creation, wishes to praise You" (I, 1).

Twice he repeats it: man is part of God's creation, *aliqua portio creaturae tuae*. And at the end of the same book he comes back to the theme: all the things that make him up as man, body and soul, sense and mind, are "gifts of my God," that "most excellent and best creator and ruler of the universe." And "these things are good, and they all made up my being" (I, 31).

Something there is about man that reminds him of the problem of evil: mortality and sin enter in the second phrase of the *Confessions*. But from the first, Augustine warns us not to think of the body and sense as evils. All that makes up man is good; depreciation of it reflects on the "best and most excellent creator" of "all things, visible and invisible." Man, body and soul and all that makes him up, man is "portion of Your creation."

The Manichee View

Here, as throughout the *Confessions*—just as in his early works from Cassiciacum onwards—Augustine has in view the Manichee heresy which refused to concede that man was part of God's creation, or that the body and sense were good. The soul, according to the Manichees, was a spark of the Divine Light, of one substance with God. Originally part of that luminous sea of Divinity, it had been captured and carried off in a primordial invasion of the Divine by the hostile forces of evil. As the result of that primordial catastrophe, it found itself now in misery, immersed in a body which was Matter, hence darkness, evil. In no sense then was "man" a portion of God's creation; his soul was God, his body anti-God, and he was a kind of monstrous amalgam of both.

Phantasms and Rhetoric

Both this cosmogony and the subsequent details of the soul's return to its celestial rest were spelled out by the Manichees in a farrago of elements borrowed from all manner of eastern mythologies. For all of them Augustine has a single damning term: "vain phantasms." This is the accusation which mostly concerns him in the account of his own conversion to Manichaeism in Book III. The Manichees "spoke falsehoods" he warns his readers, and, significantly, those falsehoods were "not only of You, who are truly Truth, but even of the elements of this world, Your creation" (III, 10). As with the omnipresence problem, both God and the world are involved.

The fantasies they spelled out for him then, he goes on to say, were not so real as bodies, less real still than spiritual realities, hence far, far removed from the God Who is more real than these latter, being supremely real. But fantasies though they were, they managed to impress him then: by "voice alone and by books many and huge" the Manichees succeeded largely in persuading him. And here Augustine launches into one of his favorite themes: the need to discern between truth of content and eloquence of presentation, between the food being served and the "vessels" on which it is served.

Later, when Faustus comes to Carthage, a snare to many by his "smooth language," Augustine insists that despite his own regard for rhetorical grace, "yet I was able to distinguish it from the truth of the things I was avid to learn about. I was concerned not with what vessel of discourse but with what knowledge this Faustus . . . would put before me to eat" (V, 3).

And once again, in the same connection, he assures us he had "learned that a thing is not true because rudely uttered, nor is it false because its utterance is splendid. I learned that wisdom is like wholesome food and folly like unwholesome food: they can be set forth in language ornate or plain, just as both kinds of food can be served on rich dishes or on peasant ware" (V, 10). But the same theme is present in the account of his earlier experience with Manichee proselytism:

> Such were the platters on which the sun and the moon, Your beauteous works, but still only Your works and not Yourself, and not even chief among Your works, were brought to me while I hungered for You . . .
>
> But I hungered and thirsted not for Your . . . works, but for Yourself, O Truth, . . . But still they put before me on those platters splendid fantasies . . . [and] because I thought that they were You, I fed upon them, not avidly indeed, because You did not taste in my mouth as You are in truth . . . Those fantasies were in nowise similar to You . . . because they were corporeal fantasies . . . On such empty phantoms was I fed—and yet I was not fed (III, 10).

Food True and False

Here, undoubtedly, we are at one of the polemical roots of Augustine's nagging suspicion of imagination and its works: falsehood bedecked in grandiose imagery can be more impressive than the unvarnished truth contained, for instance, in the simple language of the Gospel. But there has been a subtle shift of wind. The meaning of "vessels" and "food" is beginning, in this last text, to slide. For there is another theme subtly threading its way through the above paragraph: Augustine's notion of Divine Truth as true food of the soul, and, in this connection, the Manichee confusion between God and His works. "Beauteous works" they were, the sun and moon of which the Manichees spoke with religious awe, "but still only Your works and not Yourself." These they "served up" to Augustine while he "hungered not for Your . . . works, but for Yourself." And "because I thought that they were You, I fed upon them," was fed, and left unfilled. His emptiness results not only from the fact that fantasies are fed him. Could he be fed real sun and moon, or even, indeed, the spiritual realities superior to them, he would not be sated. For only Truth Itself can assuage the soul's hunger, and none of God's works are Truth, only God Himself.

Divinity of Sun and Moon

Why, then, did the Manichees present him sun and moon as objects of religious awe, confusing his "works" with God Himself? The reason is that their discernment of Divine and non-divine remained on the sense-level: whatever was luminous was in that measure divine, whatever darksome, evil. These bodies then were fragments of the Divinity; their movements Mani accounted for in a fantastic astronomy calculated to show how they cooperated in the constant process of the equally luminous souls' return to the Divine.

Divinity of the Soul

This error brings us to Augustine's third complaint against the Manichees. The first two lie chiefly in the intellectual order: method of thinking and truth of what is thought are primarily in view. This third error Augustine sees as following from the preceding two, but it differs from them, being squarely of a religious sort. It consisted in the teaching that the soul was itself spark of the divine light, and plunged through no fault of its own into the evils of the material universe.

Pride

This was the Manichee's root explanation of the problem of evil, and Augustine comes to see it as almost the very prototype of satanic pride. For it refuses to admit, as Augustine "often heard"—undoubtedly from Ambrose—at Milan, that "God's just judgement is the cause for our suffering evil" (VII, 5). The evils that beset us in this life result from a sinful fall, in whose guilt we all share. Nor will the Manichee admit that connected aspect of Ambrosian preaching, that "the free will's decision is the cause of our doing evil" (VII, 5). The Manichee cannot genuinely sin, even now. Augustine explains this tenet as arising from the view

> that it was not ourselves who sin, but that some sort of different nature within us commits sin. It gave joy to my pride to be above all guilt, and when I did an evil deed, not to confess that I myself had done it, so that You might heal my soul, since it had sinned against you . . . Accursed is such iniquity, almighty God, by which I chose rather that You, You within me, should be overthrown unto my damnation, rather than that I should be conquered by You unto my salvation (V, 18).

That text reflects Augustine's mind at Rome some time after the bruising disappointment with Faustus, during a period when he "despaired of making progress in that false doctrine" and "began to hold in a more loose and careless manner those very tenets with which, if I came upon nothing better, I had resolved to be content" (V, 18). His Manichee faith is wavering, therefore; he even shakes his Manichee host's "overcredulity" in their fables. But he clings to this aspect of their doctrine because, he tells us, "it gave joy to my pride" (V, 18).

Pride: this Augustine judges to be the central religious sin of Manichaeism; for as he says earlier,

> What more proud, than for me to assert in my strange madness that *I am by nature what You are*? For while I was mutable . . . I yet preferred to think that even You were mutable, *than that I was not that which You are* . . . I would rather argue that Your unchangeable substance was necessitated to err than confess that my mutable nature had gone astray of its own accord and that to err was now its punishment (IV, 26).

It took Augustine some time to see the blasphemy involved in making God as subject as the soul was to violation by the hordes of darkness, a violation whereby He would be "so far corrupted and changed for the worse, as to be turned from happiness to misery, and as to need some assistance by which it could be rescued and cleansed" (VII, 3). But looking back on Manichaeism, he sees abominable pride as having given birth to their teaching—a pride that made them refuse all culpability for the fallen state to which they constantly pointed as the experimental basis for their teaching, a pride that shielded them from guilt even for sinful deeds committed in this life, a pride that made them claim their souls were one with God and thereby plunge Divinity into the same travails as they experienced. This was "presumption" indeed, carried as far as possible from the humble, contrite "confession" of his sinfulness that is the Bishop's burden here. Nor could they "confess" God in that other sense—the sense that makes him open his book with words of praise: equal to God, and to a God so cruelly demeaned, what possibly could prompt them to cry, "Great art Thou . . ."?

The Meaning of "Idolatry"

Facta erat rursus templum idoli sui abominandum tibi: this is what makes Augustine say that as a Manichee he had made the soul the temple of an idol, abominable in God's sight. Idolatry in the literal sense of the term is not involved here. Not only did the Manichees scorn all such observances, but even the sacramental use of suspect matter in their rites was probably nonexistent. Their "idolatry" was of another sort, a self-idolatry which ended by conceiving of creature as identical with Creator, considering the soul one substance with God, fashioning an idea of God that put Him, in a sense of the expression which Augustine views as damnable, in their own "heart."

THE PHILOSOPHERS OF THIS WORLD

Their Service to Augustine

But it was not from difficulties with this religious aspect of Manichaeism that Augustine was finally led to doubt its teaching. The initial challenge came from another quarter—from the fantastic astronomy that Mani had concocted to explain the heavenly bodies' collaboration with the soul's release and return to the celestial regions.

Even before Faustus' visit to Carthage, difficulties of this sort were simmering in Augustine's mind. He had "read many doctrines of the philosophers," men who "could number with curious skill the stars and the sands, and measure the constellations, and plot the courses of the planets"; these he "compared with the long fables of the Manichees" (V, 3). And on comparison, he "found much more probable the words of the philosophers who were 'able to know so much as to make a judgment of the world,' although its Lord they did not find. For You are great, O Lord, and . . . You are not found by the proud" (V, 3).

Their Pride

No "vain imaginings" here. We have to do with men who know, who mathematically coordinate their observations and achieve marvels of precision in predicting eclipses years ahead. And still, one feature already links them with the Manichees, their pride. Augustine insists upon this: "Men who do not understand such matters stand in amazement and wonder at all this; those who understand them exult and are elated. Out of an impious pride they fall back from You . . . for they do not seek with a devout mind whence it is that they possess this skill by which they seek out these things" (V, 4).

The Logic of Pride

Such pride, Augustine thinks, has a logic of its own. Its pathways he himself has trodden as a Manichee, but St. Paul's description of pagan philosophers in the Letter to the Romans has furnished him with a set of expectations; it was, he thought, impossible to step out on that way without following it to its end:

> They think themselves to be lifted up to the stars and to be shining lights, and lo, they plunge down to earth, "and their foolish heart is darkened over" . . . They become vain in their thoughts, and "profess themselves to be wise," by attributing to themselves the things that are Yours. In this wise, in a most perverse blindness, they strive to attribute to You even their own deeds, that is, to put their lies upon You . . . to change "the glory of the incorruptible God into the likeness of an image of a corruptible man, and of birds and four-footed beasts, and of creeping things." They change Your truth into a lie, and they worship and serve the creature rather than the creator (V, 5).

Again the language is the language of idolatry; but at this juncture we can no longer feel so sure Augustine means that language in its most literal and obvious sense.

Idols and the Ancient City

That language might, admittedly, be more applicable here than it was to the Manichees: the Roman philosopher was a member of the *cité antique*, took part in its civic rites, paid reverence to its "idols." But some of them at least, Augustine knew from Cicero, kept these compartments of their being relatively disjoined; the civic religion influenced their behavior, but did not really win their minds. Their philosophic thought was either (if they were Epicureans) atheistic or (if Stoics) pantheistic. The Academic would, if the Cotta of the *De Natura Deorum* is any indication, take a stance much like that of Cicero himself. Distinguishing the traditional civic faith, and rational philosophic knowledge, his inclination would be to believe in the civic gods and their providential care for Rome, while on the philosophic level finding the Stoic arguments for such theses only more probable and suasive than the Epicurean counter-theses. The likelihood is, therefore, that here, as with the Manichees, Augustine is applying St. Paul's "idolatry" language in a way that must not be interpreted too literally.

Sermon 197 on "Idols"

This suggestion begins to gather force if we turn to *Sermon* 197. It was delivered, according to Adalbert Kunzelmann's dating, "before A.D. 400," and from its position in his listing, very probably during the very years Augustine was composing his *Confessions*. Its interest lies in the fact that the Saint is preaching about these same "philosophers," and in terms of the same text from Romans that he applies to them in the *Confessions*. Asking why they "became vain in their reasonings, and their senseless minds have been darkened," Augustine's answer is the usual one, "pride"—a pride which led them to "arrogate to themselves what God had given them." "Humility" would "make their exoneration possible . . . But because they were proud" no such deliverance was granted them. These evils, he repeats, "they have received as a reward of pride," and it led them to " 'change the glory of the incorruptible God for an image made like to corruptible man.' " Again, it would seem, idolatry; but as soon as the thought occurs to him, Augustine begins to distinguish. There is, he advises his hearers, "no greater or more superstitious idolatry than that of the Egyptians, for Egypt has flooded the world with such statues as the Apostle mentions when . . . he adds 'and to birds and four-footed beasts and creeping things' . . . These are the idols of the Egyptians." Significantly, Augustine does not associate this sort of idol with the philosophers he has been speaking of. He goes on, rather, to spell out the "evils [which] arise from the ungodliness of pride," evils which "because they originate in pride . . . are not only sins but punishments," namely, that " 'God has given them up in their lustful desires to uncleanness, so that they dishonor their own bodies among themselves.' " The thought is being dictated by St. Paul's text. The text has brought Augustine to speak of the root of pride and God's "vengeance" and "punishment" that follows, and one of its forms is exchanging "the truth of God for a lie," which means "they substituted the image made like to 'corruptible man and to birds and four-footed beasts and creeping things.' "

And again, it would appear, the charge of idolatry in the literal sense will be substantiated.

But at this point Augustine shows he is keenly aware of the difficulties involved in substantiating that charge; the Egyptians may be one thing, but these "philosophers" are quite another. It had, as we have seen, become a philosophic commonplace to distinguish worship of the "idol" and worship of what it stood for. Augustine's familiarity with Cicero's *De Natura Deorum* would have brought this home to him. How does Paul's indictment apply now?

Augustine poses the objection himself, and his answer implicitly admits it has definite point.

> Lest any one of his hearers should say: "I do not worship the image but what the images signify," St. Paul adds immediately: "and they worshipped and served the creature rather than the creator." Understand this well. They are worshipping an image or a creature. He who worships an image, exchanges the truth of God for a lie. For, the sea is a truth, but Neptune is a lie fabricated by man when the truth of God was exchanged for a lie, because God made the sea, whereas man made the image of Neptune . . . Hence . . . the Apostle continued: "They worshipped . . . the creature rather than the Creator."

The application of St. Paul's text has been saved, but at a price. Idolatry is no longer in question, but rather, as with the Manichees the confusion of creature with Creator. Not the idol of Neptune, but Neptune, is being worshipped, and Neptune Augustine briskly identifies with the sea, a creature.

The example of Juno brings him to make this same, and then an even further, concession:

> What is Juno? "Juno," they answer, "is the air." For a long time paganism has called upon us to worship the sea under an earthy representation; now we are summoned to worship the air. They are merely the elements of which this world consists. Therefore the Apostle Paul . . . says: "See to it that no one deceives you by philosophy and vain deceit . . . according to the elements of the world." Here he refers to those who set forth idols to presumably intellectual persons. Hence, . . . he adds "according to the elements of the world," giving warning that the faithful should be on their guard against certain persons, not so much as the worshippers of idols, but as the learned interpreters of signs.

When presentation of a "learned interpretation of signs" becomes tantamount to "setting forth idols," we have indeed come a long way from idolatry in the literal sense of the term—eloquent warning to those who immediately assume Augustine's language in this regard was plain as plain could be.

Identity of the "Philosophers"

But the technique involved here is perhaps a clue to identifying these philosophers more closely. It was a favorite Stoic manner of reconciling "belief" in the civic gods with the "philosophic" knowledge of the universe, to interpret the various civic gods as poetic personifications of various elements or natural forces. Each of these elements or forces would, in turn, be but a partial aspect of the one cosmic deity that penetrated all things, the Divine Reason or Logos that was fundamentally identical with the human reason, the "All" that was fundamentally one with each of its "parts." In a way untrue of either Academic or Epicurean, this Stoic pantheism would indeed imply—charges we have not yet considered—their "attributing to themselves the things that are [God's]." It was, in fact, a central underpinning of their ethical doctrine to "attribute to [God] even their own deeds."

Successive Images of God

Augustine's later descriptions of his doctrinal peregrinations support this identification of the philosophers in question as Stoics. Having opted for them over the Manichees, he relates how he set himself to reading Aristotle; was briefly tempted by Academic skepticism; then warmed to Epicurean notions of the happy life; and finally, in his efforts to conceive of God and His relation to the world, sought inspiration in the fourth great school of the ancient world, Stoicism. The latter three comprise the selection regularly represented in Cicero's Dialogues. One had, it was assumed, to judge between them. His dawning faith eventually precludes his adopting Epicurus' practical atheism; his study of Aristotle and flirtation with Academic skepticism seem never to have gone very far. But in Book VII of the *Confessions*, sketching his intellectual situation at a time when his faith is already well advanced, he comes back to the difficulty that only Neo-Platonism would ultimately permit him to overcome. Still searching for a conception of God, he finds himself still forced to think of Him as "something corporeal, existent in space and place, either infused into the world or even diffused outside the world throughout infinite space . . . For whatever I conceived as devoid of such spatial character seemed to me to be nothing, absolutely nothing, not even so much as an empty space" (VII, 1).

This is still corporeal imagery; "infusion" and "diffusion" could well point to Stoicism. But there has been a significant step upward from the Manichee view. The Divine is now envisaged, no longer as bounded, but as "infused" or "diffused" throughout "infinite space." This is the crucial difference Augustine points to later, at the center of his Neo-Platonic reflections; it distinguishes the second phase of his theological progress from Manichaeism.

In the following paragraphs, he comes back to this topic. This time the Stoic pedigree is far more evident:

> So also, I thought that You, the life of my life, were a great corporeal substance, existent everywhere throughout infinite space, which penetrates the whole world-mass, and spreads beyond it on every side throughout immense, limitless space. Thus . . . all things would have You: they would all be limited by You, but You would be limited nowhere.
>
> The body of the air—of that air which is above the earth—does not hinder the light of the sun from passing through it. The sun penetrates the air, not by breaking it up or cutting it apart, but by completely filling it. Just so, I thought that [all] bodies . . . are subject to Your passage and penetrable in their parts, . . . so that they may receive Your presence, while all things, which You have created, are governed both inwardly and outwardly by Your secret inspiration (VII, 2).

Still corporeally envisaged, God is stressed again as "infinite." But there is more: Augustine no longer suggests that God may be "infused *into* the world." He has come to think it more proper to imagine the world as "in God," the limited in the unlimited, which, again, as in the central text (VII, 20), "fills all spaces in infinite space."

But now come the familiar earmarks of Stoicism: the allusions to air and sunlight. Their penetration of the bodies situated in them furnished frequent Stoic analogies for the Divine Presence to all limited beings. Bathed in this presence, they are, in addition, all "governed both inwardly and outwardly by Your secret inspiration"—the *pneuma* central to classic Stoic thought.

Augustine's last return to his preconversion God-image shows his thought running relatively firmly along Stoic lines.

> I made Your creation into a single great mass . . . [And] I imagined, Lord, that You encircled it on every side and penetrated it, but You remained everywhere infinite. It was as if there were a sea, one single sea, that was everywhere and on all sides infinite over boundless reaches. It held within itself a sort of sponge, huge indeed, but finite, and this sponge was filled in every part by that boundless sea. Thus did I conjecture that Your finite creation was filled by You, the infinite (VII, 7).

"Idolatry" and the Stoics

We can therefore conjecture with some confidence that, before reading the Neo-Platonists, Augustine was warming to the Stoic manner of conceiving the world and God.[1] That conjecture is partially confirmed in its result. It suggests a meaning for "idolatry" which, when applied—as Augustine does in the central text we have been investigating, *Confessions* VII, 20—to himself, the Manichees, and the physical philosophers, makes coherent sense.

When he speaks of his soul, engaged in the type of thinking he was doing, as one which "fashioned for itself a god" which it proceeded to "set up" like an "idol" in the temple of its own "heart," he is referring to a species of self-idolatry. His thought on this matter has largely been formed by St. Paul's suggestion in Romans. The process has a common root, a pride which results in each case in a sort of "blindness" that makes them "vain" in their thoughts; a common core-doctrine, which considers the central personality—soul or reason as the case may be—as identical with the Divine; and a common set of corollaries, involving the confusion between Creator and creature, the attribution to God of what are human properties and vice versa, and the service and adoration of creature rather than Creator.

Literal idolatry, then, comes only very remotely into question. In the case of Augustine and the Manichees, in fact, it must be excluded outright. This, therefore, if the suggestion developed here be correct, is not what Augustine primarily means by this sort of language.

THE *PLATONICI*

Nor is there, consequently, indisputable warrant for assuming the habitual sense of the term when Augustine uses "idolatry" language about the author, or authors, of the *libri platonicorum*. For he does use such language of them in the course of presenting a spirited apologia defending his indebtedness to them. That defense is too familiar to detail here. Suffice it to say that Augustine is at pains on the one hand to stress where these writings agree with, and frankly to admit on the other hand where they fall short of, the Gospel message. As with the Manichees, as with the physical philosophers, he quite predictably comes to the question of pride,

[1] See Gerard Verbeke, "Augustin et le stoïcisme," in *Recherches Augustiniennes* I (Paris, 1958), pp. 67–89, esp. pp. 78–80; Max Pohlenz, *Die Stoa* (Göttingen, 1948–1949), I, 82–83, 95–98.

the pride which, he has come to think, prevented the Neo-Platonists from embracing Christianity in greater numbers.

Those men who are raised up on the heights of some toplofty teaching do not hear Him as he says, "Learn of me, for I am meek and humble of heart, and you shall find rest to your souls." Although they know God, they do not glorify Him, or give thanks, but become vain in their thoughts, and their foolish heart is darkened; for professing themselves to be wise, they became fools (VII, 14).

Again, the Logic of Pride

The step from pride to self-adoration is a short one in Augustine's view. Were the *platonici*, like the Manichees and physical philosophers, led to take it? Not surprisingly, the Saint's answer is yes; not surprisingly, it comes buttressed with the familiar language of the Letter to the Romans: "Therefore I also read there that 'they changed the glory of Your incorruption' into idols and various images, 'into the likeness of the image of a corruptible man, and of birds, and of fourfooted beasts, and of creeping things,' namely, into the Egyptian food by which Esau lost his birthright" (VII, 15).

Aware by now of the slippage that can enter into Augustine's use of this text and of its language, our skepticism is aroused. The warrant for thinking the *platonici* are being accused of idolatry is a slender one at best. The mention of "Egyptian food" suggests that literal idolatry might be implied—there was "no greater or more superstitious idolatry than that of the Egyptians"—but no sooner are they mentioned, than the allusion to Esau immediately weakens the possible implication.

Esau's Carnal-mindedness

Esau's connection here seems at first no more than an illustration of that "exegesis by free association" which is so common with Augustine. The mess of pottage which cost him his birthright was, the Saint repeatedly observes,[2] an Egyptian dish: lentils were a common Egyptian product. Repeatedly, he makes Esau the symbol of the carnal-minded man who gives in to his desire for temporal goods, as the Israelites had done in the desert. On other occasions, however, he makes him symbolize "all the errors of the gentiles" of which Paul had spoken in Romans. There is, accordingly, a curious interference between these two kinds of infidelity to God in the sentence which follows: "For the first-born people

[2] Maurice Pontet, *L'exégèse de saint Augustin prédicateur* (Paris, 1944), p. 351, n. 135 and, on lentils, p. 234.

worshipped the head of a four-footed beast instead of You, 'and in their hearts turned back into Egypt,' and bent Your image, their own souls, before the 'likeness of a calf that eats hay.' These things I found there, but I did not feed upon them" (VII, 14).

"I Did Not Eat"

Here the conscientious reader must be confused. The worship of the golden calf seems surely to indicate idolatry in the most literal sense, yet it is modified immediately with the citation of Acts on the Israelites' turning their hearts back into Egypt, a text which Augustine regularly interprets as referring to their hankering—as Esau had—after "carnal" and "temporal" goods instead of the "spiritual, eternal" goods which had been promised them. How reconcile these two divergent interpretations? The final phrase, in conjunction with all that we have seen, may give us the clue: *non manducabam.* It recalls the expression Augustine used with reference to his conversion to Manichaeism: on platters of brilliant fantasy, they served his God-hungry soul "sun and moon, Your beauteous works, but still only Your works and not Yourself . . . [and] because I thought that they were You, I fed upon them: *manducabam*" (III, 10). As they did, as Esau and the Israelites had done, so did Augustine himself succumb to taking food that leaves the soul empty for the food that truly nourishes, things that only participate in Truth for Truth Itself. He took the temporal for the Eternal, the creature for the Creator. But now, no longer: *non manducabam.*

Pride, a resultant blindness, an eventual confusion between Eternal and temporal, Creator and creature—these are the properties of what Augustine means by "idolatry" which have thus far been verified of the Neo-Platonists. There remain the connected tenets of considering the central personality as identical with the Divine, and consequently attributing to God what is man's, and to man what is God's. But the indictment continues.

It pleased You, Lord, to remove the reproach of a lesser status from Jacob, so that "the elder should serve the younger," and You called the Gentiles into Your inheritance. I had come to You from among the Gentiles, and I set my mind on that gold which You willed Your people to take out of Egypt, for it was Yours wherever it was. To the Athenians You said through Your Apostle that in You "we live, and move, and have our being," *sicut et quidam secundum eos dixerunt.* In truth these books were from the Gentiles. But I did not set my mind upon the idols of the Egyptians, which they served with Your gold, they "who changed the truth of God into a lie; and worshipped and served the creature rather than the Creator" (VII, 15).

Sicut et quidam secundum eos dixerunt: the translation of that phrase we shall tackle presently. It is enough for now to note that Augustine is making two connected points. He is at once justifying his exploitation of Gentile writings for the purpose of understanding the Hebrew Scriptures, and also deftly inserting the idea that he has Pauline warrant for having exercised the very discernment in the use of these writings that Paul himself would have sanctioned. But in the process of making these two points, he reveals far more than is immediately explicit in his text.

Jacob and Gentile Philosophy

The first of these points—the use of Gentile thought for the proper understanding of Scripture—is an issue that Augustine held very close to heart. The reasons underlying, and the implications that follow from, that view we must go into at a more appropriate point. But a particularly neat aspect of his approach here is his resort to Scripture to defend that practice. For now the initially confusing mention of Esau is made to do double service. First-born as the Israelites were a "first-born people," his carnal understanding of the promises permitted his younger brother to supplant him—for Jacob is (to Augustine's mind) the figure of the Church which, come from the Gentiles, succeeded in grasping the spiritual dimension of the Old Testament in a way that had eluded the "carnal-minded" Synagogue.[3] Scripture itself therefore suggests that the "younger" Gentile mind may grasp the spiritual meaning of Scripture where the "elder" Jewish mind had missed it.

The Need of Discernment

But, the objection might be raised, this "understanding" of the faith is a tricky and dangerous process. Yes, Augustine implicitly admits, it requires great discernment; his *Confessions* in its entirety represents his plea that he has succeeded in bringing such discernment to the task. Not every philosophy is fitted to the task of aiding this understanding. Carnal-minded ways of thinking about God and world, for instance, are not the monopoly of simple-minded Christians. The Manichees themselves, and even the Stoics, were just as guilty of error here. Only in the *platonici* had he himself thought to find an adequate form of thought for this key relationship—a form of thought whose crucial recommendation was, again, its ability to cope with the fundamental omnipresence question.

[3] *Ibid.*

Even with the *platonici*, however, discernment is required. Not only were they proud, and blinded by their pride, but the punishment of their pride was just as Paul described it. They too had taken the creature for the Creator, thereby serving up, along with what gold of truth they may have discovered, "the idols of the Egyptians." Could Augustine assure his critics he had really set his mind only on the gold, and not upon the idols too?

Aratus and Omnipresence

But how can the *platonici* be said to have been guilty of confusing creature and Creator? Only the most ungenerous understanding of Plotinus' emanationism would claim he had done such a thing. At this point, Augustine gives us a valuable clue. The sensitive doctrine was the very one St. Paul had preached to the Athenians, taking for his text the saying of a Gentile poet, Aratus of Cilicia—the doctrine of omnipresence, which allowed him to assert that in God "we live, and move, and have our being."

At this point it is important to cite the text of the Acts in the Latin through which Augustine made its acquaintance. Paul speaks of men's duty to "seek for God, and perhaps grope for Him and find Him, though He is never far from any of us." He then goes on to add:

In ipso enim vivimus, et movemur, et sumus: sicut et quidam vestrorum Poetarum dixerunt: Ipsius enim et genus sumus. For in Him we live, and move, and are: just as some of your poets have said: "For we are also his offspring" (Acts 17: 27–28).

Augustine and This Text

Commentators have pointed to several curious features of the way Augustine uses this text.[4] The first is that he does not quote the verse of Aratus—not here, nor anywhere in the numerous instances where he makes appeal to this same verse of Acts. Secondly, as a kind of compensation for not citing the poet, he has regularly changed the *sicut et quidam vestrorum Poetarum* to the puzzling form, *sicut et quidam secundum eos*.

Fr. Henry, accordingly, once held Augustine guilty of a "confusion" here—as though the Saint thought St. Paul was attributing the lines preceding "in Him we live, and move, and have our being" to the Greeks whom he was addressing. François Chatillon,

[4] See Henry, *Plotin*, p. 97, n. 1; Chatillon, "*Quidam secundum eos*: note d'exégèse augustinienne" in *Revue du Moyen Age Latin*, 1: 287–304 (1945); Courcelle, *Recherches*, pp. 130–132; Clement L. Hrdlicka, *A Study of the Late Latin Vocabulary . . . in the Confessions of St. Augustine* (Washington, D.C., 1931).

however, has surveyed a number of Augustine's quotations of this same Pauline verse and finds a regularity of pattern which, he thinks, and more than plausibly, precludes the possibility of a mere slip on Augustine's part. Why, then, does Augustine quote the text so regularly in the way he does? The answer is, Courcelle has suggested, that he found Ambrose doing something substantially like it. As Augustine does here and in his other uses of the Paulinism, Ambrose thinks the doctrine involved is a philosophic one. Hence Augustine found warrant in Ambrose for attributing this teaching to the Neo-Platonic philosophers, and for changing the wording accordingly. Courcelle then cites a fragment, to which Henry had already directed attention, from *Ennead* VI, 9—its kinship with the treatise on Omnipresence we have already noted —where Plotinus teaches that "We have not been cut away; we are not separate, what though the body-nature has closed about us to press us to itself; we breathe and hold our ground because the Supreme does not give and pass but gives on forever, so long as it remains what it is (*Enn* VI, 9, 9, 7–11).

Differences from Ambrose

But Augustine's differences on this point are at least as important as his kinship to Ambrose. He never alludes to the fact that a poet is involved; indeed, he never once quotes, as the Bishop of Milan does repeatedly without blush or hesitation, the verse of Aratus: "For we are also his *genus*," his race, or offspring. Aside, then, from the fundamental questions which nag at Courcelle's thesis—when did Ambrose really pronounce his "Plotinian" sermons, and was Augustine really there to hear them?—that thesis, even if in this case granted, fails to explain the peculiarities of Augustine's use of this Pauline text. It may be that Augustine heard these sermons after all, and substantially as they were later put into writing. It is also very probably true that he read, and was strongly influenced by his reading of, *Ennead* VI, 9. But it is more than doubtful he has that treatise directly in mind when he uses the phrase, *sicut et quidam secundum eos dixerunt*—or that Ambrosian influence is really helpful in understanding how he means that troubling expression.

Secundum: "According to"

The key difficulty to Courcelle's solution here, as it was to Chatillon's, is one so elementary that one hesitates even to bring it up. Both of them must reconcile themselves to mistranslating the term *secundum*. "*Comme l'ont dit aussi certains d'entre eux*: as some *among them* said" is the way Augustine's remarks come out in both instances. Chatillon has shown himself sensitive to the difficulty. In the Latin of Augustine's age, the word regularly means "according to." Chatillon has consulted C. L. Hrdlicka's study for Augustine's own use of the term and found him holding that the Saint conformed without exception to the usage of his time. This fails to discourage him, however: a cavalier observation on "statistics," a witty allusion to the "land of Ford and Gallup," and Chatillon is off and away again to explain his grounds for translating the term as his ingenious theory requires it be translated.

Perhaps it is, after all (as the Queen of Hearts announced in her immortal declaration), a question of who shall be master, we or the words. But one may be excused for initially at least taking the words in their common usage as the things to be explained, the phenomena to be "saved," and going on from there. Once this stance is assumed, it becomes plain that each occurrence of the term from which Chatillon argues that Augustine is not using it in the accepted way does with a little patience yield perfectly good sense when translated in the accepted way. But far more to the point, such a translation goes very well here—once we uncover the fragment of Plotinus Augustine has in mind.

Again, *Ennead* VI, 4–5

That fragment, we suggest, occurs right at the start of *Ennead* VI, 5. Plotinus is making one of those appeals to "common belief" to which Bréhier alluded in his introductory *Notice*. He notes that: "The integral omnipresence of a unity numerically identical is in fact universally received for all men (πάντες) instinctively affirm the god in each of us to be one, the same in all."

Plotinus is somewhat overstating his case. The belief to which he refers is common enough, but to say that it is "universally received," that "all men" affirm it, is going a bit far. One can understand why Augustine preferred to be more modest. He changes the master's "all" to a more indefinite "some": *quidam*. Plotinus is reporting the common belief these men have held—and we may connect the subject *quidam* with its verb *dixerunt*: "some have said."

But Augustine is not himself directly reporting this belief. He is reporting Plotinus' report—or, in the vaguer language he prefers to adopt in this section of the *Confessions*, he is reporting the report of the *platonici*, the authors of these books. And so he adds, *secundum eos*: "according to them," that is, the writers he is speaking about. The question, then, is not one of Augustine's own misuse of a Latin term; it is really one of our having long assumed a faulty punctuation for this phrase. The commas which did not exist in

Augustine's time should be inserted after *quidam* and after *eos* to make the sentence read: *sicut et quidam, secundum eos, dixerunt.* The full translation, then, would read: "just as some, according to [the authors of] those [books], have said."

Why "Idolatry"?

Once again, then, we have been brought back to Plotinus' treatise on Omnipresence. Can that treatise help us to resolve the other questions raised in this perplexing section? Will it, for instance, explain why Augustine regularly leaves out Aratus' verse? The answer may lie to hand if we rephrase the question. It is obvious what there was in this treatise that makes Augustine think of it in connection with St. Paul's allusions to God's being "not far" from any of us, to the presence in which "we live and move and have our being." But what was there about it that would bring it to Augustine's mind in a section dealing with "idolatry"?

"Outspoken Pantheism"

The answer I am suggesting is that this treatise seems at least on the face of it to convict Plotinus, not only of confusing creature and Creator, but of making the central human personality identical with the Divine, indeed, of adopting the tones of what Armstrong has called an "outspoken pantheism." Not that Plotinus' philosophy more generally should be labeled pantheistic, far from that. But there are insights in philosophy that have a logic of their own, a thrust or drive that leads to the very edge of this position. Omnipresence is one of those insights. The perennial difficulty of affirming the Divine Immanence and at the same time preserving the Divine Transcendence is one that has dogged philosophers since time began. What Plotinus has seen in the writing of this twin-treatise is the complementary insight: that his favorite emanation image, although assuring the divine sphere its transcendence to the lower grades of being, does not do adequate justice to its omnipresent immanence. And so, in the course of this same series of reflections, he is brought to correct even that central image of his earlier thought—is brought, in fact, so to stress the immanence of the divine that it sometimes becomes difficult for him to account for the fact that there are "other," lower beings at all.

Now all of this could easily have escaped Augustine's attention were it not for the fact that he found this treatise so rewarding and impressive, and for the companion fact that Plotinus' closest brushes with pantheism occur in two sections of the treatise which most deeply impressed and influenced him: the finale of *Ennead* VI, 5 and the passage presenting the celebrated head-image.

The first passage mentioned presented the Truly Existent as "one Life," infinite, omnipresent, and unfailing; "denying it" we have "strayed to something of another order" and have fallen. Only when we cease to say "so much is me" shall we again "become the All." For—and here is the dangerous point—"no doubt you were the All from the first, but something other than the All has been added to you, and that addition diminished you; for the addition was . . . from what is not the All."

Were there any doubt in Augustine's mind, the head-image must only have disquieted him further. Here the identity of the "real" in each of us with the Omnipresent is even more strongly put. It is said that "we reduce to Real Being, all that we have and are . . . we are [true beings] while we are also one with all: therefore we and all things are one." There follows the image of the single head with many visages, illustrating why "we are not conscious" of this paradoxical unity. And then, in that crucial final phrase, "If a man could be turned about—by his own motion or by a lucky pull of Athena—he would see at once God, and himself, and the All."

Throughout this treatise, Plotinus has been speaking of the omnipresence problem as though the soul, the ideas, and "God" enjoyed fundamentally the same relation to the lower world of corporeal realities. Only here has the implication of that parallelism come to explicit term. Just as the Manichees had, and the Stoics after them, Augustine sees that Plotinus, too, is assuring him that his soul was literally of the divine substance: the final feature of "idolatry" as he has come to understand that concept. Twice before had this "Egyptian dish" been proferred him, but this time, he is at pains to assure his readers, *non manducabam*: "I did not eat of it." The gold of omnipresence he had "set his mind to," but the idols he had firmly rejected. For the gold had the sanction of St. Paul's words to the Athenians.

The Omission of Aratus

And yet, Augustine uniformly omits the verse from Aratus when citing that text. The reason is that against the background of *Ennead* VI, 4–5 its language was disturbing and could too easily be misunderstood. To say we are of the same genus as God might be taken by the simple to imply we were of a divine "race" in the sense in which Manichees, Stoics, and now Neo-Platonists might understand that term. Clearly to signify rejection of that view, he presents Plotinus' image of the head in two markedly distinct phases.

Augustine Splits the Head-image

If, Plotinus had declared, one were finally to think without images; if a man, either by his own power, or by a lucky pull from the goddess of philosophy, were to be twisted about, then he would see "himself, God, the All" as one and identical. *Fovisti*: "You warmed, healed, soothed, caressed and turned my head," Augustine confesses. It was not "his own power" but a mild maternal fondling action that had "closed his eyes" to the image-world of "vanity," a "lucky pull," if you will, but a better name for it is grace, the gracious action of "philosophy," if that term be understood as sheerest Wisdom, Power, Love, and therefore God. "Idolatry" alone would attribute such divine action to man. Only God's hand can heal, can turn the head, convert the soul that has turned its back to the light, incite the "return" from exterior to interior, from lowest to highest—open the soul's eye on the vision. And once turned, Augustine sees that Truth Who is Son and God's "right hand"—the Eternal Word, "all-upholding" omnipresent Law and Power from which no man can flee. This, in the first phase of the head-image, is what Augustine sees: he is careful *not* to intimate that he sees himself.

That vision of the self will come, but its quality will be markedly different from the above. This time God's action is cruel, insistent, painful. Again and again Augustine's head is yanked about to gaze at the horror he had made of himself. Ah, but this darkness, this non-being which wraps us round, Plotinus had assured him, was the "alien"; it was a diminishing addition which, in the last analysis, is unconnected with our real identity. The Manichee message had not been much different: his sin was due to another nature than the one which really was himself. But all of Augustine's subsequent religious experience has reinforced the conviction that he was, himself, responsible for his sins. He was not this monstrous amalgam the Manichees, and now Plotinus, spoke about: *totum ego eram*: "this whole thing was me!" (V, 18). This "distorted" thing is none other than himself. He can, it is true, no more escape from himself, his own "darkened heart," than he can from the "internal eternal" Who is God. His "interior" is now one, now the other, with an ambiguity that sometimes is bewildering. But these two—his central self and his God—remain eternally distinct. He spurns the invitation once again to "fashion a god" and "set it up"—in the wrong sense—in his heart. God and the heart in which He dwells are most emphatically not one and the same reality. To claim they were the same would be unutterable pride, a blindness on one's real situation, confusion between creature and Creator, satanic presumption rather than Christian confession: in a word, as Augustine means that word, "idolatry."

A Defense of Ingenuity

The task of making sense of what Augustine says imposes, now and then, a certain exercise of ingenuity. But there are points at which the foregoing explanation of what Augustine meant by "idolatry" may have seemed too "ingenious" to be entirely above suspicion.

The only defense against such suspicions is, I submit, the text itself; for the text is difficult, and its difficulties can be accounted for at two levels. First there is the tremendous activity of Augustine's imagination in his process elaborating an "understanding of the faith." The "free association" method of exegesis allowed at times for ambiguities and double-meanings that defy the ordinary instruments of logical interpretation. The meanings of Esau, Egypt, and vessels for serving food, are only three examples we have seen. But secondly, and more fundamentally, the reason why Augustine *must* profit from ambiguities is that he is constructing a basically Plotinian "understanding" of a "faith" which all too often, alas, remains alien in its import to Plotinian modes of understanding. Frequently, the only way of suggesting that Plotinus and Christianity are saying fundamentally the same thing is to put certain ambiguities into play, and it is doubtful that Augustine is always perfectly lucid on the fact that he has taken this course. His good faith, however, should hardly be placed in doubt: his firmness in rejecting Plotinus' latent "idolatry" is only one more evidence of that.

Summary, and a Question

It was, therefore, Augustine's text—the things it says or implies, the things it regularly does not say—which guided us throughout the foregoing inquiry. What Augustine does *not* mean by "idolatry" was first suggested by his application of the term to himself and to the Manichees in the central passage of Book VII. There he is concisely summarizing two stages of his own theological development—his Manichee period and a later period during which his image of God bears unmistakable Stoic traits. Closer examination of what he says of Manichaeism reveals a positive core of what he does mean by "idolatry," and this same core is found in his statements of the (presumably Stoic) philosophers who, in Book V, are said to have shaken and partially replaced his Manichee ideas. The elements Augustine includes in "idolatry" are suggested to him by St. Paul's Epistle to the Romans. He shows an obvious willingness to find these elements verified in both Manichees, the philosophers of "the elements of this world," and eventually in the *platonici*. Their pride resulted in the punishment of blindness and brought them to take creature for Creator and, notably, to consider their central personality as identical with the Divine. But despite his readiness to find in them all that St. Paul claimed was there—including "idolatry" in the more ordinary sense of the term—Augustine's respect for truth will not permit him to do so; not in any of the three cases we have examined does he take that step. His only resort is to "understand" St. Paul's idolatry in a way that makes this final step dispensable—and this he regularly does.

Clearly, then, when he uses this same language of the *platonici*, there is not the slightest warrant for searching out some group of Neo-Platonists who distinguished themselves by idolatrous practices in the literal sense, or for assuming that he is referring to Porphyry's theurgic tendencies.[5] Augustine does not mean this by the term. If, on the other hand, one looks for a Neo-Platonist who fits the description Augustine presents in his apologia for having read their works, further complexities in that description have to be ironed out—complexities such as his multi-dimensioned reference to Esau, his reference to the Egyptian "vessels" and "platters" on which idolatry was served, and the regularly truncated use of St. Paul's sermon to the Athenians. To each of these clues, one author—in fact, one treatise of that author—responds satisfactorily: *Ennead* VI, 4–5. And the same stroke resolves the puzzling problem of why Augustine "split" the image that for him so centrally represents "conversion," the Plotinian image of the head turned about.

A number of features of Augustine's thought are illustrated by this piece of detective work. Chief among them is the style of his reaction when he finds some element of Plotinus' thought unacceptable for the ticklish task he has set himself, that of "understanding the faith" without distorting it. By the time of the *Confessions*, he has come to see that the divine status of the soul is a teaching that the Catholic cannot square with Scripture: he rejects it without the slightest hesitation.

But a question arises: when did Augustine come to perceive the irreconcilability of this Plotinian teaching with the Christian

[5] O'Meara, *Porphyry's Philosophy from Oracles in Augustine*, pp. 151–152 and ff.

faith? The Augustine of the *Confessions* has rejected it out of hand; but what of the early Augustine, the convert at Milan? Was his reaction to this doctrine as immediate as one might too easily suppose? There are features of his language at Cassiciacum that would indicate the contrary.

For one thing Augustine in his earliest writings repeatedly refers to the soul as "divine." The preceding chapters have attempted to take into account three of the thought-worlds which, till then, had contributed to the shaping of his mind—Manichaeism, Stoicism, and Plotinianism. They serve to warn the reader that, not yet fully emerged from those thought-worlds, the early Augustine might conceivably have intended that term to be taken more literally than he would later have allowed. For none of these thinkers would have boggled at calling the soul "divine" and (each in his own way) meaning it.

Deum et animam scire cupio: Augustine replies to Reason's query in the *Soliloquies* that he wants to know nothing more than this, God and the soul. It has always seemed safe to presume that he thinks of them as nonidentical, in which case one decisive task of his early anthropological thinking has been accomplished. He has placed a firm distinction between God and the soul. It would follow, then, that the soul's "divinity" must be understood in a sense much weaker than Plotinus, for example, would have intended.

To follow accurately the turnings of Augustine's early theory of man, however, that presumption must be tested more severely. The provisional synthesis he arrived at in A.D. 391 cannot be understood except as a development upon, and partial correction of, his first hesitant attempt to think out man's situation in the universe. And crucial to understanding that hesitant statement of Cassiciacum is the task of giving as clear a reply as may be had to the question: what does Augustine mean by the soul's "divinity"?

4 THE SOUL'S DIVINITY AT CASSICIACUM

AUGUSTINE'S PERPLEXITY

Any attempt to discern Augustine's teaching on the soul as presented in the Cassiciacum Dialogues must first reckon with an initial phase of genuine confusion, and with the possibility that the confusion may be Augustine's own. Again and again he frankly admits his perplexity on matters concerning the soul.

Commentators who have pointed to his perplexity do not always agree on the issues that perplex him.[1] Courcelle's brief treatment of his difficulties in this regard is geared to showing that the person whom the Augustine of the *Soliloquies* hopes will come to his aid was the Milanese Neo-Platonist, Mallius Theodorus. Only in passing does Courcelle observe that the soul's immortality is one of the questions nagging at him.

O'Meara treats the matter more fully, and in some respects differently. He sees Augustine as "satisfied that the soul is immortal," but at the same time puzzled about its origin. In one sense, both writers are correct. There is much the Augustine of the

[1] Courcelle, *Recherches*, pp. 202–210; O'Meara, *Against the Academics*, p. 169. For some valuable background material, see E. L. Fortin, *Christianisme et culture philosophique au Ve siecle* (Paris, 1959).

Soliloquies "believes," but that work is certainly an attempt, to some extent at least successful in Augustine's eyes, to evolve a *reasoned demonstration* for the soul's immortality.

As for Augustine's uneasiness concerning the soul's origin, this, and several other aspects of his perplexity, we shall have occasion to consider in the following chapters. For the moment we shall limit our concern to O'Meara's confidence that Augustine has already emphatically rejected a "fundamental postulate of Neo-Platonism," that the soul is "of the same substance as God." If true, this would instance a freedom with regard to Neo-Platonism that might do Augustine signal credit. But a closer look at the evidence O'Meara adduces to support his stand soon dissipates one's certainties.

THE PLOTINIAN BACKGROUND

Before moving on to examine that evidence, however, it might be well to survey the factors that were calculated to produce the Saint's perplexity. Again, the announcement in *Contra Academicos* III, 43 comes to mind: he counts on the Neo-Platonists to help him toward that understanding of the faith to which his entire intellectual effort is directed. But how much could one count on them for unalloyed help touching the question of the soul, its status, origin, destiny, and possible "divinity"? What were the inevitable points of contact—and conflict—between Plotinus' Neo-Platonism and the Ambrosian Christianity to which Augustine has given his allegiance?

For purposes of clarity, we shall provisionally limit our survey here to three Plotinian treatises which have left clear traces of their influence in the Cassiciacum writings: *Enneads* VI, 4–5 on Omnipresence; V, 1 "On the Three Initial Hypostases"; and III, 2–3 "On Providence." This limitation excludes the possibility of accounting adequately for Augustine's theory of the soul at this point in his career, but it does allow for pointing up the problems facing him and for understanding why he must have been perplexed.

Ennead VI, 4–5

The crucial doctrine of *Ennead* VI, 4–5 we have already seen: few of Plotinus' utterances would more deeply engrave the idea that the soul was "divine," of one substance with God, than certain key passages of this treatise.

Ennead V, 1

But *Ennead* VI, 4–5 is hardly Plotinus' only word on the subject of the soul's divinity. It is, we have seen, a relatively late treatise; at points it constitutes a shift of emphasis, perhaps even a correction of the emphasis found in earlier works. And the emanationist background, against which those earlier works are set, profoundly changes whatever substantial identity may exist between the soul and God. *Ennead* V, 1 furnishes an interesting comparison. Instead of handling the soul as one of three instances—the Ideas and "God" being the other two—of essentially the same relationship to the sense-world, it represents Plotinus' effort to relate the soul to the sense-world and to the other two "hypostases" of his Intelligible World, but with a relation clearly marking off the distinction and hierarchic subordination reigning among those three hypostases. Here he depicts the *Noûs*, the world of Intelligible Ideas which are also Knowing Intelligences, as second hypostasis proceeding from the first hypostasis, the One; the All-Soul, in its turn, proceeds as third hypostasis from the *Noûs*.

How, then, do individual human souls fit into this picture? Plotinus' answer here supposes, and in part resumes, the teaching of his earlier treatise IV, 8 "On the Descent of the Soul." The individual human soul is a "part"—in a special Plotinian sense of that term—of the All-Soul, a part which has "fallen" from the All-Soul into the world of sense. That "fall" has begotten in the soul a deep forgetfulness of its true station, has made it necessary to "remind" it somehow of the "divinity of its own nature" (*Enn* V, 1, 1).[2] Yet, despite that fall, the soul remains at its topmost point still in the uppermost regions. Its identity with All-Soul is not entirely severed; the charioteer's head still is lifted into those lofty heights. The great desideratum, then, is to "remind" the soul of its innate dignity, and this, Plotinus suggests, can be done only by persuading the soul to turn inward on herself, find within herself the evidence of her linkage with the All-Soul and the other two Hypostases of this Neo-Platonic Trinity.

Once so reminded, the soul will see that each lower hypostasis is an emanation of the higher, much as the spoken word (Logos) is in some sense image and prolongation of the inner word, the thought. She will see, accordingly, that in her unity with the All-Soul she

[2] See Bréhier's Notice to *Ennead* V, 1 in *Ennéades* V, 7–8. I pass over for the moment the complications which drove Plotinus to a tripartite view of man, with a "higher" and "middle" soul. They are important for understanding Plotinus, less so for grasping Augustine's idea of his philosophy. See A. H. Armstrong's essay on "Plotinus" in the *Cambridge History of Later Greek and Early Medieval Philosophy* (Cambridge, Eng., 1967), pp. 224–235, esp. p. 225.

herself is creative Logos of the sensible universe, that all the order in it, all its pattern and beauty, is of her making.

Soul is the author of all living things, . . . it has breathed life into them all, . . . is the maker of the sun . . . formed and ordered this vast heaven and conducts all that rhythmic motion: and it is a principle distinct from all these to which it gives law and movement and life . . . And the heavenly system, moved now in endless motion by the soul that leads it in wisdom, has become a living and a blessed thing . . . It envelops the heavenly system and guides all to its purposes . . . By the power of the Soul the manifold and diverse heavenly system is a unit (*Enn* V, 1, 2).

The realization Plotinus aims to evoke is a dizzying one: that all the soul admires in the visible universe is really her own product, product of an operation carried on in unity with the All-Soul. Both that unity and operation the soul has "forgotten" in her fall, but consciousness of it must be re-excited. Then the soul will be aware once more of her "divinity"—but a divinity now implying a station distinct from, and inferior to, the two hypostases above it.

But even more interesting for our purposes is the use to which Plotinus puts the Logos comparison. Each lower hypostasis is compared to the "spoken word" of which the higher is the "inner word" or idea (See *Enn* V, 1, 3). The notion was a common one among the Stoics. Plotinus here insists on the thesis which distinguishes him from Stoicism, that the "higher" word in each case must be a distinct, subsistent hypostasis. There must be an "other" Platonic world to account for the pattern found in this sensible world. That higher "inner word" is not merely the pattern-aspect of the sense-cosmos grasped by abstraction—it is and, compared to this half-real world, "truly" is.

Ennead III, 2–3

The third treatise of interest to us strikes something of a different note. *Ennead* III, 2–3 "On Providence" is even later than the Omnipresence treatise; it shows the affinity to Stoicism that can be noted there, but now in a more advanced state. The Stoic Logos is on the scene, and with a vengeance. There is no longer question of its being identical with the soul. Bréhier remarks, and rightly, that Plotinus' efforts to situate it with respect to his customary three hypostases is an embarrassed one at best.[3] It floats uneasily between the sense-world and the *Noûs*, patterning the sense-world's

[3] *Ennéades* III, 18–21. For another view of this matter, including a different interpretation of Bréhier's remarks here, see Armstrong, "Plotinus," in *Cambridge History*, p. 252.

blend of good and evil to produce the Heraclitean beauty of antithesis, but ordering as well the fall and return of individual souls.

AUGUSTINE'S PROBLEM

The Order of the Sense-world

What, now, is responsible for the order of the sense-world: soul, or Logos? Or, to put the matter more germanely for our purpose, what was Augustine to think? For the question here is not whether Plotinus' thought is inconsistent on these issues—though that position can be fairly argued. Our question aims at ferreting out Augustine's understanding of Plotinus, and this is quite another thing. He comes to Plotinus relatively unacquainted with the Neo-Platonic tradition, with the thought currents it attempts to fuse into synthesis, with the chronology of the *Enneads*. Equally important, he comes to Cassiciacum intent on forging as far as may be a Plotinian "understanding" of the Christian faith.

Logos: Plotinian and Christian

And here, it must be said, that term Logos was indeed a poser. For Augustine knew of it through his acquaintance with the *Ratio Suprema* of Cicero, Stoicism's Divine Logos in Roman dress. He knew it, too, through his acquaintance with St. John's *Prologue*: indeed, he mentions that Simplician explicitly pointed to the Logos-resonances in Neo-Platonism when Augustine went to consult him at Milan.

Now in the Christian tradition, the Logos or *Verbum* was—as in Plotinus—a hypostasis, a subsistent reality. But Augustine has witnessed at Milan the last death-throes of the Arian attempt to interpret the Christian Logos in the very subordinationist terms he had encountered in Plotinus. Here, then, was a point where Plotinianism quite evidently threatened to pull the Christian *fides* out of shape—and Augustine's reaction, from the very first, leaves not the slightest doubt where he stands. His mentions of the Trinity are regularly couched in distinctively Plotinian language, and yet he goes out of his way to warn his reader that the "processions" involved must be conceived as implying not the slightest hint of subordinationism (cf. *Vita*, 35). Where Plotinus and Christianity clash, Augustine's manifest intention is exactly as he has expressed it: Christ is Truth, and he will stay with Him.

But, that skirmish over, the war has just begun. For the Plotinian hypostases were aimed at furnishing a systematic explanation of certain features of human experience, of certain features of the world about us. Can a key element—like the subordination of the hypostases—be scrapped without in principle scrapping the explicative value of the entire scheme? To put this question more pointedly, how will Augustine account for the order of the sensible universe: by appeal to the Logos Who is God and Son of God? or to an All-Soul of which our individual souls are fallen "parts"? or to both? In that last alternative, what will be attributed to the Divine Logos and what to the Soul? How will these two relate to each other and to the other two hypostases of the non-subordinationist Christian Trinity particularly when the Stoic Logos was often called *Pneuma*, the same term used to designate the Holy Spirit?

Two Thought-ways: Emanation and Omnipresence

But Augustine's problem goes further than that: it will take him into the troubling area of relating the "Two Worlds" of Neo-Platonism—the spaceless unchanging "beyond" with the changing spatial world of immediate human experience. Here again, the difference in emphasis between *Ennead* V, 1 and the later treatise on Omnipresence (*Ennead* VI, 4–5) presents him with a formidable philosophic difficulty whose proportions he does not ever seem adequately to have measured, one which only exacerbates the tensions already present in Plotinus' theory of the soul's fall and return.

For *Ennead* V, 1, with its stress on the hierarchic distinction between the three hypostases of the supra-sensible world, along with its explanation of the soul's presence in this world of sense as having been due to a "fall," is built essentially on the lines of the emanation-image. All inferior reality is conceived of as "cascading" downward (or "radiating" outward) from the One, the downward cascade resulting in various reality-levels, each distinct from and subordinate to the level above it. The radical distinction differentiates the higher world of the three hypostases from the lower world of sense and body, hence the special need to explain the presence of the soul in this sphere of "genesis" by means of a "fall." Its downward motion of procession should have been arrested to prevent this "immersion" in the sense-world, but, for reasons we have partially seen, it has plunged deeper than it should have. Despite Plotinus' constant effort to preserve both unity and continuity, the primary service this emanation-image renders is to allow for differentiation between as well as interior to each of the "two worlds"—a differentiation which, too often, risks being expressed in unpurified imaginative terms. Each level is pictured as "below" and at some "distance" from the level above it. Thus the accompanying risk of thinking that the soul is "down here," exiled and alienated from the divine realm "up there" and aching to pursue the upward "journey" or "flight" involved in its return.

It does not seem entirely adequate to repeat, as Bréhier frequently does, that Plotinus does not take such imagery seriously. It is doubtful whether any thinker ever succeeds in so surmounting the influence of the world-image which furnishes the starting point for his metaphysic. But in Plotinus' case, it seems quite clear that in the Omnipresence treatise he acutely feels the need for correcting some of the corollaries that earlier seemed to follow from the emanation-image.

Here, as I think Armstrong has rightly argued,[4] Plotinus calls upon the resources of Stoic monism, complemented by the powerful technique of correction by dynamic-image, in a mighty effort to think out the relation of the two Platonic worlds in such a way as to affirm the "presence" of higher to lower and still do justice to the "absence" of lower to higher. It is not our business here to judge whether he succeeds. This twin-treatise must remain, in any judgment of it, one of the most brilliant and powerful attempts the human mind has ever made to grapple with the central metaphysical questions Plato raised in the *Parmenides*. It does, though, seem exact to say with Armstrong that *Ennead* VI, 4–5 represents from start to finish a heroic "struggle between a doctrine of emanation and one of immanent omnipresence, which finally" (in several of its sections at least) "issues in an outspoken pantheism." The fundamental and primary drive of the thought is unitive rather than differentiating; all notions of "distance" Plotinus attempts to eliminate. Even the distinction and subordination of the three hypostases drift for the moment into the background: their relation with the sense-world is presented in uniform terms. Though the status of the One remains unclear, it is true of "God," "Ideas," and Soul that Being is equally present to all its inferiors, not partly to this, partly to that, but integrally to each and all of them. But if there be no difference in the way higher is present to various members and strata of the lower world; if, more crucially, by "laying aside the 'so much' " that leads to individual differentiation, we become "the All" we were "from the first" (VI, 5, 12); if "we reduce to Real Being, all that we have and are" so that "we and all things are one" (VI, 5, 7), then how account for the

[4] Armstrong, "Emanation," p. 62.

differentiations between the various levels of being in the sense-world, or, between various rational souls who find access to and recognition of the omnipresent divine diversely possible to them?

Plotinus struggles manfully with the difficulty. It is a reminder of how seldom his thought on any central issue is allowed to remain flatly unilateral. Even when distinguishing the various hypostases and levels of being in terms of the emanation-image, he takes care to complement that view by insisting on the contact of higher to lower, the continuity of the real. *Ennead* V, 1, for example, begins with the truth of differentiation as primary and works inside the emanation-frame, but precisely in order to elucidate the soul's continuing contact with, and more, its continuing presence "in" the higher world. So here, in *Ennead* VI, 4–5, though the primary stress is on the radical unity of the real, the fact of differentiation is never totally lost to view.

That differentiation he explains as arising from the diverse "competence" of various members of the lower world to "receive" the integrally Omnipresent—a diversity of competence that is accounted for by their having "turned away," "absented" themselves from the Ever-Present, allowed an "addition" from the realm of non-being to parcel them off from Being (and from each other) such that (deluded) they can say "so much is me, and no farther." Behind all this lies his tenacious characterization of the realm of being as the realm of unchange, a characterization that compels him to account for change uniquely from the side of non-being, compels him to refuse to Being the possibility of differentiating, from its side, its presence to the beings of the lower world. This in turn forces him to re-explain the soul's alienation from the higher world as resulting not so much from a downward motion of the soul as from an upsurge of the "rabble" of non-being (already "enhanced with some impress of soul") become unruly in its hunger after higher form and being. The same cast of thought accounts for his uncompromising refusal to admit that Being need, or even can, "come" to the denizens of the lower world.

The problem with reconciling these two divergent manners of thinking out the soul's ontological situation is this: the "competence" of the inferiors must logically precede their diverse reception of Omnipresent Being if it is to account for that diversity of reception. Somehow, then, this diversity of competence must be accounted for, independently of, and without making circular appeal to, that diversity of reception. Their "turning away," therefore, their acquiescence to the "diminishing addition" of non-being, must be brought into play. The result: Plotinus must shift back into a variant of the uncorrected emanation-register at a crucial point in his omnipresence argument, must admit of a "turning" that introduces change at least into the soul when in the over-world. He must, moreover, equip non-being with a quasi-independent shadow-existence, a power of "negativing positivity" with unquestionably dualistic overtones.[5] What I am suggesting, in other words, is this: to think out the soul's "fall" and alienation from the Higher World from which he claims it originates, Plotinus finds himself compelled eventually, though surreptitiously, to fall back not only on a positively, dualistically conceived "non-being," but also on some features of the emanation style of thinking that his Omnipresence treatise calls seriously into question. More generally, I mean that pure emanation-thinking facilitates, whereas pure omnipresence-thinking makes difficult, the business of thinking out the "fall" of the soul.

At very least, the propositions above are valid *for Augustine's use of Plotinus*. They are based upon a prima-facie judgment on the way two currents of thought clash in Plotinus' system—a prima-facie judgment I have come to in the course of an effort primarily focused, as here, on getting behind an analogous set of tensions as they show up in Augustine's own thought. It may be that more refined analysis of Plotinus would show him reconciling more adequately than I think possible these two modes of thought. That question must remain secondary for this study. The point is that Augustine, as we shall have occasion to see, does not seem able to synthesize them satisfactorily. When he is sketching the soul's situation as "fallen," and accounting for the diversity of reality-levels, we shall see him regularly rely on a (somewhat hybrid) variant of emanation-thinking. When, on the other hand, he drives the omnipresence style of thought to its extreme, he comes to formulations that make it difficult to account for the soul's fall, alienation, even, at times, distinction from the Divine. The habit he develops over time, of permitting omnipresence insights to fuse with, and radically transform, idea-patterns drawn from the emanation mode of thinking, succeeds in camouflaging to some

[5] On the "strangeness of [Plotinus'] conception" of Matter in the sense-world, see Armstrong, "Plotinus," in *Cambridge History*, esp. pp. 256–257. Although determined on the one hand to trace matter's existence wholly to the One, accord it no "positive quality," view it as "total negativity and otherness, absolute privation," Plotinus nonetheless accords it a "baffling quasi-existence" (256) identifies it as absolute evil and the principle of evil, "able somehow to infect the things which enter it with its darkness and emptiness, to impart a defect to them" (257). Its "total negativity" thereby acquires a paradoxically positive function. Though Plotinus, in the last analysis, may not be a metaphysical dualist, his doctrine of matter often takes on unmistakably dualistic overtones.

degree, but in the end manages only to bring their basic irreconcilability into higher relief.

Augustine's problem in reconciling these two thought-ways is only aggravated by his reverence for certain views clearly connected with the core of his Christian belief. His acceptance of immutability as the primary character of the Divine will force him to couch the Biblical dialogue between God and man in terms that fail, one is entitled to think, to do it full justice at crucial points. Can the Incarnation, for example, be made intelligible in terms that refuse to God the possibility of "coming," in any genuine sense, to the world of men? Eventually he develops a doctrine of "creation from nothing" which strips "matter" of all positivity prior to and independent of God's creative influx. But it will take him time, as we shall see, to purify his notion of matter of Neo-Platonic overtones, and once he does, it is doubtful he succeeds in finding something else to account for what that positivity was meant to explain in Plotinus' view.

But of pressing interest to us now is the way he deals with those two key features Plotinus repeatedly affirms of the soul: its essential "immutability" and its "divinity." It should be clear how those two characteristics are connected in Platonic thought; but it will simplify our task if we focus first on Augustine's treatment of the soul's "divinity," leaving for a more appropriate moment how he copes with the question of its "immutability."

GROPING TOWARD A SOLUTION

The Soul's "Divinity"

Augustine repeatedly speaks of the soul as "divine" in the course of the Cassiciacum Dialogues. The term, O'Meara reassures us, was also used by Ambrose.[6] But what Ambrose may or may not mean by it still leaves open the question of what this recent convert might have meant. He uses the same term, we are told, to describe "philosophy," but the reminder is hardly a comforting one. We have seen too many instances of Augustine's tendency, encouraged doubtless by a similar tendency in Plotinus, to begin with such abstractions as philosophy, wisdom, truth, and beauty, and to allow them to slide through a process of personification into hypostatic, subsistent entities. *Philosophia* all too often threatens to become "Some-one," a person bearing suggestive resemblances to the Eternal Wisdom—divinity indeed.

[6] O'Meara, *Academics*, p. 169.

World-Soul Doctrine

The first strong indication that Augustine means the soul's "divinity" in more than a transferred sense is his willingness to accept the doctrine of a World-Soul and his connected readiness to proclaim the individual soul's radical identity with this World-Soul. The clearest texts on this question are to be found in the two works dating from immediately after Cassiciacum, but in the light of those texts, it is easy to discern the same doctrine forming in the first works we have from his pen. "The body . . . subsists in virtue of the soul," he writes in the *De Immortalitate Animae*, "and for that reason the soul is what animates the body, *whether universally, as in the case of the world*, or in particular instances, like every animal in the world" (24). But the *De Quantitate Animae*, that effort to remind his readers of the soul's true "greatness," shows Augustine exploiting the very technique Plotinus uses in *Ennead* V, 1: the soul must be reminded that all the beauty and order of the sensible world is really, were she only awakened to it, her production. The implication is that the individual soul is one with the World-Soul which accomplishes these marvels—a thought that might disturb his friend Evodius. Were Augustine to reply to his difficulty with the answer that the soul "is one and many at the same time," then Evodius would doubtless smile, "and I would not find it easy to make you suppress your smile. But if I say that it is many, I shall have to laugh at myself, and it will be harder for me to suffer my own disapprobation than yours" (69).

Reason One with "Reason"

In the light of such remarks, it becomes plainer what Augustine at Cassiciacum means to imply by the somewhat arch observation to Romanianus that their mutual friend Lucilian belongs to "all of us who are one" (*Acad* II, 9). Reason, he points out in the *De Ordine*, is something "only a rare class of men is capable of using as a guide to the knowledge of God or of the soul—either of the soul within us, or the world-soul" (II, 30) in terms of which, presumably, we are "one" (cf. *Retr* I, 11, 4). The mind ascends the ladder of the liberal arts to eventual wisdom precisely by following the traces of a personified, subsistent "Reason" which is held responsible for all the numerical order and beauty found in visible things and in the graded sequence of the liberal disciplines that "Reason" has created. Once the philosophic heights are reached, the soul introspects itself and finds that "reason either is the soul itself or belongs to it, and that there is in reason nothing more excellent or dominant than numbers" (II, 48). The phrase is heavy with ambiguity. Does Augustine mean "reason" here as a power of the individual human soul, or as that overarching "Reason" which shortly before was led to "feel that it possessed great power, and that it owed all its power to numerical proportions. Something wondrous urged it on. And it began to suspect that it itself was perhaps the very number by which all things are numbered, or if not, that this Number was there whither it was striving to arrive . . . this Number which would be the discloser of universal truth" (II, 43).

On the answer to that question, Augustine himself seems unsure. Several paragraphs later he is at first prepared to draw conclusions from the premises that "reason is immortal, and . . . I who analyse and synthesize all those things am reason" (*Ord* II, 50). But, then, a doubt draws him back, and he entertains the possibility that "the soul is not the same as reason" (*Ord* II, 50). He is prepared to think with the Plotinus of *Ennead* V, 1 that the individual reason and the overarching Reason are at bottom one and the same, the individual soul one with the World-Soul which has produced the traces of "reasonability" in things. But he is not sure.

The suggestions of this identity between reason and Reason contained in the *Soliloquies* are quite probably contemporaneous with, and not developments or confirmations of, the hints found in the *De Ordine*. The *Soliloquies* represent Augustine engaged in a dialogue with himself which is at the same time a dialogue with Reason. When all at once that voice speaks to him, he is immediately led to ask "whether it was myself or another inside or outside of me." He must confess: "I do not know, for that is the very thing I am endeavoring to find out" (*Sol* I, 1). The dialogue constantly slides into the use of the first person plural: Augustine and Reason constitute a "we" who must advance, progress toward the vision "they" desire; "but it is not granted to us to imagine or know how deep we have sunk or how far we have risen." Not Augustine only, but "we" the day before "had announced . . . that we are now liberated from all defilement" (I, 25). Because "we are speaking to ourselves alone, I chose," says Reason, "to call [this work] by the title of *Soliloquies*, a name which . . . is quite suitable to indicate its purpose . . . It was my pleasure to seek the truth with God's help in peace and propriety by questioning and answering myself" (II, 14). The "dialogue" is therefore truly a "soliloquy"—Reason and Augustine's reason are, it is suggested, one.

Reason and Holy Spirit

It would be invaluable for our purposes to know how consciously Augustine meant such hints to be interpreted in the light of *De Ordine* II, 26. There he intimates that the Reason which plays such a key role in that dialogue is the third divine hypostasis, presumably of the Christian Trinity. Speaking of the realities, "great and hidden," which the believer comes to know once authority has opened the door, he enumerates the objects of that knowledge in an ascending series of three: "what Reason itself is, which he . . . follows and comprehends; what Intellect is, . . . which is the sum-total of all things; and what, beyond all things, is the Source (*Principium*) of all." To erase all doubts as to whether he is speaking of God, he observes that this knowledge is so privileged that "even after this life, no one can exceed it" (*Ord* II, 26).

Could he be experimenting with the idea that the Reason of the *Soliloquies* is the *Deus-Admonitio* he refers to there as the same third hypostasis (*Sol* I, 3)? The radical identity that the Stoics held between the *pneuma* in man and the divine *Pneuma* which traversed the entire sense-universe might have encouraged the experiment: and the Stoic *Pneuma* was accorded many of the same functions as the Plotinian World-Soul.

Augustine's Hesitancy

That implication may have disturbed him somewhat. The difficulties of reconciling Plotinus' Logos with the Christian Logos may well have introduced an additional factor of speculative uncertainty. Perhaps, we have seen him query, the Number which is source of all order is, after all, the Divinity whither the soul in its quest for happiness is "striving to arrive"—hence, other than the soul. If anything is clear about Augustine's thinking at this point, it is that he is unclear; the only thing certain is his uncertainty.

DE ORDINE II, 46

Of Divine Substance?

That same hesitancy envelops the very text which O'Meara adduces to buttress his contention that Augustine has rejected the notion that the "soul is of one substance with God," thereby repudiating a "fundamental postulate of Platonism." What we have seen of Plotinus' theory argues already against conceiving of "substantial identity" as adequately describing the Plotinian theory of the soul's relationship to God—and the evidence is excellent that Augustine had by this time read enough Plotinus to make him aware of that.

But the text in question (*De Ord* II, 46), especially when studied in context, holds other surprises as well.

The Context

The *De Ordine* begins with Augustine's dedication to his friend Zenobius. Here he states the problem of the Dialogue in terms as bald as one could wish. Is God's Providence universal or not? In other terms, does everything that exists and happens exist and happen in function of a divine ordering? The problem is familiar: it is the Manichee problem of evil, and the issue that the Manichees claimed to solve by their dualism is being squarely posed. For on the one hand it seems impious to deny that the Divine Order is limited in scope; yet on the other hand, the universality of that Divine Order might seem to imply that God Himself is responsible for man's sins and for other evils as well. This is at least equally impious.

The first book is essentially a preliminary skirmish on the issues. Augustine's pupils are being trained to defend their views. The second book approaches the central question not once, but twice. In both instances Augustine's pupils—and, one may think, Augustine himself—are found unequal to the challenge. They succeed in showing that evils, once existent, can be integrated into an order that owes its existence to God; but that order is subsequent (logically at least) to the evil's existence or perpetration. What of the actual coming to be, the actual perpetration of the evil? Did this occur "in order" or not?

It is significant that Augustine both times balks at this issue (II, 11–13, 20–23), both times chooses the same road out of the impasse. He takes the occasion to advise them of the need of beginning with belief on authority before going on to trying to reason things out for themselves. Then, he limns, first briefly (II, 14–17), then more expansively (II, 24–44), the "ordered" stages the mind must mount to sharpen itself for the task of solving such abstruse questions.

The Text

This, then, is the atmosphere of intellectual caution prevailing at the moment when Augustine comes to speak of the soul's identity with God. Postponing for the moment consideration of the remainder of *De Ordine* II, 46, we isolate the portion of the text which is most directly relevant to that question.

> But, if we say that evil had been troublesome and, as it were, antagonistic to God—as some opine (*quod nonnulli existimant*)—no learned man will repress his laughter, and every unlearned man will be indignant. For what harm could that indescribable nature of evil do to God? If they say it could do none, then there will be no reason for the creation

of the world. But if they say it could do some [harm to God]—why, it is an inexpiable crime to maintain that God is subject to injury (*violabilem*), or that He has not at least provided by His power that His nature should suffer no injury (*ne sua substantia violaretur*). In fact, they acknowledge that a soul suffers punishments here, although they would have it that there is absolutely no difference between the substance of God and that of the soul: *inter ejus et Dei substantiam nihil velint omnino distare.*

The Anti-Manichee Focus

The first surprise a close look at this text provides is this: Augustine is talking, not about the Neo-Platonist, but about the Manichee theory of soul and God. He would, in the first place, have been keenly aware that Plotinus was, for the most part, far from maintaining there was "absolutely no difference" between the soul and God. The phrase is entirely too strong to describe the Plotinian position, or better, shifting range of positions. But more decisively, the other elements of doctrine here show quite clearly that Augustine's *nonnulli* refers, as Jolivet[7] and others have claimed, to the Manichees. Their dualism between God and Evil, an evil imagined as originally "troublesome" and "antagonistic" to God, explained the creation (more exactly: ordering) of the sense-world, subsequent to the soul's imprisonment in the world of "darkness," as the divine attempt to salvage those precious sparks of its own substance that had been "violated." Comparison with the *Confessions* will shortly put this beyond doubt. For the moment, our analysis of the text will assume this anti-Manichee focus as granted.

A Modest Point

Is Augustine, then, rejecting that "substantial identity" that the Manichees held between soul and God? Here we come to the second surprise contained in this text. Even assuming Augustine is making a point about that precise Manichee contention (we shall be led shortly to question that assumption), it is almost disquieting what a modest point he would, in that hypothesis, be establishing. He is saying, in effect, that any such doctrine must be evaluated in connection with its logical consequences. At this juncture he grants the Manichees a choice of alternatives: they may claim either that Evil could or that it could not do harm to God. In either case, they must face a difficulty. If they say that evil could do harm to God, then they are guilty of an "inexpiable wrong": *nefas*. What is that wrong? It consists in believing that "God is subject to injury, or that He has "not at least (*nec ita*

[7] In his translation of this work, *BA* 4, p. 442, n. 1.

saltem) provided" against such violation of his substance, by the exercise of His power. If, on the other hand, they claim that evil can do no harm to God, they must find another reason for the creation of the material world than the one they hold.

Dualism

But the central point of this portion of *De Ordine* II, 46 (isolated, be it noted, from the rest of the paragraph) would in that case be quite distinct from the question of the soul's identity with God. If Augustine is to be conceived of as rejecting anything, it is the idea of Evil's being "troublesome" and "antagonistic" to God—the backdrop of aggressive dualism against which the Manichee set all his other beliefs. And even then, while he seems at first bravely to affirm that the dualistic theory of Good versus Evil is both laughable and infuriating, he does not (as he does with the notion of a "change of plan" in God) reject it directly and outright. He finds himself, rather, forced to argue through a series of alternative consequences which such a conception would necessarily implicate, and to end with an argument drawn from the soul's substantial identity with God—a view which, incidentally, he is careful not to say is necessarily implicated in the above, but only *de facto* held by the Manichees. The conclusion of his argument is that if the Manichees persist in holding that the soul is one with God, and at the same time that it "suffers punishments" in the sense-world, *then* they must *either* justify a concept of God such that He is shorn of "inviolability" even to the extent of being unable by the exercise of His power to provide against such "violation" of His substance, *or* admit the divine "inviolability." In the latter case, they must devise, first, an explanation of how the identity of God and suffering" soul is reconcilable with that inviolability, and, secondly, a fresh account of why the sense world was brought into being. In either of these major alternatives, Augustine is fairly confident that the aggressive dualism of Light and Darkness has been called seriously into question, and this, if anything, is the main point of his argument.

Again, Unsureness

Even as it stands, and isolated from its immediate context, the argumentation shows a curiously indecisive tone. But restore the immediate context and that air of unsureness is only enhanced. What is up for question is Manichaeism as one possible solution to the problem of evil, the subject of the entire *De Ordine*. The portion of the text isolated above makes it plain that any one member of that solution must be considered as impacting on a network of others. Such questions as God's inviolability, the motive of creation, the reason for the soul's presence in the world of sense, are all related to each other. But these, Augustine is warning his students, are far from constituting a complete listing of such interrelated questions. The opening portion of *De Ordine* II, 46 enumerates among them:

how so many evils come to pass, although God is omnipotent, and effects nothing evil; for what purpose did He make the world, though He had need of nothing; whether evil always was, or began in time; and if it always was, then was it under God's control; and if it was, then whether this world also, wherein that evil is curbed by divine order, always was; but if the world had a beginning sometime, how was evil held in check by divine power before that time; what need was there to construct a world in which evil, which divine power had already controlled, was included for the punishment of souls; if, however, there was a time when evil was not under God's dominion, what suddenly happened which had not happened before throughout the eternal years? (*Ord* II, 46)

This, then, is a more complete list of issues, all of which must be resolved before the problem of evil can safely be considered to have found solution. Such matters, Augustine warns his students, are "most abstruse" (*obscurissimae*), and—now we come to the central point of the entire section, to what is really being affirmed *in directo* in *De Ordine* II, 46—"any investigation concerning these and similar matters is to be made following that order of learning [outlined in the sections immediately preceding, *De Ordine* II, 32–45], or not at all." The entire section, then, considered as a unit, means to bring to a point the drive of the preceding argumentation. Such questions are difficult, more demanding than the Manichees imagine. Their solution supposes a training of the mind involving a whole ordered series of "disciplines." And it is not at all clear, finally, that Augustine assumes himself adequately equipped for the exacting task the *De Ordine* took on with its opening queries on evil and divine providence. Everything, in fact, argues to the contrary.

Echoes of Nebridius

Augustine's reasoning here shows clear resonances with the argument he attributes to Nebridius in the *Confessions*. He heard it from his friend, he tells us, back in Carthage, some time before his conversion to Catholicism. He is addressing God:

[Nebridius] asked: "What would that unknown nation of darkness, which the Manichees are wont to postulate as a hostile mass, have done to You if You had refused to contend with it?" If it was answered that it would do You some injury, then You would be violable and corruptible. If it were said that it could not injure You, no reason would be offered for Your fighting with it, fighting, too, in such wise that some portion and member of Your being, or some offspring of Your very substance, would be mingled with those opposing powers and natures which were not created by You [and] turned from happiness to misery . . . They would hold that this offspring is the soul, to whose aid Your Word had come . . . Therefore, if they should affirm that whatever You are, that is, Your substance by which You are, is incorruptible, this whole tale is false and execrable. But if they should say You are corruptible, that too is known to be false and abominable as soon as it is uttered. Sufficient, therefore, was his argument (VII, 3).

Both texts allude to the main tenets of Manichaeism: God and Evil over against each other, the primordial clash wherein fragments of the divinity were carried off into the world of darkness, the "creation of the world" conceived as a Divine intervention in order to salvage these portions of its own substance, the identity of men's souls with these fragments of divinity. Both texts, too, indicate Augustine's dissatisfaction with the Manichee manner of accounting for evil. But neither text refers to Plotinus' theory of the soul's divinity, nor do they focus on this as the central weakness even of the Manichee explanation.

With a Difference: Divine Incorruptibility

But here a significant difference enters. The argument in the *Confessions* is clean-lined and decisive. Only if God is admitted as substantially corruptible does the Manichee cosmogony stand—but then, it stands on a principle which itself is patently unacceptable. The key term is one that assumes an important role in the *Confessions*: incorruptibility. Augustine has come to see that the ontologically incorruptible is per se superior to the corruptible, and that God as "highest" is therefore perfectly incorruptible. Once the argument is made to pivot on that central concept, it concludes clearly and firmly.

But in the *De Ordine*, the concept of ontological incorruptibility does not appear. Its substitute is a far more anthropomorphic notion of "being subject to injury," *violabilitas*, for the key reference point is an anthropocentric one: the soul's own miserable condition in the sense-world. If the soul has suffered injury, and the soul is one with God, then God has suffered injury.

Augustine's Position at Cassiciacum

Does this mean that Augustine has "emphatically rejected" the Manichee thesis of the soul's substantial identity with God? One could at least wish for more emphasis. Augustine is far less decisive than that, and his indecisiveness is understandable. He knows that the soul's substantial identity with God is a central strand in the logic of the Manichee position; that as the logic of that position is spelled out, it does not answer to its own question. But where exactly is the point of breakdown? Here he quite significantly abstains from pronouncing with the confidence that characterizes the *Confessions*. There are too many "abstruse matters" involved; any viable solution to the problem of evil must involve satisfactory positions respecting a host of connected issues. He means primarily to show that a long and ordered sharpening of the mind is needed before confidence in all these matters can be warranted. There is, therefore, a long step from the *De Ordine* to the *Confessions*.

But it is significant that Augustine hopes to take this step with Plotinus' aid. The *De Ordine* echoes with themes taken from *Ennead* III, 2–3 on Providence, which tried to establish that the fact of evil and suffering could be reconciled with the universality of Providence and still not make God guilty of our misdeeds. Perhaps, then, the crucial flaw in the Manichee explanation was the dualism that would have denied that universality to Providence. This defect remedied, perhaps the soul's relation to God could be thought out in terms that accorded intelligible sense, at the same time bringing whatever slight modifications were requisite, to the Manichee belief in the soul's substantial unity with God.

At all events, nothing Augustine says against the soul's substantial identity with God refers to Plotinus' doctrine on the subject. In fact, all the indications in the Cassiciacum writings point to Augustine's willingness to experiment with a Plotinian conception of the soul, of its origin, status, destiny, and—in a qualified sense at least—of its "divinity." And when shortly afterwards, in the *De Quantitate Animae*, he firmly announces that the soul is "not what God is" (*non esse quod Deus est:* 77), that announcement comes after an extended *ascensio animae* has attributed to the soul, one in its functioning with World-Soul, all the magnificent order of the sensible universe for which *Ennead* V, 1 makes it responsible. Gone, to all appearances, is the temptation to consider the soul in any sense "divine"—though here, too, it is only fair to note that Plotinus' terminology more usually prefers to reserve that title in its strict application to the second hypostasis.

The soul is not divine, but Augustine now claims it is created and the pinnacle of creation, "nothing among His creatures being closer to God": *nihil . . . Deo propinquius* (*Quant* 77). Significantly, the crucial distinction between God and soul is couched in terms more closely akin to those attributed to Nebridius in the *Confessions*: God is "unchangeable Principle, unchangeable Wisdom, unchangeable Love": *incommutabile* (*Quant* 77). *Letter* 18, dating from the year A.D. 390, follows the same line of reasoning: what distinguishes God from creature is God's changelessness. But there, a suggestive element of precision is added. Augustine presents it as something *grande et breve* for Caelestinus' consideration. The body is changeable in both time and place; God is in nowise changeable; but the soul, interestingly enough, is said to be changeable so far as time, but not at all so far as place is concerned: *per locos nullo modo, sed tantum per tempora* (*Ep* 18, 2).

Immortality

That distinction represents a concession to, but, more important, a serious departure from Plotinus. I cite it here, however, chiefly because it is puzzling enough to remind us that there is still much to understand about Augustine's early conception of the soul.

Among the other features requiring such understanding, there is one that would seem to lie at the very antipodes to the theory we have just been examining. How can Augustine at one and the same time toy with the "divinity" of the soul and manifest such deep disturbance about its possible mortality? Despite some of the *De Ordine*'s brave statements on the soul's immortality, he still feels the need, in the *Soliloquies* and in the *De Immortalitate Animae*, to wrestle with this troubling topic.

Again, the clouds of Cassiciacum may part more easily before the rays of hindsight. Much of what is still perplexing in the earlier works may be illumined if we turn now to examine how he goes about the composition of his dense little work on the soul's immortality. That examination will compel our asking more precisely how the Augustine of this period envisages the soul's relation to body—what he means when he speaks of the soul as "fallen."

TWO: THE FALLEN SOUL

5 THE DE IMMORTALITATE ANIMAE

When reporting on the *De Immortalitate Animae* in his *Retractions*, Augustine admits to an impression every reader must himself have felt: "The reasoning is involved and too briefly expressed, and its resultant obscurity was such that my attention wearied as I read it: I could hardly understand it myself" (I, 5, 1). The scarcely digestible character of the work is due to several factors, but among them one must count first that it was intended merely as an outline-draft for the third book of the *Soliloquies* and second that it requires a key, and the key is Plotinus' treatise of the very same title, *Ennead* IV, 7 "On the Immortality of the Soul."

INFLUENCE OF *ENNEAD* IV, 7

A Tell-tale Argument

The *De Immortalitate Animae* is, then, a continuation of the *Soliloquies*. There, throughout the second book, Augustine was grappling with the difficulty of finding some rational demonstration of the soul's immortality. His central argument, and the first one he brings to completion in this work, starts from the conviction that mathematical truths are immutable and eternal, that "truth" therefore is eternal. But truth must have a "reason" in which to "dwell"—hence reason itself, and therefore the soul which reasons, must itself be eternal.

Its Neo-Platonic Cast

Scholars had long attributed this argument to Plato's *Phaedo:* the soul which knows the eternal forms must be akin to them, and hence itself immortal. De Labriolle,[1] however, and after him Verbeke,[2] have shown convincingly that the reasoning is characteristically Neo-Platonic rather than Platonic. It pivots on the notion of the soul as subject in which eternal truth dwells. Scouring Plotinus for the "source" of Augustine's argument, they both agree it is *Ennead* IV, 7: This treatise, then, Verbeke concludes, must be added to the list of those familiar to Augustine at Cassiciacum. For even if the *De Immortalitate Animae* was written on his return to Milan, the substance of this characteristically Plotinian argument has already appeared in the final portions of the *Soliloquies.*

We need not re-establish what those two scholars have established. There are, however, pieces of corroborating evidence that may be added to their proof, not only to confirm it, but to follow up some corollaries of their discovery.

Return to Milan

The first piece of evidence rests on the significance of that return to Milan. The Cassiciacum Dialogues testify to Augustine's perplexity on matters touching the soul. Particularly concerning the question of elaborating a rational proof for the soul's immortality, he looks for help from some one who, he thinks, can aid him—probably, as Courcelle has ably argued, from Mallius Theodorus. The *De Quantitate Animae* (70) shows that he still would put his questions on the soul "to a man of great learning [and] of great eloquence, too; yes, to one wise and perfect in every respect! . . . But now, since I have no one else to do this for me, I venture this." Quite probably, then, as Courcelle suggests, Augustine's hopes for personal coaching on this question have been disappointed.

His return from the country affords him, though, a possibility which he more than likely did not have there. Again, it would appear that he did not approach whoever in Milan had lent

[1] See his Introduction and notes to the volume containing, among other works, the *De Immortalitate Animae, BA* 5 (1948), esp. pp. 18–20. Despite his accurate location of the Plotinian source of Augustine's "proofs," de Labriolle remains unsettled by some of the arguments: *ibid.*, pp. 165–167.

[2] Verbeke, "Spiritualité," in *AM* I, 329–334.

him the *libri platonicorum* and ask to carry them off to Cassiciacum for his stay there. At Cassiciacum, therefore, it is quite conceivable he had no Plotinian texts to hand; the scattered (and, compared to those which turn up in his other writings, blurred) reminiscences of the *Enneads* found in his works there were, in all probability, engraved on a memory that years of rhetorical practice and teaching had made remarkably retentive.[3] Whether or not he found more personal help in Milan on his return, accordingly, he seems to have set himself to a close study of Plotinus' treatise on the topic uppermost in his troubled mind: the immortality of the soul. And it must be no surprise if the traces of that treatise that find their way into his own slight work of the same title are clearer, firmer, and to some extent less digested than any Plotinian echoes uncovered in the Cassiciacum Dialogues.

ADDITIONAL PLOTINIANISMS IN AUGUSTINE'S WORK

Structure of *Ennead* IV, 7

And yet, Plotinus' treatise is not thoroughly undigested. Augustine has, as we shall see, altered the problematic somewhat and borrowed from his source as the need of this altered problematic suggested. Plotinus' treatise proceeds in four main sections: the first three sections refute in turn the positions holding that the soul is a body, a Pythàgorean harmony of the body, an Aristotelian entelechy of the body; the final section presents the Platonic view as he understands it, and answers difficulties against that view. The first two sections are heavily dependent on Aristotle's refutation in the *De Anima* of materialists and Pythagoreans in turn, and on the classic Peripatetic commentators. Many of the difficulties Plotinus raises against the entelechy notion are, ungratefully, also drawn from Aristotle's work. Plotinus' vast and careful knowledge of philosophic tradition is, accordingly, in full display. Augustine's relatively impoverished mastery of that tradition will trip him up at several points, thus adding a third factor to explain the "obscurity" of his little work.

Soul, "Subject" of Truth

Augustine's treatment of the question begins, as we have seen, by continuing the argument he had begun in the *Soliloquies:*

[3] On the power of Augustine's memory, see the evidence and observations in Peter Brown's *Augustine of Hippo* (Berkeley: University of California Press, 1967), pp. 36–38.

the soul must be immortal if it be the "subject" of the immortal truths with which the various liberal "disciplines" deal. The force of his argument, Plotinus counsels, will be seen by one sufficiently purified, himself "become an Intellectual Cosmos and all lightsome, illuminated by the truth streaming from the Good, which radiates truth upon all . . . within that realm of the divine." Augustine has, as de Labriolle and Verbeke point out, dipped into sections 8 and 10 of Plotinus' treatise for the argument. In addition to its main lines, he takes the notion from IV, 7, 8 that the soul when engaged in understanding is "turned away from the body."

But it is significant for our purposes how often Plotinus speaks of the soul's "divinity"—and how discrete Augustine has already become in the use of that qualifier.

Soul Essentially Unchangeable

Paragraphs 2 and 3 of Augustine's work move on to another argument. The soul, the Saint would have it, is essentially unchangeable. The idea is a strange one. It is difficult to understand why one should think such a thing, but it is what Plotinus thought, what he tries to prove in section 9 of this same treatise, and Augustine follows his reasoning faithfully. Mover of the body, the soul itself remains essentially unmoved, unchanging, just as, "fallen" into a world of change, it remains at its topmost point "still there." Is the soul's involvement in the world of change and process, then, for Augustine as for Plotinus, the result of a "fall" from the divine realm?

Postponing for now the final answer to that troubling question, hindsight allows some clarity on two curious passages in the *De Ordine* (II, 3–7, 18–21). In his attempt to understand how evils could exist and God's omnipotent ordering power extend to all that is, Augustine had Licentius explore this notion of the mind (*mens*) remaining unmoved even while the body moves from place to place. The perfectly "wise" man, Licentius wishes to hold (and with no sign of disapproval from Augustine), ever remains in that part of his being for which we call him wise, entirely unmoved and one with God.

This notion, as we pointed out earlier, Augustine will shortly drop. The passage from unfallen to fallen existence, as well as the countermovement of return, must involve some real change in the soul; the soul must therefore be subject to time, though not, as the body is, affected by spatial situation. The religious import of this change of mind should be stressed. A Christian must admit the reality of sin, and of sin which makes a difference. The soul itself (as Augustine would have put it) sins, and is affected to its very core by the sinful condition, stands in need of real "conversion," must "confess" to its sin. Again, a crucial tenet of Plotinianism must be modified to some extent by Christianity, and Augustine very soon indicates his willingness to modify it. His over-all responsiveness to Plotinus' thought is evident, however: he is willing to experiment with it, going to lengths which he later finds subject to censure. Perhaps one might suggest that his later rejection of some notions in the *De Immortalitate Animae* made the reading of that work additionally "obscure" to the aging Bishop.

Soul the "Place" of "Art"

De Labriolle finds the arguments of sections 5 and following somewhat strained and strange. "Art" and the necessary connection (*ratio*) between numbers, "knowledge," and what Augustine calls *musica*, all these are immutable, they must be "somewhere" and not pass from teacher's mind to learner's, nor pass out of being when forgotten. The soul, therefore—the "somewhere" in which they dwell—is equally immutable. Strange the argument certainly is to modern ears. It may be another of the points Augustine found "obscure"; but set against the background of *Ennead* IV, 7, particularly sections 10, 12, and 13, some sense can be made of them. We think instinctively of "knowledge" as a function of the mind, an "accidental modification" or perfection of a power which can act or not, act this way and that, know, now this, now that. But for Plotinus, "art," "music," the *rationes* of the number-series were subsistent realities, in a subsistent Intellectual Cosmos.

Identity of Knower and Known

In that Intellectual Cosmos, furthermore, Plotinus held that knower and known were radically identical. Here was the thesis that Porphyry himself so long found difficulty in accepting. It is, I suggest, the very tenet that prompted Augustine, in sections 10 and 11 of his work, to ask what otherwise is an unaccountable question: whether *ratio* was the soul's "gaze" (*aspectus*) or act of "contemplation," or curiously enough, the very objective truth which the mind contemplates. He does not seem ready—or able—to go along with the frank identification of Intelligence and Intelligible on which Plotinus insists. He must therefore strain to show that even if distinct, truth known (*ratio* in an objective sense) is inseparable from the knowing soul, and hence the latter's immortality is safe. But despite his reserve on this point, "knowledge," "truth," "art," "music" remain for him as for Plotinus, subsistent realities, "somewhere" and immutable, which accounts for the style of argumentation that de Labriolle finds strange.

THE SOUL AS *TEMPERATIO*

A Shift in Problematic

Now, however, Augustine changes tack. In paragraph 12 he opens a new question, that of whether the soul can pass into nothingness, *interire*. At paragraph 16, he will take up the question whether the soul can die, *mori*. Having answered both these questions in the negative, he attempts to show in the final portion of his work (20–25) that the soul cannot be changed into a body, or more generally, into any being inferior to itself. Plotinus' problem was as we have described it: to refute the various theories denying the soul's immortality and then propose the Platonic view and buttress it. Having changed his problematic, Augustine may not for that reason have diverted his attention entirely from Plotinus' treatise. There are, in fact, additional fragmentary parallels which might repay more careful investigation than will be given them here.

Temperatio Corporis

What interests us is the paragraph where Augustine seems to have veered back momentarily to Plotinus' problematic.

> Or perhaps we ought to believe, as some have done, that life is some kind of organization (*temperatio*) of the body. Of course, this thought would never have occurred to them if by means of the same mind—withdrawn from bodily habit and purified—they had been able to see those things which have true being and remain changeless.
>
> Who, indeed, in the pursuit of a thorough self-introspection, has not experienced that his understanding of things became more adequate to the extent of his ability to withdraw and remove his mental intention from the senses of the body? If the mind were an organization (*temperatio*) of the body, this would have been impossible.
>
> For a thing which had no nature of its own and was not a substance, but, as with color and shape, was present inseparably in a body, would in no wise try to turn away from that body toward the perception of intellectual things . . . In no way, indeed, can . . . that organization (*temperatio*) of the body—being a certain mixture (*certa commixtio*) of the four elements of which the body is composed—turn itself away from that body, in which it is as in a subject inseparably inherent.

Moreover, those things understood by the mind, when the latter turns away from the body, are surely not corporeal—and still they are, and exist in a highest degree because they keep themselves always unchanged (*Immort* 17).

Now it would be more than interesting to know exactly what Augustine means here by *temperatio*. It might be translated either as "organization" or "proper mixture of ingredients." Both notions would be relevant, but, significantly, to different portions of Plotinus' treatment of the problem.

Proper Mixture

The first section of his treatise deals with "materialist" concepts of the soul, and being in his early period he is inclined to treat the Stoics as materialists. He must, therefore, refute their several ways of considering the soul, and one of those ways leads them to speak of the soul as just such a "proper mixture" of the constituent elements as Augustine may imply by parenthetically defining that *temperatio* as "a certain mixture of the four elements of which the body is composed." And yet, the closest thing to Augustine's argument against this view is found in IV, 7, 8, where Plotinus is arguing in most general terms against the soul's being "any form of body."

Primal intellections deal with objects completely incorporeal, [hence] the principle of intellection must know by being, or becoming, free from body . . . The soul's contemplation, then, must be of the eternal and unchanging, like the concepts of geometry: if eternal and unchanging, these objects are not bodies and that which is to receive them must be of equivalent nature: it cannot therefore be body (*Enn* IV, 7, 8).

Or Pythagorean "Harmony"?

That argument has strong similarities with the beginning and ending portions of Augustine's considerations. The stress is on knowledge of unchanging, incorporeal realities. And yet, in the central portion of his treatment Augustine seems to be insinuating something of that inner division, inner opposition between soul and body, to which Plotinus alludes in other places. Speaking, for instance, against another possible meaning of Augustine's *temperatio*, Plotinus asks: "Is [soul] a harmony or accord? [No, for] soul rules, guides, and *often combats* the body; as an accord of the body it could not do these things" (*Enn* IV, 7, 8^4).

Or Aristotelian Entelechy?

But there was a third theory refuted in *Ennead* IV, 7—Aristotle's entelechy. Is it possible that this is what Augustine refers to by that vague term *temperatio*? Here Plotinus refers not only to intellection—Augustine's main emphasis in his text—but also to the sense of inner opposition; he stresses, further, the inseparability of entelechy from the body it ensouls, perhaps accounting for Augustine's twice having mentioned that notion.

We come now to the doctrine of the entelechy . . . Since an entelechy must be inseparable from the being of which it is the accomplished actuality, . . . there is an end to the resistance offered by reason to the desires; the total must have one uniform experience throughout, and be aware of no internal contradiction . . . Sense perception might occur, but intellection would be impossible (*Enn* IV, 7, 8[5]).

Augustine's Vagueness

What, then, does Augustine mean by *temperatio*? The answer, it would seem, is anybody's guess. The term is vague enough to cover all three theories against which Plotinus is contending. The arguments used resemble arguments he has applied against one or more of them. The significant fact is that Augustine, having read this treatise, does not seem to have considered these distinctions—classic though they were and meaningful in Plotinus' eyes—of much importance. He seems to find these three theories almost equivalents for his purposes, or worse, he may not have been able to distinguish them from one another.

In either case, the consequences will be grave. His early works show him adopting a Plotinian notion of the soul without ever having carefully weighed its merits as against its most serious contender in the ancient world, Aristotle's entelechy. His failure here will introduce a certain bluntness into Augustine's subsequent analyses of the soul, particularly in its relation to the body. The dazzling logic but bewildering unreality of the *De Quantitate Animae* is a prime example. Again and again as the discussion proceeds, Evodius counters Augustine's way of treating the soul as something substantially separable from, at times inimical to, the body; his demurrals have the ring of sanity and sense. But no sooner are they registered than Augustine's dialectical gymnastics back him into a corner, forcing him to choose between the frankly dualistic relationship the Saint is defending and something like a crassly materialist identification of soul and body. There is, the assumption seems to run, no middle ground of the sort that Aristotle's theory strove to occupy.

ALTERNATIVE TO ARISTOTLE: THE FALLEN SOUL

The Backdrop: Plotinian Emanationism

Not that there are no difficulties with the Aristotelian notion. The Stagirite himself obligingly supplied Plotinus with a full armory of them. But one may think the difficulties with the Neo-Platonic notion are, especially for moderns, even more formidable. The most considerable of these was Plotinus' insistence on the soul as native to an "other" world, fallen into this, fallen and yet not fallen. Later we shall ask whether that theory does not illumine other aspects of Augustine's perplexity at Cassiciacum. Let one suggestion suffice for now: that theory of the fall may account for the Saint's having veered away from the master's problematic and undertaken in the latter portion of his work to ask whether the soul could come to nothing, could die, could turn into an inferior sort of being. For behind *Ennead* IV, 7, and behind all the elements Augustine has borrowed from it, there shimmers the image of a luminous higher world, its splendor streaming downward to a hierarchy of beings which grow less and less perfect, less and less real, closer and closer to "nothing" as their ontological "distance" from their source increases. Man's soul is native to the upper, sunlit regions of the Intelligible World; but it has "turned away," and in that turn has "fallen," become in some sense "less" though in another sense not.

The Paradox: "Fallen and Not Fallen"

Here we have the paradox with which Augustine is grappling. It prompts him in one work to speak of the soul as essentially "divine," "next in dignity to God," and in the next to tremble at the misery and menace of its existential condition. The point at which he leaves Plotinus' treatise and strikes out on his own occurs in paragraph 12. The mind, he says there, cannot turn away from "reason" in the objective sense, meaning "truth"

> without suffering a defect; for just as the mind enjoys a more perfect being when turned toward [the truth] and adhering to it . . . so, when turned away from [the truth] the mind has a less perfect being—and this means a defect. But every defect is tending toward nothing, and no destruction can be more properly conceived than if that which has been something becomes nothing. Wherefore a trend toward nothing is a trend toward destruction. Why this destruction does not fall upon the mind, although it is subject to defect, is hard to say.

Relevance of the Fall in Plotinus

Such images as these are not peculiar to *Ennead* IV, 7. They crop up in all of Plotinus' writings, but particularly in his treatises on the soul. All four treatises that Henry originally identified in Augustine's works, and that others have claimed to find influential at Cassiciacum, come eventually to a discussion of the fall of the soul. Nor was it merely a digressive tendency that brought Plotinus in the course of his treatise on Omnipresence, *Ennead* VI, 4–5, to explain at length certain aspects of his view on the soul's "fall" into the body. The soul is one of the three hypostases of the Intelligible World; its relation to the bodily universe is one that must respond to the general relationship he is spelling out in that treatise. He must, therefore, eliminate all notion of its entertaining a relation of "form," of being genuinely "proper" to the body "in which," after its putative descent, it seems to find itself. Metaphysic and the spiritual life are too tightly knit in Plotinus' thought for him to have side-stepped this topic. It was the very intent of his entire system to make them rhyme. He must, accordingly, guard against his readers' understanding the notion of "fall" too crudely.

Importance for Augustine

The importance of this notion for Augustine hardly needs stressing. It was the very point where Plotinus' explanations of the evils of embodied existence might provide an answer to the Manichaean problem. For him, as well, philosophy always feeds the spiritual life, always carries a religious, and in this case an anthropological, reference.

We have seen evidence that the Omnipresence treatise is already working in Augustine's mind and imagination at Cassiciacum. In his later works, up to and including the *Confessions*, the Saint derived much from this same treatise. The notion of a "turning away," just found in the *De Immortalitate Animae*, was there as well, and the later refinements Augustine works on that notion are, along with the counter-notion of "conversion," contributed by *Ennead* VI, 4–5. When, consequently, Augustine qualifies that "aversion" as one that turns from a common good to one that we want to make proper, private, "ours" in some exclusive sense; when he explains that it was this vainglorious desire to have something *proprium* that plunged us from the heights into the *ima*; when, even as late as the *Confessions*, he describes *iniquitas* as a turning-away from the *Summa* to the *ima* of corporeal creation, and our punishment as a confinement to "particularity," the question must arise: to what extent are we entitled to read into his language the meaning that language must have if he has really accepted the theory of the soul he found embedded in *Ennead* VI, 4–5?

Fovisti caput nescientis: the images of divine "care" so central to Augustine's portrayal of "conversion" may, after all, point to the same interpretation of the soul's departure, wandering, and return as Plotinus proposed. The thematic current moving beneath Augustine's predilection for this imagery may be his notion of the soul as fallen from a premundane existence into the human life that we experience. In fact, if the relation we have been led to uncover with *Ennead* VI, 4–5 is sound, if the pattern method we have applied there may legitimately be extended to other Plotinian treatises as well, there seems to be no other way of deciphering his language.

6 FALL OF THE SOUL

STATE OF THE QUESTION

It must seem temerarious to suggest that the man who can without exaggeration be called the father of Occidental Christianity, whose *Confessions* has exercised an incalculable influence on western spirituality, both believed and—however cryptically—advised his readers that we are all so many souls, fallen from pre-existence in a Plotinian intelligible heaven.

Nörregaard, de Leusse

Yet, that proposal is not entirely without precedent. Jens Nörregaard, in that sober, careful study of Augustine's conversion that still ranks as one of the most commendable efforts to understand the Saint's early thinking, found himself obliged to entertain just this hypothesis. But, he notes, Augustine interprets Plotinus' theory in the light of the Book of Genesis.[1] There is a further question, however: to what extent does the Saint interpret Genesis itself in the light of Plotinian theory? H. de Leusse, starting from a study of Marius Victorinus' doctrine on the soul, notes that the Plotinian teaching uncovered in that author finds suggestive

[1] Nörregaard, *Bekehrung*, p. 238.

echoes scattered through the writings of the young Augustine.[2] Do those echoes require us to believe that Augustine read Victorinus? Or can they be explained in terms of a common Plotinian source?

Analysis of Gilson's Rejection of the "Fall"

The presence of such a doctrine in the Saint's writings has been firmly rejected by no less a scholar than Étienne Gilson in his near-classic work, *Introduction à l'étude de saint-Augustin.* The position he articulates is by no means hasty or ill-conceived; it is well thought out, ably argued, and lucid enough to lay bare the nerve of the question. Gilson starts from what he interprets as Augustine's categorical refusal to regard the body and the entire sensible universe in terms that he understands as Origen's: as a place of punishment for souls that once pre-existed in heaven, sinned, and were plunged into the body as the result of that sin. There is, Gilson argues, a "latent pessimism" in that conception which Augustine would have felt "profoundly repugnant" to his own thinking. But global impressions of "pessimism" and "optimism" provide shaky grounds for conviction; one is relieved when Gilson's argument comes down to specifics. Despite his constant insistence on the soul's "absolute hierarchic transcendence with respect to the body," Augustine "never admitted, in fact he rejected with abhorrence" what Gilson evidently takes to be Origen's view, that the body was "only a prison" for the soul, the "sensible universe in general and the human body in particular" having been "created as places and instruments of punishment."

For Augustine, on the contrary, everything God made is good. Therefore, the body was created for its intrinsic goodness, not as a consequence of or punishment for sin. Finally, the soul could not have been sent down into the body as into a prison; in keeping with the description we have just given of it, the soul is united to the body in love, as an ordering and conserving force animating and moving it from within.[3]

Gilson goes on to support his view by appeal to two major texts on the question. The first occurs in the *De Civitate Dei* (XI, 23, 1–2), where Augustine expresses his astonishment that a man as versed as Origen in the *litterae ecclesiasticae* could put forth the theory he there describes. The second occurs in *Letter* 166 (27), written to

[2] Hubert de Leusse, "Le Problème de la préexistence des âmes chez Marius Victorinus Afer," in *Recherches de Science Religieuse*, 29: 197–239, esp. 198 and 236ff (1939).
[3] *The Christian Philosophy of Saint Augustine* (New York, 1960), pp. 50–51, faithfully translated from the 2d ed. of his *Introduction à l'étude de saint Augustin* (Paris, 1943).

Jerome, and there astonishment has become the horror to which Gilson alludes.

Now the first factor of uncertainty in all this is the relative lateness of these texts. They both date from the year 415, some twenty-nine years after Augustine's conversion.[4] And the period between 386 and 415 was a critical one in Occidental Christianity, precisely in regard to the theory that concerns us here, for it generously embraces the first anti-Origenist crisis in the West.[5]

The Anti-Origenist Controversy: Chronology

In the light of his subsequent fall from favor, it may seem strange that Origen's glory shone without eclipse practically up to the end of the fourth century—that Jerome himself, so soon to become the standard-bearer of the opposition to his ideas, could rank him in 381 as the most eminent of the Church's teachers after the Apostles themselves, and as late as 392 enthusiastically enshrine him in his *De Viris Illustribus*. Ambrose, called the Bishop of the West at his time, exploited his exegetical works with neither stint nor scruple, and there is good reason to think that up until 399—perhaps after the termination of the *Confessions*—Augustine remained ignorant of the details of Origen's error. His *Letter* 67 to Jerome, of that date, is plainly a request for information. If, therefore, we admit the Saint's own professed ignorance of the *litterae ecclesiasticae* during several years after his conversion, his confidence in Ambrose' orthodoxy, and the general reputation that Origen enjoyed up to the turn of the century, it must be left open at least as a possibility that Augustine could, in perfectly good faith, once have held an analogue of the Origenist doctrine which he later repudiated.

AUGUSTINE'S FOUR HYPOTHESES ON THE SOUL'S ORIGIN

But the question only sharpens if we juxtapose two affirmations Gilson makes in the course of his study. The first that interests us is this: of the four hypotheses concerning the soul's origin that Augustine presents in the third book of the *De Libero Arbitrio*, Gilson claims that Augustine never chose one to the exclusion of

[4] See Gustave Bardy, *La Cité de Dieu*, *BA* 35 (Paris, 1959), p. 10, n. 1; and Alois Goldbacher's discussion of chronology in the *Corpus Scriptorum Ecclesiasticorum Latinorum* edition of Augustine's letters, vol. 58 (Vienna, 1923), p. 44.

[5] For the details on this controversy see Pierre de Labriolle, in *L'Histoire de l'Église* (Fliche-Martin), III, *De la Mort de Théodose à l'Élection de Grégoire le Grand* (Paris, 1947), chap. 2, pp. 31–46; and his principal source, Ferdinand Cavallera, *Saint Jérôme*, 2 vols. (Louvain, 1922), esp. I, 193–286.

the others, since "faith condemned none of them . . . and none of them is imposed as certain from reason."[6] It is well to remember that the book in question seems to date from about A.D. 395, in which case the possibilities as Augustine sees them then are the following four:

> There are these four opinions about the soul: that it comes by generation, that it is newly created when each person is born, that souls which pre-exist elsewhere are sent by God into the bodies of those who are born, or that they come down (*labantur*) of their own will. We should not lightly (*temere*) accept any of these opinions. Either this question has not yet been worked out and decided by Catholic commentators on Scripture, because of its obscurity and difficulty, or if this has been done, these works have not yet come into my hands. At all events, our faith must keep us from holding anything about the substance of the Creator which is false or unworthy of Him (*Lib* III, 59).

Notice in passing that it would be difficult to find a more appropriate Latin term for the Plotinian expression of the soul's movement in falling—παρεκβαίνειν (cf. *Enn* VI, 5, 12, 16)—than the *labantur* which expresses Augustine's fourth hypothesis. It catches the sense of "deviate" and "fall" contained in the Greek original. Notice also his avowal of ignorance with respect to any *litterae ecclesiasticae* that might settle the question. His later complaint about Origen is that a man so learned in traditional teaching should have known better than to hold what he did on the soul's fall; but this complaint is entered at a time when Augustine himself has done considerably wider reading in the Fathers. Here, however, the reference obviously means to keep all four of these hypotheses open. In Gilson's phrase, the "faith" condemns none of them.

What, though, of "reason"? What the "ecclesiastical writings" might contain is one thing; what reason would compel as acceptable "understanding" of the faith is a distinct question. A priori, it would be difficult to conceive how Augustine, for whom "soul" and "God" are such pivotal and related questions for his "understanding" of the faith, could long avoid making a commitment to one or other of these four hypotheses. At least, it must be admitted, the first two (generative transmission, individual creation) impose radically different orientations toward the incarnate situation than the second two, both of which include the position that "souls pre-exist elsewhere" before being embodied. True,

[6] *The Christian Philosophy*, p. 51.

Augustine warns his reader not to "accept lightly" (*temere*) one of these positions to the exclusion of the others; but he himself could quite conceivably imagine he had serious and compelling grounds for having made such a choice.

The second of Gilson's affirmations—and here he has received able confirmation from G. Bardy (*Les Révisions*, 141–148)—informs us there was a time in Augustine's career when he had made such a choice. He chose to think of the soul as pre-existing before its entry into the body.[7] How can this be squared with Augustine's insistence in the *Retractations* (he is commenting on the *Contra Academicos*) that touching the soul's origin he "did not know then, and still [does] not know" the answer to that question: *nec tunc sciebam, nec adhuc scio* (*Retr* I, 1, 3)? The answer is, apparently, that there was a time when he *thought* he knew, but only later considered himself to have been mistaken in that view. For the phrase refers to the very period when both Gilson and Bardy find the thesis of pre-existence most clearly expressed in his writings.

How long did this state of pseudo-conviction endure? Only careful examination of Augustine's writings after Cassiciacum can answer that question. But for the moment, it will suffice to reiterate that Augustine's remarks on the four "hypotheses" in the *De Libero Arbitrio* do not warrant the conclusion that he had abandoned that conviction by the time he wrote the third book of that work. They keep the question open for the believing Catholic, while in no way forbidding a choice of one or other hypothesis by one engaged in "understanding" the faith, provided his option is not made lightly.

It is, therefore, still permitted to ask: in view of Augustine's preference for thinking of the soul as pre-existing (and hypothesizing for the moment that his preference would still be active around the year A.D. 395), which of the four alternatives would he be inclined to choose? Again, the answer is clear: either the third or the fourth. But this, in turn, raises another question: what does the fourth hypothesis mean?

To arrive at any clarity on this issue, it would be indispensable to illuminate the entire context, thereby reviving a controversy whose flames still slumber.[8] For that context bristles with difficulties,

[7] *Ibid.*, pp. 71–72.

[8] The controversy dates from the publication of an article by Fr. Yves de Montcheuil, "L'hypothèse de l'état originel . . . d'après le *De Libero Arbitrio* de saint Augustin," in *Recherches de Science Religieuse* 23: 197–221 (1933) (reprinted in his *Mélanges Théologiques*, Paris, 1946, pp. 93–111) in answer to Fr. Charles Boyer's "Dieu pouvait-il créer l'homme dans l'état d'ignorance et de difficulté?" in *Gregorianum* 11: 32–57 (1930). In 1954 it still showed no signs of abating: see the contributions of Trapé, Boyer, Le Bourlier, De Lubac to *Augustinus Magister*, and the discussion, *AM* III, 247–261.

not to say with confusion: and we would suggest that Augustine is not entirely exempt of responsibility on the latter score. What seems beyond question is the fact that Augustine is here discussing two troubling aspects of human existence, our ignorance and our difficulty in doing good (*Lib* III, 53; cf. I, 23). He begins by assuring his readers that these two aspects of our life are surely a punishment, and, since God is just, punishment for some sin (*Lib* III, 51–54). The purpose that brings him to examine the four hypotheses is, accordingly, that of proving that however the soul is conceived as having arrived in this vale of tears, God's justice is beyond reproach (*Lib* III, 53). Now this is how he reasons respecting the fourth hypothesis:

> But if souls existing elsewhere are not sent by the Lord God, but come of their own accord to dwell in bodies, we can easily see that whatever ignorance and difficulty result from the action of their own will, the Creator is in no way to blame. Even if He had sent them Himself, since He did not deprive them . . . of their freedom to beg and seek and strive . . . He would therefore be utterly without blame (*Lib* III, 58).

God's justice, therefore, is put beyond man's complaint. But the hypothesis is none other than that of a voluntary fall of the soul into the body, into ignorance and difficulty, into a place of punishment. The divine Justice is uncompromised precisely because the soul has chosen freely, and consequently deserves everything that follows from that free choice. One can only infer that this choice is itself the sin for which the soul is punished, the sin preceding birth in this life on account of which it is embodied in a sensible universe—the essence of what Augustine may much later have found to be Origen's position.

Consider now the difference between the third and fourth hypothesis. Either God has sent the soul without fault on its part, or the soul has sinned. Starting from his pre-existence position, which of these two must Augustine choose? His way of appending a hasty *quandoquidem etiamsi eas ipse misisset*—"even if He had sent them Himself"—to his treatment of the fourth hypothesis, is at least suggestive. The *misisset* seems to put us momentarily back into the framework of the third hypothesis, which has already been thoroughly treated: why go back to it?

Now it may just be that Augustine is not back-tracking at all. The distinction between these two hypotheses may in his mind not be a disjunction after all. He may not feel either obliged or entitled to choose one to the exclusion of the other. The good Plotinian, in fact, cannot choose between the soul's falling and being sent, for one of the peculiarities of Plotinus' doctrine consists in holding firmly to both ends of that chain and trying to persuade us that the apparent opposition is, in the final analysis, illusory.

And yet, the objection comes, that opposition is quite real: and here, with the sanction of more than one Plotinian interpreter, one is inclined to agree. That agreement leads us to examine another element of Gilson's text, quoted above. "For Augustine," he assures us, "everything God has made is good. *Therefore* the body was created for its intrinsic goodness, *not* as a consequence of or punishment for sin." I have italicized the terms that show a passage of the author's thought from the properly historical plane to the level of inference—an inference that shows the sure philosophic instinct that is at work, for these two views may not be, in fact, easily compatible. Can it be that Augustine's thought at this point suffers from a lack of coherence?

The possibility must be left open, at least for the moment. The justification of chess, it has been said, lies in the fact that even grand masters make mistakes. One might suggest by a distant analogy that it must sometimes be the business of the historian of philosophy to transcribe faithfully the inner contradictions that his philosophic instinct—and admiration—would tempt him to suppress. If Augustine's thought is not entirely coherent on the situation of the embodied soul, he was not the first to suffer under that stigma.

THE TENSIONS IN PLOTINIAN DOCTRINE ON THE SOUL

Soul Fallen and "Sent"

For it is precisely that doctrine of the soul, fallen, yet at the same time sent, into a world that is simultaneously bad and beautiful, which led Bréhier to speak of an "undeniable contradiction" in Plotinus' thought.[9] It arose from his desire to remain a faithful exponent of the Platonic tradition in its entirety. His basic work on the subject is the relatively early (sixth in chronological sequence) treatise on "The Soul's Descent into the Body," *Ennead* IV, 8.

His own conviction is that the soul is native to the "higher" world; its place is there, and its proper activity the blessed contemplation of the Intelligibles. How, then, account for the soul's

[9] *La Philosophie de Plotin* (Paris, 1928), p. 68. The entire chapter, pp. 47–69, is valuable for an understanding of the diverse tensions in Plotinus' theory of the soul. Note that Jean Trouillard, *La Procession Plotinienne* (Paris, 1955), pp. 30–33, 61–63, and *La Purification Plotinienne* (Paris, 1955), 22–25, 110–112, 118–122, tends to present a far more sympathetic view of these tensions.

experience of an "immersion" in the body? He begins with a careful summary of the two conflicting sides of Plato's thought on the question before proceeding to his own effort of reconciliation. The pessimistic accent found in the *Phaedo* and the *Phaedrus*, whereby some "fault" of its own has plunged the soul into matter, is balanced by the more optimistic view of the *Timaeus*, where the demi-urge, out of goodness, "sends" the soul down into the sensible universe to impart beauty to it by conferring on it the intelligible perfection of the Ideas.

Plotinus is, therefore, conscious of the ambivalence in the master's thought from the very beginning of his philosophical activity. He refuses the privilege of taking a one-sided view of the matter,[10] at least on the plane of reflective thought; but reflection and affectivity do not always harmonize. Thus there is a possibility that the "shift of accent" which is generally admitted in Plotinus' thought only complicates that original ambivalence, allowing the pessimistic accent to dominate toward the beginning and only gradually to give way to the more Stoic optimism which characterizes his riper work. The turning point in this development Harder has placed at the moment when Plotinus realized that his earlier views gave entirely too much encouragement to the Gnostics, who for a considerable time became the target of his fiercest opposition.[11] Thus, in his later works, he points much more to the beauty of the sensible world, which so reflects the goodness of God and the perfection of the Ideas that it must rightly be called God's "youngest child," indeed, the "manifest god" (*Enn* V, 8, 12).

The soul, consequently, is "sent" to confer beauty on this world. Does it follow that it has not sinned and "fallen" into that world?

[10] Many of his predecessors seem to have opted for either the pessimistic or the optimistic position. See A. J. Festugière, *La Révélation d'Hermès Trismégiste*, II (Paris, 1953), pp. 63–96. This attempt at reconciliation is already a first hallmark of the Plotinian theory.

[11] See H. R. Schwyzer, "Plotinus," *RE* XXI, 1, cols. 547–548; but see also H. C. Puech, "Plotin et les Gnostiques," in *Sources de Plotin*, pp. 159–174, and the subsequent discussion, pp. 175–190, esp. pp. 183, 185. Cf. E. R. Dodds's study, "Numenius and Ammonius," in *Sources de Plotin*, pp. 1–32 (discussion, pp. 33–61). The resulting picture is one of more decided development than Schwyzer was prepared to admit when writing his article for *RE*. Its direction generally is away from a semi-Gnostic dualism toward a more Stoic optimism. (Armstrong, "Plotinus," in *Cambridge History*, p. 218, attenuates this shift; but cf. *ibid.*, pp. 205–206). Unaware of this development, and taking his Plotinus without regard for chronology, Augustine shows the tensions more clearly, perhaps, even than the Plotinus of any given treatise. This quite deliberate departure from consideration of Plotinus' "sources" and the difficulties in reconciling them may well account for the more positive view Trouillard takes of his finished systematic.

Not in the least; the two theses remain true and still require reconciliation, or, in Bréhier's term, perpetuate the undeniable contradiction.

Choice and Cosmic Law

Plotinus repeatedly attempts to dissolve this "contradiction," and writers differ on how well he has succeeded. More important for us here, however, is the solution he proposes. There is, he must admit, some "fault" involved in the soul's fall. We are fallen because in some sense we desired to fall, or desired something that entailed the fall. And yet, the cosmic laws are perfect and inexorable. This semblance of liberty involved in our original fault he feels he must integrate into the necessary operation of those immutable laws. The soul's freedom and cosmic necessity are really one and the same. The mute, spontaneous desire which entailed our fall is itself identical with the Logos' work interior to us, that Logos which irresistibly rules our falls and our returns to the upper world.[12]

Fallen, Yet Still "There"

There is an additional paradox in Plotinus' personal view of the fall, however, one which we have met before. Here, he frankly admits, he is proposing a personal view, one for which he finds no clear warrant in the Platonic tradition. The soul is "fallen," true, but in a sense not entirely fallen: its capacity for intellectual knowledge shows it still retains a link with the Intelligible World. This link he describes in a term familiar to the Platonic tradition, "reminiscence"; but here, too, he gives the notion a personal twist. For the capacity for intellectual thought shows not only that the soul once, before its fall, contemplated the Intelligible Archetypes. It also indicates that the soul is even now being "illuminated" by those Archetypes, is even now to some extent "still there" (*Enn* IV, 8, 8, 1–9). This paradox of soul-fallen and soul-still-"there" will only be heightened when Plotinus sets himself to thinking out the fall in omnipresence terms. That added complication we can, however, leave for later consideration.

Memory and Return

How, then, is the soul to "return" from its fallen condition? By taking advantage of the foothold this intelligible "memory" affords. One way of doing this leads upward through the study of

[12] *Enn* IV, 8, 5 entire. Plotinus returns to this nettling problem in *Enn* III, 2, 18, 29ff and IV, 3, 12–13. Note that the latter two treatises are expressly referred to in *The City of God* and are generally admitted as figuring in Augustine's earliest readings in Plotinus.

the liberal disciplines, studies, which sharpen the mind and strengthen the soul's eye for eventual contemplation of purely intelligible reality—a power that has been weakened by our involvement in the body and sense. But not all souls are equally adept at this demanding intellectual task. This inequality Plotinus accounts for by the suggestion that some souls are "less fallen" than others. Those that are less advanced on the downward path will mount back to the vision more easily than others (*Enn* IV, 8, 5, 17–29).

The very lucidity of Gilson's estimate of the situation, therefore, was sufficient reason for examining his position. He has pointed to one area where Augustine's adaptation of the Plotinian theory of the soul would result in a certain strain or even incoherence in his thinking. That incoherence is, however, only one of several that troubled Plotinus. Taken together, the ensemble of his statements on the soul give his doctrine a characteristic set of inner tensions which may serve to make it all the more identifiable if found reproduced in Augustine's works.

But one must not expect this doctrine to appear in each of Augustine's works with such sharpness of detail as will clearly betray its Plotinian pedigree. Whether it forms the backdrop for Augustine's anthropology, from Cassiciacum forward, is a question that will occupy us later. But for the moment we must pass on to a series of works in which Plotinian echoes occur with a fidelity that is surprising and revealing. For nowhere is Augustine's debt to Plotinus more starkly manifest than in the works he pens after his return from Cassiciacum: and central among those works is the *De Genesi contra Manichaeos*.

THE PLOTINIAN FALL IN AUGUSTINE

The Soul's Ideal Situation: Mid-rank Being

Plotinus' speculations on the soul's present condition in the body are regularly cast against the backdrop of what he considers to be the soul's ideal situation. Still focusing our consideration on his fundamental treatise on the question, *Ennead* IV, 8, we find that the key term which Plotinus there uses (IV, 8, 7, 5) to describe the soul's ideal station is *μέση τάξις*, drawn from Plato's *Timaeus*, and a classic expression in Neo-Platonism. Theiler (*Porphyrios*, 17ff) has shown the importance of that notion in Augustine's works, at the same time endeavoring to demonstrate that Augustine found it, not in Plotinus, but in Porphyry. But had Augustine drawn the notion of *μέση τάξις* from Plotinus, where would he have found it?

Oddly enough, in only two loci. The first of them is in *Ennead* III, 2, 9 on Providence, which we know he read, but where the notion is found without extended development. Its only other occurrence is in *Ennead* IV, 8, where Plotinus describes the soul's position in reality as an intermediate one, between the pure intelligibles and the sensible realm, such that it pertains to her very nature to govern and order the sensible world, communicating to it the perfection she draws from the contemplation of the ideas.[13] This function, he is careful to note, she can fulfill while remaining entirely recollected in contemplation, enfolded in the unity of the universal soul, with which she is fundamentally at one. Her government of the sensible world does not necessitate her entering "into," engaging in intimate contact with it. Like the entourage of a king who never leaves his palace, she can govern that world "from afar."

The *De Genesi Contra Manichaeos* and the Soul's *Medietas*

If one were looking for a work as revealing on Augustine's anthropology as *Ennead* IV, 8 is on Plotinus', one would have to point to that little-studied (perhaps because highly disconcerting) book, the *De Genesi contra Manichaeos*. Here, Augustine's "spiritual exegesis" permits him to take extraordinary liberties with what is often the most obvious meaning of the Scriptural text, something of which he seems at times uncomfortably aware. He justifies his resort to the transferred sense with a number of reasons, laying particular stress on the need to explain Genesis in a manner "worthy of God" (*Gen Man* II, 3) and therefore calculated to retort the "sacrilegious" exposé of the same work proposed by the Manichees (*Gen Man* II, 3; cf. II, 19). His sincerity in all this, his "Catholic spirit," is beyond question; he is undoubtedly serious in proposing as his aim an interpretation of Genesis "according to the faith of the *Catholica*" (*secundum Catholicam fidem*: II, 3) to which the Manichees, with their pretensions at "enlightened" Christianity, were so opposed. But it is well to remember that his model in exegetical method is almost certainly Ambrose, whose "subjective, capricious, arbitrary" manner of interpretation so frequently succeeded, as Dudden puts it, in making virtually "anything mean anything."[14] From Ambrose, too, Augustine may have received

[13] *Enn* IV, 8, 7, 5. Here its connection is different from the above, as we shall shortly see. I am indebted to G. Pollet for this information on the occurrence of the *μέση τάξις* notion in Plotinus, information he was enabled to furnish thanks to his researches toward a Plotinian lexicon.

[14] See F. H. Dudden, *The Life and Times of St. Ambrose*, 2 vols. (Oxford, 1935), II, 459. See also *ibid.*, p. 458 for the principle of interpreting Scripture in a manner "worthy of God."

occasional encouragement for one or other concrete piece of interpretation. We are reminded, for example, that the Milanese Bishop followed Philo in reducing the Scriptural author's very substantial Eve to a kind of *exemplum*, a symbolic figure standing for the inferior "animal part" of human nature, subject to the "virile" *ratio*.[15] And this does not exhaust the series of points at which Augustine's interpretation corresponds with that of Ambrose.[16]

But even taking these points of correspondence into consideration, Ambrose's contribution in this regard seems far more likely to have been similar to his contribution in Augustine's conversion. He establishes an atmosphere and provides a method whereby Augustine is both encouraged and equipped to find the faith of the *Catholica* in fundamental resonance with the "understanding" of human life proposed in the *Enneads*. For what Ambrose did not furnish, and Plotinus did, was the firmly structured view of the soul and of its situation in reality which presides over the recent convert's exegesis of Genesis. Ambrose's relatively arbitrary manner of interpreting the scriptures leaves Augustine free to unearth, beneath the *verba* of the sacred text, the *res*, the view of human existence, presented in Plotinus' writings as he understood them.

The very reduction of Eve to an *exemplum*, for example, Augustine performs inside a framework where the feminine, "animal part" of human nature is "fitted to obey" (*accomodata ad temperandum*). All this seems Biblical enough in inspiration, until we note that the governing "reason" must itself remain in constant contemplative contact and submission to the subsistent Wisdom which is Augustine's counterpart of the Plotinian "Intelligible World" (I, 30; cf. I, 27–28). At this point one begins to ask whether the "animal part" is really a "part" of a substantially unified and individualized "man" in the usual acceptance of both those terms. The Platonic use of μέρος when speaking of the "parts" of both soul and man immediately comes to mind and bids us be cautious; the symbolic atmosphere pervading the entire *De Genesi contra Manichaeos* counsels further caution. Augustine may not be using

[15] G. Madec in *REA* 11: 374 (1965). The argument Madec proceeds to draw from such correspondences can be retorted: they may only have encouraged Augustine in thinking that Ambrose and Plotinus would agree in his interpretation of Genesis, as Boyer and Courcelle have given us reason to suspect.

[16] Piero Rollero, *La Expositio evangelii secundum Lucam di Ambroggio come fonte della essegesi Agostiniana* (Turin, 1958), pp. 14–17, 129–132, 137–140. My contention, again, is that Plotinus furnished the comprehensive matrix into which Augustine sets such borrowings, not only from Ambrose, but from others as well.

the term in a sense that would seem most immediately obvious to the modern reader. He has already proposed an ingenious theory whereby all "copulation" in paradise would be "spiritual," the marriage of "man and woman" destined to bring forth only "spiritual progeny of immortal joys" (*spirituales foetus immortalium gaudiorum*: I, 30). He has then gone on to make the soul part of the "invisible" and "spiritual creation" symbolized by the vegetation of the fields (*viride agri*: II, 4), a "spiritual creation" irrigated by the intelligible light of the Verbum (II, 5).

Noteworthy here is the fact that the original sin is regularly imputed not to "man" but to "soul." Augustine seems bent on distinguishing the ideal state "before the soul sinned" (*antequam anima peccaret*) and a post-lapsary state where the term "man" (*homo*) appears for the first time to become an entirely appropriate designation. Only after the fall, he observes, was there "man laboring upon the earth" (*homo laborans in terra*: II, 5). How can this be, when the sacred text obliges him to admit that "man" was created from the clay of earth? Augustine immediately reduces the force of that Biblical statement by reminding his reader that this refers to the "animal" and not to the "spiritual man"—to man *before* he was transported into paradise, "to be consummated by God's Word" (*ut a Verbo Dei consummaretur*: II, 10). This would seem to mean that the very process of man's creation was incomplete before that "consummation": the normative idea of man is therefore that of the "spiritual man," a "spiritual creature," a contemplative "soul" enjoying that detached relation to all sensible reality whereby it governs the whole in the absent kind of way Plotinus insists upon. Intrinsically *related* to the sensible, the soul is nonetheless far from "embodied."

On these grounds, then, Augustine can say that the basic flaw in the Manichee interpretation of Scriptural anthropology lies in the fact that they "err in considering man after [the] sin, when he had been condemned to the mortality of this life" (*post peccatum considerent hominem, cum in hujus vitae mortalitatem damnatus est*: I, 29). Or, in terms he uses elsewhere to express the same post-lapsary condition, it is an error to draw one's idea of "man" from this creature "in this mortal [condition] of body" (II, 29), "in this body" (II, 34), "cast down to the mortality of beasts" (II, 32).

The same "spiritual" status of the newly created soul is indicated by what the Saint says of our ultimate destiny. We look forward to a "renewal" (*re-novatio*), a "liberation" (*liberatio*) which he boldly terms a "change into angelic form" (*commutatio in angelicam formam*: I, 29 and 32); but this would appear to mean the restoration of our original state, since he advises us that by following the "spiritual" Adam, Christ, we shall become *once more* the "spiritual creation" (*iterum fieri viride agri*: II, 6) be "restored" (*restituamur*) to the paradise we lost by sin (II, 10).

This, then, would appear to be the "understanding" of the faith which led him, at the climax of the *De Quantitate Animae*, to portray Evodius as proclaiming his firm conviction that he is "soul," but adding that Augustine's arguments have led him to see a corollary he had not thought of until now: that our "souls are not *in* bodies" (*Quant* 61). Shortly afterwards, Augustine warns his companion that the soul is by its nature "equal of the angel" (*par angelo*), any present inferiority being a consequence of its sin (*Quant* 78).

It begins to dawn that this is no earthly Paradise, that the soul has been given a position and function in the hierarchy of being entirely analogous to the soul in Plotinianism. Such suspicions are only further alerted when he describes the situation of the soul in the pregnant term, *medietas animi*, taking his starting point from the happy coincidence that Genesis speaks of the "two trees" situated "in the middle of paradise" (*in medio paradisi*).

Ennead IV, 8

7, 1–17: As there are these two realms, the intelligible and that of sense, it is better for the soul to dwell in the intelligible (ἄμεινον μὲν ψυχῇ ἐν τῷ νοητῷ εἶναι); but such is its nature, it is necessary that it live also in the realm of sense. Accordingly it occupies only an intermediate rank among beings (μέσην . . . τάξιν ἐν τοῖς οὖσιν ἐπισχοῦσαν). Yet there is no cause for complaint that it is not in all respects the highest. By nature divine, it is located at the nethermost limit of the intelligible realm, bordering on the realm of sense, and there gives to the realm of sense something of its own. In turn it is itself affected when, instead of controlling the body without endangering its own security, it lets itself be carried away by an excessive zeal and plunges

De Genesi contra Manichaeos II

12: "Every tree produced from the earth" we take to mean every spiritual joy, that is to say, [the soul's] rising aloft from earth (*supereminere terram*), and not being enveloped and buried in the entanglements of earthly desires (*non involvi atque obrui terrenarum cupiditatum implicamentis*). The "tree of life set in the midst" (*in medio*) of the garden, however, signifies that wisdom whereby the soul should understand itself as ordered at a certain mid-rank among realities (*in meditullio quodam rerum se esse ordinatam*), such, that, though the entirety of corporeal nature be subjected to her, she understand that God's nature is nevertheless above her: so that she turn aside neither to right (arrogating to herself what is not: *quod non est*) nor to left, through deep into the body and ceases to be wholly united to The Soul (*εἰ μὴ μετὰ τοῦ αὐτῆς ἀσφαλοῦς διακοσμοῖ, προθυμίᾳ δὲ πλείονι εἰς τὸ εἴσω δύοιτο*). Yet the soul can rise above this condition again (*πάλιν ἐξαναδῦναι*), and turning to account the experience of what it is above and can know more clearly what is better by contrast with its opposite (*ἱστορίαν ὧν ἐνταῦθα εἶδέ τε καὶ ἔπαθε προσλαβούσῃ καὶ μαθούσῃ, οἷον ἄρα ἐστὶν ἐκεῖ, εἶναι, καὶ τῇ παραθέσει τῶν οἷον ἐναντίων οἷον σαφέστερον τά ἀμείνω μαθούσῃ*). Indeed, knowledge of good is sharpened by experience of evil (*Γνῶσις γὰρ ἐναργεστέρα τἀγαθοῦ ἡ τοῦ κακοῦ πεῖρα*) in those incapable of any sure knowledge of evil unless they have experienced it (*τὸ κακὸν πρὸ πείρας γνῶναι*).

negligence, despising what is (*quod est*). This, then, is [what is intended by] the "tree of life set in the midst of the garden."

By "the tree of knowledge of good and evil," however, is meant that very mid-station and ordered integrity of the soul (*ipsa item medietas animae et ordinata integritas*), for this [tree] too is set in the midst of the garden (*in medio paradisi*); and so it is spoken of as the tree of discernment between good and evil, because if the soul, which ought to "stretch forward to the things which are before" (*in anteriora*), that is, to God, and "forget the things which are behind" (*posteriora*) (*Phil* 3, 13), that is, bodily pleasures, should desert God and turn about to herself (*ad seipsam, deserto Deo conversa fuerit*), wanting to enjoy her own power (*sua potentia*) as though [she could exercise it] without God, she swells up with pride (*intumescit superbia*), which is the beginning of all sin. And once punishment follows on this sin of hers, she learns by experience what separates the good which she deserted and the evil into which she has fallen (*experiendo discit quid intersit inter bonum quod deseruit et malum in quod cecidit*). And that will bring her to taste of the fruit of the tree of discernment between good and evil.

Now the most significant similarity between these texts is one of doctrinal pattern. Plotinus' key term, *μέση τάξις*, is translated by the term *medietas animi*, which Augustine paraphrases with the explanation that the soul is "ordered" *in meditullio quodam rerum*. The paragraph from the *De Genesi* then presents a finely compressed statement of the doctrine presented in *Ennead* IV, 8: the soul must *supereminere*, retain her natural relation of governor of the sensible world, without letting it degenerate into an *involvi*, *obrui*, an *implicatio* in earthly pleasures. Her *gaudium* should remain *spiritale*, and we have noted that Augustine has already explained this as referring to the delights of intellectual contemplation, exactly in accordance with Plotinus' mind on the matter. So firmly has he grasped the doctrine concerned, he can re-express it in terms reminiscent of various other treatises, reminding us that the things in this spiritual world really exist, those in the sensible universe not "existing" in the true sense of that term. The *dextera-sinistra* couple furnishes a semi-Biblical hook for a perfectly Plotinian insight (cf. *Conf* VII, 16–17). The spiritual is, for both thinkers, what is prior, *ante*, while the corporeal is posterior, *post* (cf. *Conf* III, 10), in a realm which the soul should school itself to forget in order to revive that other kind of memory, the Platonic reminiscence of the intelligible: again, good Plotinian doctrine.[17] The notion of an *aversio* whereby the soul has "deserted" God, turning "to itself" and to the delighted exercise of its "own" powers, Augustine probably drew from the opening of *Ennead* V, 1. The term "desertion," however, will eventually bring him to interpret the flight from God in the light of *Ennead* VI, 4–5: the soul deserts God, but God never deserts the absent soul.

The doctrinal pattern, then, is identical in both texts: was the one modeled on the other? An indication that this is probable is found at the end of Augustine's exegesis of the verse in question. Why should Augustine insert that peculiar assurance, one that seems to have nothing to do with his exegetical task at the moment, concerning the fruit the fallen soul can draw from her fallen existence? The spiritual meaning of "tasting the fruit of knowledge of good and evil" provides a starting-point, but one whose meaning must be slightly adjusted by the interpretation he gives it. The fall has a positive side: the soul can gain an experiential and comparative knowledge of the good she has deserted. We shall see that this parallelism of association points to an identity of problematic in both authors. But the effort to "justify" the fall is, at the same time, arbitrary enough in the context which is Augustine's here. Its explanation becomes easy, however, once we admit that it was suggested by the same reminder occurring in the same context in Plotinus' *Ennead* IV, 8.

Ennead IV, 3 and the Properties of the "Fallen" State

For Augustine, the "beginning" of the fault lies in "pride." We are reminded that for Plotinus as well, the fault which can disturb

[17] As contained in *Enn* IV, 3, 25ff, which Augustine read, and which Klaus Winkler finds active at Cassiciacum: see "La Théorie augustinienne de la mémoire à son point de départ," *AM* I, 511–519.

this delicate balance is a desire whereby the soul tires of being with the intelligible whole, and wishes to be "on her own"—*ad seipsam*, as the Saint puts it. The result of this desire, Plotinus explains in the same treatise (IV, 8, 4, 11–28), is that the soul retires into hesrelf, leaves the whole-soul to become isolated and partial, a fragment capable of surveying and dealing only with fragments—notably, with that part of the corporeal universe which she chooses to be her own body. Thus she plunges into the very heart of the sensible universe, becomes sunk in sense, enters into contact with a part that becomes her own and entirely preoccupies her. This preoccupation, immersion, intimate contact—in Augustine's term, this *involvi*, *obrui*, *implicatio* as distinct from her former *supereminentia*—is what weakens the soul, draws her attention away from the vision of intelligible truth, and constitutes her fallen state.

To the mechanism of that fall we shall return shortly; but for the moment it must be remarked that one term in various forms suffices to describe man's fallen state which Augustine sees as ensuing *post peccatum*, in contrast with the soul's existence *ante peccatum*. The *Confessions* will describe it as a "dying life and living death" (*vita mortalis, mors vitalis: Conf* I, 7). But even at this epoch, he designates it as "the mortality of this life" (*hujus vitae mortalitas: Gen Man* I, 29); or, in more condensed form, it is, when compared with the "other" life which sin has forfeited, simply *mors* (*Gen Man* II, 15; cf. *Lib* II, 53). Augustine may well have found Plotinian encouragement for selecting this term to capsule the properties of our fallen situation.[18] What is more manifest is that Plotinus, rather than Genesis, warranted his treating as consequences of our fall a number of features of human life that the Hebrew author unquestionably thought proper to man as God created him. Thus, labor (*Gen Man* II, 15), carnal procreation (I, 30), the need to resort to sense-knowledge, language, symbolic communication of all sorts (II, 5–6), the opacity of a body which makes concealment and simulation possible (II, 32)—none of these, in Augustine's view, were proper to man (or, more exactly, to the soul) as originally intended. All such things came upon us "because we became

[18] Cf. *Enn* IV, 7, 11 and *ibid.*, 9, line 23, where the term is applied to wood and stone in contrast with the soul. Augustine's distinction *Immort* 16, between *anima-animata-exanime*, with the latter then termed *mortuum*, seems an echo of this terminology. See also the coincidental but striking grouping of the same terms (wood, stone, death) in the Plotinian original of Augustine's death-bed quotation, *Enn* I, 4, 7, 20–26: "One that sets great store by wood and stones, or, Zeus! by mortality among mortals, cannot yet be the proficient, whose estimate of death, we hold, must be that it is better than life in the body." Such verbal correspondences mean very little to us; there is much evidence to suggest that they meant very much to Augustine.

mortals after sin." Again, a comparison with *Ennead* IV, 3, which we know Augustine read, makes the structured correspondence of teaching almost transparent.

Ennead IV, 3

18, 1–4: There remains something still to be said on the question whether the soul uses deliberate reason (λογισμῷ) before its descent and again when it has left the body.

Reasoning is for this sphere; it is the act of the Soul fallen into perplexity, distracted with cares, diminished in strength (Ἢ ἐνταῦθα ὁ λογισμὸς ἐγγίγνεται ἐν ἀπόρῳ ἤδη οὔσης καὶ φροντίδος πληρουμένης καὶ μᾶλλον ἀσθενούσης); the need for deliberation goes with the less self-sufficing intelligence; craftsmen faced with a difficulty stop to consider; where there is no problem, their art works on by its own forthright power.

18, 9–22: [In the unfallen soul] we may represent to ourselves a reasoning that flows uninterruptedly from the Intellectual-Principle in them (τὴν ἐκ νοῦ ἀεὶ γινομένην), an inherent state (καὶ οὖσαν ἐν αὐταῖς διάθεσιν), an assertion that is real; in this way [the souls] would be users of reason even in the over-world.

We certainly cannot think of them, it seems to me, as employing words in the Intelligible realm, nor as having bodies, quite, in the heavenly region (Οὐδὲ δὴ φωναῖς, οἶμαι, χρῆσθαι νομιστέον ἐν μὲν τῷ νοητῷ οὔσας, καὶ πάμπαν σώματα δ'ἐχούσας ἐν οὐρανῷ). And very surely the deliberation of doubt and difficulty which they practice here must be unknown to

De Genesi contra Manichaeos II

30: For the very fact that everyone born in this life has difficulty in finding the truth (*difficultatem inveniendi veritatis habet*), because of the corruptible body ... and "thorns and thistles" stand for the pricking of involved questions (*punctiones tortuosarum quaestionum*) ...

And because we are necessarily admonished through these eyes and ears (*per hos oculos et per has aures*) about the truth, and it is difficult to resist phantasms ... in this perplexity, accordingly (*in ista ergo perplexitate*), whose brow does not run with sweat in order that he may eat his bread?

5: But before sin [had been committed] ... [God] watered [the spiritual creature] by an interior fountain (*fonte interiore*), speaking to its understanding (*loquens in intellectum ejus*), so that it did not receive words from without (*ut non extrinsecus verba exciperet*) ... but was satiated by His fountain, that is, by the truth pouring forth from its own interior (*de intimis suis manante veritate*).

6: And therefore, "laboring upon the earth" [man] finds teaching by means of human words necessary (*laborans jam in terra necessariam habet ... doctrinam de humanis verbis*) ... For on this account Our Lord ... poured forth ... the dew of the holy Gospel ... so that [the soul comes to a state wherein] it no longer seeks rain from without (*forinsecus*) ... [Scripture means them there (Ὅσα μὲν διὰ χρείας ἢ δι' ἀμφισβητήσεις διαλέγονται ἐνταῦθα, ἐκεῖ οὐκ ἂν εἴη); all their act must fall into place by the sheer force of their own nature; there can be no question of commanding or taking counsel; they will know, each, what is to be communicated from another, by present consciousness (οὐδ' ἂν ἐπιτάττοιεν οὐδ' ἂν συμβουλεύοιεν, γιγνώσκοιεν δ' ἂν καὶ τὰ παρ' ἀλλήλων ἐν συνέσει). Even in our own case here [below], we know many things through the eyes [of those we behold] though they keep silence (καὶ ἐνταῦθα πολλὰ σιωπώντων γιγνώσκοιμεν δι' ὀμμάτων); and there, all is pure; every body is, as it were, an eye; nothing is concealed or pretended; one knows by seeing before the other speaks (ἐκεῖ δὲ καθαρὸν πᾶν τὸ σῶμα καὶ οἷον ὀφθαλμὸς ἕκαστος καὶ οὐδὲν δὲ κρυπτὸν οὐδὲ πεπλασμένον, ἀλλὰ πρὶν εἰπεῖν ἄλλῳ ἰδὼν ἐκεῖνος ἔγνω).

us to understand that] divine teaching by means of human words (*de humanis verbis divinam doctrinam*) is necessary, like rain from clouds, for man laboring upon the earth, that is, placed in the aridity of sin [-fulness] (*in peccatorum ariditate constituto*).
32: Nor should it be believed that in those heavenly bodies (*in illis corporibus coelestibus*) thoughts were concealed as they are concealed by these bodies [we now are in] (*sic latere cogitationes . . . quemadmodum in his corporibus latent*): but just as certain acts of mind are manifested on the countenance and particularly in the eyes (*apparent in vultu et maxime in oculis*), so, I opine, all acts of mind without exception were unconcealed in that transparency and guilelessness of [those] heavenly bodies (*sic in illa perspicuitate ac simplicitate coelestium corporum omnes omnino motus animi latere non arbitror*).

The adjustments Augustine has worked here are all in function of his exegetical task and of the modification of problematic imposed by his Christian preoccupations. None of them however, can hide the fact that the inner logic of Plotinus' position has been grasped with admirable acuity. Thus, the use of reasoning is due to difficulties, perplexities, which are symbolized by the "thorns and thistles" of "this life" (ἐνταῦθα). This "labor" to earn the "food" of truth, Augustine assures us, is what the author of Genesis must mean by Adam's punishment. In the higher sphere of existence (ἐκεὶ, ἐν τῷ νοητῷ), all our knowledge was poured into us by that *fons* spoken of in Genesis, one that irrigated the spiritual creation, symbolized by the *viride agri*. This was done, according to both authors, "from within"—and at this point the Augustinian *manans* is reproduced by Ficinus' Renaissance translation of the Plotinian γινομὲνην. Having lost contact with this interior font, the soul must turn outwards in its pursuit of truth. Human words, all the work of communication, symbol, advice, and consultation (and this for Augustine includes the entire regime of Scriptural, Prophetic, and Apostolic authority), all these are consequences of the *peccatum animae*, the fall from paradise.

Remarkable is the fact that both authors seem to entertain the idea of the soul's embodiment in the paradisiac state, though Plotinus is careful to observe that it will not be a body "quite" (πάμπαν), that is, of the kind we usually experience.[19] If the "body" there is σῶμα it must at the same time be "pure" (καθαρόν) or in Augustine's comparable terms, "heavenly," "transparent," and "guileless" (*coeleste*, *perspicuum*, *simplex*)—a set of adjectives the last of which especially recalls MacKenna's translation of the συνάμφω whereby Plotinus in *Ennead* VI, 4, 14 characterizes our constitution after the fall: "We have lost that first *simplicity*, we are become the *dual thing*" (italics mine). This same idea Augustine further develops in *Gen Man* II, 23 by linking the "tunics of mortality" to the possibility of dissimulation and hypocrisy. But in contrast to that opaque duality, both authors portray a heavenly situation wherein everyone's inner thoughts are immediately known to his companions, no concealment or dissimulation being possible. It is significant that both describe this reciprocal awareness in identical analogies, appealing to the expressiveness of the human visage and the human eye (δι' ὀμμάτων; ὀφθαλμός; *vultus*, *oculus*).

Now the parallel just cited proves at least that Augustine's evaluation of these properties of human existence faithfully echoes Plotinus'. The fact that we know from other evidence that he did read this treatise, and the tight pattern whereby he reproduces the same interconnected scheme of consequences, make it highly probable that he had the translation of this passage clearly in mind (if not before his eyes) when writing his Genesis commentary.

We are not, therefore, in the world of "pure spirits": the "change into angelic form" means that the soul will once again don a celestial body it once had. We are entitled to think of this *corpus coeleste* as a body, and yet in a sense quite different from our ordinary use of the term. It would hardly be just, therefore, to

[19] This seems the force of Plotinus' πάμπαν where Henry-Schwyzer (accepting Vitringa's reading) place it. Cf. *Enn* V, 8, 3, 21ff for Plotinus' acceptance of corporeality in heaven. Here he seems to warn that that body will not be the kind familiar to our ordinary experience. Both MacKenna ("though they may occupy bodies in the heavenly region") and Bréhier (tant qu'elles ont leur corps dans le ciel") seem to work from a different positioning of πάμπαν.

speak of paradisiac man as truly "incarnate." Certainly, the robust author of Genesis would hardly have recognized the Adam he wrote about.

The Soul Never "Entirely" Fallen

The soul, therefore, retains even in paradise her natural relation to sensible. It is a radical degeneration of that relation which constitutes its fallen state. And yet (and here Plotinus admits he is advancing an opinion that may "clash with the general view": it is distinctive of his personal theory) the soul is never entirely fallen. His final suggestion in *Ennead* IV, 8, 8 would have it that the soul's highest portion remains in unbroken contact with the intelligible order, still engaged in contemplation. Of this highest activity, our everyday consciousness would seem to bear not the slightest trace. The objection from experience, therefore, is a normal one, and Plotinus must contend with it. In *Ennead* V, 8 (on Intellectual Beauty) one of his hearers poses the question squarely: how can the soul be in (the realm of intellectual) beauty, and yet fail to see it?

That question, allowing for modifications of problematic, is entirely analogous to the difficulty that faces Augustine in the *De Musica*. For both authors admit that sense experiences would at times vividly persuade us that we are naturally "embodied." The reply in both cases tacitly supposes the Plotinian doctrine that true health, which correlates with our exercise of the higher and therefore most proper activity, is invariably accompanied by a "diminution," at least of such corporeal consciousness.[20]

[20] In *De Musica* VI, 7–8, Augustine is dealing with the everyday impression that the body can act upon the soul in its fallen state; he counters that impression by elaborating in VI, 9–10 (with help from Plotinus, we may think: see *Enn* IV, 4, 22ff, which Augustine seems to have interpreted in the light of additional suggestions in *Enn* I, 4, 10 where the present problematic is remarkably paralleled) his celebrated theory of sensation as an active "attention of the soul to the passive modifications of the body." (For more on this question, see Chap. VII, n. 4, below.) That attention becomes sharpest, he avers, when the soul encounters some "difficulty" in its normal animating activity, one which produces the distraction from the higher activity of contemplation which is then traced to its cause in *De Musica* VI, 37ff. The cause is, one might guess, the fall of the soul. He then goes on to explain that when the soul is absorbed in its higher and ideal form of activity, it can lose consciousness of such lower activities. For this doctrine cf. *De Musica* VI, 49 and *Enn* I, 4, 10. Cf. also *Quant* 55, which describes the soul's highest activity as closest to a "suspension of activity." On whether, in Plotinus' system, *all* elevation corresponds to a "diminution de conscience" (Bréhier, *Ennéades*, V, 149, n. 1,—apropos of the exact passage from *Enn* V, 8, 11, cited above) see H. R. Schwyzer's careful "'Bewusst' und 'unbewusst' bei Plotin" in *Sources de Plotin*, pp. 341–378. Augustine may be excused for holding, as regards corporeal consciousness, essentially the same view as Bréhier.

Ennead V, 8

11, 24–39: We must consider this too, that the perception of evils has a more violent impact, but produces less knowledge as a result of the impact (*ὡς τῶν μὲν κακῶν αἱ αἰσθήσεις τὰς πληγὰς ἔχουσι μείζους, ἥττους δὲ τὰς γνώσεις τῇ πληγῇ ἐκκρουομένας*). Illness strikes our consciousness harder, but the quiet companionship of health gives us a better understanding of it (*νόσος γὰρ μᾶλλον ἔκπληξιν, ὑγίεια δὲ ἠρέμα συνοῦσα μᾶλλον ἂν σύνεσιν δοίη αὐτῆς*); It presides over our being as something which belongs to it, and is one with us (*προΐζει . . . γὰρ ἅτε οἰκεῖον καὶ ἑνοῦται*). Illness is alien and not our own (*ἀλλότριον καὶ οὐκ οἰκεῖον*) and therefore particularly obvious because it appears so very different from us (*διάδηλος τῷ σφόδρα ἕτερον ἡμῶν εἶναι δοκεῖν*). We have no consciousness of what is our own (*τὰ δὲ ημῶν καὶ ἡμεῖς ἀναίσθητοι*) . . .

There, then, when our knowledge is most perfectly conformed to *Noûs* we think we are ignorant (*ἀγνοεῖν δοκοῦμεν*) because we are waiting for the experience of sense-perception (*αἴσθησις*) which says it has not yet seen: and it certainly has not seen, and never will see things like these. It is sense-perception which disbelieves (*τὸ οὖν ἀπιστοῦν ἡ αἴσθησίς ἐστιν*) but it is some-one else who sees; and for him to disbelieve would be to disbelieve his own existence (*εἰ ἀπιστοῖ κἀκεῖνος, οὐδ' ἂν αὐτὸν πιστεύσειεν εἶναι*): for he cannot after all put himself outside and make himself visible so as to look at himself with his bodily eyes.

De Musica VI

9–10: And so, whatever corporeal things hurtle against or come into contact with this body (*ingeruntur aut obiciuntur*) . . . effect something in the body either opposed to or in consonance with its operation (*aut adversetur aut congruat*). Hence, when [the soul] withstands something opposed to it and only with difficulty forces the matter subjected to it into the pathways of its activity, it becomes more attentive to [those] actions because of the difficulty (*cum renititur adversanti et materiam . . . difficulter impingit, fit attentior ex difficultate*) . . . and this is named pain or trouble (*dolor, labor*) . . . The soul also occupies itself attentively with any sickly disturbance of the body (*Morbidam quoque perturbationem corporis attente agit*) . . . But sense . . . is an instrument for the soul . . . to the end of joining like things with like and repelling what is harmful (*similia similibus ut adjungat, repellatque quod noxium est*) . . . The soul acts quietly (*cum quiete*) if the things within [the body] are unified in health as if agreeing in a sort of domestic harmony (*si ea quae insunt in unitate valetudinis, quasi familiari quadam consensione cesserunt*). But when things affect the body with some "otherness" if I may use such a term (*ut ita dicam, alteritate*), [the soul] exerts its activity more attentively . . . By such actions it willingly brings together suitable things and with annoyance resists unsuitable ones (*congrua libenter associat, et moleste obsistit incongruis*).

Here an identity of doctrine is expressed in the same basic analogy, and vested in a constellation of corresponding terms: Ficinus' translation reproduces Augustine's *sanitas* and *morbus*, *quietior*, *familiare*, *tranquilla*, changing his *consensione* to the cognate *consensu*. Vivid sense-impressions leave "shocks" rather than clear knowledge. They go with a state of sickness—alien, unnatural, incongruous—rather than with the more natural, "familiar," congruous state of health. Their evidence, accordingly, is more deceptive on our real ontological condition than informative. Their clamorous claim on our attention both authors associate with disturbance, tension, "otherness," and Augustine feels obliged to add an apologetic *ut ita dicam* to the *alteritas* which he may well have found translating Plotinus' *ἀλλότριον*—a disrupted state contrasting with the companionate, tranquil "unification" proper to health—a tranquillity whose upper extreme is, in both authors, the soul's ability to abstract entirely from bodily concerns. Thus Augustine's reminder in *De Quantitate Animae* 70 that only those activities obtrude upon our attention that we exercise with greater difficulty. The truth of the matter *may* be—*potest esse*—that the soul is constantly engaged in all seven levels, even in the highest contemplative activity, its noblest portion never, in Plotinus' term, having "come down." For this reason, too, he has previously observed that the soul's reascent resembles nothing more than a *cessatio*, less a kind of knowing than a lack of it—*ἀγνοεῖν δοκοῦμεν*—a "diminution of consciousness." From this standpoint it becomes plainer why the Saint has felt obliged repeatedly to return to the subject of the soul's "immobility" in his early works. It was a corollary of the Plotinian teaching whereby the acme of the soul remains entirely at peace, tranquil and changeless in the empyrean. *Potest esse:* the Augustine of the *De Quantitate* abstains from affirmation, and the uncertainty does him credit. For Plotinus' doctrine ultimately implies the rejection of any need of "being saved." Salvation is already an accomplished fact, and the only thing the soul need do is grasp that fact by an effort of intellectual ascent whose function is to bring consciousness into line with what her true ontological status unalterably *is*. But such was Augustine's enthusiasm for the Neo-Platonic illumination of Milan—after which (*Conf* VII, 17) he could more easily doubt his own existence (*οὐδ' ἂν αὐτὸν πιστεύσειεν εἶναι*) than the reality of that Supernal Truth these books had told him of—that it took him some time to grasp the dangers implied in this personal, characteristic, and therefore eminently recognizable feature of Plotinus' teaching on the soul.

The Mechanism of the "Fall"

Fault and cosmic order identical

We come now to another example of Augustinian spiritual exegesis which, on the face of it, seems utterly inexplicable. Why does Augustine take such pains to insist on the expression in Genesis whereby God is said to "dismiss" (*dimittere*) the sinful soul, rather than "excluding" it from paradise?

The reason for that insistence is that another problematic in both Plotinus and Augustine is fundamentally the same; the soul's "falling" and its "being sent" are at bottom identical, with an identity rooted in a firm affirmation of universal cosmic order. The difficulty involved in this position Augustine poses squarely in the opening paragraph of the *De Ordine*. To say that providential order is universal seems, at first, tantamount to blaming God's action for all the evils in the world. How, for instance, can it be said that the evil actions of the "unwise" (*stultus*) are performed "in order"? This question he raises twice in the course of that early dialogue (II, 11–13 and 18–21). The difficulty he experiences in answering it arises from the fact that the underlying issue troubling him has been phrased in a way that seems to follow from participation theory, which implies that all actions of the participants ("the secondaries") ultimately reduce to the action of the "First" cause. What must be saved in his answer to the difficulty is each word of the proposition that *Deus agit omnia ordine*, "God does everything" (we paraphrase for emphasis) "and everything He does, He does in order." How is it to be understood that the sinner can commit sin, God not commit it, and still the exigencies of participation theory be conscientiously observed?

In the sections of the *De Ordine* referred to above (as well as in *Ord* II, 22–23) it is plain that Augustine can for the moment offer only the solution that the actions of the *stultus* (translate, "sinner") do not elude God's *logically subsequent* ordering activity. It is also plain that he keenly recognizes this is an escape from, rather than an answer to, the problem as he has all too brutally posed it. He takes refuge in both instances by pointing out the soul's need for an "order of studies" before it is fitted to gain insight into such questions. In the *De Libero Arbitrio* (cf. I, 4) he returns to this problem, eventually proposing his answer at the end of Book II in a definition of "sin" (II, 53) which substantially anticipates the description of "iniquity" lying at the core of the *Confessions* (VII, 22; cf. *Quant* 78)—the action of the soul in "turning away" from God the Highest to the "lower realities" it proudly desires to have for "its own." That action is essentially a negative contribution, a *nihil*.

But there is something positive about that action: it has, at very least, the positive effect of situating the soul in the lower world it has chosen for itself. And so, to this extent at least, the problem still clamors for a solution. The innermost key to that solution seems to have been suggested by *Ennead* IV, 3, and particularly from the two lengthy sections (IV, 3, 12–13) which Plotinus devotes to showing that identity of fault and universal cosmic necessity which is one of his most unshakeable convictions (cf. *Enn* IV, 8, 5 and III, 2, 12). That Augustine was familiar with this work is clear from the fact that in the *City of God* he cites, as Henry has shown (*Plotin*, p. 123) the precise section of *Ennead* IV, 3 that concerns us here. The *De Musica*, written at roughly the same time as the *De Genesi contra Manichaeos*, presents a remarkable parallel which shows Augustine's mind adopting Plotinus' cyclic view of history with a fidelity that is downright disturbing. The translation represents a combination of MacKenna and O'Brien.

Ennead IV, 3

12, 12–26: The cosmos possesses all that it needs to be self-sufficient and always will. The limits of its duration are determined by unchanging forms (*κατὰ λόγους ἀεὶ ἑστηκότας ἐν χρόνοις περαινόμενον*). At the end of a given time, it always returns to the same state in the measured alternation of its cyclic lives (*καὶ κατὰ χρόνους ἀεὶ εἰς τὸ αὐτὸ καθιστάμενα ἐν μέτροις βίων ὡρισμένων*). It leads things of this realm to be of one voice and one plan with the intelligible realm (*εἰς συμφωνίαν ἀγόμενα ταῦτα ἐκείνοις*). All is determined by subjection to one single form. All is thereby regulated, as well the descent as the ascent of souls and all things else. The proof of this lies in the accord that exists between souls and the cosmic order (*τὸ τῆς συμφωνίας τῶν ψυχῶν πρὸς τὴν τοῦδε τοῦ παντὸς τάξιν*): they are not dependent,

De Musica VI

29: Let us not be envious, then, of things inferior to ourselves, and let us . . . order ourselves (*nosque . . . ordinemus*) between those below us and those above, so that untroubled by lower, we take delight only in higher things. For delight (*delectatio*) is a kind of weight of the soul (*quasi pondus est animae*). Delight, therefore, orders the soul . . .

But what are higher things, but those where resides the highest, unchangeable, undisturbed, eternal equality? Where there is no time, because no changeability; whence the [epochs of] time are produced and ordered and changed, imitating eternity as they do when the turn of the heavens comes back to the same state, the heavenly bodies to the same place (*dum coeli conversio ad idem redit, et caelestia corpora ad idem revocat*), so that in months, years, centuries and all the other periods of stellar but, by their descent, they have put themselves in contact, and they stand henceforward in harmonious association with the cosmic circuit (συναπτουσῶν ἐν ταῖς καθόδοις ἑαυτὰς καὶ μίαν συμφωνίαν πρὸς τὴν περιφορὰν ποιουμένων), to the extent that their fortunes, their life experiences, their choosing and refusing, are announced by the patterns of the stars; from this concordance arises, as it were, one musical utterance (σημαίνεσθαι τοῖς τῶν ἄστρων σχήμασι καὶ οἷον μίαν τινὰ φωνὴν οὐκ ἐκμελῶς ἀφιέναι). The music, the harmony, by which all is described, is the best witness to this truth (καὶ τὸ μουσικῶς καὶ ἐναρμονίως μᾶλλον τοῦτο εἶναι ᾐνιγμένως).

revolutions (*caeterisque siderum orbibus*), the times obey the laws of equality, unity, and order (*legibus . . . ordinationis obtemperat*). So terrestrial things, subject to celestial, join their temporal circuits in numbered sequence to the poem of the universe (*Ita coelestibus terrena subjecta, orbes temporum suorum numerosa successione quasi carmini universitatis associant*).

30: Many of these things seem to us disordered and perturbed, because we have been knitted into their order in accordance with our merits (*quia eorum ordini pro nostris meritis assuti sumus*), not knowing the beauty that Divine Providence produces from us (*nescientes quid de nobis divina providentia pulchrum gerat*).

Starting with a recall of the soul's intermediate position in the "order" of reality (just as Plotinus does in the section preceding) Augustine goes on to sketch the fall as one which "binds" us to the order of temporal realities. The accent is characteristic of the *De Musica* which stresses the fall into time as much if not more than the fall into the body; but it reflects Plotinus' reminder that the souls "by their descent . . . have put themselves into contact, and they stand henceforth in harmonious association with the cosmic circuit," tied to it (see context) with "bonds" which Zeus the father periodically dissolves. Fall and return are both, therefore, the work of the cosmic order, of that providence which rules the periods of history (a cyclic conception which Augustine was later [*Civ* X, xxx] firmly to reject, and in explicit connection with this same text) after an eternal and unchangeable pattern so that from all that happens there arises one single "musical utterance," the *carmen universitatis*.

But in the section following (IV, 3, 13) Plotinus goes to some pains to show that the inalterable law does not draw its power "from without"; it is interior to the beings that execute it; its action is also theirs. How does it operate? "Each several entity is overruled to go, duly and in order, towards that place and Kind to which it characteristically tends, that is towards the image of its primal choice . . . to which its individual constitution inclines it; there is therefore no need of a sender . . . of its own motion it descends . . . as by a magician's power or by some mighty traction . . . neither under compulsion nor of freewill" but more by a kind of "leap of the nature as moves men to the instinctive desire of sexual union, or, in the case of some, to fine conduct." And Plotinus ends with another image, one which illumines both Augustine's *Delectatio . . . quasi pondus est animae*, and his curious exegesis of Genesis' *dimisit illum:*

Ennead IV, 3
13, 27–33: If the time comes, what [the universal cosmic law] wills to happen is brought about by the beings themselves in whom it is present; they accomplish it themselves because they bear it about and it is strong by its firm establishment in them; it *makes itself a sort of weight in them* and brings about a longing, a birth-pang of desire to come there where the law within them tells them to come (*οἷον βρίθοντα εἰς αυτοὺς καὶ προθυμίαν ἐμποιοῦντα καὶ ὠδῖνα ἐκεῖ ἐλθεῖν, οὗ ὁ ἐν αὐτοῖς ὢν οἷον ἐλθεῖν φθέγγεται*).

De Genesi contra Manichaeos II
34: The expression is a good one, [God] dismissed, and did not exclude [man from paradise] *dimisit, non exclusit*: so that it would be plain that [man] was driven by the very weight of his sins to a place which suited him (*ut ipso peccatorum suorum pondere tanquam in locum sibi congruum videretur urgeri*). This often happens to a bad man if, having started living among good men, he refuses to change for the better: he is expelled by the very weight of his evil habits (*pondere malae suae consuetudinis pellitur*) from such association with good men. They [for their part] do not "exclude" him [as though he were] reluctant [to leave]; they "dismiss" him, rather, as one who wishes to leave (*non excludunt reluctantem, sed dimittunt cupientem*).

Pondus meum amor meus: "my weight is my love." The celebrated phrase of *Confessions* XIII, 10 is not so different from the *De Musica*'s "Delight, the weight of the soul." Nor is it a *hapax*. At each of his life's turnings Augustine finds God has governed him by those "interior goads" which are none other than his own profoundest inclinations, those "weights" in the deep heart of that mystery, man. When we come to the Augustinian doctrine of freedom and grace that underlies his "conversion" account, we shall be led to ask how far he went in adopting the Plotinian problematic of freedom and cosmic law that is suggested here.

The nature of the "fault": pride, concupiscence, and "curiosity"

Law and fault are, therefore, one: another characteristic tension in Plotinus' teaching can be found in Augustine, and related persuasively to a precise text which we have every evidence he read. But what of the fault itself? Here another set of tensions greets us, for Plotinus' doctrine is not entirely easy here. The root fault Plotinus designates by the term *τόλμα*. The likelihood that a Latin, especially one interested in erecting a Plotinian understanding of the Biblical faith, would translate this with the term *superbia*, pride, has already been suggested by scholars of the question.[21]

But the identity of that primal fault is more complex: we have seen already that Augustine relates it to a *superbia* whereby the soul, "arrogating to itself what is not," chooses at the same time "to delight in its powers as though without God." And yet, in that very paragraph, he speaks of an "implication" in "earthly cupidities," in "bodily delights": are we to understand that the fault of *superbia* is identical with a species of *cupiditas*?

This tension too is found in Plotinus, whose *τόλμα* frequently contains a note of "excessive zeal" for the ordering of the sensible universe, not entirely unconnected with the kind of desire for sense-delights which the Orphic strain in the Platonic tradition, complicated by Plotinus' own semi-Gnostic leanings, finds uniformly reprehensible. Thus, in the early treatise on Beauty which so struck Augustine, he describes the soul's ugliness—"dissolute, unrighteous, teeming with all the lusts . . . thinking only of the perishable and the base . . . the friend of unclean pleasures" (*Enn* I, 6, 5). The terms only too faithfully echoed both Augustine's experience and the Manichaean revulsion toward the sexual reproduction which they held to be the chief of all sins. It is interesting that the Manichees traced that sin to the principle of concupiscence, *Hulê*, just as Plotinus traces it, both here and in his last word on the question, to the alien principle, matter (*Enn* I, 8). It is not, therefore, surprising that Augustine's first serious efforts to seek out a definition of sin start with the terms *libido* and *cupiditas* (*Lib* I, 8ff), and that his later efforts to make this emphasis rhyme with the more Christian *superbia*, found the ambiguity of Plotinus' *τόλμα* ready and waiting to help him. Even more relevant to the text

[21] See W. M. Green, "*Initium omnis peccati superbia.* Augustine on pride as the first sin," in *University of California Publications in Classical Philology*, 13: 407–431 (1949). Theiler, *Porphyrios*, p. 28 tries to show that the concept which he finds so important in both Augustine and Plotinus must *therefore* have been in Porphyry.

that concerns us here, is Plotinus' insistence that matter is the primal evil, that consequently the initiative for the fall of the soul comes from below, from that sensible universe which like an undisciplined "rabble of pleasure, desires and fears," sets up a howling for the soul's attentions (*Enn* VI, 4, 15). This may explain Augustine's curious insistence, not once but twice in the *De Genesi Contra Manichaeos* (II, 20, 39), that the only path temptation can take to the virile *ratio* is the lower, animal-"feminine" principle in each of us.

There is, however, actually a triad of sins that dominates Augustine's moral thinking from the *De Genesi* onwards. Theiler has underlined the important role played in the *De Vera Religione* by what at first sight appears to be the "triple concupiscence" of St. John's first Epistle, and he has labored to show that it reproduces a Neo-Platonic moral triad that "must have been" in Porphyry (*Porphyrios*, pp. 36ff). *Concupiscentia*, *curiositas* and *superbia* are, assuredly, terms that would seem to derive from the Johannine "concupiscence of the flesh, concupiscence of the eyes, and pride of life" (*ambitio saeculi*) to which Augustine later on explicitly relates them (*Mus* VI, 44).

But the difficulty here is explaining the explanation. Why in the world should Augustine have chosen, as his constant set of moral categories, a triad of sins to which nothing in the ecclesiastical tradition seems to have accorded a similar importance? What we wish to suggest as an explanation is this: Theiler is correct in thinking that Augustine found the Johannine triad in more or less reasonable accord with an appealing Neo-Platonic triad, but the Neo-Platonist in question was, after all, most probably Plotinus. The possible correlates for Augustine's *superbia* and *concupiscentia* we have already suggested. The key facet of the question, consequently, is the origin of the *curiositas* notion.

Having supposed that this final category was taken bodily from Porphyry, where it was presumably directed against the imagination and its works, Theiler must suppose a constancy in Augustine's use of it, which precludes the tentative work of adaptation that in point of fact characterizes his initial introduction of the category into his writings. Theiler's mistake, if mistake there be, is partly accounted for by the fact that he starts his investigation of Augustine with the relatively systematized *De Vera Religione*, then somewhat blandly assures his readers that the earlier works present *ein ähnliches Bild* (*Porphyrios*, p. 57). Partly, too, his confidence reposes on the use of the triad in the second book of the *De Libero Arbitrio*, which he mistakenly assumes is prior to the *De*

Genesi Contra Manichaeos,[22] when it is, in fact, subsequent to it, and profits accordingly from the initial effort of systematization which we are about to observe.

The first occurrence of the triple concupiscence in Augustine's writings is found, unless we are seriously mistaken, in the finale of the first book *De Genesi Contra Manichaeos* (I, 40). But its very firmness there suggests that it may have been inserted after the second book was completed, to lend the entire work a certain unity of design. For its appearance in the course of the second book is nowhere near so firm.

In the course of his exegetical task Augustine is led to comment on the punishment imposed on the serpent. The Biblical text he is using presents a triadic structure which has been eliminated from our modern translations, and he reads God's words as: *Pectore et ventre repes, et terram manducabis*, "You shall crawl on breast and belly, and eat earth" (II, 26).

His taste for parallelism leads him to see in the condemnation of the serpent a reference to the same sins as provoked the fall of the soul: the *pectus* means pride, *superbia*; the *venter* refers to "fleshly desire" (*desiderium carnale*). Alas, what is to be made of the *terram manducabis*? Augustine hesitates. This, he suggests at first, could refer once again to earthly "cupidities." But the solution does not satisfy: it involves duplicating the symbolic force of the *venter*. Only then does the happy idea seem to occur to him that this third member arms him with a neat sally against the materialism and sensism of his Manichaean adversaries. He proposes that "surely a third kind of temptation is figured by these words, namely, curiosity (*curiositas*). For he who 'eats earth' penetrates into [matters] which, though deep and darksome, are nevertheless both temporal and earthly: *temporalia atque terrena*" (II, 27).

Examining its next occurrence, one is at first tempted to grant Theiler that the "curiosity" notion might originally have been directed against imagination and imaged thinking; it may reflect a Porphyrian polemic against the *phantasia*. But Theiler's chief piece of evidence that there existed such a Porphyrian emphasis is the fact that "curiosity" is found in that connection in Augustine's work, something which in its turn could easily be explained by the influence of *Ennead* VI, 4–5 on omnipresence. But there is more. In the case before us, as in so many instances, the exigencies of

[22] See Gustave Bardy, *Les Révisions*, *BA* 12 (1950), pp. 567–568. He dates *Gen Man* in 389 and Books II–III of *Lib* between 391 and 395, the work having been completed closer to 395. I cannot share Du Roy's confidence (*L'Intelligence de la Foi*, p. 344, n. 1) that this triad is already consciously employed in *Mor* I, 37–38.

controversy must be taken into account. Augustine is hardly bashful in making adaptations when they serve an apologetic cause. Once arrived at the *prophetica explanatio* of this same punishment, all his hesitation has left him. The triad is directed squarely against what he conceives to be the major errors of the Manichees. It is this polemic reference that has molded the "triple concupiscence" into final shape.

For [the devil] deceives only the proud (*superbos*), who arrogate to themselves what they are not (*quod non sunt*) and quickly come to believe that what belongs to the supreme God and to the human soul are one and the same (*una eademque sit*); or, those entangled in carnal desires (*desideriis carnalibus implicatos*), who love to hear that whatever lascivious actions they perform are not their doing, but that of the "race of darkness"; or, the "curious" (*curiosos*), who savor earthly things, and search into spiritual matters with earthly eyes (*spiritalia terreno oculo inquirunt*) (II, 40).

To "search into spiritual matters with earthly eyes": we are back with what *Ennead* VI, 4–5 had convinced him was the main defect in the Manichees' and in his own former intellectual comportment. But again, it took time for "curiosity" to assume this meaning. The likelihood is, therefore, that Augustine did not find this triad already neatly packaged for him in Porphyry. And yet, the riddle concerning the origin of this *curiositas* notion is still not completely resolved. I suggest that Augustine found a corresponding term in the Plotinian treatise on Time and Eternity, *Ennead* III, 7. In the *De Musica*, he briefly tips his hand and cues us in this direction.

Guitton has well characterized the preoccupation of the *De Musica* with the title, "Le Temps Poétique,"[23] for Augustine seems to have done little but transpose Plotinus' considerations on temporal measures, intervals, and their relativity into a series of metrical applications. All creative activity, in fact, he there links to the soul's "general love of action" (*amor generalis actionis*) which urges her to create a "mendacious" array of numbers in imitation of the immobile perfection of the eternal world. In all this, the

[23] *Temps et l'Eternité*, pp. 102–130. I have suggested elsewhere that study of the Eleventh Book of the *Confessions* confirms the view that Augustine's discussion of eternity and time there follows quite faithfully the pattern of Plotinus' own treatise, *Enn* III, 7. See my "Plotinian Fall," n. 117 and "Riddle of Augustine's *Confessions*," pp. 355–358 (both articles cited in Preface, n. 1, above). In a fuller analysis of the *Confessions*, soon forthcoming, I will take up the question in greater detail.

context of *Ennead* III, 7 is faithfully reflected; but as if to clear up any remaining doubts, Augustine gives an etymological definition of *curiositas* wherein its Plotinian origin becomes manifest.

That definition, however, is rooted in a context that speaks of the fall of the soul. What possible connection could there be here? Plotinus describes the process of the fall in *Ennead* IV, 8, 4 as beginning with the stage at which the souls "come down from the universal, become partial and self-centered (ἑαυτῶν); in a weary desire of standing apart they find their way, each to a place of its very own (ἑαυτῶν) . . . Intent upon the fragment, severed from the whole, [the soul now] administers the particular . . . is caught into contact . . . and tends to the outer to which it has become present, and into whose inner depths it sinks far." In all this, the term τόλμα is never explicitly mentioned. But as Bréhier has alertly remarked in his *Notice* to *Ennead* V, 1, the description of the "fall" presented there (and which we know Augustine read) is in the main a résumé based on *Ennead* IV, 8, in which the term τόλμα is expressly related to the description of the fall presented in the earlier treatise. But now Plotinus adds another note as well. He mentions that the fall plunges the soul into a sphere of "genesis," of time and becoming. On that connection Augustine has seized, studied the description of the origin of time in *Ennead* III, 7, and found there a potent image of the soul's fall. Struck, finally, by its resemblance to a Biblical image of *superbia*, he has evolved a description of the fall from its contemplative paradise in terms of this entire array of connected elements. The translation of Plotinus (MacKenna's generously emended) strives to preserve the literal sense of the original.

Ennead V, 1	*De Genesi contra Manichaeos* II
1, 1–8: How is it then that the souls forget the divinity that begot them so that—divine in nature, divine by origin—they know neither divinity nor self? The source (or beginning: ἀρχὴ) of the evil that has befallen them is self-will, becoming (Ἀρχὴ μὲν οὖν αὐταῖς τοῦ κακοῦ ἡ τόλμα καὶ ἡ γένεσις), the primal differentiation, and the desire to be their own (or belong to themselves: τὸ βουληθῆναι δὲ ἑαυτῶν εἶναι). Once having tasted the	22: From these words we see that sin was brought on through pride (*superbia*) . . . such that they refused to be under God (*sub Deo*) but [preferred] to be in their own power without the Lord (*in sua potestate potius sine Domino*) . . . as though God were jealous lest they rule themselves (*ne se ipsi regerent*) . . . Thus they were persuaded, therefore, to love their own power to excess (*ut suam potestatem nimis amarent*), and since they wished to be God's equals, they

pleasures of power over themselves, they use their self-propulsion (τῷ δὴ αὐτεξουσίῳ ἐπειδήπερ ἐφάνησαν ἡσθεῖσαι, πολλῷ τῷ κινεῖσθαι παρ' αὐτῶν κεχρημέναι) to go in a direction that leads away from their origin. And when they have gone a great distance (πλείστην ἀπόστασιν πεποιημέναι), they even forget that they came from it.

Ennead III, 7

11, 12–29: Before, when [the soul] had not yet in fact produced this "before" or felt the need of what comes after, it was at rest with it in real being; it was not yet in time, but itself, too, kept quiet in the reality [of *Noûs*] (ἡσυχίαν ἦγε). But since there was a restlessly active nature which wanted to control itself and be its own (φύσεως δὲ πολυπράγμονος καὶ ἄρχειν αὐτῆς βουλομένης καὶ εἶναι αὐτῆς), and chose to seek for more than its present state, this moved, and time moved with it. And so, always moving on to what comes after and is not the same, but one thing after another, we made a long stretch of our journey and constructed time as an image of eternity (αἰῶνος εἰκόνα τὸν χρόνον εἰργάσμεθα).

For because the soul had an unquiet power, which wanted to keep on transferring what it saw There to somewhere else ('Επεὶ γὰρ ψυχῆς ἦν τίς δύναμις οὐχ ἥσυχος, τὸ δ'ἐκεῖ ὁρώμενον ἀεὶ μεταφέρειν εἰς ἄλλο βουλομένης), it did not want the whole (πᾶν) to be present to it all together; and as from a quiet seed the logos, unfolding itself to largeness, as it thinks (ὥσπερ δ'ἐκ σπέρματος put to bad use that mid-rank character (*medietas*) whereby subject to God, they held bodies in subjection to themselves . . .

24: Who is it "hides himself from the sight of God" but he, who, having deserted God, begins to love what is his own (*qui deserto Deo ipso, incipit amare quod suum est*)? . . . The one who speaks lies speaks "of his own" (*de suo loquitur* (John 9:44) . . . Whoever, therefore, is turned away (*aversus*) from that [divine] Truth, and turned toward himself (*ad seipsum conversus*), so that he rejoices (*exsultat*) not in the God Who rules and illumines, but rather in his own movements as though they were free (*de suis motibus quasi liberis*), is darkened over with lying . . . Hence, having turned away [from God] and turned toward himself (*aversus et ad seipsum conversus*) . . . he saw his nakedness, and was displeased at having nothing of his own (*ex eo quod non habebat aliquid proprium*; *scil.*, the "coverings of mendacity" [*coopertimenta mendacii*] which symbolize the corruptible body).

6: When, however, the soul was watered by that fountain [of divine light and truth] it had not yet spewed forth its insides through pride (*nondum per superbiam projecerat intima sua*). For the beginning of man's pride is the apostasy (*apostatare*) from God. Swelling outwards through pride (*in exteriora per superbiam tumescens*), he ceased being watered by this interior fountain—a thought well-expressed in those prophetic words: "Why does earth and ashes pride itself? For in its lifetime it has spewed forth its insides ἡσύχου ἐξελίττων αὐτὸν ὁ λόγος διέξοδον εἰς πολύ, ὡς οἴεται, ποιεῖ), but does away with the largeness by division, and, instead of keeping its unity in itself, squanders it outside itself and so goes forward to a weaker greatness (ἀνθ' ἑνὸς ἐν αὐτῷ οὐκ ἐν αὐτῷ τὸ ἓν δαπανῶν εἰς μῆκος ἀσθενέστερον πρόεισιν); in the same way the soul, making the world of sense in imitation of that other world (κόσμον ποιοῦσα αἰσθητὸν, μιμήσει ἐκείνου), moved with motion which was not that which exists there, but like it, and intending to be an image of it (εἰκόνα), first of all put itself in time.

(*Quid superbit terra et cinis? Quoniam in vita sua projecit intima sua*)" (Ecclus. 10: 9–14).

De Musica VI

39: The love of operating on bodies turns [the soul] away [from contemplation of eternal realities] and makes it restless (*Avertit amor de corporibus operandi et inquietam facit*) . . . Love . . . of empty knowledge (*amor vanissimae cognitionis*) also turns [the soul] away (*avertit*) . . . and this knowledge it pursues in terms of those sensual numbers in which are found certain rules, as it were, which rejoice in imitating art (*regulae quaedam artis imitatione gaudentes*): thence curiosity (*curiositas*) is born, enemy—as the term "care" indicates (*ipso curae nomine*)—of peace. 40: But the general love of action which turns the soul away from God, proceeds from pride (*a superbia proficiscitur*), the vice whereby the soul preferred to imitate God rather than serve Him (*anima maluit Deum imitari quam servire*). Rightly, then, is it written in Holy Scripture: "The beginning of man's pride is the apostasy (*apostatare*) from God"; and, "The beginning of all sin is pride (*superbia*)." What pride is could not have been shown better than where it is said: "Why does earth and ashes pride itself? For in its lifetime it has spewed forth its insides" (Ecclus. 10: 9–14).

If we are willing to concede Augustine no more than a schoolboy's power to adapt timidly and unimaginatively his Plotinian sources, the work of synthesis we are claiming here is, of course, incomprehensible. Augustine was, however, no mere schoolboy. He was a highly talented thinker and had at this point been engaged for about five years in the demanding task of erecting this Plotinian "understanding" of the faith. His close study of Plotinus—one in which verbal correspondences played a frequently exaggerated role, since he was by profession a *grammaticus* and *rhetor*—has resulted in insights that permit him to read one treatise in the light of others, juxtapose, combine, superpose, even upon occasion fuse elements from one with analogous elements from others. Thus the pivotal idea of the first text here cited is the *medietas* notion from *Ennead* IV, 8, with its subordination implications. And yet, the love of its own power (*potestas:* cf. αὐτεξουσίῳ) which tempts the soul to insubordination, is taken from *Ennead* V, 1, 1, where the connection with τόλμα—the "beginning of evils" for the soul—gives it an almost Christian ring. This connection to *Ennead* V, 1 is further confirmed by the soul's "exultation in its own free movement" found in the second text, reproducing almost verbally the αὐτεξουσίῳ . . . ἐφάνησαν ἡσθεῖσαι . . . κινεῖσθαι παρ' αὐτῶν of *Ennead* V, 1, 1. Instead, however, of the flight theme, "running away," Augustine here prefers to think in terms of "apostasy" (*apostatare:* cf. Plotinus' suggestive ἀπόστασις) and of the "desertion" which resonates neatly with the *aversio-conversio* couple that so impressed him in *Ennead* VI, 4–5. It was, moreover, that same treatise on Omnipresence that reinforced the attraction of the *commune-proprium* dialectic which is here represented by the terms *proprium*, *amare quod suum est*, and their analogues. It is clear from the context that Augustine means this *aliquid proprium* to stand for the animal skins that symbolize the corruptible body conferred on the soul after the fall. Having lost the original transparency of the "heavenly body" the soul is plunged into the realm of *mendacium*, "untruth," and that for two reasons: first, because the opacity of the corruptible body allows for simulation and concealment of private thoughts, and hence the deceptions of hypocrisy; but secondly, and more fundamentally, because the entire corporeal world is, for Augustine (*Sol* II, 9ff) and for the Neo-Platonist, a "lying image" which the soul, fallen into time and action, fabricates in "imitation" of the superior, intelligible world. Among other things involved in the soul's primal sin, however, is this desire to have a body, *aliquid proprium*, something *suum*—something it can independently control, and at the same time "delight" in controlling. Pride? or bodily "concupiscence"? The ambivalence of Plotinus' τόλμα seems, for the moment, to gloss over the difficulty.

The play on interior versus exterior is common both to Plotinus and to St. Paul, making it a choice item for the type of concordism to which Augustine is committed. Its value here is governed mainly by the background of *Ennead* III, 7 and notably by the image of the soul as a seed, desirous of ruling itself (*se ipsi regerent: ἄρχειν αὐτῆς βουλομένης*) and uncoiling its insides out to a "weaker greatness," an image which Augustine has found evocative of that other, present in Ecclesiasticus, whereby the proud man *projecit intima sua*. Here, moreover, the process on both sides is one of abandoning a spiritual unity in itself to deploy that unity in an outgoing search of the material non-self, a close analogy of Plotinus' assurance in *Ennead* VI, 5, 12 that the "alien" which cloaks us from without is really unconnected with our authentic self, our true identity. The way of return to primal unity consists accordingly in abandoning that non-self which is non-being, the likely source of the "abundant poverty" (*egestas copiosa*) whose paradoxical structure recalls Plotinus' "weaker greatness" here: *εἰς μῆκος ἀσθενέστερον*. The soul's sin, therefore, involves a loss of spiritual unity in both authors, a "swelling outwards" into the spatialized world of body, a *distentio animi* into the dispersion of time.

Once again, the thought-movement of the text from *Ennead* III, 7 is framed by the notions of the soul's "imitative" action, creative of an image of eternity—a reminder that brings us to the *De Musica* text, where the same preoccupation with "imitation" is evident. In both authors, the fall from eternity to time is a fall from the superior occupation of immobile contemplation to the essentially degraded sphere of action. The root of the fall Plotinus places in the soul's desire to be "its own" (*βουλομένης καὶ εἶναι αὐτῆς*), and, given the *βουληθῆναι δὲ ἑαυτῶν εἶναι* of *Ennead* V, 1, 1, Augustine is entitled to supply here the *τόλμα* which he found in a perfectly identical connection there. Hence, the *amor generalis actionis*, the *amor de corporibus agendi* which reflects Plotinus' concern in *Ennead* III, 7, the Saint roots quite legitimately in *superbia*.

But Plotinus' diagnosis goes further. There was in the soul, he tells us, a "restless" principle. Or should that term be translated as "curious"? *Πολυπράγμων*: the term is, in fact, deliciously ambiguous, meaning both "restless" (thus Ficinus' translation, *inquieta*) and "curious" (hence Bréhier's, *curieuse*). It is revealing that both poles of the ambiguity are preserved in Augustine's text: the love of action on bodies makes the soul *inquieta* and at the same time gives rise to *curiositas, ab ipso curae nomine*, and sends her out on the quest for *vana cognitio*. The text then goes on to portray *superbia* by citation of the very same text we have seen in *De Genesi* II, 6, the *projecit intima sua* of Ecclesiasticus. There is, therefore, a connection between the *De Genesi* II, 6 text and *De Musica* VI, 40. The later text actually illuminates the genesis of the former, by bringing together the two key images that collide there: Plotinus' ἐκ σπέρματος . . . ἐξελίττων αὐτὸν and the Biblical *projecit intima sua*. Finally, the origin of Augustine's *curiositas* is also laid bare. Its counterpart is none other than Plotinus' ambiguous πολυπράγμων. Far from finding it ready-made in Porphyry, the Saint has gone to considerable pains to elaborate that concept, and in his elaboration of it numerous disparate elements have entered, chief among them being Plotinus, the Bible, and his anti-Manichaean polemic.

Summary

We began with Gilson's perceptive reminder that if Augustine holds a fall of the soul, his theory must be fraught with incoherence. The body must simultaneously be a place of punishment, and, as a creature of God, beautiful in its own right. The same tension we found characteristic of Plotinus' view of the matter, a view which showed other important strains as well. The μέση τάξις explanation allowing for a fall of the soul through its own fault is immediately followed by a reminder of the good that the soul can draw from its fallen experience, and the same pattern is reproduced in Augustine. The properties of the fallen state, the *vita mortalis*, are perfectly Plotinian as well, including a third peculiarity of Plotinus' theory, to wit, the suggestion that the highest portion of the soul never "comes down," remains immobile in contemplative bliss. To an objection drawn from experience, both authors reply in strikingly similar terms, and in function of the same basic theory whereby consciousness diminishes as the soul reascends.

Why does Plotinus pass from his description of the soul's fault to a reminder of the good it can draw from the fallen experience? The reason is that the soul's spontaneous choice is ultimately identical with the operation of the Logos, the principle of cosmic order, and he is anxious to "justify" that order as far as possible. The identity between choice and cosmic law, we noted, is something he strains to prove, eventually coming round to an image. His desire, "weighing on" the soul, we suggested, is the counterpart of Augustine's celebrated *pondus*: the soul is not "excluded," it is "dismissed" from paradise; the soul's choice and the working of Divine Law exactly coincide.

Nor have we exhausted the list of tensions in Plotinus' theory. There is a final one, regarding the fault that results in the fall. The τόλμα concept temporarily attenuates the difficulty of choosing between "pride" and "fleshly concupiscence," but the situation again becomes confused if we take into account the third member of Augustine's moral triad, *curiositas*. Tracing the genesis of this triad in his work, we are led to Plotinus' ambiguous πολυπράγμων, its ambiguity entirely preserved in the Saint's explanation of *curiositas* in a text where its origin becomes manifestly Plotinian after all.

Do the parallels we have presented actually prove a direct Plotinian source for each of these items in Augustine? The issue may remain secondary, but it has its importance nonetheless. It seems beyond question that Augustine drew these ideas from a faithful exponent of the Plotinian doctrine in all its complexity. That Porphyry may have found some of the tensions in that theory indigestible, and modified his master's teaching to eliminate some of them, is a possibility to be envisaged. But the tendency in recent scholarship to expand once more the circle of Plotinian treatises the Saint probably read tilts the scales even further in Plotinus' favor. I have made no effort to hide my own conviction that Augustine read each of the treatises I have used in this explanation of his teaching on the soul, and more. But whether one choose Plotinus, Porphyry, or both, the service they render must be the same: to sharpen our reading of Augustine's text, and help us, when we read it, to believe our eyes. The main contention of this chapter is exactly this: during the years A.D. 389–391, Augustine said, and meant to say, that we were "fallen souls."

Are we then to conclude that Augustine came to consider the soul in these full-blown Plotinian terms only after his return from Cassiciacum? For any clear estimate of his intellectual development, for any trustworthy evaluation of the soundness of his early views, the answer to that question is imperative.

Once again, hindsight may come to our aid. Having surveyed his later, firmly articulated view of the soul, having situated with some confidence the treatises from which it was drawn, we are equipped with a set of clearly focused questions for rereading the Dialogues wherein this view may, after all, be undergoing groping formulation.

7 AUGUSTINE'S THEORY OF MAN AT CASSICIACUM

Centuries of tradition, forming around thought and language of a thinker like Augustine can blind us to the need of taking an occasional fresh look at that thought and language. Spiritual writers since his time have spoken tirelessly of the "soul" and its salvation; by effect of habit, we automatically correct that language and understand them to be speaking of "man." And well we may, for this, more often than not, is undoubtedly what they mean. It is not easy to recapture that pristine surprise which comes from realizing that the Augustine of the period we are studying speaks constantly, deliberately, of the "soul," that his theory is far less an "anthropology" than a theory of the soul.

Nor is this merely a way of speaking, a peculiarity of language which, if taken at face value, would be pressed too far. Such assumptions are, again, anachronistic. As a Manichee, and as a Neo-Platonist, Augustine would quite naturally speak of man as fallen soul, and mean each word of it quite literally. And the same, to judge from any number of expressions in his sermons, might conceivably be true of Ambrose.

These remarks are only intended to reopen a question that the habit of centuries would tempt us to consider closed. Refusal to take Augustine's language literally here may be merely inherited prejudice; if it is possible that he meant exactly what he said, then such prejudice must first be discarded, or at least suspended, before his meaning can become clear.

Assume, then, that we can examine Augustine's writings afresh, without the dusty overlay of centuries. Assume, too, that when the terms he uses suggest that man is literally a fallen "soul," he quite possibly meant just that—possibly, at least that. But, read in the light of Plotinus' theory, do the Dialogues of Cassiciacum tell us that is what he *de facto* intended us to understand?

THE REAL "SELF"

Beginning his treatise on "The Immortality of the Soul," Plotinus makes a characteristic observation. It is indispensable, he says, when discussing the question of immortality, to decide first whether the body "is really a part of us." For, if it be, rather, "an instrument of ours . . . put at our service for a certain time," then "the sovran principle, the authentic man, will be as Form to this Matter, or as agent to this instrument, and thus, whatever that relation be, the Soul is the man" (*Enn* IV, 7, 1).

The view is not peculiar to this treatise, but given the confidence we can have that Augustine read this work early in his studies, it is significant that the observation occurs there. The force of such remarks was by no means lost on him. For him, too, "the Soul is the man," the authentic "I"—and the idea appears from Cassiciacum onward.

In the first words we have from his pen, Augustine prays that God may "give back" Romanianus "to himself" (*te tibi reddat: Acad* I, 1), and assures him that his own philosophic activity at Cassiciacum has permitted him to "return to myself" (II, 4), and that his platonic readings were what stimulated him to "return entirely to myself" (II, 5). The underlying notion is one that makes the "I" essentially soul. The composite of body and soul becomes accordingly an uneasy amalgam, its semi-accidental unity being explained by a "fall" of soul into body, a fall that (at this point in Augustine's career) seems to require that the soul "return" to a pre-embodied state, "unencumbered" even by the "heavenly body" spoken of later in *De Genesi*. This, Augustine claims, is the truth enveloped in the definition[1] "ancient philosophers" have given of man.

[1] It has frequently been noted that Augustine's several early "definitions" of "man" (cf. *Quant* 21 and 47; *Mor* I, 6 and 52) regularly imply the slack Platonic union of a soul "using" a body as its instrument. (See Frederick Copleston's *History of Philosophy*,

Man is an animal, rational and mortal . . . By those distinguishing notes [rational and mortal], man, I believe, was to be admonished both whither he is to return (*quo redeundum*) and what he ought to flee, for, just as the soul's forward movement (*progressus*) has fallen down to the things that are mortal (*usque ad mortalia lapsus est*), so ought its return be to reason. By the one term, rational, man is distinguished from brute animals; by the other term, mortal, he is distinguished from God; . . . unless it turns aside from the mortal element, it [the soul] will not be divine: *divina non erit* (*Ord* II, 31).

Relation to the Body

The text has implications which, we know, frightened Augustine after a while. The soul's identity with reason seems to suggest its identity with the third divine hypostasis. But one corollary of this view Augustine draws with firm clarity: that "if reason is immortal, and if I . . . am reason, then that by which I am called mortal is not mine" (*Ord* II, 50). The body, then, is something alien to our true identity. But for such a view of body it is not necessary to hold the soul is identical with "reason." Even "if the soul is not the same as reason, and I nevertheless use reason, and if through reason I am superior, then we ought to take flight from the lesser good [the bodily] to the greater, from the mortal to the immortal" (*Ord* II, 50).

This view of man as fallen soul is what warrants Augustine's frequently stiff language of the body: prisonhouse, filth, stain, birdlime, even excrement are terms that come to his pen in this connection.

Beginning and Ceasing to Be "Man"

This same view illuminates the suggestion that Licentius makes—with no expression of disapproval from his master—that the searcher after truth "is not always a man" but at some time "begins to be a man": *non semper homo est . . . incipit esse homo.*

II (Westminster, Md., 1950), p. 78; more recently, R. A. Markus' chapters on Augustine in the *Cambridge History*, esp. pp. 355–357). It then frequently depends on the commentator's preoccupations whether he stresses the slackness (as Copleston does) or the union (as Markus is rather more inclined to do). My own tendency, obviously, is to stress the former aspect. Augustine wishes us to realize that "we" are really "souls," and that the "fall" accounts for the soul's being involved in the relationship it *now* experiences with body. This view implies that when he defines "man" he is defining a post-lapsary composite which careful reflection would refuse to identify with "us." For the complex, but quite real relationship the soul in the unfallen state enjoys with the bodily and sensible universe, see above, Chap. VI. This crucial attenuation of Plotinus' dualism does not yet figure importantly in the writings at Cassiciacum. It may have been the problem of the body's resurrection—first mentioned in *Quant* 76—which alerted Augustine to it, bringing it to the surface in the *De Genesi contra Manichaeos.*

Licentius here is defending his interpretation of Academic doctrine—that only "God, or perhaps the soul of man once it has abandoned the body" (*Acad* I, 9) can know the truth. This Augustine later interprets as implying that the soul "unencumbered" attains to wisdom only "after this life, that is, when you have ceased to be a man" (*Acad* III, 20). The same view also underlies the repeated praise of "temperance"; the stress on the soul's "purification" from the body, sense, and sensual desires; the insistence that in loving friends and knowing them it is the soul that must be known and loved (*Sol* I, 7); such curious self-corrections as warn us that the Divine Spouse "seeks other men—or, to speak with greater precision, other souls" (*Ord* I, 24); and the ignorance Augustine confesses on the "usefulness" of the "mortal body" which he "moves and bears" (*Sol* I, 6).

The *Soliloquies* represent him "seeking himself" as usual (I, 1), a real self shorn of all that is "alien" to it (*aliena nostra:* I, 3). Again, the reference, presumably, is to the body.

"Nothing" and Creation

But, it may be asked, how can Augustine take so stern an attitude toward matter and the body if he is a Christian and believes that the visible world was created from nothing by an all-good God? Augustine's answer seems to lie in a concept of "nothing" (*nihil*) uncomfortably close to the Neo-Platonic non-being (*mê on*): *nihil* he defines as "all that flows, that is dissolved, that melts and steadily perishes" (*Vita* 8). The term for "worthlessness" (*nequitia*) he takes pains to derive from *necquicquam*, "not-anything," explicitly connects it with non-being (*non esse*), as well as with "want" (*egestas*), and reminds his hearers that the latter signifies "a sort of sterility or lack" (*Vita* 30). He is groping; his thought is hardly fixed. It is, he warns his students darkly toward the end of the *De Ordine* (II, 44), not a simple matter to understand what "nothing" really means. He raises the possibility that "nothing" may be distinguished from that "unformed matter" which Plotinus holds eternally exists and is the "source of all evils" (*Enn* I, 8), but he does not pronounce on the question, yet.[2]

Profit from the Fall

This theory of the soul as fallen and aching for "return" is what lends existential urgency to Augustine's quarrel with the Academics. He is "concerned with life, with morality, with

[2] For more on this issue of creation from "nothing," see Chap. X, n. 8, below.

the spirit," with "that spirit which hopes to overcome the antagonism of every kind of illusion, and possessing itself of truth, to return in triumph over the passions to that region, so to speak, from which it sprung (*quasi in regionem suae originis rediens*), and . . . to reign, safer in its return to heaven" (*Acad* II, 22).

"Safer in its return"—*securior rediturus in coelum*—up to this point Augustine's Cassiciacum theory of the soul's fall and return could have been drawn from a number of sources in the ancient world. But here we come close to a personal hallmark of the Plotinian view: the soul will profit from its experiences in the fallen state, and, as Augustine puts it in another text, return to God "with added vigor" (*in eum firmior redeas: Ord* I, 20), more stable now in possession of the good that it had left.

OTHER FEATURES OF PLOTINIAN FALL

Not All Equally Fallen

But there are other indices at Cassiciacum of this specifically Plotinian view. First, Augustine's conviction, like Plotinus', is that not all souls are equally fallen; consequently, "return" is not so easy for some as for others. Speaking of the soul in the familiar Odyssey image, he offers the suggestion that

> there are apparently three classes of seafarers, so to speak, whom philosophy is able to embrace. The first is made up of those who . . . go only a little distance away . . . Others . . . have chosen to proceed out into the middle of the sea and venture to journey far from their homeland, which they then often forget . . . Between these two is a third class, consisting of those who . . . still perceive some familiar signs and remember, even amid the waves, the great sweetness of home (*Vita* 2).

In another image, that of the eye beholding the Sun of Truth, he makes the same point. Here, however, he speaks of two classes only.

> There is more than one way to wisdom. In fact, each one grasps that unique and most true good according to his health and endurance . . . There are some eyes so healthy and vigorous that they can fearlessly turn toward the sun as soon as they are opened . . . Others, however, are dazzled by the very luster they so ardently desire to behold . . . These are, therefore, first to be trained . . . their love is to be restricted and nourished (*Sol* I, 23).

He echoes this view when warning his students that although it is the common lot of all the foolish to "have their minds immersed in darkness," nonetheless "it is not in one and the same way that wisdom extends a helping hand to the sunken. There are some—believe me—who are called to rise high; others are let fall into the depths" (*Ord* I, 29).

It is not "granted to us to imagine or know how deep we had sunk, or how far we have risen" (*Sol* I, 25), Reason warns him. Here we enter into an atmosphere of mystery, the mystery of that Providence which, perhaps, accounts for some being called to "rise high [while] others are let fall into the depths."

The Mechanism of Fall

Choice and cosmic law

Indeed, it raises the entire question of why we are fallen in the first place, a point on which, O'Meara has shown, Augustine is frankly perplexed. Plotinus, we have seen, tries manfully to explain our state in terms of a cosmic law that integrates our own faulty "choice." Augustine's earliest reactions to this are, as one would expect, both puzzling and puzzled. On the causes of our fallen state, he writes to Mallius Theodorus that: "God or nature or necessity or our own will, or a combination of some or all of these, would have us founder in this world heedlessly and by chance as in a stormy sea—the matter is indeed not clear" (*Vita* 1).

A like perplexity runs through his speculation on the need of providential misfortunes to stimulate our "return": "But the fact is that, whether because we have deserved it, or because this is necessary by nature, the divine spirit that is united to our mortal bodies can never reach the harbor of wisdom . . . unless fortune herself, good or bad—but only seeming so—bring it thither" (*Acad* I, 1).

The prayer in the *Soliloquies*, however, shows the convert's basic willingness already to accept Plotinus' identification of choice with, or at least its integration into, cosmic law. In a passage presaging the *De Musica*'s image of the *carmen universitatis*, he speaks of God's "laws by which the poles revolve, the stars follow their courses," those laws which rule the "orders and recurrences of seasons," the "cycles . . . and the great eras of time." "O God," he prays,

> by whose ever-enduring laws the varying movement of movable things is not suffered to be disturbed and is always restored to a relative stability by the controls of the encompassing ages.

O God, by whose laws the choice of the soul is free, and rewards to the good and chastisements to the wicked are meted out in accord with inexorable and universal destiny (*Sol* I, 4).

Fault and its nature

If there was fault, however, what can be its nature? Here again Augustine's later theory is illuminating, though he has not yet brought Plotinus' varied suggestions into line with the help of that sin-triad referred to in St. John's Epistle. We have seen how Plotinus speaks of *tolma* as the root-fault in the fall, describing it as the soul's audacious desire to be "on its own," to delight in its own "power" to control a body.

Tolma, *audacia*, *superbia*—the step from one term to another was an easy one. Augustine's stress on the sin of pride "the most heinous of all vices" (*Acad* II, 21) may well have Plotinian overtones already. It is, he warns Theodorus, the "proud yearning for empty glory" which constitutes the last obstacle to the soul's voyage toward wisdom's haven (*Vita* 3). The first book of the *Soliloquies* closes with Reason's advice to the same effect, but now Augustine's adaptation of Plotinian language is more manifest: "Do not seek to be your own (*quasi proprius*) and in your own power (*in tua potestate*), but profess yourself the servant of the most merciful Lord whom it is most advantageous to serve" (*Sol* I, 30).

And yet, virtually every page of the Cassiciacum Dialogues is studded with that emphasis the Augustine of the *Retractations* later goes to such lengths to correct: the "flight" from both body and sense. The recency of his conversion from sensual excess has something to do with this, of course; a certain residue of unresolved Manichaean suspicion of the body makes itself felt as well. But the Plotinian tendency to let the soul's "audacity" slide over into a kind of "itchy desire" for sense-delights and "unclean pleasures" has something to do with it, too, as has the allied stress on "purification" as the essential virtue of "return." It will take Augustine some time to bridge this gap between what he translates as *libido*, *concupiscentia*, and "pride" (*superbia*)—a process which, as we have seen, he brings to term only in the *De Genesi contra Manichaeos*. But there a third member will be added, the *curiositas* which here has not yet made its structured appearance.

Augustine is not, as we shall presently see, entirely unconscious of the difficulty. His description of the soul's ideal state is, in part, an indirect attempt to deal with it. The complexity of that description is such, however, that it is better postponed until later.

"Return"

The function of the "disciplines"

Let us, then, pass for the moment to the question of the soul's "return." Remarkable in this connection is Augustine's stress on the aid that the "liberal disciplines" can offer in "purifying" the soul, "strengthening" and "nourishing" it for its return to the ideal, unfallen state. The accent at Cassiciacum is, in the main, alarmingly intellectualistic, even more so than in certain passages of the *Enneads*. Part of the reason may be the influence of Varro's "Nine Books on the Disciplines" (*Novem Disciplinarum Libri*) and other similar works, an influence that threatens at times to flatten out Plotinian intellectualism into a kind of numerical rationalism.[3]

In any case, return requires that the soul be "nourished and strengthened" by the "understanding and knowledge of things" (*Vita* 8). "Instruction in the liberal arts," he assures Licentius, "if only it is moderate and concise, produces devotees more alert and steadfast and better equipped for embracing Truth" (*Ord* I, 24). This implies that the "souls of wise men are by far richer and greater, in their way, than the souls of the uneducated . . . The souls of people not scientifically trained and unfamiliar with the liberal arts are, as it were, hungry and famished" (*Vita* 8). Licentius' weakness, his inability to sustain the vision of "so great a God," is due to his soul's not being "nourished by erudition and training" (*Ord* I, 20). Hence Augustine's care to sketch out an ordered progression of liberal disciplines which will so nourish the soul as to fit it eventually for the desired vision (*Ord* II, 14–17, 32–51).

"Memory" and salvation

What marks the core of Augustine's view as Plotinian, however, is the salvific function he accords to "memory," the firm connection he establishes between that function and "erudition" in the liberal disciplines. He has placed himself in the class of those who have not ventured so far out into the sea of human misery as entirely to forget the "homeland" whence they fell. Those of his type "still perceive some familiar signs and remember, even amid the waves, the great sweetness of home" (*Vita* 2). He assures Romanianus that he is "beginning to know *again* (*recognoscere*)" the God He seeks (*Acad* II, 2). Memory, therefore, reaches back to the happiness the soul once enjoyed in its native

[3] For fuller details on these influences, see Solignac's Introduction to *Les Confessions*, *BA* 13, pp. 85–112, and Marrou's *Culture Antique*.

upper region and tends to draw the soul back to the vision that it once enjoyed in the pre-existent past (*Ep* 7, 2).

"Memory" and the disciplines

But the soul remains even now capable of knowing certain unchangeable truths. Augustine's examples of that capacity are regularly drawn from the "disciplines" of mathematics, geometry, and logic. The second book of the *Soliloquies* especially shows him grappling with the implications Plotinus would have drawn from all this. At the climax of the discussion, *disciplina* suddenly becomes a hypostatic reality and is said to "dwell in the soul." A few lines later, Truth itself "proclaims that it dwells within you." The exhortation follows, "Turn from your shadow, return to yourself," and Augustine's answer comes once more in the language of memory: "I hear, I regain my wits, I begin once more to remember" (*Sol* II, 33).

The problem of "oblivion"

But some ticklish problems still call for attention. One of them affects the Plotinian teaching itself. Plotinus had to cope with the ordinary testimony of human consciousness, which shows no overt trace of the fallen soul's still being "there," in the intelligible world. Augustine, we have seen, alludes to this problem in the *De Quantitate Animae*; later, in the *De Musica*, he faces it more squarely. His solution follows both the reasoning and phrasing of Plotinus' *Ennead* V, 8. But here again, through hindsight, his awareness of the problem can be detected as early as Cassiciacum. It takes the form of a question revealing how closely he links "memory" and the kind of learning characteristic of the "disciplines."

I do not see how a branch of learning, particularly that of argumentation, exists always in the soul, whereas so few know of it, and whoever does know of it was for a long time in childhood unaware of it. For we cannot say that the souls of the unlearned are not souls, or that there can be in the soul learning of which they are not conscious (*Sol* II, 25).

The question recurs two paragraphs later (*Sol* II, 27), but no direct attempt to answer it is given until the end of the *Soliloquies*. There, Reason distinguishes the kind of forgetting that clouds the events of our infant life and that other kind of "oblivion" which is relevant to the specifically Plotinian memory. A comparison is offered to illustrate this second type of "recall."

We see something, recognize for certain that we have seen it at some time, and declare that we know it. But where or when . . . it came to our attention, we struggle to review and remember. As, for example, if this were to happen to us in the case of a man, we ask him where it was we made his acquaintance. When he has reminded us of it, all at once the whole affair floods back to our memory like a light (*Sol* II, 34).

The application then is made to "persons who are well-trained in the liberal arts." They "bring to light in the process of learning, knowledge that undoubtedly is buried in an oblivion within them, and, in a way, they disinter it. Moreover, they are not content . . . until they behold . . . the whole countenance of Truth, whose splendor already glows in a certain measure in those arts" (*Sol* II, 35).

The answer is not a demonstration; it does, however, offer an analogy that encourages adoption of the Plotinian hypothesis. Once this hypothesis is granted, there is reason to hope that objections against it can be handled. The "oblivion" in question is "surely not entire." The "discernment that refuses to accept a false suggestion is itself a kind of memory," a guarantee that we are still, to some extent, "there" (*Sol* II, 34).

Augustine will not rest content with that; he will come back to this question again and again, until he formulates his later theory of memory and illumination on another basis. That new basis, he will see, is required by the view of salvation peculiar to Christianity. Over the years, the proper character of the Christian view of man in his relation to God will penetrate his thinking more and more deeply until it makes him sharply aware of the difficulties involved in his early intellectual project—that of showing the profound consonance of Roman philosophy with Neo-Platonism, and the accord which he once thought held between Plotinus' "true philosophy" and the "true religion" to which he has returned.

MEDIETAS ANIMAE: ROMAN PHILOSOPHY AND PLOTINIANISM

A careful scrutiny of the Cassiciacum works reveals that Augustine's project is no less ambitious than that. Significantly, too, his bold effort at synthesis compels him to expend his greatest energy—and ingenuity—in persuading his reader that the central tenet of Plotinianism, the soul's mid-rank position in reality, was obscurely insinuated by Roman philosophy adequately understood. The personal history of philosophy he presents in the *Contra Academicos* (III, 37–42) reveals his assurance that Aristotle really agreed with Plato, that the Academics were really crypto-Platonists. Plotinus, consequently—that *Plato redivivus*—represents the "true philosophy" which assumes all that is true in Aristotle and the Academics, bringing them at last to say what they dimly wanted to say.

Throughout that history of philosophy, one might think the Stoics play the part of villains. They are the materialists whose vision is limited to the world of sense. Yet this is a unilateral view of Augustine's attitude toward Stoicism. They too spoke some truth, and that truth also must be assumed and integrated into Plotinianism. Augustine is not content merely to show them they are wrong: he wants rather to demonstrate, as Plotinus (especially in his later works) strained to do, that the deepest inspiration of their system found completest expression only in Neo-Platonism. Plotinus is particularly intent on this in *Ennead* I, 4 "On Happiness," that treatise which much later provided the Bishop of Hippo with his deathbed quotation, but with which, even at Cassiciacum, he could well have been familiar. Its topic was surely apposite for the section we are about to consider from the *De Beata Vita*. There, as Bréhier's *Notice* puts it, Plotinus is trying to show that "the Stoics were not wrong in placing happiness in judgment and reason . . . But for happiness to be independent of the quest for exterior realities, as they contend it is, reason must have an object superior to its quest, an object in the intelligible world . . . Stoicism can stand, therefore, only if it transcend itself through a mystical interpretation" (*Ennéades* I, 67–68).

Now in *De Beata Vita* 22–32, Augustine is strenuously grappling with a much similar task. Key Stoic notions, such as independence of exterior goods of fortune, "measure in all things," the limitation of desires to what one has, liberally dot the entire section. Three times Terence is quoted approvingly. Cicero is brought to bear at crucial steps in the argument. Roman thought, and in the Stoic strain, is ostentatiously represented.

But then, it is forced to undergo a transformation. The trick is not an easy one for Augustine to manage. He brings it off by dint of verbal correspondences as much as, if not more than, by grasping the two contending doctrines in depth. He has already shown that the food of the soul is knowledge and thoughts. But happiness, the "fullness" of the well-fed soul, requires possession of a lasting good, beyond the reach of fortune's vicissitudes. The eternal God being such a good, it follows that the soul which possesses God is happy.

Now, however, things shift back into a Stoic register. Unhappiness is "want" (*egestas*), but not the want of exterior goods which the subject could lose even against his will. The want that is crucial would deprive the soul of "wisdom." The wise soul will not extend its desires beyond its reach, will not desire "anything too much." Where there is measure (*modus*), he observes, there is "nothing either too much or too little." He is preparing us to accept a kind of "middle state" as the soul's ideal; this is why Cicero is correct in calling "frugality" the highest of the virtues. This, too, is why the term "fullness" (*plenitudo*) is more apt a description than "riches" (*divitiae*) or "abundance" (*abundantia*). The latter, especially, suggests "a profusion and a sort of pouring forth of something excessively plentiful" (*Vita* 32), and we are reminded of Plotinus' image of the seed "going forth from itself" and "uncoiling outwards" (*Enn* III, 7, 11). Wisdom, then, is "the measure (*modus*) of the soul . . . through which the soul keeps its equilibrium so that it neither runs over into too much nor remains short of its fullness" (*Vita* 33).

Here the Stoic could not but agree; but to this point both "wisdom" and "measure" are properties qualifying the soul itself. A moment later they have suddenly become the subsistent realities which Neo-Platonism's correction to Stoicism requires they be.

When the soul beholds the Wisdom found, and, . . . devotes itself to it, and without being moved by mere empty vanity, is not seduced to the treachery of images, weighed down in whose embrace it generally deserts God and finds a pernicious end, it then fears no immoderateness, and therefore no want, and hence no misery (*Vita* 33).

Medietas Animi

At this point, another curious anomaly falls into place. Once in passing Augustine has made the unexpected observation that the opposition between *nequitia* and *frugalitas* corresponds to that between *esse* and *non-esse*, being and non-being (*Vita* 30). He returns to this theme with the oppositions between "want" and "fullness," and makes a further point of connecting "fruit" (*frux*) with "being" (*esse: Vita* 31).

There is, I submit, no way of making sense of these remarks except against a Plotinian background. Augustine is bent on associating the soul's ideal state with the unchanging Plotinian realm of "Being," and describing its fall as into the realm of non-being, *nihil*—that realm of change where everything "flows . . . is dissolved . . . melts and steadily perishes" (*Vita* 8). Here, as in the *Confessions* and *De Genesi contra Manichaeos*, he thinks of that fall into relative non-being as due to the "weight" of image-realities which drag the soul downward and "immerse" it.

In its happy state, therefore, the soul is engaged in contemplation. That contemplation is a "possession" expressed in the familiar erotic terms of a mystical embrace (*habere*, *tenere*, *ad ipsam se tenere*) of that subsistent Wisdom and Truth which answers both to Plotinus' *Noûs* and to the Christian Logos. The resulting condition is a sort of "middle state," an "equilibrium" or balance between too much and too little. The soul is able to resist the seduction of "vanity" and "images." These would act as a "weight" (*pondus*) on the soul, bringing it to desert and fall away from God: that fall, finally, is into a changing realm of non-being.

The picture lacks the firmer structure it will take on later. It is complicated by the tormented attempt to show that both Roman and Plotinian notions really say the same thing. But there are enough indicators to suggest that the pattern of the soul's *medietas* is already taking shape at Cassiciacum.

Roman, then, agrees with Greek: liberated from its usual sensist interpretations, and understood mystically, Stoicism was stammering the same deep truths as can be found in Plotinus' "true philosophy." The Stoic thought wisdom empowered the soul to attain "measure," and he was right—provided the wisdom spoken of is understood as the subsistent Wisdom of Plotinus' intelligible world.

Lines for a Later Picture

Even as early as the Cassiciacum writings, therefore, Augustine shows clear signs of working toward the Plotinian theory of man whose far firmer structure we have seen in the *De Genesi contra Manichaeos* and contemporary works. It is not hard to understand why it took him time to grasp more surely the contours of that theory, but the key elements are already at work in the earliest writings we have from his pen: the notion of soul as the real self; of souls as diversely fallen, through an interplay of fault and cosmic law; of "memory" as resource for the way of "return" to the ideal state of *medietas*. The implications of this *medietas* have not yet fully dawned on him. The "flight" of the soul is simplified to suggest a more total rupture from the body and from the sensible world than either Plotinus or Christianity's doctrine of the resurrection would countenance. The problem of Plotinian "forgetfulness" rightly bothers him, and he vaguely senses a difficulty with the concept of creation from "nothing." Only in time will he come to face that difficulty frontally, structure the "fault" in its eventual triadic form, make relative the salvific function of the "disciplines," and smooth out the wrinkles caused by his somewhat forced attempt to make Roman philosophy rhyme with Greek. It will be even later that he begins to suspect that this attempt to think out the Christian faith in Plotinian terms is fraught with more fundamental difficulties than he originally imagined.

VERA PHILOSOPHIA, VERA RELIGIO

For the moment, however, he is largely convinced that Plotinus' "true philosophy" presents the same view of soul in its relation to God as contained in the "sacred mysteries" of Christianity (*Acad* III, 43). The manifestly trinitarian climax of the *De Beata Vita* equates Plotinus' Wisdom with the Wisdom and Truth that St. John's Gospel assures us is the Son of God: possessing Him, the soul has access to the Supreme and ultimate Measure Who is the Father (*Vita* 34).

Admonition and Memory

Having found place in his scheme for Father and Son, Augustine completes his trinitarian consideration by alluding to the Holy Spirit as "a certain Admonition, flowing from the very fountain of Truth, [which] urges us to remember God, to seek Him, and thirst after Him tirelessly" (*Vita* 35). The prayer of the *Soliloquies*, again trinitarian in structure, speaks in third place of the God Whose prerogatives are that He "admonishes" us to be watchful, "converts" us, "calls us back to the Way," and eventually "leads us into all Truth" (*Sol* I, 3).

Christian teaching, then, insinuates essentially the same view of memory as Plotinianism does. Frequently at Cassiciacum, Augustine implies that the soul needs to be "reminded," or, in the term he regularly prefers, "admonished." This is the service which, he claims, the Platonic writings had performed in his own case: they "admonished" him to "return to himself" (*Conf* VII, 16). The *Confessions* attribute the same function in earlier stages of his life to Monica, a dying friend, and Ambrose. Augustine himself performs it on Alypius' behalf. The contexts imply that the one admonished is normally, and the one admonishing often, "ignorant" of the service being rendered, particularly "not knowing" that the reminder transmitted really comes from the Omnipresent God, Who works in and through all to "turn around" the soul fleeing from Himself: again, *fovisti caput nescientis*.

But it took time for the omnipresence theme so thoroughly to penetrate the theory involved in "admonition." What is remarkable at Cassiciacum is how frequently the term and its cognates already occur, and how consciously Augustine already applies such terms in a firm, semitechnical sense. For a Platonist, the deliverances of sense "remind" the soul of the knowledge it has brought from its pre-existent vision of the higher world of Forms. For Augustine, as for Plotinus, the religious import of that doctrine comes to the fore. The entire sensible universe is ordered by the overarching Reason (which, we have seen, he identifies with the Holy Spirit), as one harmonious concert of such reminders. Licentius confesses he has found Augustine's words a reminder (*commonear*) to devote himself to philosophy, "our true and tranquil abode." His expressions evoke all the resonances of the *fovere* image. He would have nothing "twist away and break off (*detorqueat atque disrumpat*)" [his] hold "on the divine reality, I know not what (*nescio qua divina re*) which begins to reveal itself to me, and to which I am passionately attached (*cui me inhiantem suspendo*)" (*Ord* I, 9–10).

Unus Magister

Certain kinds of soul, less fallen than others, Augustine thinks need only such an "admonition," not an "instructor" (*doctor: Sol* I, 23), and Licentius promises to be of this type. "There is no further need for me to be a teacher," Augustine informs him (*Ord* I, 12). Licentius underestimates himself while overestimating his master, for, Augustine confesses, "in philosophy I too am a boy. And when I ask questions, I do not care very much through whom He answers Who daily hears my lamentations, and whose oracle you will be some day, I believe" (*Ord* I, 13).

Already the theme of the *De Magistro* is taking shape: the Incarnate Christ himself "admonishes outwardly," while the Eternal Christ "teaches inwardly" (*foris admonet, intus docet*). Indeed, the words of the Incarnate Word, much like the words of others, are admonitions, reminders, prodding us to turn inward to be taught by the Eternal Wisdom of the Father, the "only Master of us all, Christ." But the same holds for such seemingly chance phenomena as the sound of waters running in the night, the fright of a field mouse (*Ord* I, 14), the comportment of two cocks in a fight. He and his students are thence "admonished" (*inde admoniti: Ord* I, 26) to search through all such things for "beauteous Reason signaling something thence—reason which rules and governs all things, the knowing and unknowing things, and which attracts her eager followers in every way and wherever she commands that she be sought" (*Ord* I, 25).[4]

Again, the Eros-imagery of the *fovere* theme; but once again, the problem which constantly dogs the reader of the Cassiciacum dialogues: who or what is this "philosophy," this "beauteous Reason"?

We must allow for a certain slippage in the answer Augustine gives to that question at this early stage in his project. We have already seen why he cannot yet be firm and precise in answering it: he still must clear up a host of problems touching the place and function of Plotinus' troubling Logos, and of his three hypostases (including the World-Soul and the fallen, individual soul), particularly as they relate to the Christian Trinity.

But even at this stage a certain regularity of usage begins to emerge. The personified *Philosophia* which has turned his head and called him back is one and the same as the *religio* of his infancy. He is convinced that concord is possible between them. On what terms? Again, the distinction of the Two Worlds comes into play: one must situate the Second Person, Truth and Wisdom of God, in the "other," intelligible world, assigning as His "domain . . . the whole world unknown to sense" (*Sol* I, 3). Yet "from that realm, law is promulgated even in these regions" of sense (*Sol* I, 3).

That "promulgation," Augustine's language seems to suggest, must be attributed to the Holy Spirit, the divine and overarching Reason which orders the visible universe on the divine pattern—a pattern which Augustine identifies with the Son of God, Divine Intellect, and Divine Truth at one and the same time. The Spirit's ordering activity extends to everything sensible: to the

[4] For an excellent brief treatment of sense-perception and its relation to reasoned judgment in Augustine's early period, see Markus' essay in the *Cambridge History*, pp. 374–379 and 362–373. The classic work on this difficult issue remains Johannes Hessen's *Augustins Metaphysik der Erkenntnis*, 2d ed., (Leiden, 1960). Markus argues, rightly in my view (pp. 376 and 380; cf. also Copleston, *History of Philosophy*, II, 78) that the obscurities of Augustine's perception theory follow from, rather than lead him to, his root Platonic notion of "man as a rational soul using a material body." Illumination of this root-notion partially accounts for the anomalies that plague his perception theory but the reverse does not seem true. Consequently, I feel entitled to leave more detailed discussion of those anomalies to a forthcoming study of Augustine's early esthetic theory.

murmuring of streams; the fighting of cocks; all men's words and writings; everything embodying Reason's power to "admonish," turn the fallen soul around, summon it to "knock," "seek," and lead it eventually to "find" the Truth, "from Whom to turn is to fall, to whom to turn is to rise again, in whom to abide is to stand firm" (*Sol* I, 3).

The activity of the Holy Spirit must extend, accordingly, to the entire regime of Scripture and Prophecy, Church and preaching and sacrament—He it is gives us both "cup" and "bread of life" (*Sol* I, 3). His activity extends, we may assume, to the Incarnation of the Son.

The modern reader is inclined at this point to blink incredulously. However much a beginner in philosophy, however untutored in orthodox Catholicism one may count him, is it possible that the young Augustine could have been so sanguine on the possibilities of bringing Christianity and Plotinianism into harmony?

Only a closer examination of the shape his early Christianity took can authorize an answer to that question.

THREE: THE CHRISTIAN SOUL

8 VISION

The Question of Augustine's "Christianity"

Few propositions are better calculated to raise the hackles of dedicated Augustine scholars than the suggestion that the convert of Milan, and in important respects the Bishop of Hippo, was articulating so thoroughly a Neo-Platonic form of Christianity as I claim. No sooner is the suggestion made than the ghost of that *enfant terrible*, Prosper Alfaric, is immediately invoked. The mere intimation that one or other view of Augustine represents a "return to Alfaric" is calculated to cut short all further discussion of the matter.

There were, admittedly, many defects in Alfaric's monumental study of *L'Evolution Intellectuelle de saint-Augustin.* Partial, tendentious, it nonetheless remains a major milestone in Augustinian scholarship. Since its publication, things have never been quite the same. If nothing else, it left us with a tangled skein of problems scholars have been unraveling ever since. And one has the uneasy feeling that the closer the scholar surveys the evidence, the more qualifications he inserts into his rejection of Alfaric's position, the less confidently he reaches for those explosive adjectives which abounded in the earlier reactions to that work. It would be pointless to insist again upon the differences in both substance and method that separate my work from Alfaric's; the reasonably careful reader has seen them already. But it would not be amiss at this juncture to single out once again a central weakness of Alfaric's thesis: he seems to have judged Augustine's "Christianity" from the anachronistic standpoint of his own understanding of that term. According to his own norms, then, he censures Augustine for being Neo-Platonic *rather than* Christian. Scholars since have never tired of objecting to this way of asking the question, and the difficulty they press is a very real one.

But it should at the same time be kept in mind that this objection to Alfaric is double-edged. We see from historical knowledge of the fourth and fifth centuries that we must not exact too much of Augustine's Christianity; but by that very fact we are warned not to claim too much for his Christianity either. The early Augustine did, in simple fact, take seriously a number of Plotinianisms which our modern grasp of Christianity—developed, be it gratefully acknowledged, with great assistance from the later Augustine himself—would summarily rule out of court.

To dwell for a moment on one instance which would merit more extended treatment: the Dialogues of Cassiciacum regularly refer to death as the moment when the soul is liberated from the toils of the body. The *De Quantitate Animae* still refers to it as the soul's "complete escape and acquittal from this body," so that it "may not be impeded from giving full allegiance to the fullness of Truth" (76). Little wonder, then, that the same paragraph shows Augustine boggling at the first mention of the body's resurrection to be found in any of his works. He holds that resurrection "which some believe with too many reservations and some do not believe at all, to be . . . certain"—yet he cannot offer a shred of "understanding" of it. A study of Augustine's resurrection theory—and an appreciation of his theology at this stage—would be far more sharply focused if it started from the difficulties that belief presented to his Plotinian "understanding" of Christian truth, rather than beginning with the faintly anachronistic assumption that, from beginning to end, he must have understood the body's resurrection exactly as we today find it necessary to understand it (however, be it quickly added, *that* may be).

Turning to that central Christian mystery, the Incarnation, the field fairly bristles with such a priori judgments. To paraphrase one critic's view: if Augustine recognized the Incarnation as the very heart of Christianity, should we not expect that fundamental conviction so to have polarized his reading as radically to influence his understanding of Plotinus' *Enneads*?[1] Whatever his borrowings from the Neo-Platonist may have been, those borrowing were transposed into a new intellectual universe—the universe of Christianity—and must (from the start, presumably) have been transformed in the process.

But this is merely to play Alfaric's game in reverse. His a priori may not unfairly be said to have put the same case in contrary fashion and suggested that Christianity, transposed into the Neo-Platonic universe, was so radically transformed as to lose all recognizable shape as Christianity. Between these two extremes, we are left with a vast range of intermediate possibilities, and a question: which of these possibilities did Augustine's early Neo-Platonic Christianity *de facto* actualize? We are left, once again, with the hard, somewhat tedious, but indispensable business of searching through the text for the answer.

The evidence must be allowed to decide whether, even at the end of his career, Augustine's theoretical grasp of Christianity was abreast of the Christian life he so admirably lived. But meanwhile, his terminal positions must be understood as distillates of a long and arduous development in his thinking, each stage of which requires careful scrutiny. What "Christianity" meant to Augustine at each phase of his intellectual development—not what "Christianity" *must* have meant to him—is exactly what is in question.

Focus: The Quest for Vision

What, then, did Christianity mean to the early Augustine? If there is one constant running through all of Augustine's thinking, not only in this early period but throughout his career, it is his preoccupation with the question of happiness. From the *De Beata Vita* to the *De Civitate Dei*, this is always the focal question. But the answer is equally uniform: what makes man happy is the possession of God, a possession achieved by way of vision. Christianity's answer to human experience consists, for him, first and foremost in its assurance that man can truly look forward with hope to the vision that is object of the soul's consubstantial desire. Both the life of faith, the quest of reason, and the working of the Incarnation, he regularly understands in terms of this primary focus. Hence the

[1] See G. Madec in *REA* 9: 373–374 (1965). The point is, how long did it take the doctrine of Incarnation to "transform" Augustine's initial Neo-Platonic view? It is significant in this connection that H. I. Marrou, in his fine study of *The Resurrection and St. Augustine's Theology of Human Values* (Villanova, Pa.: Villanova University Press, 1966), almost uniformly appeals to much later texts than those of this early period. His lecture is also available in French, in *Revue des Etudes Augustiniennes* 12: 111–126 (1966).

importance of beginning our survey of his Plotinian Christianity by analyzing what he tells us of "vision."

The most useful starting point for investigating this question is Augustine's own description of the "vision" he eventually arrived at, *Confessions* VII, 16–17. Plotinus' treatise on Omnipresence has already afforded us some preliminary insight into what Augustine means there, but from what we have seen since it will come as no surprise that other harmonic portions of the *Enneads* are active as well. I propose to show that in the section of the *Confessions* under discussion, *Ennead* V, 8 on Intelligible Beauty is dominant, but that certain of its themes associate with the manner in which Plotinus expounds them in *Enneads* I, 6 on Beauty and VI, 4–5 on Omnipresence—with telling evidence corroborating the suggestions others have made in favor of treatises VI, 9, and V, 3.

Such harmonics, moreover, occur inside Augustine's work as well. There is, for example, a close similarity between the *Confessions*' initial statement of the reflections to which his Neo-Platonic readings prompted him and the reflections which he incorporates into the first two of his works, the *De Beata Vita* and the *Contra Academicos*. The former of these works makes clear their inner linkage, through their common focus on the question of happiness (*Vita* 13–15; cf. *Acad* I, 5–12, 24–25), the theme, as we shall see, of the section of the *Confessions* that concerns us. One need not postulate that Augustine reread those early works of his before composing this central section of the *Confessions*, but the parallels between them make that hypothesis not at all unlikely. In any event, we shall explain this initial section through three sets of cross-references—the first to the early works, the second to the treatises of Plotinus already enumerated above, and the third to other sections of the *Confessions* themselves. This in turn will lead us to propose a view of Augustine's theory of faith, reason, and vision—one which he found coherent with the major lines of Plotinus' anthropology.

THE ENTRY ON VISION

Intravi in Intima Mea: "I Entered Into My Inmost Being"

Being thus admonished (*inde admonitus*: that is, by the Platonic books) to return to myself, under your leadership I entered into my inmost being . . . I entered, and I saw.

Thus does Augustine begin the account of his personal reflections on these readings. *Admonitus*: the term implies, as we have seen, a providential "reminder" whereby the soul is summoned back to "itself," is called to a movement of conversion, to a turning-back which answers to its primordial sin of turning-away from the Highest to the "lowest," from the spiritual, omnipresent "eternal internal" to the bodily half-realities which are outside, *foras*. The reminder could have come from any number of loci in Plotinus' works—from *Ennead* I, 6 on Beauty, or from *Ennead* VI, 4–5 (which would explain the increasing insistence of its omnipresence context).

But it could also have come from *Ennead* V, 8 on Intelligible Beauty where Plotinus writes:

Those drunken with this wine . . . all their soul penetrated with this beauty, cannot remain mere gazers: no longer is there a spectator *without* (ἔξω) gazing on an outside (ἔξω) spectacle: the clear-eyed hold the vision *within themselves* (ἔχει . . . ἐν αὐτῷ τὸ ὁρώμενον), though for the most part, they have no idea (ἀγνοεῖ) that it is within but *look towards it as something outside them* (ὡς ἔξω ὂν βλέπει) and see it as an object of vision caught by a direction of will.

All that one sees as a spectacle (θεατὸν) is still *external* (ἔξω); one must *bring the vision within* (εἰς αὐτὸν . . . μεταφέρειν) and see no longer in that mode of separation but *as we know ourselves* (ὡς αὐτὸν); thus a man filled with god—possessed by Apollo or one of the Muses—need no longer look *outside* for his vision of the divine being (ἐν αὐτῷ ἂν ποιοῖτο); it is but finding strength to see *divinity within* (ἐν αὐτῷ θεὸν βλέπειν) (*Enn* V, 8, 10, 31–43).

Tu Assumsisti . . . Ut Viderem: "You Took Me Up . . . So That I Might See"

There is, however, a profound ambiguity in Plotinus' account of how the soul arrives at this vision, one which becomes apparent as soon as we bring together his words immediately preceding and following the section just cited. He has begun with a description of the vision as found in the *Phaedrus*.

This is why Zeus, although the oldest of the gods whom he leads (ὧν αὐτὸς ἡγεῖται) advances first towards that vision, followed by the gods and demigods and *such souls as are of strength to see* (αἳ ταῦτα ὁρᾶν δύνανται). That Being . . . rising loftily over them pours its light upon all things, so that all gleams in its radiance; *it upholds some beings, and they see* (οἱ μὲν ἀπ' αὐτοῦ ἀνέχονταί τε καὶ βλέπουσιν) (*Enn* V, 8, 10, 1–10).

In the portion of text which follows, however, the tone shifts slightly. The accent, as we have seen, is put on the soul's knowledge of *self* so that Plotinus can eventually conclude:

Similarly, any one *unable to see himself* (ἀδυνατῶν ἑαυτὸν ὁρᾶν), but possessed (καταληφθεὶς) by that God, has but to bring that divine-within before his consciousness (εἰς τὸ ἰδεῖν προφέρῃ τὸ θέαμα) and at once *he sees an image of himself, himself lifted to a better beauty* (ἑαυτὸν προφέρει καὶ εἰκόνα αὐτοῦ καλλωπισθεῖσαν βλέπει) (*Enn* V, 8, 11, 1–3).

"Lifted to a better beauty"—MacKenna's translation might be justified against the background of Plotinus' previous admission that "that Being . . . *upholds* some beings, and they see." But the entire context points to Plotinus' conviction that *we* bring the vision within, *we* raise ourselves to this "better beauty" which in the last analysis is *our own*, because the soul by its divine origin is substantial capacity for that vision, and attains to it by re-becoming one with the object seen. Augustine, too, will insist on the connection between the soul's knowledge of itself and its knowledge of God, but only after eliminating all such traces of pantheism, all suggestion of the soul's self-sufficiency.

Along with this dangerous ambiguity, however, Plotinus supplied Augustine with the very terms for removing it. It was not Zeus who led him, but God: *duce te.* He did not raise himself to the vision; he had to be "upheld," and by "that Being" which was God Himself. One is able to "see" if one has been en-abled: *potui, quoniam factus es adiutor meus,* "this I could do, for you became my helper." *Tu assumsisti me:* it is Plotinus' own image Augustine is capitalizing on. God it was who "took [him] up," none other than the *dextera Dei,* the Divine "right hand"—the Biblical *manus,* but penetrated now with Plotinus' omnipresence insight.

"Putting Sense Behind"

But the vision is within, so that the seer Plotinus speaks of, "retreating inwards (εἰς τὸ εἴσω) . . . *puts sense behind him* (ἀφεὶς τὴν αἴσθησιν)" and becomes "possessor of the all," "one in the Divine." For "if he plans to see in separation, he sets himself outside (ἔξω)" (*Enn* V, 8, 11, 10–14).

Augustine's observations, couched though they are in Pauline terms, are entirely parallel. The "light" he saw was not, he insists, the ordinary sensible light which "any flesh" can see. So far above the mind's eye is it that it is seen by some eye or other above the mind's eye: *qualicumque oculo animae meae supra eundem oculum animae meae.* That phrase is usually translated as though it meant the light (and only that) which Augustine saw was situated "above" his soul. The translation suggested here not only seems to fit the Latin somewhat better, it points to a probable interference from *Ennead* VI, 9—which others have found active in this section of the

Confessions[2]—where Plotinus informs us that in mystical vision "it is not our reason that has seen; it is something greater than reason, reason's Prior, as far above reason as the very object of that thought must be" (*Enn* VI, 9, 10, 7–9). But this "above" must not be interpreted in any spatial sense. The superiority is of another order, one of cause to effect, Archetype to image. This light is, in St. Paul's phrase, a *Veritas quae . . . intellecta conspicitur*, one that is glimpsed by the inner eye of understanding, not by the outer eye of the bodily, "carnal" senses.

Excursus: Interferences with *Ennead* VI, 4–5

That description, we have suggested earlier, shows striking parallels with two image-corrections contained in Plotinus' treatise on Omnipresence. But it is significant that the extremely sophisticated—and characteristically Plotinian—process of "dynamic image" is employed to excellent advantage in *Ennead* V, 8 as well. Additionally significant, it features a "transparent globe" that even more strongly recalls *Ennead* VI, 4–5, a "gleaming representation of a sphere" which the reader is now advised to "imagine . . . stripped of magnitude and of spatial differences." "Call on God," Plotinus counsels, "maker of the sphere whose image you now hold, and pray Him to enter . . . He who is the one God and all the gods, where each is all, blending into unity (*εἷς ὢν καὶ πάντες καὶ ἕκαστος πάντες σύνοντες εἰς ἕν*) . . . He and all have one existence (*ὁμοῦ δὲ εἰσι*) while each again is distinct (*χωρὶς*) . . . by state without interval (*ἐν στάσει ἀδιαστάτῳ*)." For, he goes on to explain,

> there is no sensible form (*μορφὴν αἰσθητὴν*) to set one here and another there and to prevent any from being an *entire identity* (*πᾶς ἐν αὐτῷ*) yet there is no sharing of parts (*μέρη*) from one to another. Nor is each of those divine *wholes* (*ὅλον*) a *power in fragment* (*κερματισθεῖσα*), a power totalling to the sum of the measurable segments (*μέρη μετρούμενα*): the divine is all one all-power (*τὸ δὲ ἐστι—τὸ πᾶν—δύναμις πᾶσα*) reaching out to infinity, powerful to infinity: and so great is God that his very members are infinites (*μέρη αὐτοῦ ἄπειρα*). What place can be named to which He does not reach? (*Enn* V, 8, 9, 1–24).

Once again, the uncharacteristic call on God, but with it the faintly pantheistic reminder that God and all are one. Here, too, is the abolition of magnitude and spatial differences, the distinction not by local situation but by kind of "distanceless distance," the

[2] Notably Solignac, "Reminiscences" and *Les Confessions*, *BA* 13, pp. 110–111, 688–689.

paradoxical dialectic of "whole" and "part," the self-canceling use of spatial language to express the omnipresence of the divine which defies our spatializing imagination and succeeds in showing us God as "the unfailing" from whose reach no place is excluded because no place is really distant from Him. In the light of all these elements, it would have taken a firm effort of will to exclude association with the Omnipresence treatise which so influenced Augustine's thinking on God and on His relation to the world. *Numquid nihil est veritas*, he asks, "Is truth, then, a nothing, because it is diffused neither through finite nor through infinite space?" If the question now is merely rhetorical, it is because both *Enneads* V, 8 and VI, 4–5 have so tellingly concurred in answering it.

Particularly striking in all this was the notion that each of these divine wholes is an "entire identity," not a power-in-fragment. This follows from the law found in *Ennead* VI, 4–5 which attributes such fragmentation to the imaginative habit whereby we think according to the corporeal properties of this lower world. The point has struck Augustine; climaxing his ascent of the mind in the *De Ordine* (II, 51), he advises his companions to reflect that "in that intelligible world, each part is as though it were [the] whole (*tanquam totum*) beautiful and perfect."

The interference between these two treatises was, assuredly, invited by the very terms and images common to them. But it required in addition that Augustine grasp the dynamic of the thought, something of the properly philosophical issues involved. As such, it is just one more illustration of his ability to catch such resonances and divine their deeper implications, to read his Plotinus with more than a schoolboy's perspicacity.

THE OBJECTS "SEEN"

The Divine Light

Caritas novit eam: "Love knows it"

Qui novit veritatem, novit eam: "He who knows Truth knows [that Light]." Augustine concludes his description by adding: *caritas novit eam.* Here too, he may well have found encouragement in Plotinus' own reminder that not everyone is fit for the vision, or even disposed to hear of it.

> If you are still unmoved and cannot acknowledge beauty under such conditions, then looking to your own inner being you will find no beauty to delight you and it will be futile in that state to seek the greater vision, for you will be questing it through the ugly and the impure.

This is why such matters are not spoken of to everyone; you, if you are conscious of beauty within, remember: ἀναμνήσθητι (*Enn* V, 8, 2, 41–46).

Here again, however, there is likelihood of interference from the unforgettable passage in *Ennead* VI, 9, 8–9[3] which describes the soul's nuptial love for the Father, and culminates in the advice that "there only is our veritable love and There we may unite with it, not holding it in some fleshly embrace but possessing it in all its verity. *Any that have seen know what I have in mind*" (*Enn* VI, 9, 45–48).

A few paragraphs further, Plotinus returns to this theme, citing the rule of the Mysteries: "Nothing divulged to the Uninitiate: the Supreme is not to be made a common story, the holy things may not be uncovered to a stranger" (*Enn* VI, 9, 11, 1ff).

The erotic resonances of Augustine's *fovere*-image may have been strongly reinforced by such language; his celebrated *Da mihi amantem et sentit quod dico*, "Give me a lover and he will understand my meaning," may owe much to such passages.

Happiness, "remembered"

But: "remember." Plotinus' injunction evokes both the reminiscence theory and the connected "fall" from the vision of that Beauty which once the soul enjoyed—which, in fact, it still possesses. For the highest portion of the soul, as we have seen, has never really "come down," and by resort to its "memories" it can take cognizance of its genuine ontological status, still linked with the over-world, still "there." We shall have to ask whether this theme is what earlier prompted Augustine to ask whether he pre-existed (*Conf* I, 7), to remark after his Neo-Platonic experience that he was left with a "memory" of God (VII, 23), and, later, to pursue his long quest through the "palaces of memory" to discover "where" he had found God, "whence" he had drawn his knowledge of the *beata vita* which he could not even seek did he not in some sense "remember" what he was seeking (X, 12–38).

Cibus animae: "food of the soul"

Once again we are reminded that the *Contra Academicos*, the *De Beata Vita*, and the section of the *Confessions* we are treating are all centered on that same "happy life"—a state which Augustine defines as "joy in the truth," or, better, a joy in the subsistent Truth, God Himself (*Conf* X, 33–34). That Truth

[3] See n. 2, above.

he repeatedly portrays as the "food" for which the soul "sighs," "hungers and thirsts," the only food that can "satiate." Thus in his treatment of the Manichee problems which the "Platonic books" helped him to solve, he exclaims:

O Truth, Truth, how intimately did even the very marrow of my mind sigh for you (*suspirabant tibi*) . . . I hungered and thirsted for Yourself, O Truth (*Te ipsam, veritas . . . esuriebam et sitiebam*). But still [the Manichees] put before me on those platters splendid fantasies . . . Yet because I thought that they were you, I fed upon them . . . nor did I receive nourishment from them, but rather was I myself more exhausted by them (*manducabam . . . nec nutriebar sed exhauriebar magis*). Food in dreams is very like the food of waking men (*simillimus est cibis vigilantium*), but sleepers are not fed by it: they merely sleep . . . On such empty phantoms was I fed—and yet I was not fed (*pascebar inanibus et non pascebar*) (III, 10).

Again and again the *Confessions* returns to this theme. Alypius is portrayed as "sighing" along with Augustine for "truth and wisdom." With him and Nebridius, he seeks the "happy life," so that the three of them are figured as so many "mouths" in want, awaiting the "opportune time" when God would give them "food" (*escam in tempore opportuno:* VI, 17). God's slow work in converting them is limned as "preparation" of "food" (*escam*) to "fill their souls with blessing" (VI, 24). Now that work of preparation is completed; the Platonic readings have enabled him to glimpse that Truth, true food of his soul.

O Eternal Truth, and true love, and beloved eternity! You are my God, and I sigh (*suspiro*) for you day and night! . . . I found myself to be far from you . . . I heard your voice from on high: "I am the *food* of grown men. Grow, and you shall *feed* upon me (*Cibus sum grandium: cresce et manducabis me*). You will not change me into yourself, as you change *food* into your own flesh, but you will be changed into me (VII, 16).

There were, needless to say, any number of Scriptural loci which contributed to this *cibus*-image. What may well have given them added force, however, was Plotinus' remark—already cited in connection with the *fovere*-image of God's maternal care—in the midst of his unforgettable description of the souls' beatitude in the intelligible heaven that "to 'live at ease' is There; and to these divine beings *verity* is *mother and nurse, existence and sustenance* (καὶ ἀλήθεια δὲ αὐτοῖς καὶ γενέτειρα καὶ τροφὸς καὶ οὐσία καὶ τροφή)" (V, 8, 4, 1–2).

Not only did Scripture here partially coincide with, it completed Plotinus with a complement amounting to correction. For, unlike the Platonists, it spoke of this transcendent Truth as condescending to our fallen "infirmity" thus becoming Truth Incarnate, the food of "little ones"—the "food mixed with flesh" to which Augustine returns when reflecting on the fruits of his reading (VII, 24; cf. VII, 13ff). But to this, the function of the Incarnation, we shall return presently.

Reverberasti . . . radians: "You beat back my feeble sight, sending down your beams most powerfully"

Lifted by God, Augustine has glimpsed the existence of that splendor which is "food" of the grown; but no more than a glimpse is permitted him. For, having shown him that He Himself exists, God shows him also "that I, the one who saw, did not yet exist: *nondum me esse qui viderem.* And You beat back my feeble sight (*infirmitatem aspectus mei*), sending down Your beams most powerfully upon me; and I trembled with love and awe. I found myself to be far from You in a region of unlikeness (*inveni longe me esse in regione dissimilitudinis*), as though I heard Your voice from on high."

Far from God in that "region of unlikeness": Courcelle (*Recherches*, p. 167) quite properly traces that expression to *Ennead* I, 8 on the "Origin of Evils"; but it represents, again, an interference called for here by Plotinus' mention of those souls "more remote" who cannot endure the vision. Augustine's *infirmitas* does not permit him to endure the radiance of that light. We have seen that the Zeus of the *Phaedrus* myth leads gods and demi-gods to the vision, along with "such souls as are of strength to see" (αἳ ταῦτα ὁρᾶν δύνανται). We must repeat here part of Plotinus' exegesis of that myth, appending what was omitted from our citation above:

That Being appears before them from some unseen place and rising loftily over them *pours its light upon all things, so that all gleams in its radiance* (κατέλαμψε μὲν πάντα καὶ ἔπλησεν αὐγῆς); *the inferiors are dazzled and turn away, unfit to gaze upon that sun* (καὶ ἐξέπληξε μὲν τοὺς κάτω, καὶ ἐστράφησαν ἰδεῖν οὐ δεδυνημένοι οἷα ἥλιον). Some beings it upholds, and they see; *others are troubled, all the more as they are more distant from* [that light] (οἳ μὲν ἀπ' αὐτοῦ ἀνέχονταί τε καὶ βλέπουσιν, οἳ δὲ ταράττονται, ὅσω ἂν ἀφεστήκωσιν αὐτοῦ). But the seers, those "capable" of seeing (οἱ δυνηθέντες), all look toward it (V, 8, 10, 4–10).

Upheld by God—*tu assumsisti me*—Augustine has seen. And yet, the vision is but momentary: he is one of those "inferior" souls, "more remote," *in regione dissimilitudinis*—not yet "strong enough" to sustain the blinding radiance of that vision from which he recoils like one unfit to gaze upon the sun. Capable of glimpsing, incapable of gazing on the light of Truth, he puts himself in a class midway between the two Plotinus describes in this treatise.

Diripiebar abs te pondere meo: "I was borne down from you by my weight"

Here again, *Ennead* VI, 9 casts further illumination on Augustine's text. Plotinus there describes just such a momentary vision, and attributes the soul's being dragged down again to its being "weighted from beneath"; "we should go without burden and we go carrying that which can but keep us back." The "impediment" he speaks of is obviously the body (VI, 9, 5). Explaining a similar descent from vision, Augustine portrays himself several paragraphs further as "borne down from [God] through [his] own weight," a "weight," he goes on to specify, which was "carnal custom." How is that phrase to be understood? He gives us an indication by inviting us to take the phrase of Wisdom quite literally indeed, that "the corruptible body weighs down (*adgravat*) the soul, and the earthly habitation presses down upon the mind that muses upon many things: *et deprimit terrena habitatio sensum multa cogitantem* (VII, 23; cf. *Sap* 9:15).

Ipsa Veritas: "Truth itself"

But the truth in question here—food for souls "grown up" enough to have returned to the Intelligible Heaven—is the very spiritual being which Augustine's previous habit of imaginative thought had persuaded him could only be a "nothing." Now, however, he says, "Is Truth, then, a nothing . . . ? (*Numquid nihil est veritas?*) From afar you cried to me, "I am who am" (*Ego sum qui sum*) (VII, 16)." God has "cried out" to him, and he has "heard as one hears with the heart." Truth *exists*, a Truth which is identical with God, not merely propositional, but subsistent Truth. And again, the thought is authentically Plotinian.

We cannot think that the divine Beings of that sphere, or the other supremely blessed There, need look to our apparatus of science (ἀξιώματα): all of that realm (the very Beings themselves) are noble images (καλὰ ἀγάλματα)[4] such as we may conceive to lie within the

[4] Plotinus goes on (*Enn* V, 8, 6) to explain this notion in terms of a mistaken but highly suggestive interpretation of hieroglyphic images (ἀγάλματα). He sees the Egyptians thereby figuring the "absence of discursiveness in the Intellectual Realm." The theme is not unconnected with that of the "seer become sign," which we shall shortly examine.

soul of the wise—but There not as written images but as beings (ἀγάλματα δὲ οὐ γεγραμμένα, ἀλλὰ ὄντα). The ancients had this in mind when they declared the Ideas (Forms) to be Beings, Essentials (ὄντα, οὐσίας) (*Enn* V, 8, 5, 19–25).

The *Cetera*: The Beings "Other Than God"

Quae nec sunt nec non sunt: "which neither are, nor are not"

The point of Truth's subsistent reality is emphasized by what immediately precedes in Plotinus' text—and it receives an important corollary.

The True Wisdom, then, is Real Being (ἡ ἀληθινὴ σοφία οὐσία); and Real Being is Wisdom; it is wisdom that gives value to Real Being; and Being is real in virtue of its origin in wisdom. It follows that *all forms of existence not possessing wisdom are, indeed, Beings in right of the wisdom which went to their forming, but as not in themselves possessing it, are not Real Beings* (Διὸ καὶ ὅσαι οὐσίαι σοφίαν οὐκ ἔχουσι, τῷ μὲν διὰ σοφίαν τινὰ γεγονέναι οὐσία, τῷ δὲ μὴ ἔχειν ἐν αὐταῖς σοφίαν, οὐκ ἀληθιναὶ οὐσίαι) (V, 8, 5, 15–19).

It begins to dawn both what Augustine means by claiming he himself did not yet "exist"—*nondum me esse qui viderem*—and why he will presently turn from this initial insight to a realization concerning "the lower beings" among which he finds himself.

I beheld other things below You (*cetera infra Te*) and I saw that they are not altogether existent nor altogether non-existent (*nec omnino esse nec omnino non esse*): they are, because they are from You (*esse quidem, quoniam abs te sunt*); they are not, since they are not what You are (*non esse autem, quoniam id quod es non sunt*). For that truly exists which endures unchangeably (*Id enim vere est, quod incommutabiliter manet*) (VII, 17).

Nondum me esse . . . inhaerere Deo bonum est: "I did not yet exist . . . to cleave to God is good"

Truly to exist, therefore, means to be eternal and out of the realm of change. Inferior beings *nec sunt nec non sunt*, "are," but in a diminished sense. But when Augustine says he does not *yet* exist, does he mean to imply that such a destiny awaits him—that eating the *cibus grandium* works a change such that the soul itself shares somehow in God's own eternity?

For the answer to that, and to other connected questions posed by the section we are considering, the reader must turn to Augustine's interpretation of the "Heaven of heaven" in Book XII of the *Confessions*. There, once again under the sign of the *beata vita*, and with significant recurrence of terms by now familiar to us, he vigorously defends the exegesis whereby he finds Scripture itself speaking of an "intellectual creature" which was created and fell before time began. In itself mutable, it nonetheless "participated" in the immutable eternity which is naturally God's own, by "clinging" to God (*inhaerendo*, *cohaerendo*, are the terms he uses). This he has learned from God Himself, "calling (as in *Conf* VII, 16) with a loud voice in his inner ear," calling him back, for he had himself turned away and fallen off into those realities which "are, but are in lesser fashion." What depth in these words of Scripture, he exclaims, and once again he "trembles with love and with dread" (XII, 9–17).

Pro iniquitate erudisti hominem: "You have corrected man for iniquity"

Let the fallen soul, therefore, whose wandering has put it "far from God," lift up its eyes to that Heaven of heaven, for it still harbors a "memory" of that blissful life. Let his readers seek, knock, and "sigh" for it, as he does. For all of us need conversion, all of us being, in our souls, a spiritual creature turned away like the fallen angels, from God our Light, by a movement of the will whose name is sin. Against the Manichees, Augustine wishes to emphasize that this iniquitous "turning away" accounts for our estrangement from God in the "region of unlikeness," and for this reason, ending his account of the first great insight gleaned from his Neo-Platonic readings, he appends a "confession" wherein the omnipresence theme of the "self-abiding" God interpenetrates with the notion of the soul's happiness consisting in "clinging" to Him.

> I knew that "you have corrected man for iniquity, and you have made my soul to waste away like a spider" . . . "But it is good for me to adhere to my God," for if I do not abide in Him, neither will I be able to abide in myself. But He abides in Himself, and He renews all things. "You are my Lord, for you have no need of my goods" (VII, 16–17).

Augustine, then, like all "souls," once "was." He has sinned and fallen into the realm of beings which "are, but in lesser fashion." Now, pursuing the way of return, he "is not, yet," but hungers, thirsts, sighs once again to "be."

Quoniam bonorum meorum non eges: "You have no need of my goods"

Once again, though, *Ennead* VI, 9, 9—the very same section as we have seen before—appears to have left its resonance. The emanation of secondary beings from the supreme "wellspring of Life" and "fount of Good" works neither diminution nor fragmentation in the eternal principle itself. The doctrine could not but remind Augustine of the almost tiresome way Plotinus, a few paragraphs earlier, had harped upon the theme that:

> Something there must be supremely adequate, autonomous, all-transcending, *most utterly without need* . . . Unity *cannot need itself* . . . [and] the sovranly self-sufficing principle will be Unity-Absolute . . . a nature *above all need* whether within itself or in regard to the rest of things . . . It *needs no standing-ground* as if inadequate to its own sustaining . . . A First *cannot go in need of its sequents* . . . [but] principle to all, *must be utterly without need* . . . Whatever may be said to *be in need* of a good is *needing* a preserver; *nothing can be a good to the Unity*, therefore (*Enn* VI, 9, 6, 17–39).

Once more Augustine has found Plotinus speaking the same message as Scripture—Scripture, that is, as his translation read. "Thou art my Lord," he cries, and citing Psalm 15 appends the reason: "for you have no need of my goods" (*quoniam bonorum meorum non eges*).

ANTHROPOLOGICAL CONDITIONS FOR "VISION"

The Purified Intellect

Implied in all this is the classic Neo-Platonic teaching emphasized in *Ennead* V, 8, 3, 16ff that "we learn in this matter from the purified Intellect in ourselves, or, if you like, from the gods and the glory of the Intellect in them"—a teaching which Augustine relays in the *Soliloquies* in the *Phaedrus* language by now familiar from the *Confessions:*

> There are some eyes so healthy and vigorous (*tam sani et vegeti*) that they can fearlessly turn toward the sun (*in ipsum solem sine ulla trepidatione* [*se*] *convertant*) as soon as they are opened . . . Others, however, are dazzled by the very luster (*fulgore feriuntur*) which they so ardently desire to behold . . . To these . . . it is dangerous to want to show what they are as yet incapable of seeing (*videre non valent*) . . . They are, therefore, first to be trained (*exercendi sunt prius*) and . . . their love is to be restricted and nourished (*differendus atque nutriendus est*) (*Sol* I, 23).

The Soul's "Knowledge of Self"

But there is a discreet suggestion of a deeper understanding of that text, of something Augustine makes more explicit in his Cassiciacum writings: that his previous inability to attain to this knowledge of God as beatifying object of the soul's yearning was directly connected with his ignorance of his own true nature and situation, that is, as soul and fallen soul. That the soul seeks happiness among corporeal realities which are inferior to her, the Plotinus of *Ennead* V, 1, 1 explained by the fact that in her flight from the Father she comes eventually to forget and ignore both the Father and her own nature and "divine" station. The same message rings clear in *Ennead* V, 8, 10–11, and Augustine has not missed it. The greatest cause of our error, he has assured Zenobius in the *De Ordine* (I, 3), is that man is unknown to himself. The order of studies must therefore include the vital step whereby this ignorance is banished and the soul is brought to recognize her dignity.[5] In short, the *noverim te, noverim me*—"to know Thee, to know myself"—of the *Soliloquies* is fundamentally one desideratum and not two (*Sol* II, 1; cf. I, 7).

"Ceasing to Be a Man"

But this recognition of himself as really a soul implies for the Plotinus of *Ennead* V, 8 the complementary insight that "become man, he has ceased to be the All; *ceasing to be a man* (*παυσάμενος δὲ τοῦ ἄνθρωπος εἶναι*)—we read—'he soars aloft and administers the Cosmos entire'; restored to the All he is maker of All" (*Enn* V, 8, 7, 33–35).

We have already seen how literally Augustine is prepared to adopt the conclusion. He has had Licentius defend the Academic position with the claim that the happy life in possession of wisdom awaits man once he has stripped off all the "envelopments" (*involucra*) of body (*Acad* I, 23). He himself later expresses their insight as implying that wisdom is not for the man still "living here" (*dum hic vivis*). Wisdom cannot be the prerogative of "man"; only "after this life," when the mind (*animus*) has been fully "exercised and purified," when he has "ceased to be a man" (*cum homo esse desieris*) will he enjoy that vision (*Acad* III, 20).

"Growing up" to the stature required for eating this "food of the grown" implies, therefore, that one put off the mortal body, cease to be a man. For, as Augustine (who pictures himself as a "little one" on God's breast) puts it in a paradoxical word-play: *Quis homo est quilibet homo, cum sit homo?* In the light of what has preceded, we may translate quite literally: "What man is any kind of a man (that is, a "grown-up") while he be a man?" (*Conf* IV, 1).

[5] *Ord* II, 16–17, 30–31, 43, 48–50. This arrival at self-knowledge is the "point" both of the *De Quantitate Animae* and of *Ennead* V, 1, on which it is partially modeled. It is also the dominating concern of *Ennead* V, 3.

RESULTS OF THE VISION

The Seer Becomes "Sign"

To credit the Academics with a secret Platonic teaching is one thing; to follow Plotinus' personal theory is something else again. If the soul be not entirely fallen, then it may be possible even during this life to "cease to be a man," to arrive at the heights of beatifying contemplation even while still "in this body." In that case, accordingly, on returning from the vision of the Intelligible Beauty, the seer himself should, in Plotinus' phrase, "*radiant* with the Divine Intellections (ἐκλάμποντα τοῖς νοήμασι) be no longer the seer, but, as that place has made him, *object for another's vision* (θέαμα ἑτέρου θεομένου)"[6] (*Enn* V, 8, 11, 17–19). This, as Augustine explains to Mallius Theodorus, is one of his reasons for composing his early Dialogues. Having entered into the tranquillity of philosophy's haven, certain souls "send up some *luminous sign* [in the form of] some work of theirs (*lucidissimum signum sui alicujus operis*) to those citizens they can reach, that once admonished they may bend their efforts to [return to] themselves (*quo admoniti conentur ad se*)" (*Vita* 2). And this is Augustine's own intention:

To let you know of my activities and of how I am shepherding my dear ones (*necessarios meos*) toward this port, and to give you some fuller understanding of my soul—for *I can find no other signs by which to manifest myself* (*neque enim alia signa invenio quibus me ostendam*)—I have thought [it fitting] to write to you and dedicate to your honor, this initial discussion of mine (*Vita* 5).

The Banishing of Doubt

But there is another resultant of this initial reflection on the Platonic readings, the very fruit which issues from the *De Beata Vita* and the *Contra Academicos* combined, namely:

And I said: "Is truth, then, a nothing . . . ?" (*Numquid nihil est veritas?*) From afar you cried to me, "I am who am." I heard . . . [and] there was no further place for doubt, and it would have been easier for me to doubt that I live than doubt the existence of Truth, which is "clearly seen, being understood by the things that are made" (*faciliusque dubitarem vivere me quam non esse veritatem quae . . . intellecta conspicitur*) (VII, 16).

[6] It is likely that Augustine interpreted this observation against the background of chapters 4–6 of the same treatise, where Plotinus speaks of the souls above as "transparent . . . every being . . . lucid to every other" (4, 4–6), all of them "visible images projected from themselves" so that "all becomes an object of contemplation" (4, 42–44). It is in chapter 6 that Plotinus spells out his interpretation of hieroglyphics (see n. 4, above).

Numquid Nihil est Veritas? "Is Truth, then, a Nothing?"

The discovery recounted here refers to Augustine's former difficulties in coming to an adequate conception of the Omnipresent.

Whatever I conceived as devoid . . . of spatial character seemed to me to be nothing (*nihil mihi esse videbatur*), absolutely nothing (*sed prorsus nihil*), not even a void (*inane*). For even if a body is removed from a place, and the place remains empty of any body whatsoever (*locus . . . vacuatus*) . . . yet there remains that empty space, as it were a spacious nothing (*locus inanis, tamquam spatiosum nihil*) (*Conf* VII, 1).

Plotinus uses language analogous to this in *Ennead* VI, 4, 2. The omnipresence theme is surely in Augustine's mind; and still, its interference with *Ennead* V, 8 was natural. For it, too, handles this temptation to doubt the existence of a purely intelligible reality beyond the range of sense-perception—the inclination to think of it as an airy nothing.

Nihil: that key term recalls the curious passage of arms in the third book of the *Contra Academicos* (5–13), in which Alypius is defending the Academic definition of the "wise man" as one whose quest for wisdom is unflagging during this mortal life. For here below, he seems to think, that quest alone, and not the final "possession" of Wisdom, is possible to us.

This, Augustine counters, is to abuse the only definition of the *sapiens* which is reasonable and acceptable. By definition the wise man *knows*, that is, "*possesses*" wisdom, so that the Academics should logically have admitted that their system condemned man to un-wisdom during this mortal life—unless they (and Alypius) are willing to fly in the face of reason by contending that the wise man can know wisdom and at the same time know "nothing," which is tantamount to asserting that wisdom is a "nothing."

That argument is a strange one at best, and perhaps not entirely justifiable, or even understandable. But the difficulty does not seem to lie quite on the surface. It does not, for instance, lie in the fact that Augustine is entirely unaware of the fallacy that appears most obvious on examination, that of passing from the logical to the real order. If this criticism were valid, he would be arguing from a definition which *supposes* man's ability to possess truth, to the entirely illegitimate conclusion that such possession is *existentially* realizable. Whatever the weakness of the argument, we suggest, it is not this. For once Alypius concedes this definition as the only reasonable one, Augustine then announces (III, 10) that the next step in their considerations must be to air the question whether there can exist a wise man in the terms of this definition. Further on (III, 24), when developing his own systematic, he himself redefines the commonly accepted term *mundus* to accord with that systematic—a right which he would seem to have denied to his companion in regard to the equally common notion of "wise man." And this right Alypius now accords him without demur: why?

Part of the reason we have already seen. Not only Augustine, but even Alypius is subtly attracted by the idea of "Wisdom" as a subsistent reality, the knowledge of it being properly termed "possession" (III, 5), something in the nature of a mystical "embrace" (cf. *Sol.* I, 7ff). They both start their philosophizing with the tacitly shared belief in what Plotinus holds in *Ennead* V, 8, that Wisdom is but another name for Truth and that both are identical with the one Divine hypostasis, the possession of which makes men "wise": the Plotinian *Noûs* which Augustine has expressly shorn of subordinationism and implicitly equated with the Christian *Verbum.*

This reality, however, lies entirely beyond the range of sense. The temptation is, in fact, to think of it as nonexistent, *nihil.* Indeed, the question put in these terms leaves but two alternatives: either Wisdom is "nothing," or else it is a being of another, superior order, one which, compared to the diminished existence of sense-realities, "truly exists." It is clear which of these alternatives Augustine has chosen: not only does Wisdom truly exist, it has, in addition, invited the sense-bound mortal to believe in its existence, to "seek, and you shall find" (*Acad* II, 9).

This Plotinian backdrop goes a long way to showing why this passage seems to Augustine, and eventually to Alypius as well, far more than a mere verbal quarrel. But the Christian point implicit throughout is indispensable to explaining the discussion of *fortuna* which prefaces it (III, 1–4) and the delight which Augustine expresses in Alypius' re-evocation, in the same context, of the Proteus myth (III, 13). This, he declares, shows the two friends at one in the most important area of "religion."

Facilius Dubitarem Vivere Me: "I Would More Easily Doubt My Own Existence"

But to this Christian "point" we shall return. For the moment, there is another aspect of Augustine's critique of the common understanding of the Academic position which calls for attention. The most poisonous element in such a system, he tells us, would lie in its corollary that even the wise man is condemned to ignorance of why he lives, how he should live, *even of whether he lives at all* (III, 19). To be a true Academic, one would have to doubt everything, even one's own existence. Hence Augustine's care throughout his early works to show that even if one pretends to doubt everything the fact of one's own existence is intuited as implied in all thinking, erring, and even doubting. Aside from this existential judgment, however, the remainder of his certitudes in the *Contra Academicos* comprise a set of propositions which are purely analytic, hence purely "intelligible." Though not yet indicating he has arrived at "possession" of Intelligible Truth, they show that he can grasp some truths of the intelligible order, pertaining therefore to the "other" world of which Plato and Plotinus taught mankind. It is, once again, with the mind's eye, not with the eye of the body, that he has glimpsed them.[7]

Mention of this certainty of his own existence takes a more condensed, and a significantly altered, form in the *Confessions*: "there was no further place for doubt, and it would have been easier for me to doubt that I live than doubt the existence of Truth." It is the momentary intellectual vision of subsistent Truth, which "is glimpsed, *understood* from the things which are created,"[8] that has swept all doubts from his mind. Though not corporeal, not diffused in space or visible to the bodily, fleshly eye, such a subsistent world of intelligible Beauty exists, and once seen, it becomes easier to doubt of one's own than of its existence.

Here again, the methodological lesson of *Ennead* VI, 4–5 is faithfully echoed in the passage from *Ennead* V, 8, on which this paradoxical reasoning-process is almost surely based.

This is why in that other (intelligible) sphere, when we are deepest in that knowledge *by intellection* (*κατὰ νοῦν*), we seem to be in ignorance (*ἀγνοεῖν δοκοῦμεν*); we are expecting some impression on *sense* (*τῆς*

[7] Augustine's artfulness here seems to have escaped even O'Meara's piercing eye. Each time the Saint uses the neutral term *tale* (*Acad* III, 18–21, esp. 21 for the Platonic two-world background which, though mentioned only in 26, has presided over this entire consideration), O'Meara translates it as "sense-object," thus entirely sapping whatever force the argument may have. As *Acad* III, 21 makes clear, Augustine admires Zeno's definition for the double reason that it suggests intelligible objects alone as grounding certitude, and is itself, as an analytic proposition, an excellent example of such an intelligible object. One must bear constantly in mind Augustine's personal theory that Zeno and the Academics generally were crypto-Platonists.

[8] Augustine's insinuation is that St. Paul teaches (Rom. 1 : 20) that we can "glimpse" God's Truth only through the "spiritual" intelligence: not through the "senses of the flesh." Dependence on sense and inability to attain to genuine intellectual insight are, for him as for Plotinus, marks of the fall, and his spontaneously Hellenic interpretation of such Semitisms as "flesh," "spirit," etc., lead him to suppose that this was the Apostle's meaning also.

αἰσθήσεως); which has nothing to report since *it has seen nothing* (οὐ γὰρ εἶδεν) *and never could in that order see anything* (οὐδ' ἂν . . . ἴδοι). *The unbelieving element is sense* (τὸ οὖν ἀπιστοῦν ἡ αἴσθησις); it is the other, the Intellectual-Principle, that sees; *and if this too disbelieved* (ἀπιστοῖ), it *could not even credit its own existence* (οὐδ' ἂν αὐτὸν πιστεύσειεν εἶναι), for it can never stand outside (ἔξω) and with bodily eyes apprehend itself as a sensible object (ὡς αἰσθητὸν ὄντα) (V, 8, 11, 33–40).

THE WAY TO WISDOM: "UNLESS YOU BELIEVE, YOU SHALL NOT UNDERSTAND"

"Belief" in Plotinus

Sense and disbelief

I adjusted MacKenna's translation of the foregoing passage to underline Plotinus' curious linkage of "belief" and vision, a connection which is by no means a *hapax*. To confine ourselves to those treatises which other evidence points to Augustine's having read, *Ennead* VI, 4, 13 teaches that dependence on sensation makes us "disbelieve" (ἀπιστοῦμεν) by forcing us to think of omnipresence in terms of a spatial extension which renders it contradictory. But the outspokenly mystical treatises are even more insistent. *Ennead* V, 3 echoes the text from V, 8: so far is the vision from our habitual sense-experience, Plotinus assures us, that even in the moment of enjoying it we must "believe" that we are seeing (τότε δὲ χρὴ ἑωρακέναι πιστεύειν) (*Enn* V, 3, 17, 25).[9]

Believing one who "points the way"

It is, among other things, this human propensity for thinking of the real in sensible terms that makes belief a necessary prelude to the attainment of vision. Thus, in the great mystical treatise which more and more evidence indicates that Augustine read, *Ennead* VI, 9, he speaks of the One from which all lower goods derive (the terms are familiar) "as from the sun all the light of the day." Alas, he admits, it is

> not to be told; not to be written . . . In our writing and telling we are but urging towards it: out of discussion we call to vision: to those desiring to see, we indicate the path (ὥσπερ ὁδὸν δεικνύντες); our teaching is of the road and the travelling (τῆς ὁδοῦ καὶ τῆς πορείας); the seeing must be the very act of the one that has made this choice (VI, 9, 4, 11–14).[10]

[9] For Solignac's suggestion regarding this work, see *Les Confessions, BA* 13, pp. 683–687.

[10] *Ennead* VI, 9, 4, 11–14. Note that Solignac (*Les Confessions, BA* 13, pp. 688–689) adduces precisely this section to prove that Augustine read this treatise.

Belief, renunciation, and likeness to God

The choice in question is the familiar one: total renunciation. To attain to vision, one must cut away everything, be prepared to fly alone to the alone. The question is how to ground this total renunciation? How persuade one who has never seen, that the vision is there and that the renunciation required will be more than repaid? The novice must *believe* the word of him who has seen, and in that trust strike forward into his task of self-purification. "Failure to attain," accordingly,

> may be due [either] to such impediment [that is, the body] or to lack of guiding thought which establishes belief (*ἢ δι' ἔνδειαν τοῦ παιδαγωγοῦντος λόγου καὶ πίστιν περὶ αὐτοῦ παρεχομένου*); impediment we must charge against ourselves and strive by entire renunciation to become emancipated; where there is disbelief for lack of convincing reasons (*ἃ δὲ ἐν τοῖς λόγοις ἀπιστεῖ ἐλλείπων*), further considerations may be applied (VI, 9, 4, 30–35).

Given the numerous thematic parallels between them, it is hardly surprising that *Enneads* VI, 9 and V, 8 should stress this same interconnection of ideas. The key text from the latter being a difficult one, we give it here in full, appending a literal translation:

> *Ἀεῖ δὲ καταμανθάνοντα μὲν ἔν τινι τύπῳ αὐτοῦ μένοντα μετὰ τοῦ ζητεῖν γνωματεύειν αὐτόν, εἰς οἷον δὲ εἴσεισιν, οὕτω μαθόντα κατὰ πίστιν, ὡς ἐπὶ χρῆμα μακαριστὸν εἴσεισιν, ἤδη αὐτὸν δοῦναι εἰς τὸ εἴσω . . .*
>
> It is necessary for the novice [or learner] while on the one hand remaining *under the image of the Divine Being*, together with his *searching, to come to some understanding* of it; on the other hand, he must give himself to a kind of entry *as the learner by faith does*—so must our learner give himself to this most blessed entry, now, indeed, to the inmost [depths] (V, 8, 11, 13–17).[11]

To recapitulate then, Plotinus exacts "belief" of the novice who has not seen, a belief that will ground the complete renunciation needed to arrive at the vision to which he can but point the

[11] Ragnar Holte, *Béatitude et Sagesse* (Paris: Etudes Augustiniennes, 1962), p. 60, suggests that Augustine could have drawn an entirely comparable doctrine of "belief" from *Ennead* I, 3, notably from its first and third chapters. The suggestion is a good one and it seems far from unlikely that Augustine read that work; but Holte does not manage to prove convincingly that the Saint, in this period of his development, enjoyed any direct acquaintance with the analogous tradition stemming from Clement of Alexandria, one which he later (pp. 316–317) offers to obviate any appeal to Plotinus as the source of this doctrine. Nor does he ever seriously argue that Ambrose mediated such a doctrine to Augustine. The likelihood stands, therefore, that Augustine came quite independently to a comparable understanding of faith-and-*gnôsis* by starting with a comparable problematic under comparable Platonistic influences.

"way," indicate the "path." Along with this belief and renunciation, however, there are two connected prescriptions: while "remaining under the image (τύπος) of the Divine Being," the novice must "search" for some "understanding."

The "image of the Divine Being" here is the *Phaedrus*' language for the classic Neo-Platonic theme of "similarity to God." Plotinus stresses it in the finales of *Enneads* I, 6 and VI, 9, as well as in the very section of the latter treatise just cited, where he warns that the vision is for "those capable of receiving (τοῖς δέχεσθαι δυναμένοις) . . . to touch it closely by their likeness (ὁμοιότητι) and by that kindred power (δυνάμει συγγενεῖ) within themselves through which . . . they are enabled to see" (VI, 9, 5, 25–28).

Only thus, he concludes in *Ennead* VI, 9 can the "image" (ὁμοίωμα, εἰκών) which is our soul hope to reattain the Divine Archetype, the "Term of all our journeying" (τέλος . . . τῆς πορείας), the end of the soul's Odyssey spoken of in *Ennead* I, 6 in words that Henry has shown (*Plotin*, pp. 107–109) burned themselves into Augustine's memory.

How come to the vision of the inaccessible Beauty . . . ? . . . He that has the strength (δυνάμενος), let him arise and withdraw into himself . . . 'Let us flee then to the beloved Fatherland' . . . What, then, is our course [or: "fleet," στόλος], what the manner of our flight? This is not a journey for the feet (Οὐ ποσὶ δεῖ διανύσαι); the feet bring us from land to land; nor need you think of coach or ship to carry you away (I, 6, 8).

A QUESTION

Plotinian "Belief" in Augustine

"Not on foot . . . do we return to you" avows the Augustine of the *Confessions* (I, 28). The Prodigal did not look for "horses or chariots or ships" or "fly away on visible wings." And summarizing the same text with explicit reference to Plotinus, he asks in the *City of God: Quae, igitur, classis et fuga*? "What is the fleet, then, what the [manner of] flight?" He answers his own question: *similem Deo fieri*. "Likeness to God is the way of return" (*Civ* IX, 17).

The theme is classic both for Neo-Platonist and Christian; nonetheless, its conjunction here with *Ennead* I, 6 is suggestive. Is there trace in Augustine of the other elements of Plotinus' "belief"?

A question parallel to that one has been asked, and the answer given to it suggests that not Plotinus, but Porphyry, is the more illuminating source on Augustine's theory of faith and reason. The Porphyrian theme of the "universal way," O'Meara has proposed, provides the pattern that inspired Augustine's thinking on the way of authority and faith.

The elements collected in this chapter insinuate another pattern, however. They indicate that Plotinus accounts for all the salient features of Augustine's thought on this question—for the doctrinal details, their accompanying imagery, their dynamic interconnections, and several disturbing corollaries.

But *ibi legi, ibi non legi*: his theory of faith and reason, one might object, Augustine could not possibly have gotten from Plotinus. If we reduce even the *credo ut intelligam* to a result of Plotinian influence, does not Augustine become, even more than Alfaric had thought, a Neo-Platonist with the merest veneer of Christianity? And does not Christ become the "Plato of the mob"?

Those two questions are, obviously, not unconnected. One can hardly treat of Augustine's theory of faith and understanding without examining the matter of faith in Christ, and vice-versa. But they are distinguishable questions. At the price of a certain overlapping, therefore, I propose to handle in the next two chapters, first, Augustine's theory of faith and understanding, then, the place of Christ within that general frame.

9 FAITH AND UNDERSTANDING

Intellectual Salvation and the Problem of Monica

One of the most pathetic themes traversing the Cassiciacum Dialogues concerns Augustine's treatment of his mother, Monica.[1] We have already seen the importance he accords to the liberal disciplines. The intellectualism of his Plotinian way of salvation—exacerbated, it would seem, by the influence of Varro's mathematical semirationalism—helps us understand why he thinks them so important. But the connection Augustine has forged between the disciplines and the way of return by "memory" will cause him serious difficulty from the very start. In the case of one who is "ignorant" but capable of the learning embodied in the disciplines, his theory of intellectualist salvation has relatively clear sailing. But how is Augustine to understand the fact that not all Christians are apt candidates for such a course of studies, equipped for such an intellectualist way of "return"? The question he asked in the *Soliloquies* apropos of memory was, in effect, a double one: the "ignorant" is a wide class, covering both Augustine and Monica, but in a vastly different sense. The

[1] On Augustine's relation to Monica, see Brown, *Augustine of Hippo*, pp. 28–34 for both bibliography and perceptive comment.

exacting course of studies he describes in the *De Ordine* may be all very well for him and for his pupils—but for his mother?

Fortune, Leisure, and Talent

Augustine seems to be coping with the difficulty toward the end of the *De Ordine*. His way of return requires that one be "of good talents and leisure," the leisure being conferred either "through the privilege of age or any kind of good fortune." A moment later he acknowledges more: the proper use of the liberal arts "is very difficult except for some gifted person who even from boyhood has earnestly and constantly applied himself" (*Ord* II, 44). For both Christian and philosopher, this poses a problem. Neither talents nor fortune seem to be within the power of the man possessing them; neither depend on his "good will." Virtue, happiness, the perfection of human life are therefore—if the obvious implications of Augustine's stand be drawn—out of the individual's control. One is either fortunate or not and there is the end of it. Augustine's speculations on the hidden identity between fortune and God's Providence come momentarily to his aid. Good fortune is God's doing, and He may be trusted to guarantee all that is due us for attaining the perfection He requires of us.

Talent

But talent? Has Monica the inborn gifts required for what Augustine suggests will lead her back to vision? More than one writer has pointed to her function as witness, if not personification to Augustine's unconscious eye, of both the "faithful mother" and the Church who is "mother of faith." Not surprisingly, her inescapable presence at Cassiciacum furnishes Augustine with a clear test case of his theory, one that confronts him with a thorny difficulty. For if his view of Christianity cannot cover Monica, who can claim to be Christian?

Monica's *Superstitio*

In the first book of the *De Ordine*, Licentius has no hesitation in using the term "superstitious" to describe the scruple that led Monica to reprimand him for bellowing psalmody while attending to the humble needs of nature (*Ord* I, 22ff). Far from defending her, Augustine shows his sympathies are entirely with Licentius. He is delighted with the youth's conversion to philosophy; this leads him—significantly—to a comparison between those who pass from acceptance of authority to the further stage of cultivating reason. For those content to stay with simple faith he reserves harsh terms, the gentlest of them being "wretched," *miseri*. Hence it is not surprising that Monica's appearance in mid-discussion (I, 31ff) provokes an immediate reflex of defense. St. Paul's warning against philosophy is directed, he assures her, against those who dabble with the *elementa* of *this* world; true philosophy, on the other hand, has to do with the other, intelligible world, the one whose existence is implied in Christ's assurance that his Kingdom was "not of this world." She must not, therefore, consider it her Christian duty to despise *philosophia*, the love of wisdom. Her own love of Wisdom, her arrival at the very height of philosophical detachment, is entirely too evident. Gladly, in fact, would Augustine become her disciple (32). Never, says Monica (with as much sweetness as good sense) did he lie so grandly! (33).

Monica's Talent and Leisure

Augustine in the grip of an idea is not so easily discouraged. His acknowledgment of her virtue, perhaps his regret at condemning her and her like to a "wretched life," seem to have worked on his mind. Between the first and second books of the *De Ordine*, there occurs the birthday discussion of the *De Beata Vita*, and all the family members are invited. There is little stretching of the evidence involved in saying that Monica is unquestionably the star of this dialogue. Here a liberal amount of fiction[2] may well have entered into Augustine's account, but again and again[3] it is Monica he features as furnishing the crucial distinction, the insight that resolves some knotty problem and brings expressions of wonder to the lips of all.

Flushed with his success, he begins the second book of the *De Ordine* with explicit mention of her presence. Long had he remarked on her talent (*ingenium*), he says, on her ardent love for divine realities; but the *De Beata Vita* discussion had disclosed to him a "mind (*mens*) . . . so rare that nothing seemed more adapted for true philosophy" (*Ord* II, 1). Hence he has decreed she should be included in their meetings whenever her leisure (*otium*) permits it.

[2] In the Introduction to his translation of *Against the Academics*, *ACW* 12, pp. 23–32, O'Meara has argued (convincingly, I think) against naïve acceptance of such indices as Augustine might seem to have left to persuade his readers they were being offered an exact transcription of the ensuing discussions. Such indices, O'Meara points out, were part of the "dialogue" *genre*, and the informed reader was expected to know they were not to be taken literally. What O'Meara has said (p. 31) of "fiction" in respect to Trygetius' replies, I have applied to Monica. For an expansion of his argument in this regard, see "The Historicity of the Early Dialogues of St. Augustine," in *Vigiliae Christianae*, 5: 150–178 (1951).

[3] See her interventions at *Vita* 8, 10, 16, 19, 21, 27.

But Her Unwillingness

If "fortune" be Providence, we can be sure it will lavish its gifts on Monica. The requisite "leisure," too, is at least intermittently hers. Now she has been accorded the last vital piece of equipment for the way of the disciplines: the mind and talent for them.

Mens, ingenium: both terms are frankly intellectualist. We are promised a renewal of the *De Beata Vita* scenario. But somehow the script has been altered. Only two of Monica's interventions punctuate the discussion (II, 22 and 23), the first calling for correction by Licentius, the second a mere *reprise* of something already contributed at an earlier stage. Augustine seems to have been disenchanted on his mother's brilliance. Soon afterwards, he is describing the "discipline of learning which is required to supplement the "discipline of behavior"; both are needed for the soul's effort toward the desired vision of Truth. Once again we are greeted with the distinction of authority and reason, and another observation on the faithful who are either incapable (*non valentes*) or contemptuous (*contemnentes*) of the "disciplines" which lead to the fullness of "erudition." Now it is no longer a question merely of ability: the willingness to enter Augustine's school of Christian Platonism is expressly brought into focus, and one cannot quite suppress the suspicion that Monica had meanwhile made it clear to her son that she was having none of it. She has held her ground, but then, neither the first nor last of sons to inherit obstinacy from their mothers, so does he. Whether it be inability or unwillingness that keeps them from pursuing the course he has outlined, he makes clear, he cannot call such people happy in this life (*Ord* II, 26). After the acrobatics of the *De Beata Vita*, it is not hard to guess how much this admission costs him.

A Hope Dashed

The discussion of the way of reason then leads into an ascent through the various *disciplinae* that are the works of Reason (II, 30ff). The series of studies imposed there as preparatory to philosophy becomes more and more exacting, and Augustine's frank admission of this (44) prompts a last despairing appeal to Monica. She need not be terrified as though this way involved an immense forest of studies; a few principles, wide and powerful in application, will certainly suffice here, considering her *ingenium* and her detachment from all bodily filth. She already knows, for instance, the thoroughly divine nature and force of grammar, as though having grasped its very soul, she has left its body to the savants (45). The same thing is true of the other arts, he assures her. And yet (what was Monica's facial expression throughout all this?) if her contempt for them still be complete, let her hold to her faith and good life as now (46). The impression is unavoidable: Augustine's wild hope of making a philosopher of Monica has met with shipwreck. Her "mind" and "talent" for such matters were probably more than anything a creation of her son's perfervid imagination; in any case, her "contempt" for his way of reason seems quite emphatically to have "remained complete."

There is quiet resignation in the final remarks he addresses to his mother. The "ascent" of the mind through the various disciplines has led him to a glowing description of the culminating vision which he is confident will make both him and his disciples both good and happy. For a last time he turns to Monica, but not, this time, inviting her to accompany them. Rather, he charges her to "prize nothing more highly than the finding of the Truth, to wish for, to think of, to love nothing else" and to pray that "we"—Augustine and his disciples—"obtain the great blessing which through your meriting we have come to desire" (*Ord* II, 52). Off they charge, Augustine and his pupils, to the conquest of the happy life; the woman, as so often, must remain behind and pray.

Reasons for an Impasse

One may speculate on whether Augustine's defeat in this battle toward his Plotinian synthesis of Christianity was really unavoidable. There is reason to think that he left untapped some of the richest resources Neo-Platonism could have brought to bear on the problem that has stymied him here. Part of his difficulty, again, stems from a heavy Varronian stress on the "liberal disciplines" which threatens to drain off the subtleties of Plotinian intellectualism, deforming it into an abstract and disincarnate rationalism. But another factor in the situation is Augustine's temperamental preference, in this period of his life, for the world-negating aspects of Plotinus' earlier work. In a recent convert, still affected by years of Manichaeism, this may be understandable.

But can Plotinus' theory of man, even at its best, be brought into strict coherence with the Christian view of conversion and salvation? This is not at all clear. When Augustine views human life as the life of a fallen soul, when he adopts Plotinus' view of the fault which produced that fall, when he adopts Plotinus' manner of integrating that fault into a thoroughly necessitarian view of universal law, when, more relevant to our purpose, he assents to a view of the soul's return which is, though not exclusively, crucially intellectualistic, then he must expect to encounter serious difficulties with Christianity.

For the stage machinery of the liberal arts which Augustine has set inside the Plotinian theory of memory is designed to sharpen the mind for the recovery of an intellectual vision: the vision of a world beyond all sensible embodiment. It must, therefore, put a certain premium on mental gifts, on leisure, on the luck—or Providence—which allows one to study what another cannot. Christianity, on the other hand—as Augustine later came to see more clearly and remind his readers—puts a premium on man's free consent to believe, to hope, to love: and one may think that in such matters Monica was no novice, after all. She is content to walk by faith. Augustine is impatient to understand what he believes—to understand, and to "see."

Behind the difficulty which his mother represents, there stands a theory of faith in its relation to reason, reason in its relation to vision. That theory follows more or less neatly from the Plotinian anthropology with which Augustine is experimenting at Cassiciacum. With modifications of varying importance, it is the theory he holds up to and including the *Confessions*.[4] It is time we studied it in greater depth.

Few facets of Augustine's thought bite so deeply into his conception of Christianity as his theory of faith and understanding of the faith. Part of the reason is that few preoccupations plunge so profoundly into the quick of his personal experience, an experience with the faith which was not uniformly happy.

THE IMPORTANCE OF "UNDERSTANDING"

African Catholicism: "Simple Faith" and "Superstition"

Augustine was, to begin with, brought up an African Catholic. The most prestigious Bishop of African Catholicism was undoubtedly Cyprian. Each evening, it is said, he would bid his servant hand him down the writings of "the master"—and by the

[4] One of the more important of these modifications is insinuated by the fact that at Ostia, and despite Augustine's avowal of her lack of formal education (*Conf* IX, 17), Monica enjoys the "vision" (IX, 23–26). Augustine has come to think that Christian "charity" and detachment can effect what he formerly thought the "disciplines" could provide. But his development on this question deserves a study in itself.

"master" he meant Tertullian. Tertullian it was who had thrown down the gauntlet to the very effort on which Augustine eventually embarked: the effort to seek some understanding of the Hebrew scriptures in the philosophy of the Greeks. What kinship could there be between Athens and Jerusalem, he cried—and assumed the question was purely rhetorical.

There is much evidence that this uncompromising spirit still held in the Catholicism of Augustine's boyhood.[5] Africa's theological conservatism was one important feature which laid it open to the inroads of that "heresy of the intellectuals," Manichaeism. And after his return to Catholicism, Augustine tends to think that conservatism was, in part at least, to blame for his having been so long away.

Recording his spiritual itinerary for Mallius Theodorus, he reports that at nineteen, having read Cicero's *Hortensius* and been "inflamed by such a great love of philosophy that I considered devoting myself to it at once," nonetheless "a childish superstition deterred me from thorough investigation, and, as soon as I was more courageous, I threw off the darkness and learned to trust more in men that taught than in those that ordained obedience" (*Vita* 4).

Superstitio: the same term was applied to Monica's scruple about Licentius' psalmody in the "darkness" of the outhouse (*Ord*, I, 23–24). The incident starts Augustine reflecting on the need for faith's passing on to a second phase of understanding. The context makes it clear that Courcelle's interpretation of the term is quite correct: "superstition," for Augustine, is connected with deterrents "from thorough investigation"—with the kind of Christianity which merely "ordains obedience," but does not "teach."[6] The superstition he refers to in the text to Mallius Theodorus is, therefore, not Manichaeism, but the sort of intransigent, obscurantist Catholicism he had experienced as a youth. With this attitude he instinctively associates his mother, Monica. Thus his reflex of defense when she enters the *De Ordine* discussion (*Ord* I, 32)—and his bruising disappointment when he finds his darkest suspicions on her are fulfilled. She is content to stay with "simple faith" and not proceed on the quest for understanding—and for the vision that lies beyond.

Were there any doubt of this interpretation, Augustine's words to Honoratus would clear them up. He is trying to show his

[5] On this authoritarian cast of African Catholicism, see Brown, *Augustine of Hippo* pp. 42–43.

[6] See Courcelle's *Recherches*, pp. 64–67.

friend, still a Manichee, the *Usefulness of Believing*. The theme was central to Manichaean proselytism of Catholics: they openly scorned the Church who exacted such simple, unthinking faith of her children; they offered reasoned insight into what the *Catholica* held up as inscrutable mysteries. In the course of the work, Augustine makes some serious admissions on his friend's, and his own, youthful experience of Catholicism.

You know, Honoratus, that for no other reason did we fall in with such men [the Manichees are meant] than that they kept saying that by pure and simple reason, apart from all fearsome authority, they would lead their willing listeners on to God and free them from all error. For, what else forced me . . . to follow these men and diligently to listen to them, save that they said we were terrified by superstition, and that faith was demanded of us before reason (*Util* 2).

Augustine admits that his own youthful disputatious temperament only made him more easily persuadable to spurn "what seemed to be old wives' tales" (*Util* 2). The Manichees, he goes on to say, "disputed widely and vigorously . . . over the errors of the unlearned" so that both he and his fellow-victims thought they should "necessarily retain whatever they implanted in us of their own doctrine, since we met with no other with which we might be satisfied" (*Util* 2).

Here the term *superstitio* is more explicitly connected with the *Catholica*'s demand for "faith . . . before reason." That demand, the Manichees succeeded in convincing Augustine, was backed up by a "fearsome authority" which "terrified" rather than enlightened. The "old wives' tales" it peddled were tantamount to "errors of the unlearned," and yet, in the face of the Manichee objections, Augustine admits to having met no other counter-position with which he "might be satisfied."

He gives us several examples in his works of the kind of reaction Catholics were known to exhibit in the face of Manichee attack: the old woman who greeted their claim that the sun was divine by "stamping her foot on the spot where the sun shone through the window and cried—quite foolishly (who will say otherwise?) and womanlike—'Lo, I am trampling on the sun, your god' " (*Util* 13). He himself will refuse to "give the answer that someone is said to have given" to a favorite Manichee objection against the opening verses of Genesis: what was God doing through the ages which preceded "the beginning" when He created heaven and earth. "Evading by a joke the force of the objection: 'He was preparing hell,' he said, 'for those prying into such deep subjects' " (*Conf* XI, 14).

The Need for "Understanding"

Such tactics were not calculated to still the doubts of a restless, inquiring mind; quite the contrary. Many of the difficulties the Manichees brought up were real, worthy of better treatment than this. It would not do to command belief in doctrines which, as they were explained to him, Augustine found senseless and contradictory. But the difficulty, he later found, was not in the doctrine itself, but all too often in the manner of its exposition. He advises Honoratus to "seek out someone both good and learned" in order to "become better and more learned by his instruction. Such a one was not easily found? . . . There was no one in the land in which you lived? What purpose, then, should more profitably send you travelling? He was . . . on the continent . . .? A sea voyage should then be taken" (*Util* 17). There is an obvious echo here of his own experience: not until encountering Ambrose did he hear an exposé of Catholic doctrine that failed to insult his understanding.

And for Augustine understanding was important. Its importance helps explain several instances of what might otherwise seem anomalies in the *Confessions* story. The first of them we have touched on already: he stresses the moment in Book VII when he arrived at some understanding of the issues which long had troubled his intelligence, far more than he does the moment of his return to the faith and to the Church. For it was Augustine's lifelong desire to be a Christian, and in one sense he could rightly feel he had been a believing "Christian" all along. The Manichees had the name of Christ forever on their lips, they pretended to be "enlightened" Christians. Christ's name is what he had found missing in Cicero's *Hortensius*, for all its powerful effect on him. But despite this difference between them, the *Hortensius* and the Manichees had this in common: they honored understanding, encouraged the quest for it.

Understanding a Step to "Vision"

This, then, is one of several reasons why Augustine marks the moment of his encounter with the *Hortensius* as the pivot point in his life: it made him desire "undying wisdom with incredible ardor of heart" and, like the Prodigal, he "began to rise up, so that I might return to you" (*Conf* III, 7). The darkest colors of the *Confessions* appear in Book II. The books which follow, even those describing the Manichee period, are already lightened with the aura of slow, painful "return," fired by the Eros, wavering but never thereafter quenched, to "love, and pursue, and attain and catch hold of, and strongly embrace . . . wisdom itself" (*Conf* III, 8). But the very wording of that text, and of others we have seen, indicates that the problem is not simply one of faith and understanding: there is a third dimension to it. The problem involves the passage from faith, through understanding, to vision.

For this, Augustine and Plotinus think, is the goal of all understanding: the vision which is "embrace," "possession," final "enjoyment" of Truth subsistent. Not so much an end for man, it is the connatural end of the soul. Augustine's dialogues at Cassiciacum show him seriously entertaining the possibility that this end is attainable even during "this life," even while the soul "bore the body": attainable, not only for a moment here and there, but in a semipermanent way. Even while "in" the body, the soul could become so purified of bodily desires, so liberated from bodily preoccupations, that it could enter this circle of lasting joy, the "happy life."

The doctrine strikes our modern ears as a curious one. Again, the dusty overlay of centuries makes it difficult to fathom how Augustine could have brought himself to take it seriously. And yet, there is no other way to make sense of the Cassiciacum Dialogues, or, more generally, of Augustine's early works.

GROUNDWORK OF A VIEW: THE *CONTRA ACADEMICOS*

The majority of loci where the Augustine of Cassiciacum discussed the relations between faith and understanding, authority and reason, are to be found in the *De Ordine*. But the groundwork of the theory he proposes in that work has been carefully laid in the two preceding works—the *Contra Academicos* and its companion-piece, the *De Beata Vita*. The point of the former work is often assumed to be the refutation of Academic skepticism, but a close examination of it in the light of Plotinian theory suggests a more exact expression of Augustine's governing intention. He means to show that the Academics were not skeptics after all; they were, in fact, the inheritors of Platonism and of its "way" of salvation for the soul. How does this way cohere with the Christian way? This is the second question Augustine sets himself to answer in that Dialogue. He answers it subtly, artfully, by situating the Incarnation inside the Plotinian scheme of "return." His answer to both these questions implies the view of faith and reason he then proceeds to expound more explicitly in the *De Ordine*.

Seeking or Finding?

"Seek, and you shall find," Our Lord has said. Only when he cites this text in the remarks to Romanianus which open the second book of the *Contra Academicos* (II, 9) does it suddenly dawn on the reader that the argument of the first book has turned on the two key words "*quaerere*" and "*invenire*." True to his theory, Augustine sets his two pupils to an *exercitatio animi* throughout the entire first book. This sharpening of the mind's eye will eventually, he hopes, prepare them for vision. The question thrown out to them is this: does happiness consist in the "seeking," or the "finding" of truth? Licentius sets himself to defend the Academic position as he understands it: the search for truth is all that is possible to man, and therein must human happiness lie. Trygetius takes the opposite view: happiness implies that truth has been "found."

An initial skirmish ensues. Cicero's authority is appealed to, and the appeal is ruled out of court. "Philosophy"—and it is significant here that Christ is quoted—promises to liberate from the yoke of authority: "The Truth shall make you free" (John 8: 31). Authority, then, for both philosopher and Christian, must yield to reason (*Acad* I, 8–9).

What is "Like to Truth"

The discussion between the two youths takes up the first book, and as might have been expected, it is inconclusive. It was, Augustine informs them, merely an *exercitatio* for them. The second book will therefore take things up in far more serious style: Alypius goes to the defense of the Academic position, while Augustine takes the other side. Augustine summarizes the doctrine of the Old Academy, and Alypius that of the New. In the course of those two summaries, a crucial term enters the debate. Because the wise man will admit, according to the common understanding of the Academic doctrine, that he cannot know the "true," he will, for purposes of action, rest content with the "probable" or—another term they used—the *verisimile:* "what is like the truth." At *Acad* II, 16 Augustine begins to press the point that it is laughable to say one can know "what is like the truth" unless one also knows the truth that it is like. The other discussants in turn make efforts to bring him off this line of argument; why haggle over a word? What the Academics meant was that man could grasp only the "probable." This, effectively, is what they meant by the term *verisimile*. But Augustine stands to his guns: this is a serious question, touching substance and not mere expression (II, 24). Cicero, for example, knew Latin as well as anyone. He used this term and we must suppose he meant it to say what it says: "like the truth" (II, 26).

The Academics' Secret Doctrine

Here Augustine hints at the theory of Academic philosophy he will fully unveil in the third book. It is important to remember that he has that theory in mind throughout everything that follows.

> [The Academics] seem to me to have chosen these terms both at once to conceal from the unintelligent and reveal to the more alert, their real opinion. Why I think this and how I understand it, I shall explain when I have discussed first the points which, as men think, they, as the apparent enemies of human knowledge, advance (II, 24).

There is, then, a difference between what "men think," what the Academics "apparently" hold, and what "their real opinion" is. Augustine goes on to indicate he thinks that "what we read in their books" was advanced "merely to conceal their true opinion, lest certain sacred truths should be betrayed rashly by them to minds defiled, and, so to speak, profane" (II, 24). Plotinus' citation of the rule of the Mysteries immediately comes to mind: "Nothing divulged to the uninitiate . . . the holy things may not be uncovered to a stranger" (*Enn* VI, 9, 11, 1ff). It may not be entirely coincidental that Augustine later explains the Academics as crypto-Platonists who veiled their positive doctrine from outsiders as though it were an ensemble of "mysteries." That positive doctrine, he prefers to believe, has received its purest expression in Plotinus. The whole discussion of the *verisimile* notion was, accordingly, keyed to prompting the reader's mind to ask the question: what is this world of Truth, to which this world we sensibly experience is only "similar"?

The Way to Become Wise: Fortune and Providence

The argument that opens the third book we have already examined: it turns on the need of "fortune" and of her gifts for the one aspiring to become wise. Like the breasts that nourished our infancy, like the ships or wings needed for voyage or flight across the sea, these things are needed for the going, even if they can be discarded once one has "arrived."

But "gifts of fortune" are, Augustine is convinced, really gifts of Providence. Even while writing the *Contra Academicos* he has in mind the solution he will spell out in the *De Ordine*. Romanianus' aid was necessary to the "fledging" process which allowed him finally to fly to the "haven," to the "lap" of "Philosophy"—from whose "breasts," he notes, in contrast to the breasts that nourish infants, "no age group can complain it is excluded" (*Acad* I, 4). But in that process Romanianus was acting as "agent" (*minister*) for someone else: but for whom? Augustine admits the answer to this "is as yet conceived by me in faith rather than comprehended by reason" (*Acad* II, 4). The *De Ordine* will seek an "understanding" of that faith.

The same implication is present in a later illustration, that of a journey to a distant city. The "seeker" may have to ask his "way" and take the word of some merest peasant, who seems purely by chance to be working in a field along the road (III, 34). But nothing, as the *De Ordine* will demonstrate, nothing is mere chance, all is Providence. Even this peasant is, as Romanianus was, an "agent" of that Divine Logos which presides over our lives down to their minutest detail (*Acad* II, 3–4; III, 1–4, 11, 13).

Proteus, the "Pointer"

The following section (III, 5–11) has already come up for consideration. Augustine presents a definition of the "sage" as one who knows "wisdom"; the philosopher, on the other hand, is still in quest of it—or "her." Alypius' counter-position is constantly threatened by Augustine's contention that it reduces "wisdom" to a "nothing." The implicitly accepted notion of Wisdom as a subsistent entity exercises a surreptitious influence on both minds in the argument. Alypius' last defense consists in comparing the truth they seek to the god Proteus: "his pursuers were never sure that what they had was still he, unless some divinity pointed him out to them (*nisi indice alicujus numine*)." "May that divinity be present to us," Augustine prays, "and may he deign to show us that truth for which we strive so hard! I too shall then confess, even if the Academics do not agree—though I think they will—that they have been overcome" (III, 11).

It must seem strange how enthusiastically Augustine leaps upon Alypius' illustration: the only question the Academics now can ask is "who will indicate (*demonstrabit*) truth to us?" (III, 12) Alypius has told them "who it is can point out (*ostendere*) truth . . . Only some divinity (*numen*) could point out (*ostendere*) truth to man"—an utterance, Augustine exclaims, "as concise as it is pious." If but that *numen* "be present to us" (*adsit*), nothing could be truer. Proteus, indeed: what "profound understanding and sensitiveness" led Alypius to hit upon that illustration of the need to cast aside deceiving images in order to get hold of truth. Augustine finds his dearest friend in agreement with him, not only in philosophy, "but also in religion itself" (III, 13).

Augustine's enthusiasm may have much to do with the strong preference Alypius had voiced (cf. *Conf* IX, 7) against mentioning the name of Christ in these dialogues. That preference could well have been dictated by a desire for accommodation to a cultivated public which might be repelled by a more overt apologetic approach. Hence the exaggerated discretion which has veiled Augustine's Christian intention in these early works, even from modern scholars. But the "divinity" which is "present to us" and "pointer to the truth," one whose entry into this discussion makes the two friends one in "religion"—these are an ensemble of elements calculated to arouse suspicion. Augustine is alluding in a code all his own to the Incarnation.

Zeno's Dictum and Eternal Wisdom

Those suspicions once alerted, their confirmation does not keep us waiting too long. Augustine passes on to consider Zeno's "definition," which he expresses with exquisite care: "that object of vision (*id visum*) can be comprehended which so appears that it cannot appear as (something) false"; such an object (*tale aliquid*), Arcesilaus had claimed in pleading his case for skepticism, "cannot be found" (*non . . . inveniri potest*) (III, 21). The assumption that would seem most ordinary in reading this text is that *visum* refers to "seeing" of the sensible sort, that *inveniri* may be taken in its everyday connotation.[7] But Augustine has already subtly reshaped these terms to fit his own special problematic. "Seeing" must be taken in the most general sense, one which covers intellectual vision as well as sense-perception; "finding" for him refers to that "embrace" and "possession" which is the desired term of all quest. Taken in this meaning, Augustine finds the definition "entirely true" and "worthy of the greatest praise" as both "a definition and example of things capable of being comprehended" (III, 21). He retreats momentarily to a less advanced position, adding that even were one not to hold this truth as certain, one would nonetheless admit "we know that the definition itself is either true or not true; that is, we know something." But his own conviction is that Zeno's definition is true and can be known for certain and the reason is that it is a purely intelligible, analytic truth—just like the disjunctive proposition stating it must be

[7] See Chap. VIII, n. 7, above.

"either true or not true." The entire series of examples Augustine then presents of what can certainly be known—examples drawn from "physics," "ethics" and "dialectics"—support this interpretation. For they, too, are all analytic statements, in almost every instance complete either-or disjunctions (III, 23–29).

Wisdom and the Intelligible World

Purely intelligible truths, therefore, can certainly be known. One can know something, even be it only Zeno's definition which so often buttresses the conviction that nothing can be known for certain. What, then, of sense-certainty? Can you know that a sensible world exists? Yes, answers Augustine, but with an interesting restriction: "by the term world . . . I mean all this, whatever kind of thing it be, . . . which presents itself to my eyes and seems to me to hold earth and sky or quasi-earth and quasi-sky . . . If . . . you deny that that which presents itself to me is the world, you are raising a question merely about a word; for I have stated that I do call that appearance the 'world' " (III, 24). The position he has taken on sense-certainty is almost pure subjectivism: "Do not assent more than you know that it appears so to you," he later puts it, "Then there is no deception" (III, 26). And the Platonism implicit in his entire discussion comes out plainly in the course of it. The Academic arguments against sense-perception

> are not valid against all philosophers. There are some philosophers, for example, who maintain that whatever the spirit receives by way of bodily sense can generate opinion indeed, but not knowledge. They insist that the latter is found only in the intelligence and, far removed from sense, abides in the mind. Perhaps the wise man whom we seek is to be found in their midst (III, 26).

Though stated here only as a suggested possibility, this view of knowledge—as being accessible only to intelligence, the senses being capable of generating mere opinion—has in fact commanded Augustine's entire presentation since he spoke of the Academics' "secret doctrine" toward the end of Book II. Everything is carefully couched to prepare for the main contention of his history of Academicism in Book III: the Academics were secretly Platonists.

Academic Crypto-Platonism

Having prepared his hearers' minds for the view which has surreptitiously presided over his entire exposé, he presents his personal history of philosophy, and in the course of it, his personal theory of what the Academics really meant to teach. There are, as Plato said, "two worlds, one intelligible, where Truth itself resides, and this sensible world which, it is clear, we apprehend by sight and touch. The first was the true world, while the latter was made *like* the true world and *after its image*. Truth . . . shines from the former in the soul which knows herself; but only opinion, and not knowledge, can be generated from the latter in the souls of those who are not wise" (III, 37). In the face of the "multitude's" tendency to believe everything is corporeal, Arcesilaus and the other Academics, he opines, although remaining faithful to Plato's positive teaching, "acted in a most prudent and useful way, . . . in concealing completely the doctrine of the Academy and in burying it as gold to be found at some time by posterity" (III, 38). Better to "disabuse them of their error" than to try and teach men "who could not be taught at all" (III, 38). It was not "right or convenient" to disseminate their hidden meaning of the *verisimile* "to the profane" (III, 40).

Had Zeno but been more alert, he would have seen that this was the authentic truth hidden in his formula: "that nothing could be comprehended except that which answered his definition of what was comprehensible, and that nothing such could be found in things corporeal" (III, 39)—the things of "this world." This, Plato's doctrine, "the purest and most clear in philosophy," has again finally "shone forth especially in Plotinus" who, one would think, was actually "Plato come to life again" (III, 41). Disciples of Plato, therefore, the Academics now can salute the positive expression of their secret teaching, Plotinus' *Enneads*.

The Assent to Wisdom "Within"

Granted, then, this Plotinian interpretation of Academicism, the first of the Academic roadblocks to the quest for Truth is removed. It is at least probable that man can attain Truth—the Truth which dwells in that other world of which this sense-world is but "image," *verisimile*. The second of their pretended maxims, that "the wise man will assent to nothing," really depends on the first, and hence falls with it. Once granted the probable existence of a true "sage," he can know intelligible truths. In a lively "spat" between the wise man and "Wisdom speaking within him" Augustine tries to demonstrate that it would be even more "monstrous that the wise man should not assent to Wisdom than that he should not know her" (III, 30). Where will he find this Wisdom? "In his very own self" (III, 31)—a good Plotinian position, one that brings Augustine round again to refurbish the argument that otherwise, "Wisdom is a nothing" (III, 32)—again, as we have seen, a stand on Plotinian principle.

THE WAY TO WISDOM FOR THE MULTITUDE

The Question of the Way

All this is very well—for the sage. But the real question of the *Contra Academicos* is, how does one *become* wise? What has thus far been proved is the probability that man can see, embrace, possess Truth. An end for the journey can be envisaged, but how lies the "way"? The Academic arguments long succeeded in holding Augustine back from the very "quest" itself, from the "search for wisdom," robbed him of "hope of reaching" Truth (III, 43). The existential question, both for him, his students, and the mass of mankind, is how to "cross over that barrier which confronts those who are beginning philosophy," a barrier which threatens that the "whole of philosophy is obscure, and does not allow one to hope that any light will be found in it" (III, 30). The thesis of the *De Vera Religione*, dedicated to Romanianus and promised him in the course of this very work, is already forming. The Platonists may have succeeded with the "few," but what of that mass of mankind who are not wise but only journeying toward wisdom?

The difficulty has occupied Augustine earlier in the dialogue: it forced him to discuss the need of "fortune" and her gifts to "become wise," the need of breasts, of wings, of boats. The same difficulty in another form he had pressed against Carneades' distinction between things about which philosophers inquire, and other (everyday) matters. It will not do for him to "appeal to those obscurities that are impenetrable to the unskilled, and penetrable only to a certain gifted few with eyes that are divine," for the Academic principle invoked "is at once the formulation of a philosopher, and is placed firmly at the entrance to philosophy." It implies Carneades has "found" some truth, yet undercuts the very "quest" which must have allowed him to find it in the first place. We all begin our lives "unskilled" and in time cultivate the "eyes that are divine." Deeper probing may force Carneades to admit, after all, that something can be known, "which is very like that which is untrue." That phrase introduces a very puzzling passage indeed. Zeno's definition, which Carneades has converted into the ground-principle of the Academy's ostensible skepticism, he has thereby made a "lurking-place" from which he pounces fiercely "on the unwary who wish to pass on their way: *transire*." Some Hercules, Augustine warns him, "will strangle you, half-human as you are, in your cave, and will crush you with the weight of that principle. For he will show that there is something in philosophy which cannot be demonstrated by you to be uncertain on the plea that it is like to what is not true" (*Acad* III, 22).

But how, the Platonist was bound to ask, can something merely "like the truth" be object of genuine knowledge? What is Augustine suggesting here?

Images of Incarnate Wisdom

That text in its entirety is a tangle of obscurities. But, once again, the suspicion that Augustine's obscurities are artful ones may help in the effort to disentangle the text. The choice, in fact, seems to lie between such artful sense and no sense at all. The topic of ordinary as against philosophic knowledge is to the fore. Just three paragraphs earlier Augustine had expressed the fear that dominates this section, that the mass of mankind "would be driven away entirely from philosophy" unless the Academics formulated their popularly understood position in more candid terms (III, 19). Here that unphilosophic multitude reappears in the guise of those who would "pass on their way" (*transire*)—over the obstacle, we may presume, which Carneades has placed at the very "entrance," the "barrier which confronts those who are beginning philosophy" (III, 30). How, then, we may decode, are such beginners on their "way" toward wisdom ever to arrive, if Carneades and sages like him block the way? A moment later Augustine will gird himself for further battle with the hope that "God will readily help me" (III, 22), and our suspicions are again alerted. The franker expression of the Academic position he had urged shortly before was couched in a curious phrase. They should, he suggested, rather have taught that "Wisdom cannot fall into man (*non posse in hominem cadere sapientiam*), a Wisdom which, they knew, was "with God: *apud Deum*" (III, 19).

Christ the Way for the Many

Again, Augustine is forcing the Academics into the Plotinian posture he will make them assume at the end of the dialogue: the Wisdom being talked about is subsistent Wisdom, "with God." What the Academics do not see is that this Wisdom can "fall into man"; it can be "perceived, even though it manifest itself by signs which are shared in common with what is not true" (III, 21). Again, Augustine is speaking a veiled language of Incarnation. The Hercules who will come to slay Carneades is a Christ-symbol, just as earlier Proteus was. He will show philosophers something which is "like what is not true" and yet, not demonstrably uncertain. Incarnate, he will exhibit the nature which makes all corporeal realities "not true," yet Truth Itself, Wisdom in the cloak of humanity, he will be the very fount of certainty.

Without such an Incarnation, the mass of mankind would be condemned to "seek" with no hope, in this life, of ever "finding" Truth. To the traveler questing for a distant city, the Academic's advice seemed peremptory and forbidding: any information given him on the "way" must be uncertain, and if he is wise he will not assent to it. But, objects Augustine, "not only does he err who follows the wrong way (*viam*), but he as well who does not follow the right one" (III, 34). The disastrous moral implications of this the Academics themselves must have seen (III, 35–36). This persuades Augustine that men as intelligent as they must have had a deeper, hidden doctrine: Platonism (III, 37–42), a philosophy "not of this world" but of "the other, intelligible world." That other world, Augustine asserts in the *De Ordine*, is the "kingdom not of this world" Christ claimed was His (*Ord* I, 32). "To that intelligible world," he now makes clear, the "subtle reasoning" of the Platonists "would never recall" the multitude, "had not the most high God, *because of a certain compassion for the masses* (*populari quadam clementia*), bent and submitted the authority of the divine intellect even to the human body itself" (III, 42).

Having Plotinized the Academics, now Augustine Christianizes Plotinus. *Ego sum veritas*: "I am the Truth." These are the words Augustine cites at the climax of his *De Beata Vita*. *Ego sum via*: "I am the Way" would be the partner member of that same quotation which, but for the discretion Alypius imposed upon him, could well have captioned the *Contra Academicos*. "I only point the way" Plotinus had exclaimed. And in a phrase reminiscent of it, the Augustine of the *Confessions* replies that full-grown Christians "no longer stand in need of a man to be pointer to the Way" (XIII, 32).

This, then, is the burden of the *Contra Academicos* as well: that to the ordinary "seeker" after Wisdom, to the sense-bound man hesitantly standing on the threshold of philosophy, Christ has come, Divine Authority Itself in human guise, to "lead him on." Far from being an intrusion ill prepared for, one that strikes from the Christian blue at the end of the third book, the problem of Incarnation is subtly at the heart of the entire argument. The artfulness attributed to Augustine here at times surpasses belief; but the choice is all too often between an artful sense and no sense at all. Besides, the artfulness attributed to him is equaled, and perhaps to some extent inspired, by the incredible artfulness he attributes to the Academics.

Christ Himself, then, is *Veritas* become *index veritatis*, divinity come to "point the way" to God. He is *par excellence* seer become "sign," Protean Truth both hidden and revealed behind the folds of His humanity, behind the changing imagery of Scripture's allegorical utterance of the Word, behind the preaching of the Church whose maternal breasts nurse our infancy on the milk of faith and who purifies our love by her salutary precepts, until we are strong enough for the "grown-up food" of spiritual vision. No longer need we depend on Plotinus' human authority to attain the vision. Divine Authority, divine Truth, has (in some mysterious sense of the term) come down to point the way back to Himself.

Plotinus Completed by Christianity

Verbum: this is the Light which Plotinus saw was the soul's beatitude, the "Light that enlightens every man who comes into this world." What he did not see was that this Light had "come unto His own," and despite the fault of desertion which made them fallen souls, had become a human light for human beings. Wisdom had, after all, "fallen into man," supernal Truth become Truth Incarnate, become the Herculean giant who strangles Carneades precisely by *being* that double-natured reality, that "something" both certain and yet "like to what is untrue": *Verbum caro factum.* The archetype has been glimpsed amid the world of copies, the true "food of the grown soul" become "food mixed with flesh" out of unutterable condescension to our fallen weakness. To feed on that grown-up's food the bulk of mankind must first be humble, "little" enough to drink in faith the milk of the Church's teaching.

The task of bringing fallen souls back to the Intelligible, Plotinus observes, is accomplished by Providence in a thousand ways. What he did not suspect—*ibi non legi*—was that Truth Himself had assumed the task, entering our fallen world to lead us by Divine Authority to vision of Himself in His eternal splendor.

THE "TWO WAYS"

There is, therefore, no fundamental dissonance between Plotinianism and Christianity, as Augustine understands each of them. That statement of the case, however, is entirely negative: how, positively, do they relate to one another? Is Augustine thinking in terms of "two ways" of salvation, suggested to him by

Porphyry's teaching on the "universal" theurgic way as over against the philosophic way of the "few"? So O'Meara has contended, and his corollary is that these two ways—the way of "faith" in authority and the way of "reason"—are coordinate with each other; the way of faith is not "subordinate" to the way of reason.[8] But to answer that question, it will be useful to attack the issue from another standpoint: is the Christian "way," the Incarnate Truth, the necessary and universal way for all mankind?

Those Who Do Not Need Christ

The central text of the *Contra Academicos* would seem, at first, to impose an affirmative answer to the second of those questions. The way of "subtle reasoning," as practiced by the Platonists, would never succeed, never manage to "recall" to the intelligible world souls which are "blinded by the manifold darkness of error and stained deeply with the slime of body" had not God "bent and submitted the authority of the divine Intellect even to the human body itself" (*Acad* III, 42). Yet, to say nothing for the moment of the difficulties raised against that interpretation by other texts in the Cassiciacum Dialogues, the very context in which this text is rooted seems to call for another explanation. Augustine's personal history of philosophy implies that the inheritors of Plato's doctrine were brought to just such an awareness of that "other world" by the masters of their school. Never does Augustine take the tack of insisting that Plato or Plotinus made contact with the Incarnate Christ or with the Hebrew Scriptures in any form. At one point, it is true, he briefly entertains the possibility that they may not have "known" the things they spoke of, but only "believed" in them (*Sol* I, 9). That supposition remains, however, a temporary aberration, hardly disturbing the structure of his view. These philosophers, then, "arrived" at the vision, and without the aid of that Divine Authority disclosed to the world in the Incarnate Christ. That fact alone calls for closer examination of the text; and it commends the Plotinian hypothesis being argued for here, that it cues us to look for, and to find, the qualifications Augustine has entered to resolve the difficulty his text presents us with.

Those Who Need Christ

The first thing such closer examination reveals is this: Augustine is affirming the indispensability of the Incarnation for those souls whom he describes as "blinded by the manifold darkness of error

[8] See esp. *Against the Academics*, pp. 191–198.

and stained deeply with the slime of body." But do all souls merit that description? Surely it fits the materialistic cast of mind which refused to accept the Platonic teaching on the "other," intelligible world, beyond the reach of sense. But does it fit the Academic who holds to Platonism as his secret doctrine? Significantly, Augustine describes them as "purifying themselves from every vice" and living a "life at a level higher than is human" (*Acad* III, 38). That superhuman purity may well account for the fact that into such souls as these, come to knowledge of themselves, "Truth, bright and serene, shines from the [intelligible world]" (*Acad* III, 37)—they have fulfilled the anthropological conditions for vision which Plotinus set down, and to which Augustine, we have seen, subscribes.

The More and Less "Deeply" Fallen

What, then, accounts for their having arrived at this purity and vision, while their adversaries remained "deeply stained with the slime of body," and consequently "blinded"? Though not explaining everything, part of the answer seems to lie in the Plotinian theory that all souls are not equally "fallen." Some are more "deeply" immersed than others; consequently, some find return to the vision easier than others. We have seen evidence that the Augustine of Cassiciacum is prepared to accept this view. In its bearing on the present question, it implies that "it is not in one and the same way that Wisdom extends a helping hand to the sunken" (*Ord* I, 29); rather, He deals with all according to the health and strength they have. Some need a teacher and a lengthy course of "disciplines" to strengthen and sharpen the soul's eye for the desired vision. Others need no teacher (*doctor*) but only an "admonition": they "turn, open their eyes, and they see" (*Sol* I, 23).

The Many and the Few

But the Plotinian distinction between souls more and less deeply fallen now intersects with another: Augustine's whole discussion of faith and reason pivots on a distinction between the "many" and the "few." The "unlearned" and the "learned" is another set of terms he uses, thus bringing the connection of "return" and "disciplines" once more on the scene. Not all are capable of pursuing the arduous upward way through the study of the liberal disciplines. Not all, in other words, are candidates for the way of "reason." More deeply fallen than the others, these are the "many," the others the "few." "*Philosophia*" it is, Augustine says, which sends forth "reason"; but reason "frees scarcely a few"

(*Ord* II, 16). For the "uninstructed multitude," as he puts it in another text, "the authority of upright men seems to be the safer guide," but "reason is better adapted to the educated" (*Ord* II, 26). The way of "authority," then, is the indispensable way for the "many," the "unlearned," for those both "uninstructed" and, indeed, incapable of the instruction demanded by the way of reason. This explains why Augustine was careful to attribute the Incarnation to God's "compassion for the masses": *populari clementia* (*Acad* III, 42).

It would seem to follow from everything we have thus far seen that some "few" have no need for the way of authority at all, but that the "many" have such need, and more particularly, need to hearken to the authority of Christ incarnate. Yet none of these apparent implications is exact.

Authority: The Door for All

For even the "few" begin by needing some reliance on authority. However favored we may be by being less fallen than others, we all begin as "unlearned," and none of us knows "in what quality he ought to present himself to instructors, or by what manner of life he may become docile." Hence "it happens that for those who seek to learn great and hidden truths, authority alone opens the door" (*Ord* II, 26). The work of that authority may be simple "admonition" rather than instruction of a more extended sort; it may be we shall quickly find ourselves able to turn, "see" (*Sol* I, 9), and from that point follow the upward path of reason without an instructor (*doctor*) to guide us. In any case, we all begin by relying on *some* authority or other.

The Value of Human Authority

But need that "authority" be the one represented by the Church and the Scriptures? Is Christ, the "way," the *only* way? It would not seem so. For here Augustine repeatedly brings another distinction into play: there is human authority, and divine. The "true, solid and sovereign authority is that which is called divine" (*Ord* II, 27), but nowhere is it affirmed as indispensable for the "few" as well as for the "many." Divine authority has indeed "debased itself" for man's sake. The "sacred rites into which we are now being initiated" permit of purification "not by the circumlocution of disputation, but by the authority of the mysteries" (*Ord* II, 27). But the implication is that for those capable of such "circumlocution," philosophy remains a possible way of "purification."

Which means that one who takes this way must start with some human authority—a risky step, because "human authority is very often deceiving." But not always: it is best embodied "in those men who propose various proofs for their teachings, insofar as the mind of the unlearned can grasp them, and who do not live otherwise than they prescribe one ought to live." If they be commended by their moral stature (and for all of this Plotinus would surely have qualified), then "it is most difficult to lay blame on anyone who puts trust in those men" (*Ord* II, 27). Is it too much to imagine that Augustine has the Platonists in mind? Given his description of them in the *Contra Academicos*, the thought is hard to suppress. But to those, on the other hand, who would identify salvific authority with Christ, he seems to be directing the warning that "the divine assistance fulfills its office of mercy to all peoples more abundantly than some imagine (*latius quam nonnulli opinantur: Ord* II, 29). "No one seeks [God] unless he be admonished (*nisi admonitus*)" (*Sol* I, 3). But such admonitions can come from sensible phenomena of all sorts: from the waters that murmur in the night, the ordered beauty of a cock-fight. Or, as we have seen from the *Confessions*, they can come from the writings of philosophers.

FAITH, UNDERSTANDING, AND VISION

Up to this point, then, it would seem that O'Meara's view is substantially correct: the two ways, of "authority" and of "reason," seem to be coordinate with, and relatively independent of one another. One can arrive by choosing either "way," at least if one be numbered among the "few," less fallen, capable of following the way of reason after some human authority has done its liminal work of admonition. Faith in Christ, accordingly, with its attendant "purification" by the sacraments (*mysteria*), would be a substitute, providentially designed for the "many" whose deeper immersion in body and sense make them incapable of taking the way of philosophy. Our only difference with O'Meara then would come down to this: instead of requiring a substructure of Porphyrian thought, the contention here would be that Augustine's conception of these ways and their relationship can more adequately be explained along Plotinian lines.

But if Augustine's thinking on this matter be Plotinian, one would expect it to develop in a different direction from the one O'Meara's "Porphyrian" hypothesis suggests. For faith, in Plotinus, although grounding the requisite "renunciation" of sense, is ordered toward "understanding," "understanding" in its turn being ordered toward "vision." Plotinianism will not permit the way of "authority" to be coordinate with, it requires that it be subordinated to the quest for understanding and eventual arrival at vision. Again, it may commend the Plotinian hypothesis that it prompts us to ask a sharper set of questions, and find them answered largely according to our expectations.

Faith versus Vision

Significant in this regard is Augustine's definition of the three virtues of faith, hope, and charity. It occurs in the *Soliloquies* and, suggestively, in direct connection with the vision-language familiar from *Enneads* V, 8 and VI, 9. He believes, he protests to Reason, but belief is not enough for him. He has renounced all else in quest of vision: why is it not granted him? We must, Reason reminds him, *believe* that this purification, this renunciation, is necessary before the divine "sun" can be seen, *hope* the vision is possible to us, *desire* that vision above all else. Otherwise we would never tolerate the arduous process whereby our eyes are healed, strengthened to gaze upon the sun which is none other than God (*Sol* I, 12). Faith, then, the Augustine of the *Soliloquies* thinks of as contrasted with the blinding radiance of vision. Magnus Löhrer puts it well: faith, for the Augustine of this period, is an act with no kernel of "insight" (*ohne innere Einsicht*).[9] It grounds a kind of blind adhesion to what remains utterly unseen. The questing eye is turned in the right direction, prompted to peer insistently, but at a "veil" behind which, it believes, the beatifying Light is shining.

Authority and Spiritual Infancy

How is that veil to be broken through and the desired vision attained? Not by the believer's resting content with belief and authority: he must take a further step. For the way of authority is only a cradle for our infant beginnings in the Christian life: *cunabula* (*Ord* II, 26). It seems to pain Augustine that not all Christians —or preachers of the faith—would agree with him. They seem persuaded to stay with faith, authority, and sense. Too often, "when wisdom begins to admonish" the many who repose in authority's cradle, they refuse to "bear with the physician and permit themselves to be healed. They return to their swaddling clothes . . . rather than bear with and submit to the physician's injunctions . . . and be restored to the health of sound men and to

[9] P. M. Löhrer, *Der Glaubensbegriff des hl. Augustinus* (Einsiedeln, 1955), p. 111. See also, Charles Couturier, "*Sacramentum* et *Mysterium* dans l'oeuvre de saint-Augustin," in Henri Rondet and others, *Études Augustiniennes* (Paris, 1951), esp. pp. 189–194 where the same opacity of the "symbol" is regularly in evidence. For a different treatment of this whole question, see Holte, *Béatitude et Sagesse*, chaps. 7–9 and 24–25.

the light." They remain "content with the name of the most high God and with their sense-faculty." Their punishment is that though they "live," they "live wretched" (*Ord* I, 24). "Content to follow authority alone," they may even "apply themselves constantly to right living and holy arts." But because they "make no account of the liberal and fine arts, or are incapable of being instructed in them—I know not how I could call them happy as long as they live among men" (*Ord* II, 26).

The Need for "Understanding"

Augustine is convinced that to be "happy" they must attain to "vision"; but for that, they must take the necessary intermediate step of renouncing their "sense-faculty" and seeking after "understanding." His course in the "disciplines," he thinks, would sharpen and strengthen their eye for vision. Here he claims to echo the message of Divine Authority itself which "in the very act of leading a man onwards . . . bids him not to be confined to the senses . . . but to soar upward to understanding" (*Ord* II, 27).

The fate of those who reject this call he finds difficult to square with his view of the soul's return. He must settle back on a "firm belief" that "upon leaving the body, they will be liberated with greater facility or difficulty according as they have lived the more virtuously or otherwise" (*Ord* II, 26). For one so bent on understanding, this is an admission that there is a difficulty. Such things do not fit in well with his dawning systematic, but God "suffers no one that rightly believes in Him through the mysteries to perish." By the bond of faith He will "draw them to Himself and free them from these dreadful, entangling evils" (*Ord* II, 15). The attitude is characteristic of this period: Augustine's own faith is thrusting to break through the doctrinaire frame his Plotinian understanding of the faith tends to set up.

Faith Ordered to Understanding

Yet for the moment he clings manfully to both contending views. It is "not by faith alone, but by trustworthy reason, that the soul leads itself little by little to the most virtuous habits and the perfect life" (*Ord* II, 50). Though the way of authority be first "in point of time" and "takes precedence in operation," reason remains "prior in the order of reality" and "more highly prized as an object of desire" (*Ord* II, 26). Once having entered by the door of authority, we are not meant to rest content with mere belief; the Divine Spouse seeks souls "for whom it is not enough merely to live, but to live the happy life" (*Ord* I, 24). This means He requires us "to understand [the mysteries] insofar as they can be understood" (*Ord* II, 16). Augustine's estimate of the "disciplines" and their value toward this end is dizzying: he thinks believers "are to be instructed in all branches of learning," since "by no other means can these things be so thoroughly understood that they become clear as day" (*Ord* II, 15). Such instruction in the liberal arts, if moderate and concise, "produces devotees more alert and steadfast and better equipped for embracing Truth," they "more ardently seek and more consistently pursue and in the end more lovingly cling to that which is called the happy life" (*Ord* I, 24).

Vision, Embrace, and Happiness—Now

Embrace, cling: the terms are familiar. They denote the "possession" of Truth subsistent which takes the form of mystical vision—but a possession undisturbed by fear of loss or remission, for this, Augustine has made clear, would interfere with that life's being truly "happy" (*Vita* 26). One should have thought such happiness was reserved for the next life. Augustine's thought on the matter is plainly otherwise. The man whose mind has been sharpened, his inner eye strengthened, "comprehends" at length the triadic divinity of Reason, Intellect, and even "what, beyond all things, is the Source of all things." Although he must admit that "to this knowledge few are able to arrive in this life," still he maintains that "even after this life, no one can exceed it" (*Ord* II, 26). Heaven can be dwelt in even now; even in the body, the soul can achieve effective disincarnation, unabating contemplation, unbroken happiness.

The "Usefulness" of Believing

Such, then, was Augustine's conception of faith in its relation to both understanding and vision—at least, at the time of his Cassiciacum writings. It has its difficulties. It would seem a safe assumption that his more extended experience of the Christian life of faith would bring some of them to the surface of his consciousness. His thought, one readily supposes, will unquestionably develop on this point as it will on others. To test the exactness of the above presentation, however, and initially to estimate the pace at which such development moves, the reader is advised to turn to the little work, written some five years afterward, *On the Usefulness of Believing: De Utilitate Credendi.*

The title itself is significant. Belief is to be classed among those things which are "useful." It has merely instrumental value; it is a step toward the intuitive perception of that "sun" whose existence is believed in, but which the soul, "darkened" and "blinded" by sin and by the residue of past misconceptions, finds itself not "fit" (*idoneus*) to contemplate (4). The spiritual meaning of the Hebrew Scriptures (which his Manichee addressee, Honoratus, would naturally have despised) can be uncovered only if Christ is allowed to lift the "veil" which "covers" it from our eyes (8–9). But this requires the subjective dispositions of openness and sympathy on the part of one who would discover that spiritual truth; it also suggests that he inquire from those authorities most qualified to inform him of their message (10–13).

The existential urgency of this "quest" for the "true religion" should, Augustine thinks, be obvious. As always, it answers to man's desire for immortal happiness, a consummation which will affect either the soul alone, or at least principally (*maxime*) the soul. The soul's present condition is limned in familiar terms. It "wanders and is foolish (*errat . . . et stulta est*) . . . until it attains and perceives wisdom (*donec adipiscatur percipiatque sapientiam*) . . . Immersed and entangled in error and foolishness (*errore ac stultitia irretita et demersa*) our soul is seeking the way of truth, if there be any: *viam, si qua est, quaerere veritatis*" (14).

The cause of this condition Augustine avows is a most obscure matter (*obscurissimum*). The very language he uses betrays, however, that he still thinks of the soul as "fallen" in the way accounted for in his other works of this same period (cf. 34). It is not to his purpose to go more deeply into that question here. What concerns him is where the quest for the true religion should begin. Why not, he suggests, among those teachers commended by their celebrity and by the vast number of their followers? At least one would have the consolation here of "erring with the human race itself" (15).

He knows what Honoratus will object to this: the likelihood is just opposite, for truth is more probably to be found "among a certain few" (*apud paucos quosdam*). Augustine fully appreciates the force of the argument. The multitude, he admits, is "entangled in lusts and far removed from pure understanding," it is "in large number, ignorant." And yet, in religion as in other matters, it is conceivable that the "few" who lead the multitude by their "authority" possess the truth after all (16). Sometimes, too, common consent can be an index of where the most solid authority is to be found. It still remains incumbent on Honoratus, then, to consider the masters of Catholic teaching (17–19), just as Augustine himself was eventually brought to do (20).

But would it not be better to stay with the Manichees who "do not impose the yoke of believing on their followers, but rather reveal the source of their teaching" in the "name of reason"?

> At this promise [Augustine concedes] the human soul naturally rejoices, and without considering its own strength and health (*nec vires suas valetudinemque considerans*) by trying to get the food of the strong (*sanorum escas appetendo*) which is unwisely prescribed except for the strong (*nisi valentibus*), and it rushes right into the poisons of deceivers. For unless those things are believed, which later, if he has succeeded and been worthy (*si se bene gesserit dignusque fuerit*) each one attains to and perceives, and without a certain weighty power of authority, true religion cannot at all be rightly entered upon (21).

It is not, Augustine goes on to say, "credulity" he is asking for from Honoratus (22). Belief of the sort he recommends is necessary for the most ordinary social intercourse. The masters of the *Catholica* are, moreover, reasonable in exacting belief because it would be wrong to cast the pearls of Christian mysteries before the "unworthy" (23, cf. 25–26).

Yet what is important is that Honoratus "come to the knowledge of God by reason" (24). Granted: but only the "few" are "capable" of reaching this understanding of the divine. Is Honoratus of this number? Let that, too, be granted. Would he exclude the others, the "many" not "endowed with so serene a nature"? "Or should they be brought gradually by certain steps to those exalted recesses" (*summa penetralia*)? For the man less endowed than he, at least, Honoratus must admit that "unless he first believes that he will arrive at the [goal] he has set for himself . . . obeying certain important and necessary precepts, and completely purging himself by a certain way of life, he will not in any other way attain to that which is pure truth." But then, even the few, like Honoratus, who can "very easily, with sure reasoning, accept the divine mysteries," will come to no harm if they consent to travel the way of those who must "first of all believe." Still, Honoratus will say, "what need is there for them to delay" by taking this lower, slower route?

Augustine's answer betrays both the inability of his anthropology to parry this objection out of its own resources, and at the same time his developing willingness to accept in faith a view that does not easily fit the Plotinian matrix of his theory. The man who spurns the way of faith may not harm himself, but he "will harm others by his example." He will tempt those incapable of reason's way to be "carried on headlong in [their] boldness" and vault over the stage of faith their weakness requires. It is entirely right that "those who are strong enough to fly" be "forced for a little while . . . to walk on a way which is safe for others." This has, accordingly, been "divinely commanded" and "handed down to our blessed forefathers." The "interests of human society," then, the danger of being "an example of rashness" to those not "already perfectly fitted" (as he is) for the "reception of truth," must convince Honoratus that refusal to believe would be a sacrilegious way to the true religion. Those who choose to take it "even if their desires be granted, cannot arrive whither they intend. For, whatever kind of excellent ability they may have, unless God is present, they creep along the ground;" and God is present to those who manifest this regard for their weaker brothers (24).

The argument, from a Christian point of view, constitutes an advance over Augustine's earlier position. It grounds the universal need for belief in Christ through acceptance of the *Catholica*. But it has something of a forced, artificial ring: the implicit tenor of the discussion up to now has uniformly been that the soul is essential desire and consubstantial aptitude for intuitive vision of the divine "sun." That aptitude can be impaired in "many" cases, but is not so impaired in all: Augustine repeatedly admits Honoratus may well be numbered among the "few." To prevail on him to consent to a way essentially inappropriate for one of his endowments, therefore, Augustine must make appeal to a divine command with all the airs of a juridical imposition involving ontological injustice. He appeals to regard for human society, to the duty of becoming an example for others less equipped for the way of reason than he is—all of which has a manifestly extrinsic sound, to say the least. The endowments relevant to reaching vision have been laid down too much in accord with Plotinian intellectualism for such an invocation of brotherly love to cohere organically with that intellectualism. Two radically diverse estimates of the human condition have been set alongside each other; they differ in their selection of what is centrally important in man's moral endeavor. Augustine is manfully trying to bring them together, but the joint shows all too painfully.

To put the difficulty in another way: Augustine's disincarnate view of man as soul in quest of vision will not ground an "understanding" of incarnate man's permanent exigency for living a life of faith in a community which claims to be the continuing Incarnation. He seems vaguely aware of this; yet he persists in thinking out the problem in substantial fidelity to his earlier views. The equation between the "unwise" (*stultus*) and the sinner is all too easily made (27); the sage, on the other hand, is limned as one who has arrived at the direct vision of the Divine which joins his mind directly with God (33). The work of authority is designed to "convert" the soul from its love of "this world," institute the "mind's suspension of its earthly habitation," send the "unwise hurrying to wisdom" (34), purify and strengthen the inner eye for this highest exercise of "reason" (33). The entire process is described as restoring the soul to a health which it presumably possessed and lost: it is question of health's "returning" (*redire*) to the soul (31). It is clear, finally, that he thinks there are some who are no longer "seekers" but have "found" the Truth; they have arrived at the state of vision-possession even during this life, and merit our calling them the "happiest" of men (25; cf. 27).

The structure of his earlier position, then, has held firm, including the corollary that one could become "happy" even during this life. This is why Augustine took such pains to persuade Monica that she too could be of the number of the "few." Her "superstition" recalls too forcibly the contempt of understanding prevalent in the African church of his youth. His own experience has shown him that, even to remain an orthodox believer, one must seek some understanding of the faith. But now, Plotinus has persuaded him that understanding is itself an intermediary step. The life of accomplished virtue and the happy life have become, to his eyes, one and the same—a life which God in Christ offers to us not only as reward after this earthly pilgrimage, but a vision He wills we strive to enjoy even now.

Plotinianism, Christianity—or Neither?

But, it must be said, there are dangers in the intellectual project Augustine is pursuing: a Christian "faith" when "understood" with the aid of Plotinus, may no longer be the Christian faith after all. Nor is this, perhaps, the best point of view for trying to understand Plotinus. The climax of that history of Academicism leaves little doubt on Augustine's subjective disposition. He thinks, sincerely, that the Platonists will help him understand the faith, their reasoning will not compel him to part seriously from the "authority of Christ"—from which, in case of any conflict, he intends in no way to depart (*Acad* III, 43).

But is there not a danger that the Truth Christ *is* may come to be measured by the truth Plotinus—and Plato—saw? That the "kingdom not of this world" has slid into too easy an equivalence with the "intelligible world" to which the Word Incarnate would recall us?

Could it be that Augustine's Christ—in Alfaric's inflammatory phrase—has become the "Plato of the mob"?

10 THE MAN CHRIST JESUS

AUGUSTINE'S CRITICISM OF HIS EARLY VIEW OF CHRIST

What, then, did Augustine think of Christ, particularly during the period of his Neo-Platonic fervor? One of the factors that ultimately illuminates, but initially only complicates, the answer to that question is the criticism of his early views which he himself presents in the *Confessions*.

> I conceived my Lord Christ as only a man of surpassing wisdom, whom no other man could equal. Above all, because he was born in a wondrous manner of the Virgin, to give us an example (*exemplum*) of despising temporal things in order to win immortality, he seemed by the godlike care he had for us, to have merited such great authority as a teacher: *auctoritatem magistri meruisse*. But what "sacrament" (*sacramentum*) was contained in those words, "The Word was made flesh," I could not conceive (VII, 25).

It was only "somewhat after this" (*aliquanto posterius*) that Augustine learned "how, with regard to those words, 'The Word was made flesh,' Catholic truth is distinguished from the false teaching of Photinus" (VII, 25).

It may safely be assumed Augustine is referring to his own error as Photinian; it is quite likely that Alypius had similar ideas. He thought "that Catholics believed that God was clothed in flesh in such wise that in Christ there was no soul in addition to his divinity and his body. Nor did he think a human mind was attributed to him."

Far from being an Apollinarianist, as some have thought, Alypius had difficulties with such Appollinarianist conceptions of Christ. "He was firmly convinced," Augustine notes, "that the deeds recorded of [Christ] could only be done by a creature possessed of life and reason" (and hence that Appollinarianism was to be rejected). It was because he thought Church teaching was Apollinarianist that Alypius "moved more slowly towards the Christian faith" (VII, 25). Here, perhaps, was additional motive for his preferring that Christ's name be stricken from the Cassiciacum Dialogues. But the text is interesting for other reasons as well. The sketch of Alypius' thoughts on Catholic doctrine, as he misunderstood it, helps illuminate the background situation against which Augustine's critique of his own thinking must be understood. For it shows that in A.D. 386 a man of Alypius' intelligence and seriousness could be confused about what orthodox Catholic Christology was.

Augustine's admission concerning Photinianism has furnished still another argument for Porphyrian influence at the time of his Milanese conversion. More serious still, it has grounded the suggestion that Augustine could not have been a believing Christian when he first read Plotinus, for how can one be a Christian and not believe in Christ's divinity?[1]

Augustine's Christian Faith

As to the first suggestion—that touching Porphyrian influence—a closer study of the situation must be allowed to decide on that. But the second of these contentions seems at very least lacking in psychological finesse. Augustine's entire account, as we have seen, from the end of Book Five when he enrolled as a catachumen (V, 25) through the intervening period (VI, 4–8; VII, 1 and 4) to the present juncture of his story, insists upon his gradual growth in

[1] See Pierre Courcelle "Saint Augustin 'Photinien' à Milan," in *Ricerche di storia religiosa*, 1: 63–71 (1954), and the discussion of this issue in *AM* III, 99–100. Courcelle starts with the simplifying assumption that Alypius was on the side of the *Catholica* (p. 54), then argues from Augustine's later practice of laying Photinian implications at Porphyry's door—essentially the same tack O'Meara takes in *Oracles*, pp. 153ff. On the reality of Augustine's "belief," see Brown, *Augustine of Hippo*, pp. 41–43.

"the faith of your Christ, our Lord and Savior, the faith of the Catholic Church." This, he repeats, "was firmly fixed within my heart. "In many ways I was yet unformed," he then admits; "I wavered from the rule of doctrine, but my mind did not depart from it, nay rather, from day to day drank in more of it" (VII, 7; cf. VII, 11). Even in our modern day, adhesion to the Church's faith seldom brings and never requires full cognizance of what the content of that faith involves. In Augustine's day, moreover, one could count oneself a Catholic and still indefinitely postpone baptism. Whether or not he was a Catholic must therefore be allowed to depend on his readiness to accept what the Church holds to be her belief, once it becomes plain to him what it is. And here there can be not the slightest question of his willingness to do that. Everything we have seen at Cassiciacum argues for it. But what did the Church hold on the mystery of the Incarnation? Here confusion of minds was possible—and wide-spread. Alypius' attribution of Apollinarianism to the Catholic Church is only one instance of that regnant state of things.

The Situation at Milan

Milanese theology was just then being forced to face the difficulties on the Incarnation that had been festering elsewhere. During the time Augustine was listening to Ambrose, the crucial battle against the Arians was still the center of attention. The focal question was Trinitarian. Was the Son of God truly God, Divine and co-equal with the Father? Or was he in some fashion subordinate to the Father, the latter alone being God in the most "proper" sense of the term? Against the Arians, Ambrose is finally victorious, and his victory is fresh in Augustine's memory at Cassiciacum.

Quite distinct, though ultimately inseparable from the Trinitarian question, was the quarrel on the Incarnation. The focus here was the "man, Jesus of Nazareth": what status was to be accorded him? How was one to understand his relationship to the Eternal Son of God? This question raged for years before it came to settlement at Ephesus and Chalcedon—the former Council one year after Augustine's death, the latter twenty-one years after. We cannot, therefore, assume Augustine capable of the refined statement possible only after Chalcedon.

Photinus and Appollinaris

It is significant that the *Confessions* mentions the two opposing poles on Incarnation theology which were the points of reference in his mind: Photinianism and Apollinarianism.[2] One useful way of explaining these two views would stress their opposing ways of expressing, respectively, the distinction and the union of humanity and divinity in Christ. Apollinaris seems to have held that the Word became so intimately united to the "flesh" that a human soul, mind, and will in Christ was excluded. Photinus, on the other hand, insisted on the reality and totality of Christ the man's humanity: there must be human soul, mind, and will in Jesus of Nazareth—and consequently, the intimate union Apollinaris held was impossible.

In this battle, Photinus represents a variant of the Antiochean *logos-anthrôpos* emphasis: the Word was united to a "man," an integral humanity. Apollinaris, on the other hand, reacts against the associated tendency in Antiocheanism to set a certain distance between the divinity and the "flesh" of the Incarnation. That "flesh" should put the believer in direct contact with the divinity, if salvation is to result from the work of Christ. This *logos-sarx* accent, more native to Alexandrian theology, tended to stress the unity of Word and flesh to such a point that its adversaries could accuse them of having generated a "confusion" and produced a kind of "mixture" of the two.

The Reasons for an Antiochean Choice

Given the confused theological situation of his early years, it is possible Augustine is being somewhat too severe on himself. It is obvious from the text that he was not formally a Photinian; only later was he apprised of the heretical nature of Photinus' doctrine. He tells us exactly what he held at that time, and many features of his thought then were unexceptionable. He had learned that "flesh did not cleave to your Word except together with a human soul and mind." He understood quite rightly "that in Christ there was a complete man: not merely a man's body, nor an animating principle in the body but without a mind, but a true man" (VII, 25).

His rejection of the possible variants on Apollinarianism is firm; but what was the alternative as he saw it then? Christ must be a man "to be preferred above all other men, because of some great excellence of his human nature and a more perfect participation in Wisdom" (VII, 25).

The support for his position he explains in two connected points: first, that the Gospel accounts show Christ performing such human

[2] Alois Grillmeier, *Christ in Christian Tradition* (New York: Sheed and Ward, 1965), pp. 175–270, esp. pp. 254–255 and 220–233.

actions as eating, drinking, sleeping, moving his limbs about, and so forth. Was it the realism of the Gospel account, therefore, which persuaded him Christ must possess an integral humanity? Not precisely; and here Augustine's reasoning is a key to the evolution of his thought on the Incarnation. All of these actions "belong to a soul and a mind which are *susceptible of change*": *propria sunt mutabilitatis animae et mentis*. They must not therefore be thought the "property" (*propria*) of the word Himself. "Anyone who has knowledge of the immutability of your Word (*incommutabilitatem Verbi tui*) knows this: I knew it at that time as far as I could know it, and had no doubt whatsoever concerning it" (VII, 25).

Alexandrian Standpoint of His Later Self-criticism

The Augustine of the *Confessions* is criticizing this position, but it is essential to grasp the standpoint from which he now views his earlier understanding of the Incarnation. Here Tarcisius van Bavel points out[3] that between the years of A.D. 386 and 400, Augustine moved from clearly affirming the distinction between Christ's humanity and divinity, toward a set of formulae that place far stronger stress on their union. One corollary of this shift involves his speaking of the humanity of Christ as *persona veritatis*. Van Bavel seems on solid ground when he cautions the reader not to assume that Augustine means *persona* in the properly metaphysical sense. To embrace the "man Jesus Christ" is to embrace one "who is over all things": *qui est super omnia deus* (*Conf* VII, 24). But there is little or no warrant for interpreting that *qui* as implying the doctrine of person suggested at Chalcedon and developed in later centuries of Christological reflection. The original sense of *persona* as referring to an analogue of the theatrical face-mask is very much to the fore in Augustine's thought in this period.

Weaknesses in the *Confessions* View

One result of this manner of viewing the Incarnation is that it seriously reduces the fullness of Christ's humanity. The Alexandrian stress on the unity of Word and flesh, characteristic of Augustine's thought here, was later seen to have this corollary. Its natural drive is toward the very Apollinarianism which Augustine's early thought meant to reject.

But there was another defect inherent in this view: it tended toward the very "confusionism" against which Augustine's early thinking was aimed, and which Chalcedon was later to repudiate.

[3] Tarcisius Van Bavel, *Recherches sur la Chrisologie de Saint Augustin* (Fribourg, 1954), pp. 1–20.

The "man Jesus Christ," Augustine confesses, "mediator between God and men," is the heavenly "food" of Wisdom "*mixed with flesh*": *cibum, cui capiendo invalidus eram, miscentem carni* (VII, 24). Divine Word and eternal Truth, He has "built for himself in the lower regions (*in inferioribus*) a lowly dwelling out of our clay," and thereby become "*Godhead, weak* because of its participation in our 'coats of skin' " (VII, 24). How Augustine felt such expressions could be reconciled with the Divine Immutability of the Word, which his early thought was an earnest effort to safeguard, is another question that comes to mind.

Augustine's Development

But such questions need not directly detain us for now. What should be clear from the above is that Augustine's criticism of his early thinking on the Incarnation is substantially an Alexandrian critique of a relatively Antiochean position. That Alexandrianism is itself not a fully satisfactory formulation of the mystery, and Augustine's thought, as van Bavel has shown, develops out of the position expressed in the *Confessions* toward one which strives to do more justice to those complementary aspects of the Incarnation that he slighted there but honored in his early views. Furthermore, the Alexandrian view is hardly the standpoint from which one might expect Augustine to furnish a just appreciation and fair presentation of the more Antiochean emphasis which presided over his earlier understanding of the mystery of the God-man. The Augustine of the *Confessions* is, therefore, being unnecessarily hard on the Augustine of Milan.

"Somewhat Later"

The reasons why Augustine earlier held a relatively Antiochean view of the Incarnation were good ones; so good, in fact, that one wonders how he could have come to his later Alexandrian position at all. The depth of those reasons, however, creates a presumption that it would take him some time to evolve toward a view that tends to undervalue them. Speaking of that development in the *Confessions*, the Saint avers that he dropped his preconversion view "somewhat later": *aliquanto posterius*. The phrase is vague, but clear enough to make one hesitate in interpreting it as meaning "very, very soon." This is what scholars have effectively done by assuring us that, at Cassiciacum, Augustine had already clearly abandoned his alleged "Photinianism." For, the argument goes, at Cassiciacum he unhesitatingly confesses the divinity of Christ, something which a Photinian position would not have permitted him to do.

But everything we have seen to this point suggests that answer may be imprecise, premature, and therefore inconclusive. Imprecise, because it is not a question of what Augustine "believed"; he firmly willed to believe what the Church believed. The question troubling the minds of Christian thinkers was what that belief entailed, how one was to "understand" the Incarnation which everyone believed. The answer normally given is also premature, for it assumes that Augustine's pronouncements at Cassiciacum on the divinity of Christ are to be interpreted in the light of Incarnation theology, an assumption which is open to serious question.

CASSICIACUM: PLOTINUS CORRECTED FOR ARIANISM

On the contrary, it seems much more natural to interpret such remarks as bearing on the theology of the Trinity, and as directed against the Arian heresy. Here Augustine could be quite clear on what the Church believed: the air was full of Ambrose's recent victory over the Arians and Arianism was very much the question of the day.[4]

When, accordingly, the Augustine of Cassiciacum protests that Christ is God in the "proper sense" (*non improprie: Ord* I, 29), it is far more natural to connect that affirmation with his clearly anti-Arian denials of all intra-Trinitarian subordination (*degeneratio: Vita* 34; *Ord* II, 16). He is referring to the divine nature in Christ—to Christ inasmuch as, in that divine nature Son of God, He is the "very Wisdom and Power" of the Father (*Acad* II, 1; cf. I Cor. 1: 24). As divine, He is supernal Truth, which "receives its being through the Supreme Measure [that is, the Father] from which it proceeds and back to which it is converted when perfected" (*a quo procedit et in quem se perfecta convertit*). The Neo-Platonic image is manifest, but the Neo-Platonic corollary, so readily accepted by

[4] Dudden, *Life and Times of St. Ambrose*, makes it clear (p. 198) that Ambrose had preached against Apollinarianism as early as the year A.D. 381, well before Augustine's arrival at Milan (autumn, 384). The Council of Apuleia, moreover (attended by Ambrose) requested the suppression (p. 205) of meetings by known Photinians in 381. But the whole of the spring of 386, a crucial period for our purposes, was occupied with the Arian persecution of Ambrose led by Justina (pp. 270–293), and this, along with the finding of the remains of the martyrs Gervase and Protase, is what seems mostly to have impressed Augustine during his stay at Milan (*Conf* IX, 15–16). In any event, Ambrose was hardly of the stature required to unravel the underlying issues involved in the Christological controversies which would divide Catholics until the Council of Chalcedon, sixty-five years after Augustine's conversion, and there is every likelihood that the heat of his anti-Arian polemic in favor of Christ's divinity may have caused him temporarily to underplay his true humanity.

the Arians, is squarely rejected. This Truth, Son of God, is "truly God": *profecto Deus* (*Vita* 34). He is, indeed, the divine Intellect itself (*Acad* III, 43; *Ord* II, 16, 26) "in which all things are, or rather, which is itself the sum total of things": *ipse potius universa* (*Ord* II, 26)—a notion whose Neo-Platonic ancestry hardly needs stressing. He is the "exalted and remote" (*Ord* II, 24), subsistent *disciplina*—learning, doctrine, and teaching all at once—God's very Law (*lex*) "ever abiding fixed and unshaken with Him," object of the wise man's contemplation and norm of his comportment (*Ord* II, 25), the Order (*ordo*) "through Whom all things which God has constituted are governed" (*aguntur*) (*Ord* I, 28), in accordance with which, indeed, He Himself is "sent" by the God the Father, and "comes" to us—a truth which would normally (but wrongly) tempt one to think He is not to be spoken of properly as God (*Ord* I, 29). For God He is, as the prayer of the *Soliloquies* makes clear, God-Truth by which all things true are true, God-Wisdom, Life, Blessedness, Good and Beauty, Intelligible Light (*Sol* I, 3).

Nothing, then, could be clearer. Despite his substantial fidelity to the Neo-Platonic framework and his frequent use of Neo-Platonic terms, Augustine means without any ambiguity, and in the face of whatever internal strains it may put his thinking, to deny all subordination between the Father and His Divine Son.

The Man Christ Jesus

But all of this affects Christ inasmuch as that name designates the divine nature, the divinity involved in the connected mysteries of Trinity and Incarnation. What of the other, human pole of the God-man's theandric reality? Here, despite the brevity with which he has treated this period, van Bavel's judgement is sound. Augustine's expressions depict the divinity as condescending to "assume and activate a body of our kind" (*nostri generis corpus . . . assumere atque agere: Ord* II, 16; cf. *Acad* III, 42–43), or—more in line with the Antiochean *homo susceptus* view which van Bavel finds characteristic of the Saint's early period—as "activating a man" (*ipsum hominem agens: Ord* II, 27). In all three instances where, at Cassiciacum, this union of divinity and humanity is expressly referred to, the stress is placed on the enormous Divine condescension involved, on the difficulty some might have in believing that Divinity could so closely associate with bodily humanity—a thrust directed not only at Manichees but at Neo-Platonists as well. But one senses also Augustine's own discomfort before a too intimate union, a discomfort relieved to some extent by the availability of that Antiochean *logos-anthrôpos* framework which stressed, along with the fullness of Jesus' humanity, a much less intimate union of divine and human than was proclaimed by the Alexandrians.

Christ's Soteriological Work

To this point, therefore, there is every reason for thinking that while at Cassiciacum Augustine's thought on the Incarnation was still substantially of the Antiochean sort he later indicts in the *Confessions*. His description of the Incarnate Christ's redemptive work only confirms that suspicion. Christ exercises the teaching function of Divine Authority. It is "fitting that by deeds it show its power; by humility, its clemency; by commandment, its nature" (*Ord* II, 27), so that "souls would be aroused not only by divine precepts but also by divine acts, and would thus be enabled to reflect on themselves and *catch sight again of their fatherland*" (*Acad* III, 42).

Respicere patriam: Christ's soteriological function, then, is to be understood in terms of the Plotinian fall and return of the soul. The prayer of the *Soliloquies* implies the same view: for the Second Person is God "from whom to turn away is to fall, to whom to turn is to rise again, in whom to abide is to stand firm. God, from whom to depart is to die, to whom to return is to be revived, in whom to dwell is to live . . . God, whom to abandon is to perish, whom to heed is to love, whom to see is to possess (*Sol* I, 3).

The interaction of Plotinianism and Christianity in Augustine's thought is, therefore, not a simple thing. When speaking of the Trinity, his Christianity brings a firm corrective to Plotinian subordinationism, but the Incarnation of the Second Person is fitted far more easily into the Plotinian theory of man, as soul, fallen and bent on return to the intelligible beauty "whom to see is to possess."

Christ's Authority-Role

As far as the soul's return is concerned, accordingly, Augustine can still feel that the understanding to be found in the Platonists in no way compels him to depart from the "authority of Christ" (*Acad* III, 43). Recalling that text, however, brings us back to the topic of authority and understanding, but now, in terms of its Christological implications. Augustine's view is that the Incarnate Christ represents the way of authority, the Platonists the way of "subtle reasoning." Or, put in more classic terms, the humanity of Christ—the man, Jesus—has, in the expression taken from the *Confessions*, "merited great authority as a teacher." The divinity of that same Christ, however, is the other-worldly Truth, Wisdom, and Intelligible Light "whom no one seeks unless admonished" but "whom to see is to possess" (*Sol* I, 3). As man, therefore, his words and acts are admonitions—issued to souls so deeply fallen that they could be reached in no other way—but admonitions directing them to rise to understanding, and eventual vision-possession, of the divine splendor identical with His Divinity.

AFTER CASSICIACUM

At Cassiciacum, therefore, once Trinitarian and Incarnation resonances are carefully distinguished, Augustine's thinking about the man Christ Jesus falls readily into the Plotinian matrix, and substantially under the indictments leveled in the *Confessions*. What may legitimately trouble the reader is the fact that the formulae used in the *Confessions*' indictment are not closely duplicated in the Cassiciacum Dialogues. Ironically, those formulae are far more closely duplicated in the post-Cassiciacum works. Instead of moving *away*, as one might have hoped, the writings stretching from A.D. 387 to A.D. 391 show Augustine steadily advancing toward an even firmer expression of the Incarnation theory he was later brought to condemn.

De Vera Religione

Consider, for instance, the question Augustine asks of Plato as late as A.D. 391 in the *De Vera Religione*: If some "great and divine man" were to succeed in persuading the multitudes (*populis*) that Plato's teachings about immutable, other-wordly Truth "were to be at least believed if they could not grasp them by the mind," should he not be judged "worthy of divine honors"? Plato's answer, he believes, would be:

> That could not be done by man, unless the very virtue and wisdom of God delivered him from natural environment, illumined him from his cradle not by human teaching but by personal illumination, honored him with such grace, strengthened him with such firmness and exalted him with such majesty, that he should be able to despise all that wicked men desire, suffer all that they dread, do all that they marvel at, and so with the greatest love and authority convert the human race to so sound a faith *ad tam salubrem fidem summo amore atque auctoritate converteret.*

As to the honors "due to such a man," Plato continues,

> It is easy to calculate what honors are due to the Wisdom of God, Which would bear and govern him (*qua gestante et gubernante*) in the interests of

the true salvation of the human race, so that such a man would have merited a reward all his own, above all other men (*Ver* 3).

Even more markedly than his Cassiciacum views, though in clear continuity with their logic, Augustine's expressions here, anticipate the formulae of his indictment in the *Confessions*. Surely the Christ spoken of here has "merited great authority as a teacher"; surely, too, he is portrayed as an "example of despising temporal things in order to win immortality." His work, moreover presented as that of teaching by authority and example, receives its natural complement in the second portion of the *De Vera Religione*, which traces the "way of reason" corresponding to Platonism.

More than that, however, there is a sharp distinction between the "man" who is "borne and governed" by Divine Wisdom and that Wisdom itself, which is as it should be. But the expression used to couch that distinction is not at all reassuring: praise must be given to the Divine Wisdom, but the man Jesus, for his part, would surely merit something of "his own" (*proprium*). He would occupy an eminence "above all other men." These phrases are far closer to the *Confessions*' indictment than any to be found in the Cassiciacum writings.

The Road to Chalcedon

But that very distinction between the immutable divinity and the changing humanity in Christ was Augustine's key reason for holding to the view he later stigmatized as Photinian. The fathers of Chalcedon would have applauded at least this feature of his intention. Their confession acknowledged Christ the "only-begotten Son and Lord, in two natures without confusion, unchangeably, undividedly, inseparably, the difference of natures in no way taken away because of their unitedness, but [rather] what is proper to each nature being preserved." *Inconfuse, immutabiliter, indivise, inseparabiliter*: the Alexandrian stress on unity which Cyril expressed in his *mia phusis* and which had its brief moment at Ephesus has now been balanced by a complementary stress on distinction. There are two natures, *phuseis*, nevermore to be "confused".

And that complementary stress, ironically enough, was contributed partially by Augustine's own later development in thinking out this central Christian mystery. Fr. Alois Grillmeier[5] has

[5] Grillmeier, *Christ in Christian Tradition*, pp. 480–487. See also pp. 389–392, 460–477 for the subsequent development. For some prehistory of the *discrete-confuse* formula, see pp. 299–302 and 319–328. Pages 400–477 are important for the whole development from Ephesus to Chalcedon which is handled so summarily here.

pointed to the services rendered at Chalcedon by the celebrated *Tomus ad Flavianum*, composed by none other than the devoted Augustinian, Prosper of Aquitaine. But in writing the *Tomus*, Prosper took as one of his models the *libellus emendationis* which Augustine principally authored for the correction of the Pre-Nestorian, Leporius. There is, therefore, a direct line running from the later Augustine to Chalcedon's classic formula. And its crucial feature is the effort to balance union and distinction in Christ, without implying either separation or confusion: *neque discrete, neque confuse.*

To the Roots of a Formula

That final expression—*neque discrete, neque confuse*—is taken, not from Chalcedon, but from Augustine, and, paradoxically enough, from a work of this early period we have been scrutinizing. It is, as one might expect, a crucial formula in Augustine's thinking. But it—and its analogues—occur in contexts which, given the later history of the expression, are initially baffling. Careful study of those occurrences will cast a special light on the force this formula had for him—its ancestry and implications—and in that light we shall discover whether Augustine's belief in the Incarnation prevented him from remaining true to the Plotinian matrix he chose for understanding Christianity.

De Quantitate Animae

The first mention of this formula occurs in the *De Quantitate Animae*. Augustine has consented to answer a number of Evodius' questions on the soul, but a long *exercitatio animi* makes it impossible to get to all of them. The only question treated at length is that of the *quantitas animi*, an ambiguous phrase which for the early portion of the dialogue means "quantity," but for the second and climactic portion means "greatness" of the soul. Augustine's presiding conception is to eliminate all notions of the soul's being "great" on account of "quantity," then to show its "true greatness," one which is measured by its power and dignity. This is accomplished by describing the "seven levels" of the soul's increasingly disincarnate achievement, including the ordering and beautifying of the temporal world which it achieves in virtue of its unity with the All-Soul.

This permits Augustine finally to correct any hesitations he may formerly have had: the soul is "not what God is," and yet, "nothing among the things God has created is nearer Him" (77). The soul should therefore adore and reverence nothing but God

Himself, "unchangeable principle, unchangeable wisdom, unchangeable love"—should adore him *neque discrete neque confuse.* The later history of the expression makes us look for some mention of the Incarnation, but we are disappointed. Augustine's entire effort in the passage is concentrated on distinguishing the various grades of reality. The "unchangeable" must be distinguished from the "changeable." Sensible reality is lower (*deterius*) than the human soul. The spiritual creature one might be tempted to consider its superior, the [soul of the] angel, is in reality its equal (*par*). Any inferiority the soul may show in respect of this latter is due not to its nature but to sin (*hoc peccato ejus fit, non natura*). The argument implies, therefore, not only Augustine's central doctrine of the soul's fall, but also the stratified hierarchy of being he has adapted from Plotinus.

But now he draws an astonishing conclusion.

> But man, no matter who he may be, and be he ever so wise and perfect (*quanquam sapientissimus et perfectissimus*), or any soul at all endowed with reason and bliss supreme, is at most to be loved and imitated; deference is to be shown it in keeping with its merit and proper rank. For *the Lord thy God shalt thou adore, and Him only shalt thou serve* (78).

The conclusion is astonishing precisely on account of its universality. No man—or rather, "soul"—none, whoever he may be, however perfect, wise, or happy, is to be more than "loved and imitated." Augustine has constructed his phrase to leave no exception, even for Jesus of Nazareth!

That realization forces re-examination of his mention of the Incarnation a few paragraphs earlier. It occurs (predictably) in the familiar context treating of the way of authority. Once arrived at the seventh and highest level of the soul's activity, "the very vision and contemplation of truth," Augustine notes that "here we have no longer a level but in reality a home at which one arrives via those [lower] levels" (76). The soul which has "found" Truth, he means to say, will enjoy unbroken contemplation and bliss, even in this life.

But at that moment of "return," the soul looks back on the way it has traveled, discerns "how great a difference there is between these [vanities in the sense world] and the things that truly exist." Beautiful though they are, such sense realities "are as nothing in comparison with the things that truly exist." Again, the two-world division is on the scene, in customary dress. But the reflection goes on.

Then we shall acknowledge how true are the things we have been commanded to believe, and how excellently we have been nurtured in perfect health by Mother Church, and how nourishing is that milk which the Apostle Paul declared he gave as drink to her children.

The image is familiar. Augustine's point till now is to justify authority and faith—even the "command" to believe—as suited to our spiritual infancy. What is suitable to infancy, however, is not suitable to adulthood: "To take such food when one is fed by a mother is most proper; to do so when one is already grown would be shameful" (76).

Once "arrived" at vision, therefore, one no longer needs the milk of authority and faith. It would, in fact, be "shameful" to continue to drink it in. The message of Cassiciacum has held firm.

But now Augustine's reflection touches on the Incarnation. Here his terms must be weighed carefully.

Then indeed we shall contemn all those who ridicule the assumption of a man (*susceptum hominem*) by the almighty, eternal, immutable Son of God—as an example (*exemplum*) and as first fruits of our salvation—and his birth from a Virgin, and the other marvels (*miracula*) of that historic account (76).

Every characteristic of the doctrine he later criticized is here; and yet, the implications of the text are not immediately evident. But everything falls into place once we suppose Augustine is addressing himself to the Manichees, in an effort to show them that his brand of Plotinian Christianity not only is immune from their attacks, but answers to their problem better than they themselves can. They distinguished themselves by rejecting the marvelous birth of Christ from Mary; proposed a docetist view of the Incarnation; claimed the Catholic understanding of that mystery "soiled" the divinity through contact with mortal flesh; resented the Church's "command" of faith and assumed that faith would lead to no further phase of understanding; and finally, adored sun and moon and other heavenly bodies, thereby "confusing" them with God, and yet, on the other hand, their dualism put the Divinity at such a "distance" from the rest of visible creation that He was "discrete" from it.

The Incarnation Augustine understands, accordingly, within the context of the soul's "return" to God. Jesus is a *homo susceptus*, a man "taken up" by the "eternal and immutable" Son of God. He is "example" of our salvation. Again, all of Augustine's complaints about his early Christology are fully justified—justified, and better understood. For if we be souls, questing through an initial stage of understanding for return to vision, it is logical that the work of authority eventually be left behind. No man, whoever he be or whatever be his perfection, should retain our permanent interest or be held worthy of our adoration.

All this is perfectly consistent with his judgment on the "third level" of the soul's activity, one "which belongs to man exclusively." The description of human achievement is enthusiastic, almost rapturous: arts and crafts and all the marvels of human ingenuity are passed in review, "duties, prerogatives, honors and dignities . . . in profane and sacred institutions." These things, he concludes, "bear the mark of greatness, and they are characteristically human" (72). Yet, only on leaving this human level does one reach the disincarnate realm "which goodness and all true worth call their home" (73). Only when the soul has completely "left sense behind," turned its back on all the "admonitions" of the sensible order—including those embodied in and emitted by the man Jesus of Nazareth—has that vast providential strategy, set in motion to promote its "return," achieved its purpose.

De Moribus Ecclesiae

Augustine's moving apostrophe in the *De Moribus Ecclesiae*, spoken to the "Catholic Church, truest mother of Christians" (I, 62), only confirms the interpretation just given. Compelled by his adversaries' insistence on reason, he has reluctantly begun his work on that plane. In the course of it, he situates the "way of authority" and its function. The soul, he reasons, will arrive at perfect virtue by following either a man or God. But a man can be taken away from us, even against our will. He infers, then, that:

> God remains; if we follow Him we shall live well; if we attain to Him, we shall live happily . . .
>
> But how are we to follow some one we cannot see? Or how shall we see Him, men, and more, foolish men, as we are?

The answer comes in imagery familiar from the *Phaedrus* and *Ennead* V, 8: our soul's eye is too weak, is repelled by the radiance of the divine splendor.

> On this account, by the dispensation of ineffable Wisdom, that opacity of authority has come to our aid, desirous as we were to take refuge in darkness; by marvelous deeds and written words it charms us, as by so many shadowy and tempered signs of truth. What more could have been done for our salvation? What more benevolent, what more

generous than divine Providence, which has not entirely deserted man, fallen as he was, unfaithful to the divine ordinances and rightly [condemned to] propagating mortal progeny, since it was desire of mortal realities which caused his fall? (*Mor* I, 11–12).

The entire regime of authority, therefore, all its symbolic deeds and words, is a providential accommodation to the fallen soul—an accommodation designed to lead us back to the vision of God's splendor. If as a provisional step we drink in the light of truth in the tempered fashion of symbols, if in our early stages we even "follow a man" to achieve the virtue which eventually unites us to God, all this must finally pass. Once strengthened, it is the invisible God Whom we must both "follow" and "attain."

It is significant, though, that Augustine attributes the crucial role in following God no longer to the disciplines, but to love: *eum sequimur diligendo*. That "love," however, he interprets as the longing for happiness (*appetitus beatitatis*), so that its term remains what it formerly was: "making contact with Him in a marvelous and intelligible fashion, [we shall be] thoroughly illumined and enveloped by His Truth and Holiness" (I, 18). The Platonic Eros, dressed as Christian *caritas*, still makes room for a radically intellectualist understanding of the "way" to, or rather, "back" to God. For the description of the fall two paragraphs beyond is couched in terms familiar from and perfectly consonant with those used in the *De Genesi contra Manichaeos* (I, 20).

Where then does Christ fit into this picture? Augustine prefers to dwell on His Divinity: He is the Power and Wisdom of God, the Truth "which knows no conversion or change," the love of which is sanctity. The "conformity" St. Paul speaks of is conformity not to Christ as "man" but to Christ as object of our *caritas*-desire, Eternal Truth, unchanging Word (I, 22; cf. 27–28).

Whether one consider the *Confessions* or any of the works here cited, this unchangeability is the character that marks Divinity and that must not be either "confused" with, or too radically "separated" from, the world of change. This is the clue to what Augustine means by Chalcedon's later formula.

Rightly then, Catholic Church, truest mother of Christians, do you preach most purely and chastely not only that we worship God, Whose possession is the happy life; you urge us also to adore no creature, order us to serve none; you exclude from that incorruptible and inviolable eternity—to which alone man ought to subjected, cleaving to which alone the rational soul escapes from misery—you exclude everything which is made, or subject to change, or set in time; *you neither confuse* what eternity and truth and peace itself keep distinct, *nor do you* on the other hand *separate* what one majesty has joined together (I, 62).

The Two Worlds: Omnipresence Again

Neque confundens . . . nec rursus separans: what is eternal and unchangeable must neither be confused with nor divorced from the temporal changing realities of the sensible world. The principle is the same as Augustine admits guided his early thinking on the Incarnation, and yet, as here invoked, it is a general principle, of absolutely universal application. Where its expression comes from, whether Augustine took it from some one else or hammered it out himself, need not detain us here. It is significant, though, that it expresses that relation of the Higher to the Lower World on which Plotinus insisted in the *Enneads*, and notably in his magnificent treatise on Omnipresence. The influence of that treatise on Augustine we have seen. Its major effect, to his way of thinking, was to teach him how to conceive of precisely the relation in question here, and to liberate him from the sensist kind of thought that dogged the Manichees. Immediately before the *discrete-confuse* mention in the *De Quantitate Animae*, it is hardly surprising that Augustine speaks of God as "unchanging Source, unchanging Wisdom, unchanging Love, one God, who . . . never was other, never will be other than He is." He then goes on in the language of omnipresence: "Nothing is more hidden than He, nothing more present; to find where He is is difficult, but to find where He is not is more difficult still; not all can be with Him, and no one can be without Him" (77).

It has been suggested that Augustine patterned his conception of the soul's union with the body on the union of Divinity and humanity in Christ.[6] The opposite suggestion has also been advanced: he may have taken the former as pattern for the latter.[7] What we have seen intimates that neither of these proposals is necessarily incorrect, because at this epoch Augustine's views, both of the hypostatic union and of the union of soul and body, are roughly parallel, and because both these views are modeled after the more comprehensive principle he uses to think out the

[6] This is the tendency embodied in the final suggestion (pp. 549–550) of Charles Couturier's "La structure métaphysique de l'homme d'après Saint Augustin," *AM* I, 543–550. The remainder of the article, however, like the entirety of his "Structure métaphysique de l'être créé d'après Saint Augustin," in *Recherches de Philosophie,* 1: 57–84 (1954), is more suggestive of the approach advocated here: a universal cosmological principle governs both the hypostatic union and the union of soul with body.

[7] An approach suggested (but again, in carefully qualified fashion) by Fortin, *Christianisme et culture philosophique*, esp. pp. 121–122.

omnipresence of the unchanging world of Reality to the image-world of changing bodily things: *neque discrete, neque confuse.*

He has, therefore, taken the Incarnation, the central mystery of Christianity, and set it inside the Plotinian matrix of his thought. Taken together with other elements of that same matrix, the man Jesus Christ becomes the central fixture in a providential strategy to "admonish" and "recall" the fallen soul through an initial faith, subsequent understanding, to eventual vision of Divine Truth, unchangeable and omnipresent.

De Libero Arbitrio II

The same dynamic of Augustine's early theory of salvation is brought out in the *De Libero Arbitrio.* There the second book opens on a lively defense, not only of the need to begin with faith, but also of the urgency of passing on from faith, "seeking" for understanding.

> When [Our Lord] spoke of the gift itself which He would give to believers, He did not say, "This is eternal life, that they may believe," but "This is eternal life, that they may know Thee!" . . . Then He says to those who already believe, "Seek and you shall find," for what is believed without being known cannot be said to have been found, nor can anyone become capable of finding God, unless he has first believed what afterwards he is to know. Therefore in obedience to the Lord's commands, let us seek earnestly (II, 6).

The dialogue proceeds to demonstrate the existence and nature of that immutable subsistent Truth for whose embrace the Eros of the soul is aspiration. Here, then, will happiness be found; but, then, Augustine notes,

> one man does not become happy through the happiness of another man. When one man imitates another in order to become happy, he seeks to become happy by the same means by which he has seen the other has become happy, that is, by means of the unchangeable Truth which is common to all. Nor is one man prudent through another's prudence, nor brave through another's bravery, nor temperate through another's temperance, nor is a man made just through another's justice. But he becomes such by conforming his soul to the unchangeable principles and illuminations of the virtues, which have incorruptible life in Truth itself and Wisdom which is common to all (II, 52).

The *De Moribus* had emphasized the same point in different terms. One does not become virtuous by "following" another man, but by "conformity" to, by love and embrace of, that subsistent Truth and Beauty whose vision is accessible, even now, to the soul willing to leave behind the trappings of infancy, quest for understanding, strive for vision. There is no limit set to this proposition. No exception is made for the man Jesus Christ. His virtue and happiness were due to the very source from which ours derives; he was a man, "taken up" by the Divine Wisdom in a special way, distinguished, as the *Confessions* puts it, by a special "participation" in Wisdom. But his exemplary function is to lead us on toward "finding" the very immutable Truth which illumined, strengthened, and beatified him.

Other Works of This Period

This, then, is the point of that division so characteristic of Augustine's works from this early period: the *De Moribus Ecclesiae*, the *De Utilitate Credendi*, the *De Vera Religione*, all display a treatment of faith in authority, which leads eventually to the second, ulterior "way of reason" or understanding, a way which is meant to climax in enduring vision. This, too, is the point of the *De Magistro*. Its epistemology is expressed in a brief aside in the *De Libero Arbitrio*, where Christ is said during his life on earth to have "outwardly admonished, inwardly taught": *foris admonet, intus docet* (*Lib* II, 38). Admonition is proper to the sensible sphere in which authority and faith do their work. But the soul's dependence on this sensible sphere, on all the trappings of authority and language and symbol—and even Incarnation—is a result of its fall. Once they have done their work of "reminding," the soul can and should turn "inward" to be illumined by the One Teacher of all: it must "conform" itself to the Eternal Christ, unchanging Wisdom, the Intelligible Archetype containing "the unchangeable principles and illuminations of the virtues" (*Lib* II, 52). Those who would question that this Intelligible Archetype can function as model for human virtue, are like "boys who, when they see an artist painting with other pictures set up before him so that he can follow them closely, cannot believe it possible to draw a man unless the painter looks at another picture" (*Quant* 76). But more than that, they do not see as Plato saw, that the "civil" virtues proper to the active life of man are only "like the other, real virtues"—the higher, contemplative virtues as Plotinus claimed—"which are known by a few wise men only" (*Acad* III, 37). Immersion in the life of action is a result of the fall. "Whatever is done in this world" in accord with those civil virtues cannot be called "anything but 'like-the-truth,'" (*Acad* III, 37). The real business of the fallen soul is to leave the life of action and embodiment and rise to the higher life according to the contemplative virtues, a life which eventually takes as its final model not another man, be he Jesus of Nazareth himself, but Truth Eternal.

Conclusion: The Shifting Meaning of "Christ"

Throughout all this discussion, however, the reader must have been conscious of a nagging ambiguity: the term "Christ" has constantly been shifting. The shift, however, is characteristic of Augustine's own use of the term. Now "Christ" refers to the Eternal Christ, Unchanging Son, Wisdom and Power of God, the end of our desire for happiness; now the name applies to that man, more excellent than all men, "taken up" to be special participant in, but later "spokesman" (*persona*) of, Divine Wisdom Itself, the providentially appointed "way" to vision.

Was "Christ," then, "divine"? Did the Augustine of Cassiciacum believe in Christ's divinity? The answer is clearly yes. But Christ means one thing there, another when the question centers on the man of Nazareth. At Cassiciacum, the divinity of the Eternal Christ is affirmed against all Arian (and Plotinian) subordinationisms. Ambrose's recent victory over the Arians is fresh in Augustine's memory. New theological battles on the Incarnation would now begin to occupy the Church's attention. The issues here are not nearly so clear. One could object to Augustine's understanding of the Incarnation in the *De Moribus* and *De Vera Religione* with the accusation that he "denies the divinity of Christ," but Augustine himself would have been shocked at the accusation. What he finds defective in his earlier formulation of the mystery is the situation he accorded to the man of Nazareth. But even to the end, he would have resisted calling that man, *precisely as man*, "divine." The immutable, he would still have said, must be neither "confused" with, nor unduly "separated" from, the changing humanity which was Jesus of Nazareth.

The fact that the Church in his day was still grappling with the task of understanding the hypostatic union of Christ's humanity with the divinity allowed Augustine more maneuvering room than later would have been the case. Indeed, his own Christology advances as his life goes on: the *cibus miscens carni* and *persona veritatis* terms he prefers at the time of the *Confessions* must themselves, he later sees, be sharpened and modified. That task, and others imposed on him by growing familiarity with the Christian message,[8] will strain the Plotinian matrix which so long succeeded, Augustine thought, in trellising his understanding of the faith.

He will later depart in important respects from the "understanding" he earlier deemed adequate to the Christian faith. But the import of those departures are best appreciated when set against the provisional synthesis, which, piece by piece, he sets carefully about dismantling. His later views ought not, however, too briskly be used as evidence to disprove the contention that from his conversion at Milan until his priestly ordination, Augustine thought man's real "self" was soul, fallen into the world of time and body. Cared for by an omnipresent Providence—its last and greatest condescension the "assumption" of a human nature whose words and works might "outwardly admonish" us—the soul was meant to "turn," or better, be "turned about," to pass along the way of faith in Christ the Way, but eventually to pass beyond that way and glimpse the beaming radiance of Christ, Eternal Truth, the half-remembered splendor which had once, before its fall and entry into this human life, been bliss to behold. This, the early Augustine thought, was the homeland of the heart, start and term of all our journeying.

[8] Those tasks include the necessity of coping with the issue of creation from "nothing." As late as the *De Magistro* Augustine still remains impressed by the mysterious "profundity" of this dark concept (19; cf. *ibid.*, 3). In the *De Vera Religione* he takes a braver (and possibly anti-Plotinian stand (35–37; esp. 36: even unformed matter must in its turn have been made by God from "nothing"). But his language on what *nihil* has by this time come to mean to him leaves unsolved the question of how the soul's fall can be accounted for without attributing to "nothing" the shadowy quasi-existence and resulting negativing positivity it has in the *Enneads*. Whatever he means by the term, he does not yet see it as requiring readjustment of his theory of the soul's fall. Theiler's Neo-Platonic interpretation of this work still seems sound (see especially the language regarding the soul's situation, reproducing that seen above, Chapter VI, in *Ver* 18–25, 27, 51, 72, 78–79, 88–89, 101). Dinkler, *Die Anthropologie Augustins*, pp. 95–96) suggests a possible solution to this anomaly: the later Augustine may, surreptitiously, have come to attribute a kind of positivity to the "nothing" he often speaks of as though it remained a negativing ingredient in any created being.

11 EPILOGUE

Augustine, Sensibility and System

The multiple facets of Augustine's complex personality have given rise to any number of antithetic judgments. To some, he is a rich artistic mind, warm, intuitive, and impressionistic, leaping from thought to thought through a series of brilliant but unpredictable digressions. To others, he has seemed quite the opposite. So dreadful is his logic, so willing is he to follow out unflinchingly the path that leads from premise to conclusion, that he has bequeathed to Western Christianity some of its most bloodless features, among them a predestinationism that designates the vast majority of humankind as a *massa damnata*. Intellectualist or voluntarist, tough- or tender-minded, phenomenologist of Christian experience or the man responsible for having drained off its lifeblood in the interests of a theory: what kind of man was he?

On the surface, that question is easily answered: he is all of these things by turns. African in temperament, plunged from an early age into a series of literary, theatrical, and amorous experiences, his sensibilities were awakened to an extraordinary degree. Yet the whole educational process he passed through on the way to becoming a *grammaticus* and *rhetor* was, Marrou reminds us, one designed not to discipline sensibility by according it some rightful place in the equipment a man brings to assimilating experience. Rather, it tended to rationalize, desiccate. The *De Magistro* becomes a grammarian's sterile analysis of a great line of Vergil, the *De Musica* a dispiriting exercise in Neo-Pythagorean numerology, the *Confessions* a biography where beneath the surface warmth a little digging uncovers the unyielding bones of a theory of man. Too fertile and vivacious to be cabinned by a theoretical frame unequal to it, the play of Augustine's sensibility often escapes the narrow confines of his structured view. And yet, in a vast number of cases where initially it seems he is working intuitively, impressionistically, unpredictably, it is rather we who have not come to grasp the structure that secretly guides his thinking.

But how was this possible? The *Confessions* does, after all, repose on Augustine's personal experience, and the breadth, depth, pulsating life of that experience is manifest on every page. How could a man whose friendships were so vital to him (one need but recall Alypius, Nebridius, the unnamed youth of Book IV), one who had known the faithful love of Adeodatus' mother and the harrying but unquestionably tender fidelity of Monica, one who so obviously vibrates to more in a line of Vergil or Catullus than grammatical analysis could ever succeed in destroying—how could Augustine satisfy himself that he had done justice to all the contour and color of the human scene by viewing it in terms of the theory we have outlined here? And yet, we have his own words to meditate: *magna haec, et omnino humana*—none of the grandeur of the human scene would he deny, and yet, no authentic value is to be found here. His theory of friendship would dissolve the bonds that knitted him to Alypius and Nebridius, his theory of marriage cast a shadow on all the beauty we detect in his relationship with his wife and mother, his theory of art urge us to leave art behind in a disembodied flight to the purely intellectual.

The difficulty is one that constantly dogs the thinker of any sort, the artist included. Any effort to evolve categories or forms adequate to the job of making sense of one's experience eventually threatens to backlash, affecting the quality of experience itself. What reflection has brought us to think of as important does, in time, tend to occupy center-stage in our view of the world. We begin to see what we are looking for, and look for it because we have come to think it is the thing worthy of primary notice. Not even in our earliest years is experience a totally undifferentiated field, unstructured by such foci of importance: language, the cues of elders and companions, the myriad features of environment in the widest understanding of that term, all serve to direct our attentions, influence our valuations. As life proceeds, it becomes increasingly difficult to avoid, in T. S. Eliot's phrase, the fate of having "had the experience and missed the meaning." For the meanings we have progressively imposed upon experience place certain landmarks in the limelight, leaving others cloaked in shadow. A truncated theory of friendship, marriage, or art, can in time blunt our perceptions, blind us to the shifting tones that for another man, or for another age, become the very focus of contemplation and evaluation.

Human and Christian

This problem of experience and meaning only complicates when the thinker involved is at the same time trying to see his world in the light of a religious revelation. How does human experience relate to the experience of the world that revelation suggests should be the experience of the Christian? How, in modern terms, does nature relate to supernature, and, specifically, on the experimental level? How is human life to be understood, when some at least can claim, and believers themselves be sometimes tempted to think, that the understanding proposed in revelation is a different one from that which man, left to his own resources, could arrive at? Can the Christian view of man and of reality cohere with a matrix drawn from one who remained either untouched by Christianity as Plotinus seems to have remained, or from one who has frankly disavowed it as Martin Heidegger and Jean-Paul Sartre have done? That question introduces another: what is *specifically* Christian? Where are Christianity's foci of primary importance? Are they all accessible to experiential observation, whether by the Christian, the non-Christian, both, or neither? And if they are accessible, do they correspond point for point with the foci of central interest which sincere and careful reflection, unaided by revelation, would in time uncover?

Theologians and Their Philosophies

To all those questions Augustine's answer is remarkably modern, even contemporary. It stands comparison with Rahner's proposal that historical man as we know him is qualified from the depths to the heights of his being by an *Existential* which makes him "hearer of the Word," positively oriented toward, prefigured for, the revelation which illumines to his gaze the mysterious reaches of his own selfhood: *grande profundum, homo*. One knows how much Karl Rahner's philosophy of religion, like Rudolf Bultmann's, represents a bold adaptation of Heideggerianism to the task of rethinking Christianity; one wonders whether Paul van Buren and others have not chosen far less wisely in trying to bring their "secular" transposition of the Gospel message into harmony with Anglo-Saxon linguistic analysis.

It may be an occupational deformation that makes the philosopher seldom happy about the theologian's choice, and understanding, of the philosophy through which he sifts his theological views. But when it comes to the choice Augustine made, his perspicacity at least must be commended. Among the schools he had to choose from in his day, Plotinianism was easily without peer. If Christianity was to be thought out in terms of any philosophic matrix, the *Enneads* furnished one whose brilliance and power has seldom been equaled in the history of human speculation.

Obstinately convinced that the Christian view of things must make sense to the inquiring mind, that faith owed it to itself to seek for understanding, that human and Christian experience could not be held apart as though the one were irrelevant to, or the negation of, the other, Augustine was led to believe that the mode of inquiry, the categories of understanding, and the version of human experience most appropriate to his task were those embodied in Plotinus' writings. The contemporary theologian is inclined for the most part to assent to the first three of these propositions, but resolutely reject the choice Augustine made on the basis of them. He shudders when he reads in the *De Vera Religione* (7) that the "Platonists" need change but a few words here or there to bring their teaching into line with that of the *Catholica*. Countless scholars have tried to dodge that chilling vote of confidence Augustine gives to Neo-Platonism so shortly before his ordination to the priesthood; or, when they could not dodge it, they have tried every imaginable device to explain it away. Ingenious though they have been, none of the devices is quite successful. The phrase sticks stubbornly out of the text, waiting to be explained. The burden of the preceding pages is that it can be explained, and that Augustine's early theory of man and of Christianity will defy interpretation if we choose to explain that phrase away. He said it and meant it, and a conscientious appreciation of his debt to Plotinus helps us understand both why he said it and how he meant it.

Lucidity and Fidelity to Tradition

Implicit in this effort to measure the debt Augustine owed to Neo-Platonism is the supposition that it is of interest and importance to the contemporary Christian thinker to know what

Augustine said and meant. The task of measuring that debt imposes some arduous and arid searching into what both men wrote—an examination far less inspirational than the plethora of writings lyrically detailing "what Augustine means to me," far more suspicious than many would like of the multitude of faintly anachronistic comparisons one reads where an Augustine suitably misunderstood is hailed as the genial forerunner of virtually every tendency in contemporary thought. Only when we have placed him against the philosophic background of his time, can we evaluate his statements and their permanent vitality for us with the lucidity so urgently needed in the age we are living through. How much of what he says to us still echoes the Gospel note, how much of his view transmits an understanding of the Gospel but filtered through a Plotinian prism?

Letting the Mind Wander

There is a breath-catching instance of the kind of lucidity I speak of in St. Thomas' early disputations *On Truth*. The question is raised whether any true knowledge can be gained through the senses (X, 6). Aquinas lists a series of Platonist positions, from Augustine himself as well as from others, replying in the negative. His answer to that general thesis is, at one point, devastating: such an evaluation of sense, he reminds his adversaries, has regularly been connected in the history of thought with the theory of a soul, fallen from the intelligible world, into the body—a view, he goes on to add, unsupported by reason and condemned by the Church. How much did Thomas see? One wonders what would have happened if, with Plato's and Plotinus' text as close at hand as Aristotle's was, he had pursued that line of inquiry. It surely would have brought him to ask whether his proofs for the soul's immortality, which go back in a straight line to Augustine's *De Immortalitate Animae*, through Plotinus' treatise of the same name, to Plato's *Phaedo*, did not imply a similar set of corollaries. It might even have put to the test the entire theory of man he proposes in the *Prima Pars*. Who knows (historians of thought have the right to dream, occasionally), Christian thinkers might long before this have been compelled to grapple with the challenge of conceiving man in the "secular," this-worldly fashion which comes as such a shock to the tradition-bound intelligence of today.

Augustine's Use of Plotinus

But while dreams are our theme, a parallel line of speculation solicits the mind considering Augustine's use of Plotinus' *Enneads*.

He came to the reading of them with an affectivity already polarized by years of Manichaeism. The Manichee view of the soul's imprisonment in body, of sexual procreation as the darkest of sins because it perpetuated that imprisonment, was not exactly calculated to smooth his relationships with either his mother or the mother of his son. Nor was it designed to alienate him from the early Plotinus' devaluation of both body and sense. More than that, these are the very features of Neo-Platonism with which Ambrose's preaching was most likely to resonate.

But he was intellectually conditioned, too. Reading the master with eyes habituated to more rationalistic Roman thought, Augustine tends to stiffen the mathematical skeleton that is far less prominent in Plotinus than in Varro. Moreover, he is relatively ill-equipped to grasp in depth the complex tradition Plotinus was working with. It was inevitable that he remain in important respects insensitive to the tensions that affected his master's thinking from the very start, and to the brilliant subtleties, far beyond the reach of rationalism, that Plotinus brought to his effort at resolving them. Augustine seems entirely to have missed the slow development that progressively relativized early emanation imagery in order to stress the integral omnipresence of the divine in the world of man's experience, a development that also tends to replace a world-negating emphasis on the soul's "fall" by a far more optimistic acceptance of its ordering mission to the world of sense and body. He seems to have seen these opposing aspects of Plotinus' thought as merely complementary and rather too easily reconcilable.

Not that he remains, or ever was, a slave to Plotinus. From the start he pointedly corrects the Trinitarian subordinationism that came with the system. In time he comes resolutely to deny the soul's identity with the third hypostasis, to eliminate all suggestions of pantheism, to alter the status of matter in the light of creation from "nothing." The doctrine of the body's resurrection forces a more sympathetic view of the bodily and the human. His later doctrine of charity represents in part an attempt to justify the soul's involvement in action for the sake of others. More decisively, his advancing Christianity brings him to transfuse whatever borrowings he took from other treatises with the powerful insights of the *Ennead* on Omnipresence. As a result, the metaphysical underpinning of the *Confessions* represents a twilight struggle between an emanationism in which the soul can be thought of as "fallen" and "distant" from God and a fundamentally different view in which nothing can be "distant" from the Omnipresent. It is doubtful, though, whether Augustine ever really gauged the terms and importance of that struggle. We can feel confident today that had he possessed something of Plotinus' own control of the ancient philosophic tradition, things might have turned out far differently. The quest for meaning along these lines, particularly when pursued in the light of Christianity's optimism with regard to matter, the body, sense, and God's "ingredience" in the world, might gradually have tested (and partially reformed) his affectivity; it might also have purified the residue of Roman rationalism, and thus allowed for a more profound refocusing of his experience than he seems ever to have achieved.

All this may seem to be purest speculation, the archeologist's mind wandering the maze of contrary-to-fact conditionals. But in an age when the word is abroad that Western Man has been dehellenized, that Christianity, too, must therefore become dehellenized, such musings may have point. What would Augustine's thought have been had he known how fully to exploit, first, Plotinus himself, and then the additional resources of the Greek tradition which lay behind him?

Augustine and the Ancient Tradition

First of all he would have noticed that Plotinus' over-world is far more characterized by teeming images of life than by the glacial immutability a rationalistic mathematicism is tempted to project there. Alerted by that discovery, and further jostled by the revelation of the Trinity, his mind engaged in the task of envisaging the Biblical God of care, responsiveness, and involvement in human history, might have tossed about for more sophisticated forms of thought than the ones he actually brought to that task. "In heaven's name," the older Plato is brought to ask, "are we really to be so easily convinced that change, life, soul, understanding have no place in that which is perfectly real—that it has neither life nor thought, but stands immutable in solemn aloofness?" (*Sophist* 249a). That question might have received a fresh and brilliant answer, or at least have provoked a more fruitful line of inquiry than the one that ends in flatly denominating God as an absolute Unchangeable which the mind boggles at calling the God of Abraham, Isaac, and Jacob. Hegel's admiration for and debt to Plotinus is a matter of record; the temptation is irresistible to wonder what Western Christianity would be like had the *De Civitate Dei*, say, been a first daring effort to think of God from the startling standpoint that He could seriously involve Himself in human history.

The facile association of transcendence with immutability once broken, the entire problematic of immanence-transcendence with which the later Plotinus was so brilliantly wrestling might have been placed on another footing—one far more germane to the side of Platonic concern so little represented in Neo-Platonism. In fact, it can be affirmed that the later Plotinus' thought more generally begins to open on vistas which were really the starting point for all of Plato's metaphysical quest. The Gnostics' world-detestation prompts him to look more sympathetically than ever on the body, the sensible, the soul's divine mission to bring intelligible order into the world of human life. Now no one was more concerned with ordering human life, with the virtue of man living among men in the City, than the Socrates whose vocation inspired Plato's *Republic*, *Statesman*, *Laws*, in fact, his lifelong preoccupation with politics. Again, what might have happened had Augustine seen Plotinus' development as pointing toward eventually reintegrating this sympathy for political action into a systematic utterly devoid of it? *Plato dimidiatus*, one writer has called Plotinus. One may think the other side of Plato is at least as vital to the understanding of Christianity as the world-evading aspiration toward contemplative bliss. Had it not been sorely lacking in Augustine's systematic, too, the consequences might have been incalculable. The need for some concern with the "secular" is gradually borne in upon his mind, particularly through his pastoral activity. Studies he would earlier have seen as infections of "curiosity" he later justifies in the name of *scientia*. Though no longer mere "distractions" as he had thought in the *De Musica*, still, they can never become objects of autonomous value, items intrinsically interesting for themselves, so long as the soul's dominating desire is to "use" them, then pass on and upward in its restless pilgrimage back to the lost vision.

The single-minded thrust of Augustine's eudaemonism will not permit him to accord autonomous value to created realities. There is only one object of "enjoyment," and that must always be God. How often have we been told in this connection that putting the Kantian question to a fifth century thinker is sheer anachronism. One has no right to ask why he never discerned the difference between the sense of duty (*Pflicht*) and the morally indifferent "desire" (*Neigung*) which acts as mainspring to all eudaemonisms. And yet, against the background of hellenic thought one may at least ask what became of the Stoic sense of duty and of the *bonum honestum* in its original meaning: was Augustine sufficiently sensitive to the issues in this centuries-long debate, even as Cicero reports them? The Socrates who inspired Plato was a man who died at the behest of a moral imperative which did not on the face of it bring profit or advantage in its wake. The Stoics were wrestling with the difficulties that came from recognizing that the virtuous man could find himself in that limit-situation, could find himself compelled to do the *kalon* without its being manifestly an *agathon*. Their dedication to the City and to its human concerns was partially a response to that recognition. Let the early Plotinus scorn them as materialists (he becomes more qualified in later treatises), this surely was their greatness, a greatness to which Augustine seems to have been largely blind. For despite his frequent reversion to the topic of "beauty," the beautiful for him remains essentially an object of desire, an *agathon*, and never (to any thematized degree) an embodiment of value prompting the "awe and reverence" of Plato's *Phaedrus*. The drunken Alcibiades pays tribute to this kind of beauty when he speaks of Socrates as a Silenus-figure with the images of divinities inside him. Once glimpsed, it is not merely a man's habitual desires but desire itself as the unique compelling force of action that the vision calls into question.

Again and again Aristotle is forced to qualify his morality of the mean by the reminder that a man must have this sense of the *kalon*, this sensitivity to what is right, fit, beautiful—or, in the classic Stoic term, to what is "honorable," *honestum*. But obviously, such moral insight cannot be the product of abstract thought, of disembodied intellect, however sharpened by the Augustinian *exercitatio animi*.

Greek Philosophy and Contemporary Secularism

Nor can it, I suggest, be the product of the rationalistic pragmatism, the scientism, the linguistic positivism that lies at the base of so much contemporary "secular" Christianity. Nothing seems to wake more repugnance in the heart of a van Buren or a Harvey Cox than the specter of "ancient philosophy" with all its train of metaphysical problems. But when they ask us to take the human concern more seriously than Augustine could, as seriously as Socrates did, they are driven in the end to speak of the "mystery of human relationships" and ask with Unamuno whether man is "alone in the universe" or not. Both questions lie at the heart of Plato's *Apology*; it will not do to write off Greek philosophy's attempt to answer those questions before we have fully surveyed the resources which Augustine, Plotinus, even Plato and Aristotle together, were in the end unable to marshal at full strength in their efforts to answer them. We cannot now afford a succeeding generation who will say, as the youths in Plato's time were saying, that the secular dedication, the commitment to the human adventure in history, is a game not worth the candle. At the heart of the Christian epistemology of faith, I would suggest, there lies a question closer than is generally imagined to the one that tormented Plato, and will in time return to torment the secularist: what is it one can see in man—in a man called Socrates, or a man called Christ—that summons the mind to entertain the vision of a world of values, present in and to, yet stretching transcendentally beyond, the man who first embodied them in our experience? What is the depth and breadth and height of this "mystery of human relationships"? And if man be "alone in the universe," do the lives of those in whom we find the flame of human dedication burning purest, do the lives of a Socrates or a Christ, in the ultimate analysis, make sense?

The Past and Progress

It is not enough to say that Christian philosophy, due in part to its sometimes misplaced loyalty to Augustine, has failed to take up the challenge of those questions. If Christian thought is to remain organically linked with the tradition it claims to be developing, if Christianity is to avoid the fate of becoming "secular" but no longer genuinely Christian, it is essential to ask where and why that failure occurred. Then and only then does a discerning fidelity to tradition become possible.

I have tried here to prove to what extent the failure of Augustine's early thought can be traced to his confidence in Plotinus' Neo-Platonism. It can, I think, be shown that this failure largely persists in the *Confessions* and that one of its key features is a radically defective theory of sensibility. The proof of those contentions will each require a book to themselves. Their relevance lies in the facts that few works outside of the Bible itself have done more to shape traditional Christian spirituality than the *Confessions,* and that the sensibility I speak of is operative in three areas crucial to the contemporary debate on "secular" Christianity: esthetic intuition, moral knowledge, and, intimately connected with both the foregoing, the kind of insight that permits us to penetrate the "mystery of human relationships" which, once, like the Silenus-figure, they have disclosed their riches, immediately solicit the question of transcendence.

An old, old question, the central question to which tradition has always, though sometimes only half-aware, addressed itself. The

Christian thinker working out of that tradition may still find a model in Augustine; he will, in fact, find few better than the Augustine of the *Retractations*. When one of his loyal partisans, writing for clarification on his doctrine of predestination, hastens to assure the aging Bishop of Hippo that on all other points the monks of Marseilles remained his faithful and devoted disciples, the Saint's answer (*De dono perseverantiae*, 55) points to what the Christian "quest of wisdom" requires of us today. It is, he says in effect, of little interest to me whether you are Augustinians, except "for those matters where you have seen I have not erred." He tells him further that his own progress is still advancing, but significantly, by reconsideration of the past. He is engaged in the laborious work of the *Retractations* to inform future generations of Christians where he himself would reject or modify certain features of his earlier thought. "He is the man whose hope is firm," he concludes, "whose last day of life finds him still progressing: then what his progress lacks will be added unto him, for he will be judged worthy of being perfected rather than punished."

When one engaged in such a reconsideration of the past finds himself obliged to criticize an Augustine as I have done here, he should do so with the modesty that befits a dwarf astride the shoulders of the giant he is criticizing. He may in time regret that, in the tone of his observations, that modesty was less evident than he might have wished. But one comfort still remains to him: that he consigns his work to a tradition that, in its onward movement, can be trusted to ensure that "what his progress lacks will be added unto him." And, if he accepts with grace what others say to correct him, he too may "be judged worthy of being perfected rather than punished." Then the dwarf will not have been too unfaithful to the giant's spirit.

INDEX

Date Due